INDIGENOUS AND OTHER AUSTRALIANS SINCE 1901

TIM ROWSE has been writing on Australian Indigenous affairs since the early 1980s and is one of Australia's most significant scholars of Indigenous Studies. He worked for many years at the Menzies School of Health Research in Alice Springs. He has also taught on this subject at the Australian National University, Western Sydney University and Harvard University. Widely published, Tim's most recent book is *Rethinking Social Justice: From 'peoples' to 'populations'* (2012).

INDIGENOUS AND OTHER AUSTRALIANS SINCE 1901

TIM ROWSE

UNSW PRESS

A UNSW Press book

Published by
NewSouth Publishing
University of New South Wales Press Ltd
University of New South Wales
Sydney NSW 2052
AUSTRALIA
newsouthpublishing.com

© Tim Rowse 2017
First published 2017

10 9 8 7 6 5 4 3 2 1

This book is copyright. Apart from any fair dealing for the purpose of private study, research, criticism or review, as permitted under the *Copyright Act*, no part of this book may be reproduced by any process without written permission. Inquiries should be addressed to the publisher.

National Library of Australia
Cataloguing-in-Publication entry
Creator: Rowse, Tim, 1951– author.
Title: Indigenous and other Australians since 1901 / Tim Rowse.
ISBN: 9781742235578 (paperback)
      9781742244075 (ebook)
      9781742248479 (ePDF)
Notes: Includes bibliographical references and index.
Subjects: Aboriginal Australians – History – 20th century.
Aboriginal Australians – Government policy.
Aboriginal Australians – Politics and government.
Australia – Politics and government.
Australia – Race relations – Political aspects.

Design Josephine Pajor-Markus
Cover design Luke Causby, Blue Cork
Cover image Gordon Bennett, *Home Décor (after M. Preston) #21*, 2013, Acrylic on linen, 182.5 x 152cm, Photography: Carl Warner, Brisbane, Courtesy: Milani Gallery, Brisbane © The Estate of Gordon Bennett
Maps Karina Pelling, College of Asia and the Pacific, The Australian National University
Printer Griffin Press

All reasonable efforts were taken to obtain permission to use copyright material reproduced in this book, but in some cases copyright could not be traced. The author welcomes information in this regard.

Contents

Acronyms *vi*

List of maps and figures *viii*

Introduction: Deakin surveys the continent *1*

1. Missions and the state in North Australia *20*
2. Knowing and ruling Northern Aborigines *63*
3. Governments, churches, parents, spouses and children, 1897–1940 *93*
4. Did 'protection' protect? *134*
5. Global awareness and the recession of race *169*
6. World Wars and the Cold War *198*
7. Towards racial equality *225*
8. From the referendum to 'self-determination' *262*
9. The Indigenous Estate in Land and Sea *287*
10. Asserting 'Southern' Aboriginality *334*
11. The Indigenous middle class *380*
12. Family, community and the crisis of self-determination *402*

Epilogue: Within a single field of life *443*

References *450*

Notes *473*

Acknowledgments *493*

Index *495*

Acronyms

AAB	Aboriginal Arts Board (Australia Council)
AAL	Australian Aborigines' League
AAPA	Australian Aboriginal Progressive Association
ADC	Aboriginal Development Commission
AIAS	Australian Institute of Aboriginal Studies
AIATSIS	Australian Institute of Aboriginal and Torres Strait Islander Studies
AIDA	Australian Indigenous Doctors' Association
ALFC	Aboriginal Land Fund Commission
ALRA	*Aboriginal Land Rights (Northern Territory) Act* 1976
ALSWA	Aboriginal Legal Service of Western Australia
AMIC	Australian Mining Industry Council
AMSANT	Aboriginal Medical Services Alliance
ANRC	Australian National Research Council
APB	Aborigines Protection Board
ATF	Aboriginal Theatre Foundation
ATSIC	Aboriginal and Torres Strait Islander Commission
ATSISJC	Aboriginal and Torres Strait Islander Social Justice Commissioner
BCL	British Commonwealth League
CAA	Council for Aboriginal Affairs
CWA	Country Women's Association
CDEP	Community Development Employment Projects
CIM	Compulsory Income Management
CPA	Communist Party of Australia
CPD	Commonwealth Parliamentary Debates

DAA	Department of Aboriginal Affairs (Commonwealth)
FAA	Foundation for Aboriginal Affairs
FCAA	Federal Council for Aboriginal Advancement
FCAATSI	Federal Council for the Advancement of Aborigines and Torres Strait Islanders
HREOC	Human Rights and Equal Opportunity Commission
ILC	Indigenous Land Corporation
ILO	International Labour Organisation
ILUA	Indigenous Land Use Agreement
IPA	Indigenous Protected Area
NAALAS	North Australia Aboriginal Legal Aid Service
NAC	National Aboriginal Congress
NACC	National Aboriginal Consultative Committee
NSWPD	New South Wales Parliamentary Debates
NTER	Northern Territory Emergency Response
OPAL	One People for Australia League
QPD	Queensland Parliamentary Debates
RDA	*Racial Discrimination Act* 1975
SAPD	South Australia Parliamentary Debates
SEAM	School Enrolment and Attendance Measures
SNAICC	Secretariat of National Aboriginal and Islander Child Care
TPD	Tasmania Parliamentary Debates
UN	United Nations
VAAL	Victorian Aborigines Advancement League
WAPD	Western Australia Parliamentary Debates

List of maps and figures

Map 1: Remote missions (established 1877–1952), anthropology research sites 1929–39, World War II airfields, radio installations and Cold War weapons testing regions in remote Australia

Map 2: The Indigenous Land and Sea Estate (2017) and the Aboriginal and Torres Strait Islander Population (2016), by jurisdiction

Table 1: Chronology of remote mission formation 1877–1952

Table 2: Places, people and dates in field-based anthropology

Table 3: The Australian Aboriginal population in the 1901 Census

Table 4: Estimated 'full-blood' Australian Aboriginals, 4 April 1921

Introduction:
Deakin surveys the continent

For £500 per year Alfred Deakin agreed in 1900 to write anonymously a weekly essay about current political life in Australia for London's *Morning Post*. Trained in the law and experienced as a journalist, Deakin had been a member of Victoria's Legislative Assembly from 1879 to 1899, holding office in several governments between 1883 and 1890. He had also been one of the authors of the Australian Constitution in the 1890s. Elected to the new Commonwealth parliament, he had been attorney-general (1901–1903) and prime minister (1903–1904).

In February 1905, reflecting on Aboriginal Australians, Deakin's theme was regional difference in the relationships between colonists and Aborigines. He argued that the good state of affairs in the continent's south-east ('our records are on the whole respectable') would eventually extend across the continent.[1] However, while this would confirm that no region was beyond the rule of law, it would not stop the Aboriginal population dying out.

In 1881, Deakin had been appointed to the Board for the Protection of Aborigines (BPA), but he had soon resigned, having a poor opinion of some of the staff who enjoyed the board's favour. He had helped the Kulin to represent themselves when they had complained in 1882 about their superintendent at Coranderrk. Thereafter, Deakin had occasionally been at odds with the board, and the Kulin seem to have regarded him as one of the more approachable MPs. However, Deakin had participated in staging the humane elimination of the Kulin Aborigines of Victoria, supporting a board policy to expel 'half-castes' from the reserves. As the old 'full-blood' cohorts died out, the succeeding generations – more and more of mixed descent – were expected to be absorbed into the wider Victorian population; revoked reserves would then be available to settlers. When the BPA sought legislative backing for this policy in 1886, Deakin as chief secretary presented the bill to the Assembly.[2] Whatever his criticisms of the board, Deakin shared its view that Aboriginal people were fated to die out and/or be absorbed. Barwick has traced this idea back to the origins of Victoria's reserves policy in 1858.[3]

Accordingly, as Commonwealth Attorney-General Deakin had authorised in 1901 that 'Aboriginal native' in the Australian Constitution did *not* refer to 'half-castes', and he had supported excluding from the franchise the 'natives' of Australia, Asia, Africa or the islands of the Pacific except New Zealand.[4] When Deakin surveyed past and future in 1904–1905, it was common sense that the 'Aboriginal native' was a diminishing responsibility.

Deakin was frank that in some regions there remained serious problems in the colonial relationship. Vicious pioneers had taken advantage of 'the ignorance and sexual laxities of the blacks'.[5] Where there were yet no courts or police the settlers had used force to guard their property from Aborigines, resulting in 'blood-red imprints on the early pages of the history of Queensland'. However, protectors such as Walter Roth were now bringing order to that state's frontiers.[6] Some parts of

Western Australia now resembled Queensland at its worst, he continued. Authority in Perth had not yet checked the 'semi-slavery' of the interior and the 'tyranny' of the police.[7] Deakin urged Western Australia to implement the recommendations of Roth's 1904 Royal Commission: the rule of law would eventually shape disorderly and corrupt frontiers into something as admirable as Victoria and New South Wales.

History has not confirmed Deakin's belief that Aborigines were 'dying out fast from natural causes, despite the efforts of the state governments to prevent it'.[8] As recently as 1971, only 116 000 were counted – not much more than the 1901 Census (under)count of 93 000. However, rapid growth – an annualised rate of 4 per cent since 1971 – has resulted in an Indigenous population of 669 900 by 30 June 2011 (3 per cent of the total Australian population). Demographers see four factors in this recovery: declining mortality rates, high fertility rates, changes in the definition of 'Aboriginal population', and a growing propensity to identify as Indigenous, including the willingness of non-Indigenous mothers and fathers to report as 'Indigenous' the children born to their Indigenous spouses. Indigenous persistence and recovery is a central theme of Australia's post-Federation history. Indeed, in recent public (mis)perception, the Aboriginal and Torres Strait Islander population is even larger. An Auspoll survey for Reconciliation Australia in 2012 found that 58 per cent of a 'general community' sample estimated the Aboriginal and Torres Strait Islander population to be 5 per cent or more of the total Australian population.[9] A surviving and articulate Indigenous population provokes a morally troubled imagining of the nation.

In a lecture broadcast on ABC Radio in 1968, the anthropologist W.E.H. Stanner predicted that Australia's 'silence' about Aboriginal matters would not last. He wished for – indeed, anticipated – a historical narrative that would name Aboriginal men who had sought constructive dealings with obdurate whites.

> Not to scrape up significance for them but because they typify so vividly the other side of a story over which the great Australian silence reigns: the story of the things that we were unconsciously resolved not to discuss with them or treat with them about; the story, in short, of the unacknowledged relations between two racial groups within a single field of life supposedly unified by the principle of assimilation.[10]

The phrase 'within a single field of life' has come to mean a lot to me as I have written this book, for three reasons.

First, the category 'Aboriginal' is not a given or natural fact but the dynamic product of interactions within 'a single field of life' contested between colonial authority and those marked as its objects. The distinction 'half-caste'/'full-blood' was an ideological inheritance of the region that formed the outlook of founding fathers of Federation such as Deakin. Between 1860 and 1905, each Australian jurisdiction attempted to enumerate or estimate the Aboriginal population in terms that included distinguishing 'full-bloods' from those of racially mixed parentage. My narrative will show the persistence, up to mid-century, of the supposition that 'half-castes' were not Aborigines or were only a 'contaminated' version of a pristine and primitive race. The Australian state's federal relations made it difficult for non-Indigenous authority to resolve whether 'half-castes' were 'Aborigines'. When governing practices were referenced to the Constitution, 'half-castes' were not 'Aboriginal natives', as Attorney-General Deakin had ruled; but when the states distinguished those who were in need of management, as 'Aboriginals' (or as Torres Strait Islanders), they administered many 'half-castes' as 'Aboriginals'. Not only governments were undecided about the significance of the 'half'/'full' distinction; some of those who would reform the laws and institutions of 'protection' affirmed this distinction, while others rejected it. Among those rejecting it were people of Aboriginal descent subject to the states' more inclusive administrative practices; they began to espouse a pan-Aboriginal nationalism between the World Wars. By the middle of the 20th century, changes in scientific thought meant 'Aboriginal' was less biological and more cultural – without ever losing 'descent' as an essential ingredient. A more coherent state definition of 'Aboriginal' emerged around 1970, facilitating a pan-Aboriginal arena in which different *historical* (not biological) formations of Aboriginality contended. This sense of commonality blossomed as black nationalism in the 1970s.

These colonial dynamics took place in a large continent, diverse in physical and human geography, on which a new nation attempted to create 'a single field of life', a culturally coherent nation. When Australia federated in 1901, there were two 'Australias'; without pretending to geographical precision, I refer to them as North and South. The distinction is partly physical. Australia north of the 20th latitude has 'wet' and 'dry' seasons, not the four-season cycle of the south. Cutting across this axis is another, between the rainy east, south-east and north coast and the dry interior: about 60 per cent of the continent is semi-arid. Soils, in most of the continent, are deficient in what agriculture requires, and in 'northern' regions where agriculture has proved possible, the relative unpredictability of rainfall has made it precarious.

Up to 1901, almost 4 million immigrants (mostly from the British Isles) introduced land uses that displaced the hunting and gathering economy of the Aboriginal people. Agriculture (initially subsistence, but export-oriented in the second half of the 19th century) and pastoralism (export-oriented from its inception in the 1810s) were the colonists' two great land use innovations. Each colony built railway networks to connect crop-growing, herd-raising and mining regions with cities/ports, in the period 1860 to 1901. Some food-growing regions were stimulated by the discovery of minerals, but most mining towns were short-lived. Pastoral deployment of cattle and sheep was a more extensive and permanent enterprise, flourishing in the south before extending further into the north. Pastoralism expanded along two great 'arms', writes Geoffrey Bolton, one starting from Sydney and arcing south, south-west and north towards Cape York in the period 1788 to the 1880s, the other commencing in Perth in 1829 and spreading along the west coast. In the 1880s, the two 'arms' – some overlanders based in Perth, others originating in Queensland and New South Wales – met in the Kimberley.[11] On every frontier, pastoralists competed with Aborigines for the best country and enforced their occupation. Aborigines who survived the often violent frontiers adapted to become its workforce. Within the ring made by these curved arms lay the western desert; the boundaries of this uncolonised arid third of the continent have been determined, since the 1880s, by the severity of the dry spells, by the patience of banks and by the optimism of marginal pastoralists. Within that vast region Adelaide-based investors initiated a marginal pastoral zone along the MacDonnell Ranges in Central Australia in the 1880s. The towns that grew as railheads of the line from Adelaide – first Oodnadatta, Alice Springs after 1929 – were the administrative centres from which the 20th-century welfare state patrolled to the Aboriginal people of the western desert, in a series of contacts from Herbert Basedow's pastoralist-funded medical patrol into north-east South Australia in 1919 to the unexpected contact with the last 'wild' Pintubi in 1984.

By the time of Federation in 1901, the natural and financial limits of pastoral and agricultural expansion had been reached. 'Perhaps the salient feature of Australian colonization has been its concentration in urban surroundings,' Bolton remarks, for most of 'Australia' was by then concentrated in six 'bridge-heads established by British authority', so that colonisation 'carried with it a culture derived from European, and largely British models' in coastal cities of temperate climate.[12] The 'Australia' that six colonial governments compacted in 1901, with British government permission, was at that time evolving, through mostly peaceful class struggle, a sustainable social model: racially homogeneous, exported-oriented agriculture and fenced herds, protected manufacturing, with a developmental state managing public investment in railways and urban infrastructure that drew on overseas loans. In the first decade of Federation, this 'South' Australia of cities, suburbs and farms forged a durable class compromise around the protection of relatively high wages, earned by a male breadwinner supporting a wife and two or three children, from the competition of cheaper labour and from the import of goods produced from cheaper labour. This 'Australian Settlement' was geographically limited: south of the Tropic of Capricorn and confined to the coast and to zones where agriculture and urban manufacturing were possible. This was Deakin's vantage point, as he wrote his *Morning Post* article: a 'South' from which he could project the spread of the post-frontier civilisation of 'South' Australia to the 'North' Australia that he (like nearly all his contemporaries) had never visited.

That 'North' (in which I include the arid Centre, as it became available to British–Australian occupation, roughly from the 1870s to the 1960s) was different: in its more demanding geographies, in its more limited opportunities for private and public investment, in its sparser and more ethnically mixed population, and in that it was the territory, well into the 20th century, either of pastoral runs extended over extant Indigenous polities or of Indigenous polities beyond the zone of colonial enterprise. The 'North' was the hinterland of Queensland, New South Wales, South Australia (which until 1910 stretched north to the Arafura Sea, as 'the Northern Territory') and Western Australia. The Federation compact carried the seeds of a continental ambition: to incorporate all of this territory into the Australian Settlement. Australian nationhood was a continental racial hypothesis; it would require either ejecting non-white peoples – Asians, Pacific Islanders, Aborigines and Torres Strait Islanders – or incorporating them into the political culture and political economy of the Australian Settlement. However, for decades the South would exert little transformative pressure on the North, as there were so few reasons for public and private investment there, other than pastoral occupation and a few mines. By the 1960s, the 39 per cent of Australia north of the Tropic of Capricorn contained only 3 per cent of Australia's population (excluding 'Aborigines').[13] The challenge of its characteristic land uses, labour processes, modes of government and racial composition would episodically attract the South's attention, stimulated by fear of invasion, by discovery of minerals and by the political intensification, after World War II, of the mandate to assimilate a growing Indigenous ('native') population.

Political necessity, not commercial prospects, would drive the new nation's continental interest. When urging the Commonwealth to take over the Northern Territory in 1910, Deakin said: 'it is impossible for us to draw an arbitrary line anywhere in this continent so as to imply that north of it our interests are any less than they are in the southernmost portion', for 'every inch of land' is 'requisite to the rest of Australia', not to be 'severed from it either in population or in policy'.[14] What he meant by 'Northern Australia' did not include the settled north Queensland coast, with its 'exceptional advantages'; it comprised 'those portions, starting from the eastern side, where the sea communication ceases to be cheap and the climatic conditions alter right across to Derby and Broome ... down as far as Roebourne'.[15]

The 'North' encouraged distinct formations of colonial authority: the remote missions initiated between the 1880s and 1952; the militarisation of the north coast and its central supply corridor in World War II; and the further militarisation of the western desert in the Cold War. Assimilation, adopted as policy at the middle of the 20th century, continued the war-inspired impetus to normalise the societies of this 'North'. In a 'North' where pastoral colonisation and a neo-traditional Aboriginal social order had become interdependent, the introduction of the 'Southern' model of the wage-supported nuclear family brought a surplus Aboriginal population starkly into view in the late 1960s. To manage these people was one of the aims of what became known in the 1970s as 'self-determination' policy. Recent anguished reconsideration of remote Aboriginal conditions is the latest episode in this projection of the nation as 'a single field of life' within the continent.[16]

The third sense in which Australia has been 'a single field of life' in the 20th century refers to the immanent singularity of Australian sovereignty: the continental extension of law to which Deakin looked forward. We must not forget that since 1901, when Australia's South projected nationhood, much of the continent has been under the dominion of people whose political order had just begun to be disturbed. To grasp Australian history continentally we must begin by contrasting the colonial and Indigenous political orders that collided as effective colonial occupation spread from 'South' into 'North'. In pre-colonial Indigenous societies the political order was not that of a state but of many territorially defined clans whose internal and external dealings were relations of kinship. To be 'kin' has a spectrum of intensities. At one end, one is kin by a close 'blood' (consanguineal) relationship, as when parents and children call one another kin and when siblings call one another kin. At the other end of the spectrum 'kinship' is 'classificatory'. In 'classificatory' kinship, two individuals who have hitherto been strangers to each other are able to work out where each of them stands within an infinitely ramifying system of relations embracing all persons. Because individuals could be kin-related in either close or distant ways, it was possible for the idiom of kinship to be also the idiom of political life. With no state structures – no administration, no law-enforcement agencies, no legislature – people could still have a sense of themselves being part of a polity, a social universe in which widely understood and respected rules regulated conduct. Two people would behave towards each other according to whether they understood themselves to be siblings or in a parent–child relationship. A man and a woman would set their behaviours towards each other according to whether they were in a classificatory relationship of mother–son, brother–sister or man–wife. Kinship was particularly relevant in the social regulation of sexuality. A man knew that there were categories of women whom he should avoid (his classificatory mother-in-law), or to whom he should behave with circumspection; there were some who were 'off limits' to him sexually and others who were potentially his licit sexual partner or spouse.

As well as being a regulator of sexual behaviour, Aboriginal kinship had (and for many still has) the political and legal function of mapping out the inheritance of rights to live on and make use of tracts of land and sea. The groups of people that own land are constituted by widely understood and respected rules about descent and relatedness. Land-owning collectives are not associations that an individual may enter or leave at will (as one might enter or leave the membership of a body corporate, by buying or selling a proprietary interest); rather, one's membership of a land-owning group is by virtue of one's descent (and no human gets to choose their ancestors), by marriage (following customary rules of spouse selection) and by applying oneself to maintain association.

In traditional Aboriginal society, every person belonged to at least one land-holding collective of people. The most important factor determining which group you belonged to was the custom of tracing inheritance through the male line: a boy or girl was understood to have rights in his/her father's country, that is, by what anthropologists call 'patrifiliation'. Patrifiliation was a variable combination of the biological (which man impregnated one's mother) and the social (which man raised me). A 'father' was not necessarily the biological father: fatherhood was a recognised responsibility of mothers' brothers. The opinion of the immediate group of kin determined the lines of 'filiation' that mattered when people were reckoning rights to be on and to use 'country' and to inherit knowledge. So 'descent' should not be understood in a narrow biological sense, as it is a social construct; it is 'filiation' recognised as legitimate. This emphasis on the social nature of filiation and descent became particularly important when, as a consequence of frontier conditions – the arrival of sexually active non-Aboriginal men lacking non-Aboriginal women as sexual partners – many children were born to Aboriginal mothers who had little or no ongoing connection with the white men who had impregnated them. Matrilineal reckoning of the inheritance of rights has probably become more important; certainly, we have become more aware of it.

Through this clan/estate polity, Aboriginal people have dealt with the core concerns of human society: the inheritance of rights to sacred knowledge and to land use, the apportioning of resources among peoples through the practices of people/territory boundaries, the social control of sexuality, the mobilisation of fighting power against other Aboriginal people, and the socialisation of the next generation. No writer on the 20th-century encapsulation and adaptation of this Indigenous polity can grasp its significance, its vulnerability and its resilience without paying attention to research by anthropologists; it enables the historian to attempt an account of the crisis and continuity of an evolving Indigenous kin-based polity. In two papers relevant to a fully *political* history of Australia's internal colonial process, Ian Keen has suggested that we understand the traditional Aboriginal polity as a system of 'reproductive power', enacted through polygyny, the right of a man to have more than one wife at a time.[17] Polygyny was more pronounced in the more resource-rich and densely populated regions (such as those inhabited by Ngarinyin in the North Kimberley and Yolngu in north-east Arnhem Land) than in the arid interior. Throughout the Australian regions that were colonised from the 1880s to the 1940s, senior men had long been governing through their control over sacred, life-giving knowledge and over the life-giving bodies of women of reproductive age. To marry polygynously, Keen argues, enacted reproductive powers that include 'sexual prerogatives, the ability to claim one's wives' children as one's own and as members of one's group, access to exchange items, and the ability to muster support in a dispute'.[18]

Aboriginal people were thus governing the continent when Deakin wrote his concise overview of colonial law and order's difficult diffusion. However, governing through reproductive power imposed a demanding sentimental education that late-Victorian Deakin was ill equipped to understand. One of the last Australians to grow up thinking that reproductive power was the way humans normally governed is Jukuna Mona Chuguna, a Walmadjeri woman who emigrated from the Great Sandy Desert in the mid-1960s. She explains how reproductive power worked:

> The marriages were arranged like this: the grandmother of a small girl (on her father's side) chooses the man who will be the little girl's 'son-in-law'. The grandmother says to the man she chooses, 'This little girl is your mother-in-law. Now you have to keep bringing her meat until she grows up.' Then they give the girl a husband. When she has a baby – a boy or a girl – she promises that child to the son-in-law already chosen for her by her grandmother. If her first child is a boy, she will give him to her son-in-law first, and afterwards, when she has a girl, she will give her to him to be his wife. The boy will stay with his 'husband', who looks after him for some of the time until he grows up. When the boy is ready to go through the law the 'husband' has to tie the hairstring belt around him. When I was old enough, my young sister and I were sent

to our husband, whose name was Pijaji, to live with him. My sister was still only a girl.[19]

There was much in a polity conducted in this way to outrage or distress a colonising British–Australian society convinced of the decency of its ordering of intimate relationships. Deakin's references in 1905 to 'ignorance', 'sexual laxities' and incomprehension of property are items in a firmly established colonial tradition of dismissing what we now can appreciate as the Indigenous order of law and government. From 1788, this stateless political order had to deal with an extending state polity and capitalist economy, derived from Britain, from whose perspective Aborigines appeared to lack law, property, government and moral decency; instead of seeing kinship as a system of governance, the colonists saw adult–child and male–female relationships that they judged bizarre, repugnant and licentious, obliging corrective action.

Critical intervention into this Indigenous order of government began soon after the British established permanent settlement. In 1790 judge advocate David Collins and Governor Arthur Phillip sought to restrain the Aboriginal man Bennelong from killing Boorong, a daughter of one of Bennelong's enemies. A reader informed by anthropological knowledge can imagine Bennelong's perspective on his wounding and threatening of Boorong: a calculated performance of his 'autonomy, which extended in this particular matter to power over life and death' for the uniformed bearers of a new order that was enforced by flogging and hanging. Inga Clendinnen plausibly imagines Bennelong's intended message to those who counselled moderation: 'These are my people; this is my territory; and this is my law. I defy you to impede me.'[20] The (sometimes physical) assertion of social authority – by men over women, by adults over children – enacted the Indigenous political order; to confront actions that seemed brutal, licentious and unlawful was to disrupt, for what seemed the best motives, Indigenous government. To the extent that Aboriginal law was hard for its subjects to live by, colonial reformers have not lacked Indigenous allies. Both external and internal pressures continue to transform Indigenous male–female and adult–child relations.

Colonial authority has confronted, undermined and reshaped Indigenous authority in more than one way, and the reader's moral ambivalence about the colonists' civilising mandate is likely to grow with a full consideration of these processes. It has been relatively uncontroversial for Australians recently to deplore the seizure and/or sequestration of children and the frontier's *extra-judicial* violence (often called 'massacres'), and to regret the disproportionate incarceration of Indigenous Australians. However, colonial challenge to Aboriginal sovereignty has included arguably justifiable interventions to curb violence among Indigenous Australians. Feminist scholarship has highlighted some female humanitarians' aspiration to empower Aboriginal women against the patriarchy of Indigenous governance. Research on the history of criminal law reveals that the colonial state began in the 19th century to prosecute homicidal Aboriginal violence towards other Aboriginal people (*inter se*) – the beginning of the gradual disallowance of the physical enforcement of customary law. Mark Finnane discerns regional difference in this eclipse of Aboriginal jurisdiction: between the small number of *inter se* homicide prosecutions in the longer-colonised south-east of the continent and the larger commitment to such policing and prosecution in colonies with large unoccupied hinterlands: Western Australia, South Australia (including the Northern Territory) and Queensland.[21] Between 1832 and 1954, the colony/state of Western Australia convicted 321 Aboriginal persons for murder and 21 for manslaughter/unlawful killing – 'an intensive intervention into Indigenous lives as settlement spread', as in most cases the victim was another Aboriginal person.[22] The colonial state strove from 1788 to be the singular agent of *licit* violence, and the 21st century's renewed attention to domestic violence (among all Australians) continues this difficult project.

The mid–20th century experience of one government official underlines the difficulty of evading the colonising dynamic of one law and moral system asserting itself over another to create 'a single field of [legal] life'. Syd Kyle-Little was a patrol officer appointed by the Australian government in the 1940s to protect the way of life of Aboriginal people on remote reserves. He thought that World War II's encroaching on Arnhem Land Reserve (declared in 1931 as a sanctuary for Yolngu, the Aborigines of the region) had damaged the lives of residents. Yolngu were being attracted into Darwin and to points along the north–south road, thus 'drifting into the corruption and squalor that inevitably accompanies their permanent association with the white man'.[23] He wished to establish a trading post near the Liverpool River 'where the aborigines could trade the proceeds of their hunting for all the things they sought in Darwin', so that 'with a minimum of organization and without interrupting his nomadic way of life, the Arnhem Land aborigine could be persuaded to develop his own land in his own way and in his own time'.[24]

It was government policy to apply the criminal law to Yolngu, and so Kyle-Little's work included apprehending men so that they could be tried for murder in Darwin. However, he hoped that his Arnhem Land trading post would 'persuade the aborigines to stay in, and to return to, their own areas' and thus limit their exposure to whites. He hoped that his 'blind eye to tribal disputes' would further preserve 'their welfare' as an isolated people.[25] Kyle-Little wished to be less intrusive than Arnhem Land's missionaries, who had begun to affect Yolngu governance by their determination to influence the socialisation of children. Conceding that missionaries were well-intentioned (and that Yolngu seem to have consented to their presence), Kyle-Little worried that missions would deny children the skills of living on country and would confront girls with a choice between tribal ways and a missionised life partnered with a Christian mission male; to choose the latter risked Aboriginal law's brutal discipline, he worried. Kyle-Little believed that if the government was to be less intrusive than missions it must establish a regional economy compatible with continuing ceremonial life and tribal law.

However, he found to his 'confusion' that it was not possible to act as if tribal disputes were not under his jurisdiction. One night a young man and woman ran exhausted into his patrol camp; Kyle-Little, through his Aboriginal helpers, soon found that they were a 'Mission girl' and her 'half-brother' who had formed an incestuous (in Yolngu law) relationship. Soon a party of twenty-five, including the woman's promised husband, arrived and surrounded Kyle-Little. They demanded that the couple submit to punishment (the young man would be obliged to fight). Kyle-Little was torn between his instinctive wish to protect the couple and his native employees' insistence that tribal law be applied. He became angry and told his helpers that he would not allow murder in his camp. He fired a shot from his rifle, promising that his next would be between the eyes of the spurned husband-to-be. He promised to take the couple to Darwin, where they would be tried and punished if found guilty of a crime. He thus exploited not only his superior firepower but also the tribesmen's ignorant belief that a white court would view the couple as incestuous and punish them as tribal law demanded.

The incident in Kyle-Little's camp in the late 1940s revealed that even white authority sympathetic to preserving Aboriginal autonomy could not seal customary law from the intrusion of Australian criminal law. When each law made demands on Kyle-Little, his allegiance was clear; his gun and his use of Yolngu ignorance carried Australian law and polity one step further into the Arnhem Land Reserve. My point is not to condemn Kyle-Little but to illustrate that the 'field of life' that he wished to isolate through the 'Muningreda' trading post was encapsulated within a single field of sovereign law; when he had to mediate between two different conceptions of lawful sexual intimacy, he could not avoid asserting one as superior. By such decisions, the Aboriginal polity was drawn into the single space of Australia's territorial sovereignty. About forty years after the incident in Kyle-Little's camp, the Law Reform Commission made the superiority of Australian law explicit when it recommended against using general Australian law to enforce Aboriginal customary marriage: 'this would involve ... denying the right not to be coerced to marry'.[26]

What we call 'sovereignty' includes an arbitration of the customs by which humans in Australia enact their 'private' being. As a settler colonial society Australia is an ensemble of clashing and negotiated differences, and the most basic has been the long, slow and often subterranean encounter of two orders of kinship and power. This clash has few 'events' but it is the integument of the events that is narratable, and so here and there the clash appears in this history. I will show how church and state authorities intruded intimately into the kin-based Indigenous polity, in the name of 'protection' of those who seemed most vulnerable within it. When colonisation alienated the Indigenous resource base, elements of an Indigenous social order endured nonetheless in the business of forming attachments, procreating children and raising them to acquire at least part of their material and ideational patrimony. Wherever and whenever the colonists deplored and intervened in Indigenous domesticity, they confronted Indigenous 'reproductive power'.

Polygyny has almost disappeared as a mode of 'reproductive power', as Indigenous Australians have found new ways to organise the social process of procreating and rearing the next generation. Change, in this sphere, is ongoing. Australian Indigenous adaptations of family have included incorporating non-Indigenous partners into the Indigenous family. The modern Indigenous household – especially in the 'South' – nowadays commonly includes non-Indigenous partners: of 17 621 births registered as Indigenous in 2011, 4747 (26.9 per cent) were to a non-Indigenous mother.[27] Australians gained a glimpse of an adapting polity of kinship in 2007 when Anderson and Wild remarked that many Aboriginal people in the Northern Territory did not yet understand wider Australian criminal law, including the concept of 'sexual abuse' – a label sometimes applied, by outsiders, to features of their marriage customs.[28] In the 'North' (specifically the Northern Territory) the adaptations of Indigenous family life are still contestable, as they involve the relationship between domestic units with children and the education system. My book concludes with the Australian government's recent renewed attempts to hold Aboriginal adults accountable in the rearing of their children.

1

Missions and the state in North Australia

Missions as colonial authority: 1870s to 1952

In the early 20th-century colonial occupation of remote Australia – the northern coasts from Broome to Cairns and the arid interiors of Western Australia, the Northern Territory, South Australia and Queensland – the state was but one of many authorities, and not necessarily the most consequential. There were public employees such as police and the staff that looked after the telegraph lines through the Northern Territory and Cape York and saw to occasional postal deliveries. The Commonwealth takeover of the Northern Territory (from a grateful South Australia) in 1911 made remote Australia a responsibility of the new national government, but the value of all buildings (public and private) in the Territory in 1907 was just under £45 000, and in Darwin, the Territory's administrative centre, there were only 374 Europeans in 1911.[1] In their impact on Indigenous lives, state officials were secondary to the private agents drawn to the northern coast and the central deserts by the possibility of either making money or ameliorating the damage of others' money-making: the pioneer pastoral lessees, the lugger captains, the fossickers for minerals, the market gardeners and the missionaries.

Three reports – Archibald Meston's 1896 *Report on the Aboriginals of Queensland*, W.E. Roth's 1904 Royal Commission report to the Western Australian government and Baldwin Spencer's 1912–13 survey of the northern parts of the Northern Territory – had each made clear how damaging entrepreneurial authority could be.[2] By making claims on the labour time, the sexuality, the mobility and the food gathering of natives, entrepreneurs substantially changed the routines of Aborigines and Torres Strait Islanders who were attracted to goods that they issued: clothes, tobacco and sugar and sometimes opium and alcohol, and carbohydrates such as flour and rice (obviating much hard work), iron tools (durable, obviating production time). The tendency of these exchanges was to entrench the ascendancy of the aliens and to reconfigure daily life among Aborigines and Islanders. As credible accounts of their physical and moral vulnerability accumulated, regulatory, protective authority became imperative. However, early in the 20th century, the state lacked the capacity to determine, unassisted, the quality of social life in remote Australia.

One churchman recorded his observation of state incapacity. In 1908, just before the Benedictine Fulgentius Torres travelled to the Kimberley to identify a new mission site at Drysdale River, he explained his aims to Western Australia's Protector of Aborigines (Mr Hale). The Protector said he hoped to establish 'big reserves for the natives'. Torres thought Hale's intentions 'very appropriate', but as he noted in his diary, the Western Australian government lacked the personnel and the money.[3] The Roman Catholic and other Christian churches were determined to offer Aborigines an alternative authority to that wielded by pastoralists and lugger captains. By 1938, the churches had proved more able than the Western Australian government to mobilise an apparatus of 'protection' in the state's remote reserves: Beagle Bay, Lombadina, Drysdale River, Kunmunya, Forrest River in the Kimberley; Mount Margaret and Warburton Range in the desert interior. In the north, the government had only four native hospitals (Port Hedland, Broome, Derby and Wyndham), three 'native stations' (Moola Bulla, Munja and Violet Valley), one feeding (or 'relief') depot (La Grange). In the south of the state, the government ran feeding depots at Eyre and Karonie, the Moore River Settlement and the East Perth Native Girls' Home. The state had been legislatively active, but north of the Tropic of Capricorn it was secondary to the missions.[4]

In Queensland, up to World War II, the mix of state and mission effort varied from region to region. The London Missionary Society had arrived in the Torres Strait in 1871, but from 1904 the government built a strong presence, placing the Islanders under the same legislation that had controlled Aborigines since 1897; the chief protector claimed by 1914 to have taken a comprehensive census across the Strait's nineteen centres of population and to be schooling about 40 per cent of the Islander children.[5] The London Missionary Society handed mission work over to the Anglicans in 1915. On Cape York, colonial authority was effected at the local level by missions, encouraged by the Queensland government. In the grazing and agricultural regions south of the Tropic of Capricorn, the government established two institutions: Barambah (later known as Cherbourg) in 1905 and Woorabinda in 1926 (replacing Taroom settlement, established 1910), while a third settlement (Hull River, established in 1914) was relocated to Palm Island in 1918. By 1939 the government could report twenty-five reserves under supervision; of the seventeen in regular use, fourteen were missions and three were government settlements. Most of Queensland's 'protectors' were either police or mission staff.

In South Australia, the state reconsidered its responsibility towards Aborigines through a Royal Commission in 1913 that focused on the condition of Aboriginal people in the state's arable southern regions. The commissioners recommended that the government assume responsibility for two missions – Point Pearce and Point McLeay – that served agricultural regions with the longest exposure to colonial influence; they foreshadowed but never delivered a supplementary report on 'the out-back blacks, and the best means to be adopted to prevent the extinction of the aboriginal race'.[6] While the commission was sitting, the Lutherans were closing Killalpaninna, one of their two remote missions dedicated to 'protecting' those Aborigines farthest from agricultural settlement (the other was Koonibba on the relatively remote Eyre Peninsula). Having recently signed responsibility for the Northern Territory over to the Commonwealth, South Australia seemed to forget that a north-west sparsely populated by nomads remained. The University of Adelaide's E.C. Stirling mentioned them in a 1914 survey article that argued for government to focus on the 'settled districts' where there was 'a relatively small number of full-blooded aboriginals and a relatively large number of half-castes and other grades of intercrossing between the white and the native race, or between the latter and the Asiatic aliens, such as Afghans and Chinese'.[7] Walter Howchin's *The Geography of South Australia* (revised edition, 1917), from which a generation of South Australians learned to imagine their state, ignored Aborigines not in contact with Point Pearce, Point McLeay or Koonibba. The state declared the North-West Reserve in 1921 – an area of 56 721 square kilometres beyond colonial occupation. However, the only notice that Annual Reports of the Aborigines Department took of these remote people in the 1920s and 1930s was a few brief notes, by Port Augusta's senior police officer, on Aboriginal peoples' conditions across the northern half of the state. The Annual Reports for 1924 and 1933 mentioned that there were Aborigines in the North-West Reserve, and in 1937 these people (Anangu) became the responsibility of Presbyterians, who commenced Ernabella mission on the eastern edge of the reserve.

The pattern of institutional development in these three states was that the churches invested money and personnel in the more remote regions among Aborigines least affected by alien contact, in the hope of averting their extinction; meanwhile, each state developed institutions where people had been exposed to colonial occupation since before 1850, where 'full-bloods' were few or absent (unless they were removed there) and where the aim was to train 'detribalised' and 'half-caste' people for manual occupations. The fourth jurisdiction with 'northern' responsibilities, the Commonwealth in the Northern Territory, conformed to this pattern. Indeed, between committing to govern the Northern Territory in 1911 and committing to defend the Territory from Japan's invasion in 1939, the Australian government advanced little in its direct authority over Northern Territory Aborigines. With the important exception of the Administration's management of residential institutions for 'half-caste' children and youth in Darwin (Kahlin Compound) and Alice Springs (the Bungalow), the government conceded effective colonial authority over Aborigines to the missions and to the pastoral industry. By 1935, there were nine missions in the Northern Territory, most of them along the north coast.

TABLE 1 Chronology of remote mission formation 1877–1952

Mission	When	Who	Notes
Hermannsburg, NT	1877	Lutheran	Closed in 1892 and reopened in 1894
Daly River, NT	1882–90, 1891	Roman Catholic	Closed in 1899
Bloomfield River, Qld	1886	Lutheran	Closed in 1901
Cape Bedford/ Hope Vale, Qld	1886	Lutheran	
Mari Yamba, Qld	1888	Lutheran	Closed in 1901
Beagle Bay, WA	1891	Roman Catholic	
Mapoon, Qld	1891	Moravian/ Presbyterian	
Yarrabah, Qld	1892	Anglican	
Weipa, Qld	1898	Presbyterian	
Sunday Island, WA	1898 1924	Anglican? Roman Catholic	
Aurukun, Qld	1903	Presbyterian	
Mitchell River/ Kowanyama, Qld	1904	Anglican/ Australian Board of Missions	
Lombadina, WA	1910	Roman Catholic	
Roper River, NT	1906/1908	Church Missionary Society/Anglican	
Drysdale River/ Pago/Kalumburu, WA	1908	Roman Catholic	
Bathurst Island, NT	1910	Roman Catholic	
Kunmunya, WA	1912	Presbyterian	
Forrest River, WA	1913	Church Missionary Society/Anglican	

Mission	When	Who	Notes
Mornington Island, Qld	1914	Presbyterian	
Goulburn Island, NT	1916	Methodist	
Emerald River, NT	1921	Church Missionary Society	
Elcho Island, NT (moved to ...) Milingimbi, NT	1922 1923	Methodist	A mission was re-established on Elcho Island in 1942
Mount Margaret Mission, WA	1922	United Aborigines Mission	
Lockhart River, Qld	1924	Anglican/ Australian Board of Missions	
Edward River, Qld	1924	Anglican/ Australian Board of Missions	
Oenpelli, NT	1925	Anglican/Church Missionary Society	
Nepabunna, SA	1929	United Aborigines Mission	
Doomadgee, Qld	1931	Christian Brethren	
Yirrkala, NT	1934	Methodist	
Warburton Mission, WA	1934	United Aborigines Mission	
Ooldea, SA	1934	United Aborigines Mission	
Port Keats, NT	1935	Roman Catholic	
Ernabella, SA	1937	Presbyterian	
Balgo, WA	1939	Roman Catholic	
Finniss Springs	1939	United Aboriginies Mission	
Croker Island, NT	1941	Methodist	

Mission	When	Who	Notes
Angurugu, NT	1943	Church Missionary Society	
Jigalong	1945	Apostolic Church of Australia	
Cundelee, WA	1950	Australian Aborigines' Evangelical Mission	
Rose River (Numbulwar), NT	1952	Church Missionary Society	

The dangerous economies of remote Australia

The Christian missions of remote Australia were assemblages of routines and material goods that amounted to an 'intervention complex'. This phrase has been coined by historians of Cape York to refer to alien activities on Aboriginal land: by physical changes to the environment and by the attraction and coercion of people, these interventions changed how Aboriginal people used their country and how they related to each other and to the aliens themselves. Chris Anderson, for example, presents the history of Cape York's Kuku-Yalanji as a series of adaptations to the pressures and opportunities of, first, a tin-mining field and then to its sequel, a mission.[8] The missionaries' 'intervention complex' established its own pattern of reward, demand and proscription that was intended to displace what the missionaries saw as the predatory and corrupting presence of preceding aliens. Thus Athol Chase narrates the transition from one complex to another on east Cape York.

> First there was the complex of coastal/marine extractive industries which featured individual entrepreneurs operating in a largely undirected and uncontrolled frontier. The nature of the resources exploited meant that there was no pressure to remove Aborigines from their home territories. Rather the existence of small local populations along the coastline suited the purposes of these entrepreneurs in terms of exploitation. The second intervention complex, starting in 1924, was the Anglican mission [Lockhart River], and while this was part of a larger formal church structure, the process of articulation with the local Aboriginal population was *via* the series of individual superintendents, each with their own approaches which, though highly idiosyncratic, nevertheless acted as agents for the state as much as for the church.[9]

To consider missions as an 'intervention complex' is to highlight that missionaries saw 'industrial' work as central to their moral project. After visiting the northern missions of the Church Missionary Society Reverend R.C.M. Long wrote in 1938: 'Missionary work is of four kinds: evangelistic, educational, medical and industrial.' He added: 'Cultivation of the heart and training of the hand go together.'[10] At their most developed, remote missions were towns in which a number of occupations and services were located. At Beagle Bay mission, for example, there were the following materials and associated trades: stock work, fences, windmills, blacksmith, carpentry, tailoring, boot-making, saddler, tannery, butchers, bakers, cooks, kitchen gardens. One Beagle Bay missionary, George Walter, wrote in 1928: 'work inculcates discipline and practice of Christian virtues, as well as providing material means for the upkeep of the

Mission'.[11] Some missionaries saw agricultural work as especially significant. In an unpublished account of his work in Arnhem Land (evidently written in the late 1930s), Theodore Webb suggested that if the missionaries could get Yolngu to commit to agriculture, it would change their cosmology. '[T]he discovery that the food supply is to be assured and improved by the processes of agriculture, rather than by the observance of the traditional magical ritual of the Increase Ceremony, must mean a very far-reaching revolution of thought and belief.'[12] In north Queensland, Mapoon, Aurukun, Doomadgee and Mitchell River missions had acquired cattle herds by the 1910s – for food, for income and as a form of supervised employment.[13]

Missionaries who saw changing production and consumption as vital to Aborigines' preservation and reform were not stepping into a moral vacuum. Hunting and gathering had been a 'moral economy': the giving and receiving of the products of one's labour signified relatedness. We might therefore say that missionaries sought to replace the moral economy of hunter–gatherer society with the moral economy of a Christian agricultural community. However, that is an incomplete account of what missionaries intended and did. Remote missionaries understood themselves as intervening not only in the traditional Aboriginal way of life but also in the new and perverse colonising economies: the maritime harvesting industries (pearl-shells, trochus shells and bêche-de-mer/trepang) on the coasts of the Kimberley, Arnhem Land and Cape York; the buffalo hide industry on Melville Island and Western Arnhem Land; the beef-raising, peanut-growing and gold-seeking activities of the Daly River region; and sheep, cattle and dingo-scalping industries of Central Australia. The missionaries observed Aborigines' and Islanders' moral and physical degradation, resulting from their participation – not always voluntary – in these late 19th- and early 20th-century economic enclaves. They intervened in moral life by creating new sites for the production and consumption of goods mostly imported from the mainstream economy. The employers that they rivalled and even eclipsed sometimes responded with criticism of missions as too indulgent to be schools of good labour. May quotes one north Queensland beef boss ruing that

> formerly we took the wild niggers as babies and then trained them as stockmen. At 14 they were competent workmen and had a job on a station for life if they wanted it. Today [the 1940s], through the interference of the Missions, we are not permitted to sign on a nigger before 14.[14]

On sea as on land, the churches' evangelical and economic enclaves challenged the remote entrepreneur. Along the coast of North Australia, from Broome to Cairns, the harvesting of pearl-shell (and sometimes pearls), trochus shell and trepang bêche-de-mer had stimulated a demand for Aborigines and Torres Strait Islanders whose 'swimming-diving' in shallow water would bring rewards. A lugger would carry fifteen to twenty workers to a productive area of sea, and then disperse them in dinghies. The fish were cleaned overnight, apart from the trepang, which had to be taken to shore in batches every few days, and smoked. As the beds in shallower waters were exhausted, swimming-diving gave way to diving with breathing apparatus from around 1880. This industry, whose prosperity varied as world prices fluctuated from year to year, remained open to the entry of small operators who could lease boats and borrow to pay running costs until their catch returned an income. The industry's labour source shifted, in the period 1880–1900, from locals (Aborigines and Torres Strait Islanders) to imported workers from South-East Asia, the Pacific islands and Japan. This breach in the White Australia policy was tolerated for the sake of an industry that could not attract white labour with its low rates of pay and harsh working conditions and that had found Indigenous and non-white labour less tractable and reliable (in numbers available) than the imported. The working day was long, conditions on board were crude and uncomfortable, and there was high risk of injury and illness; divers aged quickly. In 1920, the writer R. Logan Jack doubted that participating Cape York Aborigines had 'freedom of contract' because of 'the lack of a common language'.

> It was therefore inevitable that the natives, tempted on board by presents and promises, were at times inadequately informed of the nature of their duties or the duration of their term of service. Again, in some instances, women were induced on board the luggers, having been 'sold' by the old men of the tribes for such cheap considerations as appeal to the cupidity of savages. It was not long before complaint, friction, violence, sudden death and reprisal began to be heard of.[15]

Cape York had been occupied in the period 1870–90 by the extension of a telegraph line, by the formation of pastoral leases along this line and by the Palmer River gold rush. Sandalwood, pearling and trepang industries had commenced along the coast, and hundreds of luggers used Aboriginal labour. The Torres Strait Islanders had come under alien influence even earlier. Trepang fishing is known to have occurred there as early as 1846; and the first pearl-shell station commenced on Warrier Island in 1868. The Torres Strait also saw the first corrective response by a Christian organisation. The London Missionary Society (LMS), having converted many residents of Pacific islands, moved into the Torres Strait in 1871. Evidently one reason for the people of the Strait to convert to Christianity was that under LMS authority islanders found protection from cruel and acquisitive lugger crews.[16] Although it was not LMS policy to develop commercial operations, from 1897 the Reverend F.W. Walker encouraged islanders' self-employment; 'Papuan Industries', founded by two missionaries in 1904, lent them money to buy boats, marketed their marine produce and sold them selected 'western' goods at fair prices. [17] Queensland had annexed the islands of the Torres Strait in 1879. The government resident on Thursday Island from 1886 to 1904, John Douglas, was aware of the protective efficacy of the LMS in the Strait. His regulatory strategy was to visit the fleets while they were at work, on his government boat, accompanied by police, and to encourage Christian missionaries by granting land on the Cape York coast and then gazetting some missions (such as Mapoon) as reformatories under the *Industrial and Reformatory Schools Act* 1865. After 1897, the Queensland government would give some missionaries the authority of 'protector'.

The pearling industry, based on Thursday Island, did not welcome the Cape York missions. As rival sources of food, shelter and other desired goods, missions made it harder for luggers to recruit Aboriginal labour.[18] The Cape York missionaries regretted that local Aborigines continued to have what missionary Nicholas Hey called 'periodical intercourse with vicious and ungodly whites and yellow individuals, whose temptations they seemed powerless to resist'. There was no 'sense of sin in the native mind'.[19] On the east coast of Cape York, missionaries saw their colonial predecessors as including men of corrupting impact – not only lugger crews but also timber-getters in north Queensland's forests. Queensland's northern protector, W.E. Roth, reported of the Aboriginal people that 'they know what drink is; they recognise and appreciate the monetary value of their women; they suffer markedly from venereal disease; they have picked up the vices of their visitors with the result that they are rapidly diminishing in numbers'.[20]

It was common for the capitalists of the West Kimberley region to invest in both land and sea industries and to recruit local Aboriginal labour to both. Credible reports of exploitation and cruelty towards Aborigines led to attempts at statutory regulation by the government in Perth from 1871, but it was difficult to appoint state officials whose interests were not implicated in the new maritime and land industries whose labour conditions they were supposed to regulate. As on Cape York, a relatively weak colonial state welcomed the churches when they offered more wholesome forms of colonial authority that would displace or limit the influence of private employers. The state had the power to gazette reserves where lugger crews could not land and the church (in this region, mostly Roman Catholics) wished to place dedicated clergy on those reserves. In cooperating in this way with the church, the government understood that the region's entrepreneurs would resent any weakening of their hold on Aboriginal labour.[21] Catholic clergy who looked for a mission site on the Dampier Peninsula soon found local Aboriginal people cooperative.[22] Magdalene Williams, born at Beagle Bay Mission in 1921, relays family stories about the Nyul Nyul people spending as little time as possible near the coast, to avoid being mistreated by aliens in the pearl-shell industry.[23] The establishment of the coastal mission camps, first at Goodenough Bay (1886), then at Sunday Island (1899), Beagle Bay (1891) and Lombadina (1910), assured the Nyul Nyul, Djaba-Djaba and Bardi people of continuing safe access to some coastal homelands.

On the two islands of the Tiwi and in the western Arnhem Land country of the Kunwinjku, the hide of the buffalo had become the freebooting entrepreneurs' prize, booming in the 1890s. Aboriginal people were involved to a limited extent in the shooting of buffalo and to a larger extent in the skinning process that followed. Mulvaney has described the labour process:

> while Aboriginal men killed, skinned and dehorned beasts wounded by Europeans, females scraped off the flesh, washed and used some 10 kg of coarse salt to preserve each hide. They then folded the hides, which weighed anything from 30 to 60 kg, so their preparation at billabongs and their pack horse transport and stacking at river boat landings was strenuous and dirty work, involving many people who became attracted to and identified with individual hunter partnerships.[24]

In both the Tiwi islands and in western Arnhem Land, missions became the successor authorities to the buffalo entrepreneurs. Buffalo hunting on Melville Island from 1892 to 1896 brought violent clashes with Tiwi. Shooting buffalo and shipping their hides restarted on Melville Island under Joe Cooper's leadership in 1905. Cooper did not recruit Tiwi labour for his trepang, forestry and lugger chartering business interests, preferring to import Iwaidja people from the mainland. Spencer described them as Cooper's 'bodyguard'; they became a source of instability.[25] In his memoirs, published in the 1950s, Father F.X. Gsell recalled that he established Bathurst Island Mission just as the trouble between the Tiwi people and Cooper's men was coming to a head, in 1910.[26] Siting Bathurst Island Mission across Apsley Strait from Cooper's camp, Gsell challenged the entrepreneurs: an unnamed 'chap' had protested that if the church started a mission on Melville Island it would harm his business.[27] At first, the Commonwealth could look to both the mission and the private employer as authorities exerting influence over the Tiwi; it appointed Cooper as a sub-protector with the power to receive Aboriginal people punished by expulsion from the mainland for infringing the *Aboriginals Ordinance*. Cooper was also the effective broker of Aboriginal labour for another businessman on Melville, the timber-getter Samuel Green. Green accused Cooper of mistreating the Aborigines whose punishment he supervised and of allowing his Iwaidja employees to abduct and rape Tiwi women and to spread venereal disease. An enquiry in 1914–15 cleared Cooper, but the government decided that it would be best to repatriate the Iwaidja to the mainland. The Administration appointed as honorary protector a Catholic missionary recently arrived to assist Gsell, Father Regis Courbon; his task was to oversee the expulsion of Iwaidja. The Tiwi story is thus a cameo of a mission succeeding a private entrepreneur, and of the mission as the local delegate of the skeletal colonial state. The Catholics were offering the Tiwi an alternative source of patronage and authority to that presented by a pioneering entrepreneur and his retinue of armed Aborigines from elsewhere.[28]

In a parallel story, people of western Arnhem Land were attracted in the 1890s by the issue of food and tobacco in exchange for labour in gardens, on cattle leases and at buffalo-hide camps. The South Australian government gazetted four reserves between Darwin and the Alligator River in 1892, but their boundaries meant little to the Aborigines attracted to work for Chinese and Europeans. From 1910, South Australia obliged employers of Aborigines to seek a licence, refusing licences to Asians. The buffalo industry was seasonal, and this seems to have synchronised with the seasonal mobility of western Arnhem Land people, resulting in movement between their home estates and Darwin or Pine Creek (in the wet) and the buffalo-hunting areas (in the dry, May to October).[29] That the authority of some buffalo entrepreneurs was seen as corrupting is suggested by Baldwin Spencer's report (in 1913) that competing for Aboriginal labour led some bosses to include methylated spirit in payment for work. However, Spencer saw Paddy Cahill – residing at Oenpelli on the East Alligator River since 1909 – as one buffalo boss who could be relied on as a protector.[30] Appointed in 1912 to supervise the newly gazetted Alligator Reserve, Cahill's reports confirmed that the Aboriginal population in western Arnhem Land had diminished because of untreated disease; land thus deprived of people attracted people from further east, such as the Kunwinjku. Cahill diversified his business, grazing a dairy herd at Oenpelli and reinforcing its importance as a gathering point for Gagudju people (west of Oenpelli) and for others coming in from the east. The Northern Territory Administration retained Cahill as manager and protector when it purchased his farm as a dairy/butter source. Cahill left in 1922, and so did many Gagudju. The Church Missionary Society took over Oenpelli in 1925, with a small government subsidy, ministering to people that were increasingly from Kunwinjku country.[31]

Further east in Arnhem Land, Yolngu had for two centuries built ties of mutual understanding and interest with the seasonally (November to April) visiting Makassans, who gathered on certain beaches and dried trepang.[32] In 1906 the South

Australian government forbade Makassans to land and camp with Yolngu. This did not end Yolngu transactions with aliens; others, less familiar to Yolngu than the Makassans and more likely to be a source of trouble, were attracted to the Arnhem Land coast by its sea products. By establishing missions on Goulburn Island in 1916 and at Milingimbi in 1923, the Methodists saw themselves as helping Yolngu to negotiate their increasing exposure to such aliens. After the Commonwealth declared Arnhem Land a reserve in 1931, the Methodists were poised to further their influence, considering a mission in east Arnhem Land. In the period 1932–34, Yolngu got into trouble for killing Japanese and Europeans, and then for spearing one of the investigating police. The Methodists established Yirrkala Mission on the Gove Peninsula, north-east Arnhem Land, in 1935.

In 1935, the Catholic Church founded a mission at Port Keats. The region had been affected by a series of colonial intrusions. To the south of the Port Keats area a number of cattle runs had formed – Victoria River Downs (1883), Delamere (1883), Rosewood (1885), Auvergne (1886), Bradshaw (1896) – causing many bloody clashes between the region's Aborigines and the incoming pastoralists. However, in the years from 1895, the pastoralists had begun to pacify the locals by attracting them into station camps with food and tobacco exchanged for labour.[33] To the north of the Port Keats area, along the Daly River, there had been an unsuccessful sugar cane enterprise in 1879–83, and then the cattle herds in 1884–89. Copper had attracted miners to the Daly, and there was even a smelter there in the years between 1882 and 1899. The Daly had also attracted Chinese farmers and a government experimental farm in the years 1912–16; a police depot had commenced in 1915. Settlers attempted cotton, dairy and peanut farms in the 1920s. People whose country lay between Victoria River and Daly River were thus being attracted out of their country, to the south and to the north, even though the Commonwealth had declared an area around Port Keats a reserve in 1920. The people of this region acquired a reputation for violent predation of aliens, illustrated by their killing of three Japanese fishermen in 1931 near Port Keats, followed by the capture, trial and sentencing of Nemarluk and his associates. When Father Richard Docherty, accompanied by anthropologist W.E.H. Stanner, arrived by boat at Port Keats and established a mission in 1935, his strategy was to attract people back into their reserved homeland in order to stabilise a people who, in Stanner's view, had become restless and competitive for access to employment and tobacco.[34]

In arid Central Australia, Lutherans had established Hermannsburg Mission on the Finke River in the western MacDonnell Range in 1877 at the same time as the stock of the earliest pastoral leases began to arrive. After a few years' interruption (1892–94), the Lutherans continued. They saw the mission as a sanctuary in a region where marginal pastoralists, sometimes assisted by police, had felt entitled to shoot Aborigines who speared their stock.[35] From the mid-1890s it became the custom for pastoral lessees to ration Aborigines in exchange for labour; at the same time, the mission began to develop itself as a pastoral enterprise. The mission formed an economic link with another cattle-grazing Lutheran mission that had struggled on the arid fringe of the pastoral estate since 1866, Killalpaninna on Cooper's Creek, east of Lake Eyre. In the 1890s, staff of the missions worked out a cattle droving route between the two missions.[36] Killalpaninna closed in 1915; it had not been able to reverse the attrition of the Dieri people and their neighbours – ravaged by disease – but it had probably contributed to the survival of the people who had migrated out of the Simpson Desert, around the end of the 19th century, to investigate this pastoral fringe.[37]

Protecting sheep from dingoes was one way to redirect Aboriginal labour in such pastoral zones. Governments (starting with South Australia in 1912, followed by Western Australia and the Northern Territory in the 1920s) put a bounty on dingo scalps. These payments became the basis of a 'dogging' industry along the western edge of Central Australian pastoral leases. Issuing tea, flour, sugar and tobacco, doggers would pay Aborigines to bring them scalps on which they would then collect the state's cash bounty.[38] Because the Lutherans were starting contact with western desert people migrating eastwards in the 1920s, the rise of the dingo scalp trade became both a threat and an opportunity. The Lutherans sought to emulate the doggers by trading food and other goods for scalps. Their intention was to make the dingo scalp trade a 'buffer' economy for people with hunter–gatherer skills. By supplying the goods that Aborigines wanted, close to or within their own country, the missionaries hoped to make it less attractive for them to migrate east to Alice Springs, where alcohol abuse and prostitution were likely. As a broker of scalps, the mission hoped not only for income but also for influence; they wished to determine what desert people would consume, where and what work they would do, and for what rewards.

Far to the south-west of Hermannsburg, but within the arid pastoral zone, Rodolphe Schenk of the United Aborigines Mission founded a mission at Mount Margaret in 1922 among people severely disrupted by gold mining since 1893. Discarded buildings and equipment enabled Schenk quickly and cheaply to form a successor township whose Aboriginal residents he sought to mobilise in harvesting sandalwood, managing a goat herd, raffia work (for women), growing vegetables and sending men to neighbouring pastoralists as shearers. Against Christians who saw in such worldly concerns a lack of faith in God's providence, Schenk wrote:

> In some places like this, there is no way to gather and help natives except by making them reproductive, and, while every member of our staff wholly trusts God for every penny of his or her support, yet we believe the natives should endeavour to earn their own living. Every penny of the proceeds of the industrial work goes to this end, and we teach them, by example as well as by precept, the Scripture truth that if a man does not work he should not eat, and all this that they may eat of the heavenly manna both now and hereafter.[39]

Mount Margaret men were also encouraged to hunt dingoes to trade with police for extra rations.

Hundreds of kilometres to the east, in the north-west of South Australia, people (now known as Anangu) had hardly been disturbed by the first decade of the 20th century. The inception of the dingo scalp bounty in 1912 gave aliens an incentive to hunt in these lands beyond pastoral endeavour, and reports of abuses encouraged South Australia to gazette the North-West Reserve in 1921, including the Musgrave, Mann and Tomkinson Ranges. In 1925 the government had refused to allow a mission in the reserve, but it had allowed pastoral leases along its eastern edge, arousing fears that pastoralism and dogging would compromise the reserve. Encouraged by Pastor Albrecht at Finke River Mission (Hermannsburg), Dr Charles Duguid persuaded the Presbyterian Church to purchase one of the leases close to the reserve's eastern border, Ernabella, in December

1936. Ernabella's interim superintendent 'sought to counter the activities of the doggers by paying full value for dingo scalps to the Aborigines'. The mission thus hoped to manage Aboriginal contact with the wider economy; using skills that they already possessed, Anangu would not leave the reserve.[40] As Ernabella was a sheep station, residents also had the option to shepherd and shear, for rations.

Four themes were prominent in missionary writings. First, Aborigines were being rewarded with harmful new commodities: alcohol and opium (and some missionaries thought tobacco harmful). Second, the attraction of even non-destructive goods, such as basic food stuffs and clothes, was rapidly diminishing their skill and motivation in hunting and gathering. Third, customs of sexuality that may have suited Aboriginal and Islander social structures of pre-colonial times had gained a new and self-destructive significance in the context of these overwhelmingly masculine frontier economies.[41] Fourth, avid trafficking of goods and female bodies occasioned misunderstanding and bad faith and triggered corrective violence by both sides; such violence was increasingly likely to draw the attention of the police, and so the possibility of an Aboriginal person becoming an outlaw and a gaolbird increased as frontier economies came under police surveillance. To provide other options for Aborigines' adaptation, the missionary intervention complex regulated access to alien material culture; it allowed and even encouraged the persistence of hunting and gathering, with associated ceremonies, while promoting new forms of labour to produce food and tradeable artefacts; it subjected women's sexuality to new authority – though missions varied in their design of that authority. These three interventions were intended to pre-empt violent incidents. To obviate the intervention of police created a local mission jurisdiction.

Work, reward and attachment in the mission intervention complex

To make the mission a moral economy required missionaries to experiment cautiously with the terms on which goods and services circulated. Bishop Otto Raible told an audience of Catholics in Sydney Town Hall in 1938 that on the Dampier Peninsula it was taking three generations to turn the Aboriginal nomad into a settled worker; some residents 'like to go for a walkabout at times' for up to a month, discarding their clothes.[42] Raible was not complaining to his audience but encouraging them to be patient. Australians had been wrong to dismiss Aborigines as hopeless candidates for improvement, he told Sydney's Catholics, but missionary experience taught patience: people could not be forced into new patterns of behaviour. Missionary patience acknowledged residual autonomy. Although access to goods was an incentive to work at the mission and to submit to its influence, in some regions able-bodied adults could support themselves by hunting and gathering, though such autonomy risked starvation.

Missions widely avowed the policy of 'no work, no rations'. This norm entailed that, for periods, people would live beyond daily mission influence. The policy had to be applied thoughtfully. Because missions needed to cultivate a certain level of goodwill, they could not be too 'hard', and it was difficult to forbid 'working' Aborigines from redistributing goods to 'non-working' associates. Some missionaries admitted that their issue of goods, in practice, amounted to gift diplomacy. Gsell, at Bathurst Island Mission, recalled in the 1950s that his approach to work discipline was 'friendly cooperation', offering tasks 'as a kind of game at which all may play who wish'.[43] The Tiwi love gifts, he recalled, and it was better that they saw the missionary as 'a benefactor, but never a master … If they realise you are helping them, the cause is won: but it is fatal ever to attempt to play the boss because authority is constitutionally repugnant to them and they will always refuse to recognise it.'[44] According to Father Walter, 'for Aborigines [at Beagle Bay], correct mission method is to let them get used to a settled lifestyle and regular work without using force or restricting their freedom. Only love and a friendly approach can lead to success, not harshness or force.'[45]

In the foundation phases of a mission, when the priority was to construct buildings and to establish gardens, missionaries learned to use Aboriginal labour opportunistically. At Pago (which became Kalumburu) the Benedictine fathers were at first in a tense relationship with the local Aboriginal people. Eight years after they arrived, the Aborigines' tolerance of their presence had become a pattern. 'The tactics of the Aborigines were now well known – to spend at the mission some time on more or less friendly visits which lasted as long as they found them profitable, and leave again on their walkabout to other places, returning when least expected.'[46] Thus 'members of wandering tribal groups were always at the mission, staying for a while, but not as long as to form the desired stable community'.[47] The Benedictines went to the trouble to record their first gift: 'a tomahawk, for constancy in work, was given to Unaratje Bodidji on 18 November 1917'.[48]

Some missions made festive assembly for receiving and giving Christmas gifts – an occasion to reach out to the less engaged Aboriginal people. Such was the enduring appeal of this custom that after the Lutherans had closed Killalpaninna (in 1915), visits by concerned Lutheran missionaries could maximise contact with the dispersed former residents if they returned to Cooper's Creek at Christmas.[49] At Oenpelli in 1929, 100 Aborigines were recorded as living at the mission, including boys and girls in dormitories, with a further 200 living in scattered nomadic groups within two or three days' walk. These more peripheral people came in for Christmas when the mission staff distributed presents and food and, on Boxing Day, conducted sports and games.[50] At Roper River, 'a goodly crowd spend their Christmas season at the Mission, parents often coming, at the special invitation of children at the station, to take part in the festivities and receive gifts'.[51] At Kalumburu, the first Christmas Day carnival, held in 1922, was another milestone recorded in the mission diary: 'sports, prizes for the best performers and presents for everyone. It was an experience they would never forget, and Christmas remained as the day of the year, which was really "their own" big day.'[52] Not only Christmas festivities attracted the more detached Aboriginal people to a mission. According to Theodore Webb, Milingimbi Mission got a reputation for healing, attracting Aborigines otherwise not engaged with the mission.[53] Those who were loosely attached could still present a problem, however; in 1930 cattle belonging to the Oenpelli Mission were speared.

Aboriginal people could choose the manner and degree of engagement with the mission as long as they could access food-yielding land and sea beyond it. Without specifying regions, Anne O'Brien has argued that before World War II, many Aboriginal people were caught between a diminishing traditional food supply and a humanitarian approach that, fearing 'pauperisation', stinted food aid.[54] The residents of the Finke River Mission (Hermannsburg) suffered malnutrition in the dry years 1927–29, with the loss of 85 per cent of the children.[55] That remote Aboriginal people could and should operate in two economic spheres at once was an assumption and even, in some places, an aim of mission policy. At Port Keats, where the priority projects after 1935 included a garden, a stockyard, an air strip, a fish trap, two wells and a beef herd, Father Docherty's policy was that people spend two weeks out of every four away from the mission, sustaining themselves on their own country and continuing their ritual life.[56] Thus people from different estates in the region alternated fortnightly as the mission's resident workforce. This may well have prevented violent competition among people vying to receive the mission's goods.[57] The Methodists at Yirrkala also assumed the continuing existence of two economic sectors: they issued potatoes, cassava and tobacco to Yolngu who assisted the missionaries, but in the expectation that a worker's family would also be out on country, getting food.[58]

A mission's layout expressed, in spatial terms, a spectrum of subjection to missionary authority, and individuals could position themselves near to or far from authority and goods. At Roper River Mission there were residents of the station compound (which consisted of dormitories for girls and boys, store house, meat house, church in the centre of the compound, and dispensary) and a camp external to the compound, for visiting Aborigines made up of six different tribes from 'many miles away'.[59] A map of Beagle Bay, presented by Father George Walter in 1927, showed that close to the missionaries themselves were the children's dormitories; further from these buildings was what the mission called 'the colony' – the huts for married couples, in orderly array; beyond them were relatives of the children, camping on the mission's periphery. Magdalene Williams, who grew up at Beagle Bay in the 1920s, recalls that those living in the camp 'had the best life for they could still go to the bush and hunt for their own foods as well as eat the white man's food at the main dining room if they wanted to'.[60]

In a lecture delivered in Melbourne in 1934 Webb referred

to Milingimbi as an 'experiment' in 'racial salvation'.[61] Like other missionaries, he knew that Aborigines' interest in associating with whites was focused, to a large extent, on accessing certain goods. Webb warned against 'gifts'. Instead, he explained, 'we have instituted a simple and generous system of trading, by means of which an individual becomes possessed of these things as a result of his or her own endeavour and enterprise'.[62] In his 1938 sequel *Spears to Spades,* Webb repeated that there should be no food distribution except as payment for personal effort (with exceptions for the sick and aged).[63] In his unpublished memoir he said that Milingimbi mission issued not only food but also money to use at the mission store, reward matching effort. Articles manufactured by men and women were purchased by the store – 'a valuable introduction to the economics of civilisation'.[64] The mission did not require a fixed working day, he wrote: people were given a week to complete a task and so could decide to devote some days to hunting. At Milingimbi, there was a Yolngu 'ganger' with 'his own methods of dealing with inefficiency or slackness, with the support if necessary of one of our staff'.[65] To shop at the mission store helped to form Yolngu character, Webb thought: he commended holding some payment in reserve until the end of a week or fortnight so that the worker would have the means to shop. Webb's ideas about rewarding work effort included recognising skill and responsibility – for example, certain sawmill tasks – with higher payments. In the production of craft goods, he recommended piece rates rather than time rates. He had found that Yolngu worked better in gangs than as individuals. Like Docherty at Port Keats and the Pallottines at Beagle Bay, Webb professed respect for ceremony: the goodwill of labourers was assured, he claimed, because the mission suspended most work when ceremonies were taking place.

Cape York missions were enterprises designed to a moral purpose. Having developed Mapoon from 1891 to 1919, Nicholas Hey wrote about Mapoon (in 1923) and other Presbyterian missions on Cape York (in a 1931 history), describing a spectrum of Aboriginal commitments to mission life. On the one hand, 'some of the old people are hard cases': they have not changed their dress though they attend the hospital and the kitchen for medicine and food. Hey mentioned a 'witch doctor and rainmaker' and another who is recognised as an authority 'on native folk lore or native history' who has two wives – 'a quite unusual thing'.[66] On the other hand there were 'the Christian educated and trained young couples' – including wives who graduated from the dormitory – who 'are actively working out their own destiny, forming a settled agricultural community' four miles away from Mapoon at Musgrave Settlement.[67] There, each couple had a block of five or more acres on which to grow produce; what they did not eat they could sell on Thursday Island through the mission's agency, receiving payment in a local currency designed for use in Mapoon's Native Cooperative Store. The Musgrave residents elected a counsellor, for a twelve-month term, 'to report any difficulty he does not feel competent to deal with that may arise among the people'.[68] Standing above the counsellor in Musgrave Settlement's hierarchy was a native pastor, whose wife kept a record of church attendance: a person could be banned from the quarterly communion service at Mapoon if they did not attend at least two-thirds of the weekly prayer meetings.[69]

The Lutherans had begun work among Cape York Aborigines in 1886 at the linked sites of Hope Vale and Cape Bedford. After persuading the Queensland government to extend the reserve by 20 000 acres along the McIvor River in 1908, they cleared the land in order to grow food and coconuts. As Germans suspected of disloyalty, the Lutherans had to fight off confiscation in the years 1919–23. In 1923 they were given fishing rights along the coast north of Cape Bedford. The Lutherans sought a maritime economy (trepang and trochus) in addition to farming, which had not been sufficiently rewarding, and they wished to keep Japanese lugger crews – with their 'starvation, misery and syphilization' – at a distance.[70] By 1926 a mission-owned boat with a non-Aboriginal skipper and a privately owned boat were using labour from the mission. When war between Japan and China in 1937 reduced demand for trepang and trochus, crews switched to hunting dugong – their prey in pre-colonial times – for oil. Further north on the Cape York coast, Lockhart River Mission, under superintendent Harry Rowan from 1924 to 1938, also encouraged residents to gather trochus shell, trepang, turtle shell and shark fin; the mission provided not only a boat but a boiler for curing fish. Following the example of their pre-mission 'boss', a Mr Giblet, people oriented to Lockhart River Mission also collected sandalwood and other timber. There were gardens, though Rowan found that people did not like working in them, and women wove mats and baskets. Lockhart River ran a store where residents could exchange their own produce for rations or cash. The inadequacy of government and mission subsidy made it necessary for residents to be employed for wages on non-mission boats. For the same budgetary reason, residents were encouraged to move beyond the mission in the dry season, foraging in family groups.[71]

In the Torres Strait, work on the fishing boats could not absorb all labour and nor was the cash return from such work reliable. Beckett calls the Islanders a 'part-time proletariat'.[72] For mission and government authority the problem in designing a protective economy was to negotiate 'the push–pull of an industrial system that required the continuance of subsistence production'.[73] That is, the 'problem was to achieve the right balance between commercial and subsistence production, under conditions of fluctuating shell prices and working conditions'.[74] On at least one occasion, the teacher–supervisor ordered people to make gardens, as insurance for a time when cash flow might be inadequate for food purchase.[75]

The mission extension of colonial authority into remote Aboriginal Australia from the 1880s to the late 1930s attempted to determine the relationships among three kinds of economy: the hunter–gatherer (perceived by missionaries as having no long-term future in the modern world, but important to sustain in the short term), the secular–colonial (perceived by missionaries as routinely corrupting – morally and physically – and episodically dangerous) and the mission–colonial (missionaries' wholesome alternative to the secular–colonial). From the point of view of the missions' enclave moral economies, there were thus two kinds of exterior world. One was the food-yielding land- and seascapes, in many cases protected from colonial occupation as 'reserve', where Aboriginal people in contact with a mission continued to gain part of their material livelihood and to honour sites of spiritual significance. Missionaries were uncertain about how long traditional subsistence could continue, but they did not want to hasten its end; they varied in their stances towards the religious belief and rituals that were integral to customary land and sea management. Father Raible conceded that he could 'find in the legends and fairy tales of the natives certain truths and sentiments which rightly can be claimed as the remnants of an original revelation.… handed down from their ancestors and … the trace of divine revelation'.[76] Of Yolngu ritual Webb wrote: 'By these ceremonies the tribal organisation, with all its social and moral implications, is maintained and enforced, and the people are brought into comforting and vitalizing communion with the world of nature about them.'[77]

The other 'exterior' of the mission enclave economy was the society and economy of Australia and the world; it was a source of desired exotic goods, but missionaries thought that it should tap the Indigenous labour supply only in ways that did not jeopardise the mission's moral and industrial project. To construct a Christian alternative to the pressures of remote colonial industries was to attempt segregation. In some regions, a high degree of labour market segregation was feasible, such as in the vast reserve of Arnhem Land and on Bathurst and Melville islands – places difficult for colonial entrepreneurs to access. However, such isolation was vulnerable to far-off investment decisions. For example, the CMS mission on Groote Eylandt was remote from labour markets until 1938, when a portion of the reserve was excised so that the Department of Civil Aviation could establish a flying boat refuelling base, operated by the Shell Company, at Port Langdon on the north-eastern tip of the island. This base created a local demand for labour which was beyond the sphere of influence of the CMS mission at Emerald River on the south-eastern side of Groote Eylandt. Fred Gray, a trader and trepanger on the Arnhem Land and Gulf coasts in the early 1930s, was on good terms with the Emerald River missionaries. They entrusted him to supply labour to the Shell base from his private Umbakumba settlement, where he had once had a trepang camp; Aborigines working at the base resided there from 1938 until 1958. Thus the mission and Gray found a way to ally their economic enclaves. In Queensland, some missions eventually let residents go out to work for other cattle stations, preferring near ones or properties managed by families they knew and trusted (such as Nockatunga, near Cunnamulla); they made judgments about how such men spent their money and sought to influence their consumption through management of wage accounts.[78]

Aborigines and Islanders were, of course, attracted by the wider world that would pay them money for labour, and to the extent that missions kept people healthy and trained them they had some prospect of satisfying their recently awakened desires. At Beagle Bay, Father Walter was 'confronted with the dilemma of being unable to offer adequate employment to all'.[79] Broome townspeople, only 120 kilometres by road from the mission, became keen to employ mission-trained workers, but the missionaries were worried that residing in Broome, with wages to spend, would undermine the morality of mission-raised people.[80] Father Walter would like to have settled Aborigines of the north-west on farms, notwithstanding that climate, poor soils and distance from market made farming precarious in that region. He thought the social argument for state-subsidised farming was strong: if they are to survive and be regarded as the equals of whites, Walter wrote in 1927, 'the Blacks are to become the future farmers of the North'.[81] When Beagle Bay graduates were allowed to work in Broome, the moral risk of getting and spending money was mitigated by Broome's convent, established in 1912 under the St John of God nuns. According to Durack, the mission encouraged those working in Broome to remain in frequent contact with family on the mission; she believed that both Broome residents and the mission ultimately benefited from mission-trained Aborigines' employment.[82] The problem of Broome's proximity provoked Beagle Bay missionaries to think about paying wages on the mission, rather than payment in kind, in the mid-1920s. Walter reported that although Aborigines were 'happy with being paid in kind, it would have been good if the Mission could have offered its grown up charges more than clothes, food, and an occasional bonus for their work ... but from where would the money have come?'[83]

In the Torres Strait we see the earliest instance of the state's economic takeover of the remote mission's moral domain – a sequence that applied, to some degree, in every remote region of Australia by the 1950s. Papuan Industries – a mission initiative – was absorbed into the Queensland government's Aboriginal Property Protection Account in 1931, becoming 'Aboriginal Industries'. The mission–government encouragement of Islander self-employment in the 'company' fleet meant that in the Torres Strait, economic segregation took a particular form. Islanders made up about 20 per cent of the workforce in the pearling, trochus and trepang industry up to 1941, but employers were of two kinds: mission/government and private/non-Indigenous.[84] The more skilful and materially ambitious Islanders had a choice to work either for Aboriginal Industries (on 'company' boats) or for the (private) 'masters'. Most worked on company boats; their operation was more suited to Islanders' wish to divide their time between hunting, gardening and generating a cash income by boat work. Whether working on a 'company' or a 'master' boat, an Islander was legally an 'Aborigine' and perceived as feckless; the government held a portion of his wages in trust, drawing on this fund when investing in boats for the Islanders.

According to Beckett, the difference between the two kinds of employer was keenly felt in the early 1930s. 'Wages on the master boats were not high, but they were predictable; on the company boats "we never knew where we were"', because officials' management of each person's trust account was not well understood.[85] Islander resentment against government authority in 'company' boat employment was fuelled by their feelings about other instances of government control; they found officials increasingly overbearing in the early 1930s. The teachers appointed to each island had powers far beyond those normally held by teachers: each was the chief administrator on his island, with little accountability to residents. The system of payment was especially irksome. Each worker had a passbook, in which his debts (including to government-run stores) and his credits were calculated. When their pay was less than they hoped for or believed they were entitled to, they suspected that the government was not handling their money honestly.[86] This feeling of resentment towards the state provoked 400 men on twenty-five 'company' boats to refuse to man them in 1936. During the strike the government imprisoned some leaders, dismissed certain councillors and sent armed white police to some islands. There was no clear strike leader, though the men from the eastern islands were the most 'intransigent'. In some communities, parents withheld their children from school, in further expression of the Islanders' anger. The strike was strong partly because of the concessions that 'company' employment had long made to Islanders' way of life. That is, the Islanders were not separated from their subsistence means of production: strikers could garden and fish. To get the strikers back on the boats, the Queensland government had to make concessions; it empowered councils vis-à-vis the teacher–administrators and it distinguished Islanders from Aborigines in the *Torres Strait Islanders Act* of 1939. However, the government's management of employees' income, through the trust, remained.

The significance of Indigenous women

Polygyny was a significant aspect of the Indigenous subsistence economy. The social organisation of labour – including the labour of producing and socialising new human beings – was expressed in the 'privilege' of older men to have more than one wife and to acquire wives, as young girls, through agreement with other adults of the child's family. That a political economy should manifest to outsiders as an exotic and (to many) offensive order of sexuality made it inevitable that colonists would experience their political relationship with the Aboriginal social order as if it were a contest between civilised and barbarous moralities. A Darwin resident wrote to A.P. Elkin in 1934 that, 'A lubra has no honour; she is a chattel, bought and sold like an animal; her husband uses her as a medium of exchange for tobacco or silver.'[87] Missionary Dick Harris thought that old men's privileged access to women encouraged resistance in the form of 'secret liaisons, elopements and fighting'.[88] Missionaries and others had to consider if and how to intervene in the raising of children and in the discipline of sex.

The counsel of anthropology was becoming available by the 1930s, issuing a caution to righteousness. Phyllis Kaberry invited readers to understand sexuality in terms of its social function, suspending moral judgment. Kaberry had spent nearly all of the 1934 dry season at Forrest River Mission (and three weeks at Beagle Bay) and she had observed 'mutual affection ... between husband and wife'. Responding critically to depictions of the Aboriginal woman as a kind of slave whose subordination began when she was bestowed, as a young girl, on an old and domineering man, she wrote that research showed the woman not 'as a slave; her work is shown to be not particularly onerous;

she does assert herself on occasion; she retains her rights to her country; and she does not assume the full responsibilities of marriage until after puberty'.[89] Kaberry sought to make 'Aboriginal woman' accessible and familiar, less an object of pity and outrage. In their motives to marry, Kaberry discerned desires similar to those evident in her own society: for economic security, for children, for sexual experience that had the blessing rather than the condemnation of 'public opinion'. 'Marriage for an aboriginal woman is a means of living a full life, of finding economic, sexual, social, and sentimental satisfaction.'[90] Kaberry further suggested that living under mission and pastoral authority had begun to intensify the Kimberley woman's interest in sex and to weaken her desire for children. The women's ceremonial life – distinct from and (she conceded) secondary in status to men's – included love magic rituals that gave a sacred dimension to their profane preoccupation with sexuality. Though women lavished care and affection on children, they saw their offspring more as a consequence of marriage than as a reason to look forward to it, she reported. Kaberry saw this reluctance to bear children as an 'injury to the social structure and activities contingent on white contact'.[91]

Some missionaries took up the anthropologists' invitation to see Aboriginal sexuality in its own terms. Theodore Webb warned that it would be unwise to attempt to abolish polygyny, as it was, in its own way, an orderly moral system, and to outlaw it would probably encourage promiscuity, 'incest' (according to Aboriginal notions of licit sex) and the neglect of discarded wives. White hostility to Yolngu marriage customs had encouraged the Aborigines to view the whites' moral code as lax, Webb thought. A decree to abolish child betrothal and child marriage would collapse the whole system, 'leaving only chaos out of which it would be impossible for these people to find their way'.[92] Webb also grasped the economic importance of women. His 1938 pamphlet explained Yolngu polygyny not by reference to a heathen lack of morals but to the economic advantages of having many females gathering food for a domestic unit in a demanding environment.[93] However, Webb did see problems in Yolngu relations between men and women. Although women were not simply pawns of men, their labour, including their sexuality, was ultimately under male command, and not only force but also shame pressured women to meet their obligations. Women at Milingimbi were habituated to their subordination and this 'has developed within them a condition of apathy and of mental stagnation which is extremely difficult to overcome'.[94] While Webb saw polygyny as an economic structure embedded in a moral code, like other missionaries he sought to give women some protection and even to refashion the female life course. 'There is certainly room for a Feminist Movement in Arnhem Land,' he remarked.[95]

Missions differed in the degree and manner of their intervention into Indigenous marriage customs, and two factors made the politics of such interventions unpredictable. First, even if custom were felt as a burden by young women, would they welcome missionary intervention? Presbyterian J.R.B. Love, on the eve of becoming a missionary in 1915, speculated that the Lutheran practice of housing girls in dormitories might not only increase a girl's reluctance to marry the old man to whom she is betrothed but also isolate her socially.

> More than likely, she desires to marry a smart young fellow on the station. The solution of this problem is one that can only be arrived at by tactful and careful consideration of

the aboriginal point of view, which would regard a girl who left her tribally betrothed for another as a moral outcast, while the offending couple are almost certain to be speared at the first opportunity.[96]

Second, if women were, to a degree, a fungible asset, would senior men accept material compensation for losing a wife? Love mentioned the possibility of buying the girls from the old men, or of encouraging young men to negotiate their obligation to the old ones.[97] In the Torres Strait, the economics of marriage were transparent: bride price was customary, and it rose as one effect of the LMS's morality and of young men's participation in the new economy.[98] Bathurst Island missionaries grasped the economic importance of women to their husbands, compensating senior men for the girls that the mission sequestered.

From the point of view of some missionaries, monogamous union was a necessary aspect of Christian conversion. The Lutheran mission to the Guugu Yimidhirr at Cape Bedford encouraged Christian approaches to marriage and sexuality. Around 1900 the mission selected three young couples to marry: the women were baptised but not the men. The incentive for women to accept baptism was that it would remove them from the perceived vulnerability of being one of several wives to physically dominant old men; for the young men the incentive was that under mission patronage they could marry young women (traditionally a privilege of senior men) and stay living on the mission.[99] The mission reassured Chief Protector W.E. Roth that the pairings did not violate custom. The marriages took place in January 1901, and the men were baptised later that year.[100]

Dormitories were the most ambitious direct intervention in the life course and thus in the customs of marriage. Not only were they a means to reshape local customs of sexuality and marriage: in those missions authorised by the state to receive children who had been removed (often with their mothers) from camps perceived as squalid and predatory, dormitories were intended as a measure of child protection. However, the dormitory was controversial. The Presbyterian founders of Ernabella were of the same view as Webb in Arnhem Land: while schooling would be offered, a dormitory would be too aggressive an intrusion into Anangu tribal life. Those favouring dormitories said that even if a girl did not have to be protected from sexual predation, she should nonetheless be trained to new wifely expectations and skills. As Hey reported of Mapoon in 1923, 'the girls ... remain in the mission compound until they get married', while the boys are trained in farming at the Batavia River experimental farm or in stock work, boat work or carpentering.[101]

At Mornington Island, the Presbyterians recruited Aboriginal assistants (from this and other Cape York missions) to help them to persuade local Aboriginal families to let their girls be housed in dormitories; an important part of their persuasion was that the Lardil families' contact with the girls could continue.[102] At Oenpelli and Roper River the CMS negotiated with parents to allow their children to sleep in dormitories and even to leave them there while they roamed their country.[103] The Catholic missions on Bathurst Island, at Port Keats and at Beagle Bay also prized the dormitory as their tool. The arrival of Our Lady of the Sacred Heart nuns in 1912 made a girls' dormitory possible from almost the beginning of Gsell's Bathurst Island mission. That children seemed to find the mission, including the dormitory, materially attractive was a 'breach in the native defences', Gsell later claimed.[104] At Port Keats, where Father Docherty saw the life of women in 1935 as 'a very hard one', the mission initiated segregated dormitories as soon as the arrival of nuns in 1941 made it possible.[105] Girls could go 'home' on weekends, and the dormitory was not locked (except at the girls' request).[106] Docherty demanded that marriage be monogamous, but with the parents' continuing right of bestowal. Visiting Port Keats fifteen years after its foundation, Norwegian anthropologists in 1950 recorded that in response to the mission practice of keeping girls in a dormitory until they were about eighteen, the Murinbata and their neighbours had raised the age at which a woman was seen as properly a sexual partner for her husband.[107]

In the Kimberley, dormitories for girls became possible when a small group of St John of God nuns arrived in 1907 at Beagle Bay and took over the school and the training of young women in needlework, cooking, washing and housework. The nuns also started a convent in Broome in 1912. Nuns did not join the Drysdale River Mission until 1931; they too initiated a girls' dormitory. Missionaries were especially opposed to women's sexual contact with the men of the pearling industry, in 'lay-up' camps along the West Kimberley coast, because they saw it as immoral, as promoting economic dependency and as ruinous to health. At Beagle Bay, first the Trappists and then the Pallottines encouraged young women to marry Catholic 'Manila-men'.[108] According to Christine Choo, women either collaborated with the missionaries or maintained a life that included extramarital sexuality – labelled 'prostitution' by the missionaries.[109] Like Mornington Island and several other remote missions, Beagle Bay was authorised to receive 'half-caste' children removed by police officers from camps across the region – some with their mothers. Clergy saw such children (and some 'full-blood' children) as being at moral risk if they were not removed. In the Beagle Bay dormitory and in the classroom, Aboriginal languages were not allowed; contact between parents and the children in the dormitories was regulated, but not forbidden.

In the arid centre, Hermannsburg established a girls' dormitory some time in the first decade of the 20th century. Reporting on the mission to the Commonwealth government in 1911, Captain Barclay referred to the forcible detention of girls, but the mission's official historian denies that any girl was forced to sleep in the dormitory.[110] Radford notes this was a 'long-running point of controversy'. It is useful to distinguish two issues: were all parents in contact with the mission forced to surrender their children to mission control? No. Were children left in the care of the school expected to sleep in the dormitories? Yes. According to Radford, girls between the age of puberty and of marriage were locked in the dormitory at night to prevent escape and 'immorality'. For both boys and girls, sleeping in the dormitory was an adjunct to their schooling, a site of training in hygiene and new personal habits. The Administration approved such moral training but persuaded Superintendent Carl Strehlow to redesign the space.[111] At Mount Margaret, Pastor Schenk began to persuade mothers to let the mission look after the children, later adding dormitories to what A.O. Neville hailed in 1930 as his 'well-ordered township'.[112]

Aboriginal memories of the arrival of missions

Aboriginal oral tradition developed stories that made sense of their accommodation to missions. We know that when the Benedictine fathers arrived at Drysdale River in 1908, they found people wary; in 1913 some of them beat up and speared (non-fatally) the terrified fathers (whose monastery was on the second level, so they could withdraw the ladder at night). A local oral tradition, reported by Ian Crawford in 1978, emphasises the Aborigines' initial fear of the newcomers, but goes on to narrate the Benedictines' reaching out to them with gifts of food, including jam for the children. Reviewing an edition of the Benedictines' diaries, Crawford explained the Aborigines' eventual acceptance of the mission at Pago, then at Kalumburu. The Aborigines became addicted to tobacco and wanted tea and sugar 'very dearly'. And the mission offered some respite from the warfare and vengeful violence that had recently been raging in the northern Kimberley. Crawford reports local Aborigines in the 1970s as 'puzzled by the actions of their elders who indulged in wanton murder'.[113] They were puzzled because, by the 1970s, they had internalised much of the mission world view.

Christian community at Beagle Bay Mission probably rested on several factors: that many residents were voluntarily attached to the mission; that contact between generations was permitted, encouraging a version of family life; that the priests and nuns were seen to be 'good and kind' (in Magdalene Williams' words) in contrast to many other white bosses; that missionaries such as Father Droste could preach in Nyul Nyul; that children who were sent to Beagle Bay under the policy of 'half-caste' removal formed bonds with each other; that 'the missionaries protected Aboriginal women from exploitation and oppression from within their own society'.[114] As well, the residents shared in a rich (Roman Catholic) ritual life.[115] Father Raible told Sydney Catholics in 1935:

> On the first Friday of each month work is suspended until 11 o'clock and the Most Blessed Sacrament is exposed on the high altar for public adoration. The different sections

of the community make their visits at appointed hours, and there is hardly anyone who does not receive holy communion on that day.[116]

Former Beagle Bay resident Betty Lockyer recalls Beagle Bay in the 1930s:

At every noon, the bell rang and everybody stopped dead in their tracks. I mean everybody. That was Angelus time and the whole mission knew it. They dropped everything to say the Angelus. The people would be out in the fields, or hanging out the clothes, or just having a drink of water at the well. They'd just stop, drop, kneel, bless themselves and pray … It wasn't a put-on act either; it was the reverence and respect of the teachings of the Church that was implanted in them and passed on to their children.[117]

Dreams remain one of the means of revelation for many Aboriginal people.[118] Before Father Docherty arrived at Port Keats, a dream left a man named Mulinthin in a state of grace and physical well-being which he was keen to impart to others. Father Docherty's arrival seemed to fulfil the promise of the dream, and Mulinthin later told Docherty that the figures in his dream must have been Jesus, Mary and God. It may have been possible for some people at Port Keats to accept Docherty's work as a continuation of Mulinthin's vision of a better life.[119]

2

Knowing and ruling Northern Aborigines

In the first forty years of the 20th century, missionaries and anthropologists became witnesses and intermediaries on troubled northern frontiers. It became their uncomfortable task to consider tactics of discipline and punishment.

Anthropology

Anthropologists who wrote for the wider public invited Australians to comprehend Aboriginal ways through unprejudiced study. Reflecting in 1931 on the Cape York people whom he had visited in 1927 and 1929, Donald Thomson urged readers not to look down on Aborigines for being 'incapable of gratitude'; giving and sharing were so unremarkable among them, he explained, that such courtesies had no rationale.[1] Writing on 'The secret life and initiation' in 1938, University of Sydney Professor of Anthropology A.P. Elkin invited the reader to imagine following the Aboriginal youth through the 'door which admits to the inner shrine and to a knowledge of the mysteries, namely initiation ... for then and only then shall we gain some conception of what life means to the Aborigines, and some idea of the hidden springs of their conduct, faith and hope, and of the depth of their thought'.[2]

Elkin's imagination was both religious (evoking 'the mysteries') and governmental (sketching better administration). The two came together in his prescriptive anticipation that programs of change guided by anthropology would manage change slowly. While training for new occupations, 'the aborigine should always have the opportunity of returning to their former manner of life with its hunting, and food collecting and social gatherings. This is essential in order that they may have some relaxation from their new economic activity, with its necessary monotony and strain.'[3] Elkin urged that assimilation must respect Aboriginal psychology and preserve their 'group' life.[4]

Elkin's invitation to look deeply and to intervene carefully rested on about sixty years of scholarship to which Aboriginal people and (more recently, in the remote regions) missionaries had played host. In what Elkin later called a series of 'fortuitous individual research projects' in the late 19th century, in regions where pastoralists were the colonial authority, amateur anthropologists such as E.M. Curr, R. Brough Smyth, G. Taplin, A.W. Howitt, W.E. Roth, W. Ridley, J. Fraser, T. Worsnop, J. Mathew, K. Langloh Parker, H. Basedow and R.H. Matthews had started to go beyond collecting objects and noting strange customs. Their writings were beginning to describe Aboriginal systems of belief and action within a scientific framework that saw human society as evolving along certain paths, through stages of increasing complexity. Aborigines were valued as 'early man'. Exchanging and synthesising data in a global network of folklorists, they built a comparative and historical science of humanity. The University of Melbourne biologist

W.B. Spencer had been captivated by Aborigines when visiting Central Australia in 1894 (including Hermannsburg Mission) and had corresponded, from Melbourne, with settlers who were on intimate terms with them. With postal official Frank Gillen, he co-authored *The Native Tribes of Central Australia* (1899) and *The Northern Tribes of Central Australia* (1904), adding substantially to a worldwide project of describing the bodies, customs and beliefs of the peoples that Europeans were colonising. In the first fourteen years of the 20th century, empirical studies of Australian Aborigines helped to ground twelve works of social theory.[5]

Australian governments invested some hope in anthropology. Queensland appointed the anthropologist W.E. Roth as first northern protector of Aboriginals in 1898, and Western Australia commissioned Roth's advice on Aboriginal policy in 1904 before appointing Daisy Bates as government anthropologist (though it declined, in 1912, to publish her findings). After assuming responsibility for the Northern Territory in 1911, the Commonwealth got Herbert Basedow in 1911 (for a stormy forty-five days) and Spencer in 1912 to describe the situation of Aborigines in the Northern Territory and to recommend protections. When the League of Nations mandated Australia to govern New Guinea in 1920, anthropologists promoted their discipline 'for its value in the government of subject races'.[6] The governmental utility of anthropology became a theme of professional publications in the years between the World Wars. Success in bidding for patronage can be seen in the University of Sydney's creation of a Chair of Anthropology in 1925, in the discipline's establishing of the quarterly *Oceania* (first issue on 1 April 1930), and in anthropologists' access to the Rockefeller Foundation's funds, via the foundation's grant to the Australian

National Research Council for the period 1926–31. Such recognition gave anthropology public and academic authority.

Between the World Wars 'functionalist' anthropology began to ask: how do the customs and beliefs of a particular people fit together as an integrated ensemble that is effective in meeting life's universal needs, given their particular physical environment? Functionalists postulated that all humans shared fundamental objectives and that 'societies' differed, ingeniously, in the social structures and symbolic traditions through which they met them. Through immersive fieldwork and language study, anthropologists aspired to formulate the 'native point of view', to convey how each people understood their own behavioural regularities and to comprehend the meanings that they found in the physical world. The rise of functionalist anthropology thus made it more possible to consider Aborigines as having a 'civilisation', albeit a 'primitive' one. By World War II, through fieldwork hosted mostly by remote missions, anthropology compiled a rich descriptive archive of Aboriginal life in the continent's north and centre, adding to the earlier 'fortuitous' research projects in the temperate agricultural zones of Australia.

An early synthesis, Elkin's *The Australian Aborigines: How to understand them* (1938), emerged from lectures hosted by the Department of Tutorial Classes and by the Extension Board of the University of Sydney. 'Surely we must admire,' he wrote, 'the nobility and depth of character manifested by such men!'[8] The poverty of settler-colonial knowledge, Elkin suggested, was an effect of strategic decisions by Aborigines *not* to share what they knew, for Aborigines had calculated that their continuing strength lay in their esoteric Law.[9] Moreover, having tasted the white man's world and finding it largely unsatisfying and usually unwelcoming, Aborigines – both 'full-blood and half-caste' –

TABLE 2 **Places, people and dates in field-based anthropology**[7]

A.P. Elkin	Kimberley 1927–28 (Forrest River), South Australia/Western Desert (Mount Margaret) 1930
Phyllis Kaberry	Kimberley 1934, 1935, 1936 (Beagle Bay, Forrest River)
Donald Thomson	Cape York in 1928, 1929 and 1932–33 (Cape Bedford, Lockhart River; Mitchell River) Mapoon, Aurukun) Arnhem Land 1935, 1936–37 and 1941–43
W.L. Warner	Arnhem Land 1927, 1928–29 (Milingimbi)
Ernest Worms	Kimberley, from 1931 (Beagle Bay)
R. Lauriston Sharp	Cape York 1933, 1934, 1935 (Mitchell River)
Ursula McConnel	Cape York 1927, 1928, 1934 (Aurukun)
Geza Roheim	Central Australia 1928 (Hermannsburg)
S.D. Porteus	Central Australia 1929 (Hermannsburg), Kimberley 1931 (Beagle Bay)
C.W.M. Hart	Bathurst and Melville Islands 1928, 1929 (Bathurst Island Mission)
R.W. Piddington	Kimberley 1930–31 (Beagle Bay)
W.E.H. Stanner	North-West Northern Territory 1932, 1934–35 (Port Keats)
Olive Pink	Central Australia 1933–34, 1936–37 (hostile to missions)
T.G.H. Strehlow	Central Australia 1932–34 (Hermannsburg)
Board of Anthropological Research (University of Adelaide)	Central Australia 1929–39 (Hermannsburg and several pastoral leases)

were now returning to a modified version of 'the secret life'.[10] It was the duty of anthropology, said Elkin, to gather that secret and vital knowledge and to hold it 'in trust'.[11] Addressing a

MAP 1 Remote missions (established 1877–1952), anthropology research sites 1929–39, World War II airfields, radio installations and Cold War weapons testing regions in remote Australia

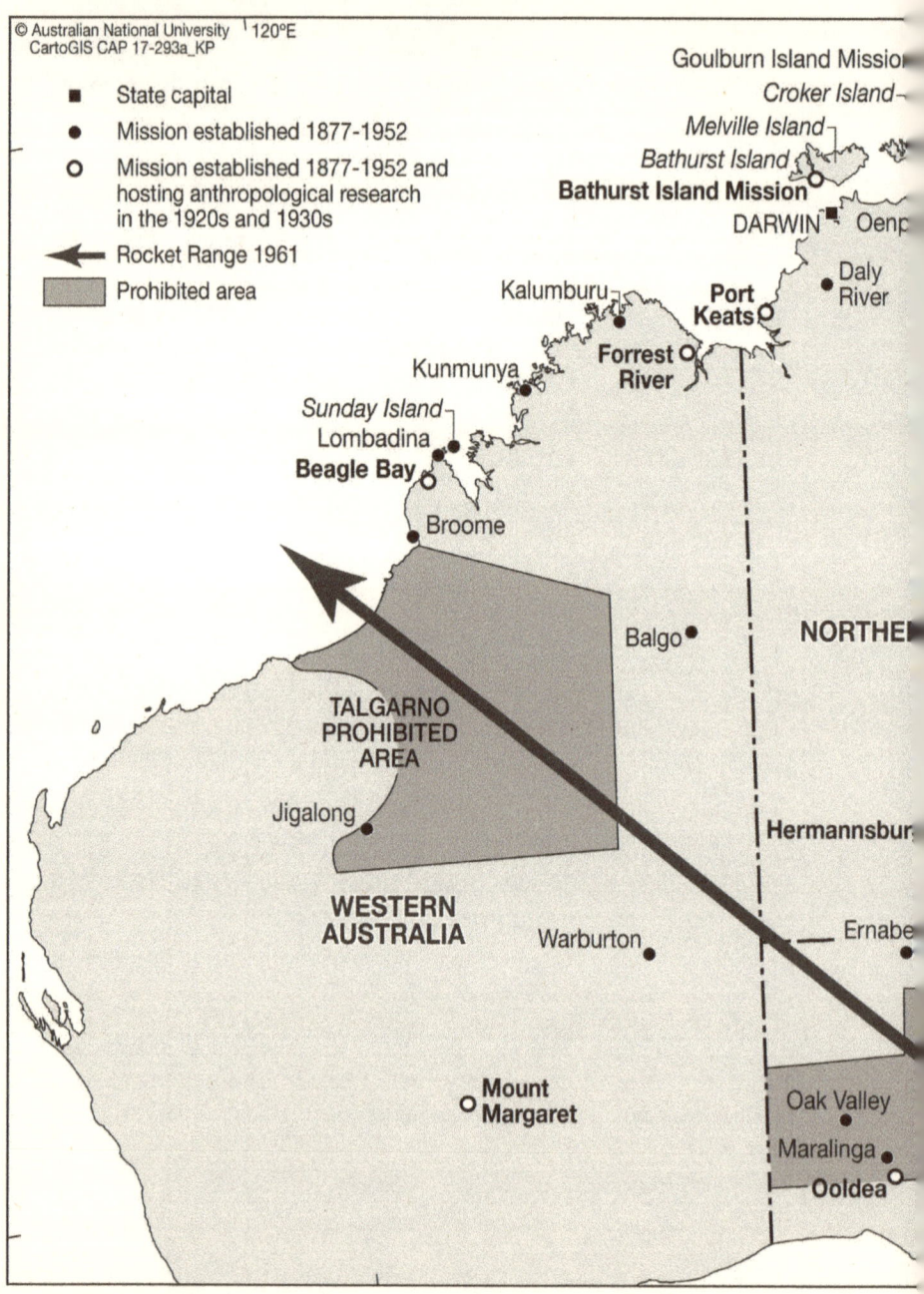

Missions, anthropology and militarisation made the Aboriginal inhabitants of remote continental Australia (the 'North') visible to Australians in the first half of the 20th century. Map 1 (pages 68–69) shows the position of missions founded in the 'North' in the period 1877–1952. It also shows which missions hosted university-based anthropology research in the 1920s and 1930s. As Chapters 1 and 2 explain, through a combination of missionaries' and anthropologists' writings, the not yet colonised nations of remote Indigenous Australia became knowable to the 'South' as an object of science

and as a 'welfare' problem. The preferred policy of missions and anthropologists was to delay for as long as possible the colonial occupation of remote Aboriginal territories. World War II and the Cold War challenged that segregative policy by revaluing the remote and 'empty' parts of Australia: these regions became important as sites of forward defence and weapons testing, as Chapter 6 explains, and assimilation began to replace segregation as the nation's obligation.

public that was only just discovering the civilisation that colonisation was putting at risk, Elkin proposed empathy with what Aborigines treasured most.

Anthropologists and missionaries sometimes clashed in their assessment of Aboriginal spirituality, ritual and sexuality, but many missionaries had come to agree that they needed to develop a sympathetic understanding of 'primitive' ways of life and to make concessions to it. An Anglican priest (as well as an academic), Elkin thought that the mandate of colonial authority included respect for the spiritual life of the colonised. He specified in 1934 the damage that missionaries would inflict if they sought to extinguish 'primitive' religion: a split in Aboriginal personality between outward conformity with mission demands and inner adherence to traditional belief; tension between generations; 'misfits' who were neither Aboriginal nor white in religious culture; neglect of the old men and women. It was impossible, he asserted, 'to understand the native's soul and his acceptance of Christian forms without a thorough knowledge of his language and the social milieu and world of thought to which he belongs'. If marriage customs and child-rearing were to be changed, the missionaries must cultivate the support of the parents and elders.[12] Theodore Webb was the outstanding example of a missionary so informed. At Milingimbi in 1927–28, he had hosted William Lloyd Warner's research; Donald Thomson wrote a warm preface to Webb's 1934 pamphlet *The Aborigines of Eastern Arnhem Land*, and Webb thanked Elkin for helping him to write his 1938 booklet *Spears to Spades*.

However, in Aboriginal society, religion and politics were densely intertwined as the Law: those with custody of sacred myth wielded reproductive power also in the allocation of spouses among interacting country-based clans and in the training of youth to their inheritance of reproductive power. Missionaries could not adopt a policy towards the spiritual domain without effecting some kind of policy – whether interventionist or laissez-faire – in the social regulation of sexuality. Inescapably, the missions were political institutions. By creating an economic enclave – coexisting with subsistence production and mediating its relations with the national and global economy – each mission established a mini-jurisdiction with its own codes of property and personhood. Any jurisdiction has sanctions. Aboriginal people who spent all or part of their time at a mission learned – with more or less enthusiasm – to adhere to its rules.

The mission as a jurisdiction

Missionaries understood their jurisdictions as means to three ends. First, to confront polygyny – without banning it outright – they could moderate the power of men to physically chastise recalcitrant youths and women. According to Eugene Perez, Drysdale River Mission was women's 'only security from the cruelty and rapacity of the opposite sex'.[13] Theodore Webb tells several stories about Milingimbi's moderation of the brutal treatment of women: 'what almost always happens now', he wrote in the late 1930s, 'is that some of our people will take a women charged with a serious offence, will care for her and protect her until tempers have cooled and it is possible to deal with the matter fairly and humanely'.[14] He gave an example. He had spoken sternly to warriors who had arrived at Milingimbi as a raiding party; the warriors had listened, modified their approach, but still had pursued their objective: a woman deemed to have misconducted herself sexually. Eva Webb had locked her in the missionaries' house, 'daring [the warriors] to interfere with her, while she sent for help [Yolngu loyal to the mission] to remove the intruders'.[15]

Second, missionaries needed to ban intertribal fighting. 'The mission station is valued as a sanctuary', Webb claimed in his 1934 Melbourne lecture, 'where these people know they are reasonably safe from their enemies.'[16] Rod Schenk at Mount Margaret felt encouraged by 'the way they call for us if some start to fight. On our appearance they drop weapons and hold a vociferous arbitration court, while we wait ... We have been able to stop many spear fights, and they recognise our loving authority.'[17]

Third, missions were enterprises with property – herds, gardens – to protect from people who presumed all plants and all animals on their country to be food for the taking. In 1930, the Oenpelli Mission punished cattle-spearers with belt and rope lashes. 'The C.M.S. supporters in the south were somewhat critical of this form of punishment, but were unable to come up with any effective alternative.'[18]

The missionaries' hosting of anthropologists resulted sometimes in critical reports. Kaberry criticised Forrest River Mission's segregation of youth in dormitories. 'Some missionaries have yet to grasp the elementary fact that needlework, cooking, housework and an occasional picnic do not in themselves constitute an adequate substitute for sexual experience.' The regime encouraged not only 'a prurient attitude towards sex' but also 'evasion and emotional instability'.[19] The Aborigines' problem with missions was not doctrinal, she argued. They accepted a version of Christian doctrine and 'will adapt Christian beliefs to their own for many years to come; in this area they call Christ Bundilmiri, and God *Wolara*', an important ancestral spirit, about whom there were creation myths.[20] She even suggested that the mission could promote the value of cattle and crops by instituting 'increase ceremonies' for them. The Forrest River problem was not spiritual but practical: the missionaries' 'senseless iconoclasm' towards authority.

> It is a great pity that missionaries have not made a practice of consulting the headman on proposed modifications in native life. Too often any respect for him finds expression in the attitude that he is a good worker, never quarrelsome, and one who may be placed in charge of a gang of men to carry out some mission task.[21]

By arranging irregular marriages, Kaberry reported, the missionaries aroused young people's disrespect for '"bush" blacks', and by emphasising the parent–child relationship, the mission undervalued other kinship obligations.[22] Yet the mission also diminished the mother–child bond. Separating mothers from children at age three to four years was a severe blow to a woman's feeling; she may pre-empt such pain by aborting a child (using hot stones).[23] Kaberry speculated that abortion may recently have become more attractive.

A determined missionary such as Ernest Gribble need not feel threatened by what was said about his authority in an academic journal, but missionaries sometimes had to contend with the police. Even if a missionary were appointed a 'protector', his processes and penalties had no legislative basis, and the local police and the nearest magistrate could still, if they saw fit, demonstrate the inferiority of mission jurisdiction. Thus Constable Kennett called upon Oenpelli's Dick Harris to witness the corporal punishment of three men Kennett had rounded up, while patrolling north of Oenpelli, for spearing cattle. 'The senior police "boy" Lumbalilli give them a good belting and let them go. Dick ... said that "it was so severe, it nearly made me sick".'[24] Missionaries were not necessarily opposed to the violent punishment of Aborigines who threatened, in some way, their projects; but they had their own ideas about the extent of their domain and what was justifiable within it.

Australia's frontiers were sites of overlapping authorities – state, pastoralist, missionary and Aboriginal – that sometimes battled for authority. How 'Northern' authority was described to Australians in the South was beginning to matter; the Southern public might be aroused to judge what should and should not be done to manage frontier relationships. Both anthropologists and missionaries had to come to terms with state power.

Political constraints on anthropology

In 1932, Ralph Piddington, Elkin's Master's student at the University of Sydney, told *The World* that at La Grange, a Western Australian government depot issuing rations to the Karadjeri people, he had seen 'slavery of natives, trafficking in lubras and the murdering and flogging of aborigines by white men'.[25] Piddington explained that because Aborigines felt such a strong bond with their ancestral country, they would put up with almost any ill-treatment by those holding a pastoral lease over their land. Piddington recommended that the Commonwealth government appoint a former Western Australian protector of Aborigines, Ernest Mitchell, to compile a report, as the state government's officials, including the police, were unlikely to know or acknowledge the suffering of the Karadjeri. In 1930, Mitchell had been retrenched by A.O. Neville, the chief protector.

Eight months after this interview appeared, Piddington read

a paper to a professional audience (subsequently published in *Oceania*). Distinguishing his 'facts' from his 'values', Piddington differentiated the four perspectives that had emerged about culture contact in Australia: the missionary's, the humanitarian's (in which he subsumed the anthropologist's), the white settler's and 'the native himself'.[26] He presented the white settler/native relationship as a clash of values, in which the less powerful and numerous native faced the greater task of adaptation. Avoiding the terms he had used when speaking to *The World*, he strove to be neutral in tone; his harshest words on the settlers referred to their 'callous indifference to the things which make life worth living for the native'.[27] 'There is some slight hope that a wide dissemination of anthropological knowledge may counteract this, but in the meantime much stricter and, it may be added, more enlightened governmental supervision is necessary.'[28]

Piddington suggested that governments would better understand their task if they heeded 'the scientific study of primitive society'.[29] He soon left for London on a Rockefeller Foundation scholarship for which the Australian National Research Council (ANRC) had recommended him.

By then Piddington's observations about La Grange had annoyed 'government' – in this case, Neville. Neville did not respond to Piddington until material from his interview in *The World* appeared in the July 1932 issue of the *Anti-Slavery Reporter and Aborigines Friend* (a London-based publication) and subsequently (again) in the Australian press. Writing to the ANRC, Neville said that his department would not assist further research by Piddington; he added that future fieldworkers would be asked to promise that they would not criticise his administration without first giving Neville the chance to refute or investigate their allegations. Judging that Neville could not be ignored, the ANRC acceded to Neville's demand. Not satisfied with Piddington's account of his conduct, the ANRC also told Piddington that it now regretted recommending his scholarship – a hint that Piddington should not seek ANRC support for future work in Australia or Papua New Guinea. Correspondence about the Piddington case published in *Oceania* in 1994 suggests that in the mid-1930s the ANRC viewed public statements that antagonised government officials as unacceptable conduct; patrons of anthropological research (Elkin the most powerful) fashioned a public voice that upheld the worth of Aboriginal civilisation without antagonising authorities responsible for the actual conditions of Aboriginal life.

The Piddington case helped to define the limits of anthropology's critique of colonial relationships in Australia. However, missions were much more powerful players in the contest about how to wield frontier authority, and how to represent it, because – unlike academics – they were effective authorities on frontiers. Missionary witness was the major source of two 'massacre' narratives that scandalised Australians in the 1920s.

Missions as witness and broker of authority

A 'massacre' is 'an indiscriminate and brutal slaughter of many people' according to *The Oxford English Dictionary* online. The qualifying adjectives 'indiscriminate' and 'brutal' imply the possibility that killings could be 'discriminate' (that is, justifiably targeted) and 'not brutal' (humanely administered) – a possibility embodied in any jurisdictions' norms of capital punishment and police and military conduct. If authority exercised violently is open to adjudication, 'massacre' is not a synonym of 'mass killing' but a censure of violence in excess. Historians who have used 'massacre' to refer to certain incidents of multiple killing on Australian frontiers have not disclosed the standard that they think should be applied. In the 1920s, missionaries could not evade that difficult question: as frontier jurisdictions, they had no choice but to consider how colonists, including themselves, should use violence.

Forrest River Mission's Ernest Gribble was admired or deplored for his strength of conviction. According to Neville Green, he 'decided what was legal and what was illegal. He made the arrests, sat as chairman of the court, decided the punishment and not infrequently carried it out with the leather strap he referred to as Black Tom.'[30] As a result, 'between 1912 and 1925 no mission Aborigines were sent into Wyndham for trial'.[31] Gribble was occasionally in contact with his pastoralist neighbours Overheu, Hay and Dunnett who ran cattle on 'Nulla Nulla' lease, land excised from Marndoc Reserve as War Service Land Settlement grants in 1918 and 1921. As a protector, Gribble was also in competition with these men about who was responsible for supervising Aboriginal labour, and he was suspicious of their dealings with women.[32] In 1926, the Nulla Nulla lessees suffered stock losses which they blamed on nomadic Aborigines who sometimes resided at the mission; it vexed them that such outlaws could exploit the protective authority of the mission and escape the punishment that was due to cattle-killers. The Wyndham police responded to their complaints with a patrol consisting of Constable St Jack and Aboriginal assistants Jacob and Windie Joe; they joined up with Overheu and his Aboriginal servants. At the Pentecost River on the Nulla Nulla lease, they raided and 'dispersed' a large Aboriginal camp – discharging rifles and pistols, but not (by their own later account) hurting anyone. Continuing to Nulla Nulla homestead, they discovered that Hay had been murdered. Informants at the mission soon named the alleged killer as Lumbia. While Gribble diarised that Hay had got what he deserved for mistreating Aborigines, he did not immediately give the alleged killer's name to the police. An armed fourteen-strong police patrol of the Marndoc Reserve began searching for a group of killers. News coverage of this patrol presented Aborigines in two ways: as the Crown's skilful servants (the police trackers) and as the reserve's unpredictable savages (the alleged killers of Hay, to be hunted and punished). Gribble eventually gave police Lumbia's name. When arrested, Lumbia said that he had speared Hay because he had not only demanded sex with Anulgoo, Lumbia's wife, he had then declared Anulgoo his to keep. This information – shaming a white pioneer and extenuating a husband's violence – was not presented at Lumbia's trial, and Lumbia was convicted of murder, his death sentence commuted to life imprisonment.

Soon after the trial, Overheu's Aboriginal servant Tommy began to admit to other Aborigines that the June patrols of the Marndoc Reserve had killed people. The rumours soon reached Gribble. Although at first he could arouse the interest of neither his bishop nor the state government, Gribble persuaded the local inspector of Aboriginals, Ernest Mitchell, to gather physical evidence – dismembered and burned bodies – at a number of sites to which local Aborigines and the missionary James Noble guided him. Further investigation of these patrols elicited testimony from Aboriginal trackers about killings by the police. By October 1926 the *Truth* was alleging a police cover-up and questioning the Australian Board of Missions' apparent lack of interest in what had happened. Growing public interest compelled the Western Australian (Collier) government to appoint a Royal Commission under Senior Stipendiary Magistrate G.T. Wood in

January 1927. After three months, Wood concluded that police had killed seven Aborigines. At the committal hearing for the two accused police – St Jack and Regan – the defence counsel cast sufficient doubt on the prosecution's evidence that the magistrate ruled that no jury could convict them. St Jack and Regan continued their careers as police, though not in the Kimberley.

Responses to their non-prosecution illustrate that on the most remote and recently colonised regions 'justice' remained a disputable ideal. For many Western Australians, it was a relief that the good name of their state had been reaffirmed and the meddlesome missionaries repudiated. The Australian Board of Missions and the Australian Missionary Council protested the reinstatement of St Jack and Regan, and even the Archbishop of Canterbury declared his disapproval. That the police were not prosecuted demonstrated to critics the depth of racial injustice in Western Australia. The region's Aborigines evidently assumed that the police would be punished, and they must have been bewildered when St Jack and Regan returned briefly to Wyndham: the two police were not executed at the scene of their crime but enjoyed the approval and shared the relief of many local settlers. One person who was executed was Lumbia's wife Anulgoo. According to information received by Chief Protector Neville, it was the view of her countrymen that 'Hay's desire to possess her had contributed to Lumbia's arrest and indirectly to the many deaths on the reserve, so she must die.'[33]

This interplay of competing Kimberley jurisdictions – leaving a sense of injustice in the minds of many Australians – was soon followed by scandalous police killings in the country of the Warlpiri and Anmatjira people, far to the south and east of the Kimberley. People in Central Australia were suffering a prolonged dry spell in the late 1920s, and authorities noticed that

Aborigines were becoming more aggressive in asking settlers for food.[34] Under the *Aboriginals Ordinance*, Aborigines' only 'protectors' in Central Australia were police officers and missionaries. Of eleven sources of rations to Aborigines three were administered by missionaries: at Finke River Mission (Hermannsburg) by Lutherans, at Harding Soak (by Annie Lock of the United Aborigines Mission/Australian Aborigines' Society) and itinerantly by Ernest Kramer (Aborigines' Friends' Association).[35] Hermannsburg was becoming a zone of authority, according to Superintendent F.W. Albrecht (appointed in 1926). In 1927 he judged that 'it will take much effort before we have established law and order'.[36] To the north of Hermannsburg, in Warlpiri and Anmatjira country, the venturesome colonists who had begun to graze stock in the previous twenty years were effectively free to negotiate their own relationship with the Aborigines with whom their cattle competed for water. Harding Soak was in this region (on Peake Hill lease).

In August 1928, when the body of Frederick Brooks was found 22 kilometres west of the outlying Coniston homestead, the story that Aborigines had murdered him soon hit the southern press, and an 'investigation' by Alice Springs–based Mounted Constable Murray immediately commenced. Murray's vigilante party (none were sworn in as special constables) comprising settlers and Aborigines soon confronted and killed several Aborigines in the area where Brooks had been found. As the party continued its journey, there were further mortal clashes. By 30 August, on Murray's later admission, they had killed seventeen Aborigines; the party then returned to Alice Springs with two prisoners, Padygar and Arkirka. In a subsequent patrol in September–October 1928, provoked by an attack by Warlpiri on another settler (Nugget Morton), Murray's posse killed more people. According to Aboriginal oral history, Murray's method included surprising camps at dawn and tying his victims to trees to ensure that shots resulted in a kill.[37] Murray's reports admitted that his two patrols had killed thirty-one. Southern press coverage of the killings in September did not characterise these patrols as punitive.[38]

The November 1928 trial of Padygar and Arkirka became embarrassing for the police when the judge (in Darwin, for the Supreme Court was not then authorised to sit in Alice Springs) acquitted them of murdering Brooks. Highlighting the poor quality of evidence against the arrested men, their acquittal intensified critical attention to Murray's expeditions.[39] The public was already receptive to the idea that all might not be well on remote frontiers. That outback police were in effect licensed to kill had been demonstrated to a horrified section of public opinion in the southern capitals by the 1926 killings on Marndoc Reserve. Murray's evidence at the trial of Padygar and Arkirka seemed another symptom of police excess. Annie Lock's stories from Aborigines visiting Harding Soak fed this suspicion in government circles, for she had got the attention of Queensland's Chief Protector J.W. Bleakley, whom the Commonwealth had appointed in March 1928 to report on 'Aboriginals and Half-Castes' in the Northern Territory. Lock talked not only to Bleakley (whom she happened to meet while travelling through Katherine) but also to a visiting Methodist pastor, Athol McGregor. Bleakley reported the stories to the Minister for Home and Territories, and McGregor repeated them to the southern newspapers and to J.A. Cawood, the government resident in Alice Springs. Missionary and humanitarian societies demanded an enquiry.[40]

In December 1928, the Commonwealth appointed a three-man Board of Enquiry comprising J.A. Cawood, the senior

Commonwealth public servant in Central Australia (Murray's boss), and two senior policemen – one from Queensland (A.H. O'Kelly), the other from South Australia (P.A. Giles). The Association for the Protection of Native Races (APNR) had suggested that a missionary be appointed to any investigating body.[41] The board invited Ernest Kramer to hear all evidence, and to comment and pose questions. The board's findings, released on 30 January 1929, were that settler actions had not been provocative of the attacks on Brooks and Morton and that self-defence warranted the killings admitted by Murray and his party. The board blamed the unruliness of the region's natives partly on the influence of itinerant missionaries who were preaching the doctrine of equality; that a woman missionary (Lock) lived 'amongst naked blacks' further reduced the natives' 'respect for the whites'.[42] The APNR and the Australian Board of Missions (ABM), in the press and in submissions to the Commonwealth government, severely criticised the board's process and findings.[43] Hartwig has commented that 'the church and mission societies were by far the most vocal' critics of the killings.[44]

However, *local* missionary testimony at the enquiry itself – Ernest Kramer, Herman Heinrich (acting superintendent of Hermannsburg), Athol McGregor and Annie Lock – was not so critical of Murray and his party. Rather, the focus of their testimony was the causes and correctives of Aborigines' restlessness. Athol McGregor's appearance was brief. After agreeing that press comments (for which he had been partly responsible) critical of the police killings were 'hearsay', he addressed the question of Aboriginal unrest: 'the cause of the recent atrocities of the blacks is the coloured relationship question'. When 'white men take the lubras', black men are upset. Government officials, where possible, should be married men. He also recommended medical patrols, more police patrols and more reserves.⁴⁵ Kramer said that he had always found Murray very helpful, that in Aboriginal opinion Murray was a good boss and that Murray was seen by some pastoralists as too indulgent. When asked about accusations against the police made by unnamed 'new Missionaries' and in some press coverage, Kramer was sceptical; he worried that such accusations, if repeated by 'educated half-castes' to 'blacks', would have 'pernicious effect'.⁴⁶ He called for more police patrols in districts where settlers reported theft by Aborigines. Though Kramer declined to say anything about settlers' interaction with Aboriginal women, he could think of no examples of settler cruelty or of settlers driving Aboriginal people away from water. There was less food for Aborigines, he acknowledged, because of the reduction in herds (and thus of pastoralists' rations from a 'killer' — a beast from the station's herd chosen for slaughter and consumption by the workers and not sent to market), because the drought had reduced wild game and because some people had lost the ability to hunt large animals, having grown up on stations, and with rabbits so abundant.⁴⁷ Of all 'semi-civilised blacks' including 'Mission blacks' Kramer generalised:

> [T]hose who have been accustomed to certain civilised
> foods such as tea sugar flour and tobacco get such a craving
> for it that after they go out into the bush they will come
> back again and in order to satisfy that craving will steal or
> kill even in order to get what they desire.⁴⁸

Thus the enquiry into what has become known as the Coniston Massacre became a forum for views, expressed by local missionaries and other settlers, about how to discipline

Aborigines in Central Australia. When the board took evidence at Hermannsburg on 4 January 1929, Pastor Heinrich recommended more frequent police patrols in his district and a police station, preferably at Boggy Hole, a former police camp near his mission. He sketched Hermannsburg's difficulties as a mini-jurisdiction. 'I have had some trouble at the station through the young natives getting cheeky and disobeying orders. The majority of these natives have been reared on the Mission Station. This cheekiness has cropped up since the strict regime of Rev. Strehlow has come to an end [in 1922].' The Lutheran authorities, he added, had allowed Strehlow to give the younger natives corporal punishment; as he explained, 'Corporal punishment is still allowed amongst the younger ones but we get the natives to administer it.'[49] Because younger natives viewed gaol as a 'holiday', corporal punishment should be legalised, Heinrich urged. Lock endorsed that recommendation in her testimony: justices of the peace should be allowed to order flogging for blacks convicted of crimes.[50] Kramer said: 'In the early days the Missionaries used to use the stock whip on the boys for disobedience and they are good boys today.'[51] McGregor did not mention corporal punishment but he commented that 'Imprisonment other than very long term does not seem to worry the blacks.'[52] Heinrich, like Kramer, thought that the key to Aboriginal discipline was access to food. His mission attended to 'the wants of the old and feeble natives … but the able bodied who cannot be profitably employed are engaged on scalping and hunting and bringing in bullock hides and curios for which they are paid. They buy tucker with the money.' He admitted that Hermannsburg Mission did not supply enough food and that game was now very scarce. Native hostility was provoked by restricting their hunting (to enable cattle grazing). McGregor also mentioned food: less should be issued to young blacks and more to older blacks.[53]

Heinrich warned that Aboriginal people lost respect for white authority when whites co-habited with blacks and when settlers were inconsistent in the manner of their interactions. His remarks would have been taken to apply to Lock, about whose judgment and credibility several settler witnesses cast doubt.[54] Kramer said that he had advised the 'old men of the tribe' to keep away from her, and he judged that 'it would lessen the respect of the blacks for the whites for an unattached women [sic] to be amongst them'.[55] Heinrich endorsed Kramer's view of 'inexperienced young Missionaries unaccustomed to the habits of the blacks'.[56] Lock's own view was that the drought explained 'the recent atrocities of the blacks'. Her portrait of Aboriginal behaviour distinguished 'semi-civilised' from 'myalls': the former had persuaded the latter to kill Brooks. '[I]t is the semi civilised natives who are causing the trouble. I do not think that the real myalls would do these things. They have never had a taste for cattle.' She too called for more policing 'to cope with these semi civilised blacks'. As well, 'a few of them should be made a real example of', by which she meant 'a little flogging'. 'I am sorry the natives who were charged with murdering Brooks were allowed to come straight back. It would have been better if they had been kept up there [Darwin] for a year or so.'[57]

In deference to local orthodoxy, Lock did not tell the enquiry all that she knew. In a subsequent letter to the APNR on 28 September 1929, Lock relayed what Aborigines had told her. Murray's party:

> simply shot them down like dogs & that they got the little children & hit them in the back of the neck & killed them

& in front of the eyes of those they left they knocked the dogs on the head & threw them in the fire. They rounded the natives up like mustering cattle & cleared or shot them out as they came to them. They had some prisoners & they took the chains off them & told them to run away & as they were running they shot them.[58]

She asked that this story not be made public 'until times when we are free to do so'.[59]

The state in Central Australia was poorly resourced: Cawood and his five police were overloaded with work and distant from Canberra's oversight.[60] The Administration devolved much of the custody and care for Aborigines to missionaries and pastoral lessees who were feeling the pressure of growing Aboriginal desperation. To deal with that pressure, witnesses recommended more policing by the state, authorised corporal punishment by non-state actors, and a more consistent approach by the state to licensing and supporting non-state actors such as missions. At the enquiry, Heinrich said that 'no Missionary should be allowed to work among the natives without the sanction of the Government' and 'any benefit to the natives can only be attained by continuous sustained Missions such as our own'.[61] Soon, in Arnhem Land, missionary action was able to pre-empt a Murray-style punitive expedition, but only by assisting the extension of criminal law into the missionary domain.

In September 1932, troubled transactions between Japanese crew and residents of Caledon Bay led people of north-east Arnhem Land (Yolngu) to kill three Japanese. A surviving crewman made it to Darwin to alert authorities, and four police officers and several trackers set out for the east Arnhem Land coast. One of the four police, Constable A.S. McColl, met his death by spearing on Woodah Island. Should the police now inflict exemplary violence on people who inhabited the recently (1931) declared Arnhem Land Reserve? Seeking an alternative to a punitive expedition, the CMS (Roper River Mission) explained to Prime Minister Lyons that alien intrusion into their homeland had provoked Yolngu. The Lyons government was sensitive to international comment on Australia's dealings with Aborigines, and it agreed that missionaries should enter the homelands of McColl's killers to explain (in the words of the CMS) 'the purpose and aims of the government and with a further view to the proper execution of justice'.[62]

Both Methodists and the CMS had been considering making a new mission in north-east Arnhem Land, perhaps on the shores of Caledon Bay. The CMS fraternally invited the Methodists on the north coast of Arnhem Land to join the expedition that would talk to the killers of McColl. Observing from Milingimbi, T.T. Webb declined this way of developing a relationship with the Yolngu. He thought it unlikely that Yolngu would give up the killers of McColl, of the Japanese sailors and of two recent European victims, Traynor and Fagan. It was not in missionaries' interest, Webb judged, to blur the distinction between police and mission authority. The CMS replied that it was not intending to do police work; they had declined the offer of a police escort. Webb counselled a year's delay, but the CMS's 'Arnhem Land Peace Expedition' went ahead in November 1932, consisting of three CMS missionaries and six Aboriginal men from east Arnhem Land and Groote Eylandt, led by Alf Dyer from Oenpelli. Fred Gray, a trepanger with long and positive experience of employing Aboriginal people from this region, joined them.[63]

Meeting the 'Peace Expedition', the Caledon Bay people

explained that the slain Japanese and two errant whites (Traynor and Fagan) had behaved badly and had deserved to die. The expedition learned the name of the man who had speared McColl, Dhakiyar (Tuckiar), and heard his account. Encouraged by these frank exchanges, the CMS missionaries canvassed the possibility of a mission, and they made a small bark chapel (St David's) as a preliminary, before the sickness of one of their party caused them to go back to Groote Eylandt. Returning to their talks with the Yolngu, they found Dhakiyar and his associates receptive to the idea that he should go to Darwin; perhaps these Yolngu anticipated that the authorities would hear their side of the story with as much sympathy as the missionaries had shown. The missionaries were not sure that they could guarantee such a reception, but CMS Headquarters made clear that the delivery of alleged killers to lawful authority was the Peace Expedition's desired result. Fred Gray, long trusted by the locals, offered to take the nineteen men to Darwin, and the missionaries hired his boat, the *Oituli*, for the purpose.

Reporting at the conclusion of the Peace Expedition, Dyer saw the hand of God in its success.[64] However, he later wondered whether his intervention had been wise. No-one was convicted of murdering Traynor and Fagan, but four of the nineteen men who had been persuaded to go to Darwin did not return. Convicted of killing a Japanese sailor, Mau, Natjelma and Narkaya were sentenced in July 1934 to twenty years' imprisonment, with the possibility of early release if they and their kin back in Caledon Bay were well behaved. When Dhakiyar, convicted of murdering McColl, was sentenced to death in August 1934, a shaken and regretful Dyer told the judge that 'a jolly good beating' back on their home territory would be the more humane way to teach justice.[65] The High Court overturned Dhakiyar's conviction, on appeal by the Commonwealth.⁶⁶ Dhakiyar disappeared soon after his release from gaol, and was never seen again, alive or dead.

Webb reflected, unpublished, on this experiment in mission–state collaboration. The incidents confirmed that the people of Arnhem Land needed to be 'patiently instructed, by word and by example, in the laws and customs to which they were expected to conform. Utterly useless was it to merely tell them what they must or must not do. Not so would the beliefs, traditions, and practices of a thousand years be modified.'⁶⁷ To illustrate the difficulty, Webb told a story about the Tjapu clan. Tjapu had recently accepted advice from Wilbur Chaseling, one of the founding staff at the new (1935) Yirrkala mission, that they should not punish some marauding Yolngu who recently had killed some Tjapu members. Chaseling had explained to them that the government was now the authority that would punish killers and thus protect Yolngu from anyone who threatened them. Tjapu questioned whether government was protective: they knew that four of the men who had gone to Darwin voluntarily to explain the Caledon Bay killings were yet to return. Chaseling had then explained that missionaries did not have authority over the government. Webb commented:

> Not a very satisfactory position for either people or missionary. Needless to say they have no understanding at all of our position in relation to the Administration. We are all of the one white-man tribe and surely we are united in action as they themselves are, so, while the missionary is powerless to carry out the promises of the Government, he is also scorned by a disappointed and disillusioned people for his failure to do so.⁶⁸

The patrol officer

In 1936, the Commonwealth appointed T.G.H. Strehlow – anthropologist and son of Lutheran missionary Carl Strehlow – as a patrol officer. A scandalous exercise of police authority triggered this innovation. The Alice Springs–based Constable McKinnon had killed an Aboriginal man who had escaped from custody, having been arrested as a suspect killer of another Aboriginal man. The Commonwealth appointed a Board of Enquiry: Professor John B. Cleland (chair of South Australia's Advisory Council on Aborigines), the Reverend John H. Sexton, President of the Aborigines' Friends' Association, and the Assistant Chief Protector of Aborigines in the Northern Territory Vincent J. White. The board received advice from Elkin and from Strehlow; its secretary Charles Mountford was a student of Aboriginal life with field experience in Central Australia.[69] They found no reason to charge McKinnon, but they asked: could such fatal police action be obviated?[70] The board recommended that Aboriginal protection be entrusted to a patrol officer who knew Aboriginal Law and who could settle tribal disputes and, if necessary, administer summary corporal punishment – 'a reasonable whipping' – consistent with that Law.[71] Appointed to this role, Strehlow soon explained to the Secretary of the Interior why he must be empowered to impose summary corporal punishment.

> The Patrol Officer can either act, with the help of his own native men, and administer corporal punishment to the offenders; or he can hold his peace, walk away crestfallen among the gibes of the triumphant youngsters, and after a few months, upon his return to headquarters, weakly seek the aid of a police constable to arrest the culprits …

[A] timely show of his authority when provoked into action will enhance his reputation amongst the natives a hundredfold, and will in no wise dim their affection for him. In order to be effective, punishment must, however, follow on the spot: a native always admires a man of just and prompt action, while despising even the best-intentioned idle talker.[72]

To extend criminal jurisdiction into the remote and foreign Aboriginal domains, the state needed that medley of knowledge and practice generated, in the first forty years of Australia's first century, as missiology and anthropology. Strehlow personified a synthesis of the practical wisdom accumulated by one kind of colonial authority – the mission – with the knowledge generated by another kind of authority: anthropology. Strehlow's knowledge of Arrernte, his studies of the religion and customary authority of Central Australia, his boyhood exposure to the practices of a mission, his sincere desire to pre-empt excessive and arbitrary force – these qualities made him a prototype of an authority ideal for remote Australia at that time. In Arnhem Land, missionary diplomacy had pre-empted punitive violence in 1934, but their actions had also revealed the incomprehensibility (to Yolngu) of the alternative: submission to criminal proceedings in faraway Darwin. For Yolngu and other Aboriginal people at the edges of colonial occupation, to become subject to criminal jurisdiction was a gamble with the unknown. Missionaries committed to corporal punishment could hope to be an educative force, offering Aborigines practice in the comportments that were now expected of them. Remote missions were sites of such tuition: semi-permeable economic enclaves whose modes of production and styles of authority could be tailored to local contingency. Christian missions localised colonial authority and made it more dialogical; and some mission practice was informed by, and helped to inform, the new academic interest in the native point of view. But missions remained accountable to a state that saw no limit, in principle, to the territorial extension of criminal law.

3

Governments, churches, parents, spouses and children, 1897–1940

During the four decades between Federation and World War II, Australian governments elaborated the legal and administrative apparatus of protection on an unprecedented scale. If you were classified as 'Aboriginal' and were within administrative reach, you could be told: where to live (banned from certain towns, removed to certain reserves under the supervision of officials not accountable to you); whether your children would be raised in an institution; how much money you could be paid as an employee and how you could spend it; whether you could marry the person of your choice; and who you could associate with (and share liquor with). In this chapter I will describe this apparatus, particularly the management of the intimate relationships between men and women, parents and children.

Laws

From 1911, when the Commonwealth assumed responsibility for the Northern Territory, there were seven parliaments making laws for the protection of Aborigines and Torres Strait Islanders.

In Tasmania there were only three pieces of legislation. One was the *Cape Barren Island Reserve Act* 1912, amended minor detail in 1934. This Act followed the creation, in 1881, of a reserve for those understood as the remnants of the Tasmanian Aborigines – the state's only equivalent to the 'native institutions' of the mainland. A schedule to the Act named those 'half-castes' who were authorised to live there and who would be entitled to apply for 50 acres of land 'in Tasmania'. The Act forbade the consumption of liquor within Cape Barren Island Reserve. An amendment to the *Licensing Act* 1932 prohibited the sale of liquor to 'half-castes'.

Victoria passed eighteen pieces of legislation implicating Aborigines between Federation and World War II. The most important were the *Aborigines Acts* of 1915 and 1928, which essentially repeated the *Aborigines Act* of 1890, defining a class of persons as Aboriginal and laying out a suite of controls over them. The *Licensing Acts* of 1915 and 1928 prohibited the sale of liquor to Aborigines. In Victoria up to 1924, there had been six managed reserves, but from 1917 the policy was gradually to concentrate all residents at Lake Tyers, with some people on other reserves rationed by police.

In South Australia twenty-five pieces of legislation implicating Aborigines in some way (including the *Northern Territory Aborigines Act* 1910) were passed between 1901 and 1939. The most important were the *Aborigines Acts* of 1911 and 1934 and the *Aborigines Act Amendment Act* 1939. The *Licensing Acts Further Amendment Act (No. 2)* 1915, the *Licensing Act* 1917 and the *Licensing Act* 1932 made it illegal for an Aboriginal person to possess or to drink liquor and illegal for any person to supply liquor. In addition, the *Aborigines (Training of Children) Act* 1923 empowered the chief protector to commit an Aboriginal child to be raised in a state institution. The state government took over two missions – Point Pearce in 1915 and Point McLeay in 1916 – but the management of South Australia's Aboriginal institutions remained largely in the hands of faith-based organisations. Until 1917 the Lutherans ran a mission in the arid north-east of the state (Killalpaninna), and they continued at Koonibba on the Eyre Peninsula. The United Aborigines Mission established missions at Oodnadatta in 1924, Swan Reach in 1925, Quorn in 1927, Nepabunna in 1929, Ooldea in 1933 and Finniss Springs in 1939. In 1921, for people who were still beyond colonial control, the government declared a large reserve in the north-west corner of the state; Presbyterians commenced Ernabella Mission on the reserve's eastern edge in 1937.

In New South Wales the parliament legislated fourteen times about Aborigines from 1901 to 1939. The *Aborigines Protection Act 1909* defined a class of persons and empowered the Aborigines Protection Board (APB) to regulate them. In 1915 the *Aborigines Protection Amending Act* added to the board's powers over the child of any Aborigine, and a further amendment in 1936 revised the definition of 'Aborigine' while extending the board's power to remove Aborigines to a reserve, to terminate their employment and to inspect their homes. In the early 1920s in New South Wales, there were about twenty reserves under state-employed teacher–managers, to which missionaries were granted access. The Aborigines Inland Mission flourished in New South Wales reserves as a fundamentalist church.[1] Charles Rowley encountered Aborigines in country towns of New South Wales in the 1950s and 1960s who believed that 'their skin colour was an affliction visited upon them by God'.[2]

In Western Australia, of the twenty-four laws implicating

Aborigines in some way passed between 1901 and 1939, the main statute was the *Aborigines Act* 1905, based on recommendations from W.E. Roth's excoriating 1904 exposé of abusive treatment of Aboriginal people (including corrupt use of police powers). As well, the *Licensing Act* 1911 prohibited the sale of liquor to Aborigines. The *Aborigines Act Amendment Act* 1936 expanded the class of people to whom the controls of the 1905 Act applied and added powers of medical surveillance and controls over marriage. There were four government stations by 1924 (Moola Bulla, Violet Valley, Carrolup and Moore River), a hospital in Port Hedland, several 'feeding stations' (issuing rations) and eleven church-run institutions – mostly in the tropical north.

In the Northern Territory, the Commonwealth took over from South Australia on 1 January 1911 and thus continued South Australia's *Northern Territory Aborigines Act* 1910. In thirty-eight subsequent Ordinances mentioning Aborigines up to the end of 1939, the Commonwealth defined the category of persons who could be regulated as Aboriginal and set out the terms of such regulation. The *Aboriginals Ordinance* 1918 (amended in 1923, 1924 (twice), 1925, 1927, 1928, 1930, 1933, 1936, 1937 (twice) and 1939) was the key legal instrument. There were seven missions by 1924. Children deemed 'half-caste' were taken to Darwin's Kahlin Compound from 1913, to Alice Springs' 'Bungalow' from 1914, to the Anglican mission on Groote Eylandt from 1921, to the Catholic Mission on Melville Island, and to the Methodist Mission on Goulburn Island. The Commonwealth declared large reserves in the south-west in 1920 and in Arnhem Land in 1931.

In legislating protection, Queensland was seen as the exemplary state in the period between Federation and World War II, not because it was the first state to legislate protection

(Victoria had passed an *Aborigines Protection Act* in 1869) but because its *Aboriginals Protection and Restriction of the Sale of Opium Act* of 1897 was the foundation of a large, comprehensive system, incorporating missions and led by 'experts'. Between 1897 and 1939, the Queensland parliament legislated twenty-nine times to define and control 'Aboriginals'. In 1939 the Queensland parliament split legislation into two almost identical statutes – for Aborigines (the *Aboriginals Preservation and Protection Act* 1939) and the Torres Strait Islanders (the *Torres Strait Islanders Act* 1939). In Queensland, there were thirteen reserves on the mainland by 1924, ten on islands off the coast. The churches ran most of the mainland reserves, and the three mainland reserves run by government were described in 1924 by Australia's *Yearbook* as 'mostly in the nature of penitentiaries'.[3]

In seeking to manage the human casualties of colonial occupation Australian governments and the public struggled to reconcile practices of segregation with a vision of homogeneous nationhood that was, by implication, integrative. This tension was not particular to Australia; 'the paradigm of protection that circulated around the globe', according to Kristyn Harman, consisted not only of 'segregating subjugated peoples for their own protection' but also 'preparing them to reach a desired standard that would enable them to re-join the wider population'.[4] For example, although some legislatures criminalised – and public opinion frowned upon – sexual contact between white and black, miscegenation was assumed to be inevitable so that, over generations, skin colour would approximate British–Australian hues.[5] The tension was felt in the very existence of special legislation, as it stigmatised, in the eyes of white Australians, those 'protected' and disciplined by it. Segregation was both physical (special institutions, reserves) and legal (disqualifying 'Aboriginals' from liberties of citizenship). Notwithstanding the widespread hope that 'the Aboriginal problem' would eventually disappear, the legal definition of 'Aborigine' was expanded either by explicit legal definition (the *Aborigines Act Amendment Act* 1936 (WA)) or by enabling officials (often the local police) to classify persons as 'Aboriginal' on the basis of appearance and behaviour.[6] By weakening self-sufficiency, contractions in the demand for Aboriginal labour sometimes swelled the ranks of those deemed the 'Aboriginal' clients of government and mission institutions.

To the extent that governments tried to train Aborigines for entry into the wider population they focused on the young and the not yet born. The tension between the stigmatising and the normalising effects of protection was sharpest in the management of the parent–child relationship and in the supervision of marital choices of Aboriginal women.

Children

Since 1981, the label 'Stolen Generations' has applied to the forced removal of the Aboriginal child from its natural parents so that it could be raised in an authorised institution or household. Testimonies illustrate how hurtful it was to treat children and parents in this way, yet recent moral revulsion may obscure the fact that the policy was based on an ethical calculation. A leading citizen of Adelaide, Edward C. Stirling, explained the mandate of South Australia's State Children's Council in 1914. Its powers, he observed,

> are hampered by the sentimental, though very natural, objections raised against the compulsory removal of native half-caste children from their black mothers, who

in most cases are fond of them, and who, according to their lights, do the best they can for their offspring. Still, in view of the gratifying success that has attended the adoption and training of such children by the State Children's Council, it would seem that the violation of the maternal feelings under such circumstances is a *less evil* than the physical and moral degradation which inevitably attends these girls if left under the influences of native camp life.[7]

Confidently distinguishing greater from lesser evil, Stirling understood protection as the difficult exercise of a duty of care for the vulnerable child. The total severance of child from family – justified by Stirling – was but one practice, at the extreme end of a spectrum of interventions. When seeking to protect a child and/or to shape a child to fit into Australian society, governments and churches did not necessarily seek total severance of child from kin. To manage the child/family relationship was sometimes thought to be sufficient.

In 1883, the colony of New South Wales had begun to take responsibility for indigent Aborigines through the Aborigines Protection Board (APB), a citizen initiative. While the colony's political elite was well represented on it, the board had no legislative base. By 1900, the government had assumed full control over the board's managed stations. Difficulties for Aboriginal people caused by the drought and depression of the 1890s had presented the board with (in Heather Goodall's words) 'an increasing financial burden of pauperised mendicants and an expanding alien cultural and racial threat [to white Australia]'.[8] Peter Read's study of the Wiradjuri, whose country had become the basis of much of the state's agricultural wealth since the 1820s, shows that while their initiation ceremonies were almost extinct by 1900, they had adapted their nomadic way of life to the resources available.[9] When the Wiradjuri required food and shelter, they sought Warangesda, Brungle and Maloga Missions and other such places (including some unmanaged reserves). They were otherwise free to move around their country, visiting relatives, camping on stock routes and watercourses and working where opportunities arose. The APB's managers were increasingly frustrated by their lack of power to settle such people down and to train them in work and domestic order; property owners and townspeople were also sometimes perturbed by these mobile families.

It was not clear how to govern such people so as to extinguish their difference and reduce their dependence. Emulating Victoria's policy (since 1886) of restricting many Aborigines from the entitlement to live on a reserve and receive rations, in the hope that the excluded would be absorbed into the wider population, the NSW *Aborigines Protection Act* 1909 narrowed the definition of 'Aboriginal'. This created opportunities to satisfy non-Aboriginal land hunger by revoking Aboriginal reserves, releasing land to white families keen to farm, as in Victoria. The success of some Aboriginal farmers on land granted at their request had demonstrated the land's quality. However, the contrary view of reserves held that, if retained, they could be the basis of Aborigines' independence of the APB's charity. Aiming to inspire Aborigines' economic self-sufficiency – on or off reserves – the APB was critical of Aboriginal parents who, in the APB's view, were doing too little to ensure that their children would be employable. In this matter, the white public of New South Wales was no help, for many whites wished to exclude 'coloured' children from schools.

Exclusion from school was against the law. The New South

Wales' *Public Instruction Act* 1880 did not distinguish the entitlements of Aborigines: any child living within 2 miles of a public school must attend at least seventy days per half-year. However, in some regions white parents said they would keep their children home if Aboriginal children were enrolled. Because such withdrawal threatened the viability of many small rural schools, Ministers of Education were reluctant to prosecute such parents, as the Act required, for not sending their children to school. Although the APB opposed this 'exclusion on demand' policy, it accepted that the Department of Education was developing a distinct system of 'Aboriginal schools': there were twelve in New South Wales by 1900, forty-two by 1920. The APB in 1894 asked the Department of Education to dilute the curriculum for such schools, removing geography, history and drawing, and not requiring music (though hymns were permitted). Reading, writing, dictation and arithmetic remained. By 1910, the Department of Education was classifying certain teachers as 'eligible for appointment to Aboriginal schools only'.[10] In 1916, the state issued a Syllabus for Aboriginal Schools that assumed the low skill of teachers (recruiting couples of 'Missionary spirit', though they had to be literate): boys were to become farm labourers and girls domestic servants. The syllabus prescribed hours of instruction in 'laundry work, gardening, sewing, cookery and manual work' and it set limits to 'indoor study' in deference to these pupils' inherited 'cravings for free out-door life'.[11] Even before New South Wales legislated to remove children from parents who 'neglected' them, it was institutionalising its own neglectful public education system, over the protests of Aboriginal parents who demanded education.[12]

As part of its accommodation to the Education Department's policies, the APB needed legislative power to determine the training of children: first through the *Neglected Children and Juvenile Offenders Act* 1905, then via the *Aborigines Protection Act* 1909 and finally through amendment of the latter Act in 1915. The places to which a child could be removed were multiplying. The United Aborigines Mission had opened a home for infants and children at Bomaderry in 1908; the APB had opened the Cootamundra Girls' Home in 1911 and was soon to open the Kinchela Aboriginal Boys' Home in 1918 (it moved to Kempsey in 1924). Meanwhile, to add to the funds that it required for supervision of reserves and for training institutions, the board began in 1911 to lease some of the reserves that it had been defending. This combination of circumstances favoured the APB's request for more power to seize children for 'uplift' through institutional supervision. In 1915 parliament removed the need for a magistrate's declaration that a child was 'neglected'; if the board saw 'neglect', police and officials could remove the child to an institution. Circumstances made 'neglect' likely: excluded from reserves, towns and schools – or disdaining their disciplines – some Aboriginal homes were no more than riverbank camps. New South Wales MP John Cann conceded that many children might appear not to be neglected, 'if the aboriginal child happens to be decently clad or apparently looked after'.[13] Board inspectors could see through such deceptions, he assured the parliament, to the degraded environment in which children were being reared, and so officials should be empowered to seize such children. Parents could object through the Children's Court. Assuming that few such appeals would be successful, Cann predicted that 'the aboriginals will soon become a negligible quantity and the young people will merge into the present civilization and become worthy citizens'.[14]

Cann's view prevailed, but there were some MPs in 1915

who contested child removal in speeches evoking the respectable Aboriginal family. Patrick McGarry, whose electorate (Murrumbidgee) included some of the Wiradjuri camps described by Read, objected: 'the mothers and fathers of these children love them just as much as the birds and animals of the bush care for their offspring'.[15] He had witnessed much abuse in the boarding out of white children, and he feared what would happen to 'half-caste' children if the 'mean settler' was enabled by the 'mean policeman'.[16] The parents of seized children, he predicted, would not be able to use the Children's Court effectively. McGarry wanted the APB to exert authority over the child and its mother *together*, on better funded 'stations' that would teach agriculture and morality. Thomas Thrower, representing the region that included Dubbo, said that the board did too little to encourage hard-working Aborigines who aspired to self-sufficient respectability and sought to live apart from the 'wasters' who thrived in camps and stations. He also worried that the board might 'farm out' children as young as seven years.[17]

George Black, from the north-west of New South Wales, compared his state unfavourably with the United States and New Zealand, where 'the original owners of the soil' were guaranteed arable land and training.[18] Refusing to assume that black parents were immoral, he too evoked the respectable Aborigine, contrasting him/her with immoral half-castes ('the scum of the community', heading towards extinction) whose existence, he said, demonstrated governments' failure to realise the potential of Australia's natives. Black explained that the removal of girls from their mothers through the 'boarding out system' had helped give rise to the half-caste who, having inherited the vices of the white man and the 'defects of the black mother', is 'inferior' to 'the aborigine'.[19] He had intervened to prevent the

APB apprenticing girls in his district, he reported. Like McGarry, Black wanted children to be trained alongside their parents, 'who have been so tutored and brought up that they are the best curators of their children's welfare'.[20] Contrary to the board's evocation of Aboriginal New South Wales as a culture of immorality and helplessness, these critics evoked Aboriginal families as able to meet the demands of a superior civilisation. Black reported Port Stephens blackfellows to be 'well respected ... they made a good living. They played cricket matches, and met the white people on equal terms, and the white people were not ashamed to meet them and shake their hands when the games were over.'[21] The member for Murray, Mr Scobie, thought that a better funded board could support Aborigines without severing children from parents; he had heard an Aboriginal man at Darlington Point

> explaining in the best of English how the aborigines were being plundered of their rations, robbed of their lands, and reduced to the position of slaves. I do not say the man was right in all his contentions, but when you meet men who understand all these things, you cannot expect them to calmly submit to an order to take from them their girl or boy.[22]

Mr Cann defended increasing the board's powers, with cameos of abject children and hopelessly degenerate parents.[23] Only three members out of thirty-four voted against the 1915 Bill.

'Neglect' and the state's duty to rescue children from it were empowering ideas for protective, forward-looking authorities. South Australia's *Children's Act* 1895 had authorised a magistrate to decide whether a child was neglected. According to Anna

Haebich, many magistrates thought that this Act did not apply to Aborigines; they leaned to the view that an Aboriginal child should be brought up 'in a wurley' – a traditional dwelling. But if such a child was of mixed parentage, how could the state ignore its duty to children of genetic potential? Perceiving as significant genetic distinctions among Aborigines, by 1909 the South Australian police had compiled a list of all known 'half-castes' – 766 children, listed by age, locality and camp or house. South Australia's *Aborigines Act* 1911 empowered the chief protector as the legal guardian of every Aboriginal or 'half-caste' child. By 1914, there were fifty-four children of Aboriginal descent under some State Children's Council (SCC) care. Many of South Australia's Indigenous children continued in attenuated association with their parents, separated from them in a dormitory, at Point Pearce, Point McLeay and at Koonibba and Killalpaninna missions.

When South Australia's parliament debated a 1923 Bill to allow the chief protector, in consultation with the SCC, to determine whether an Aboriginal child should be taken away for training, critics (including some Aboriginal people) questioned the Bill's humanity and the power it gave to one government officer. Although the bill became law, one effort to implement it in full view of the public (at Adelaide railway station) in 1924 embarrassed the protector; subsequently, his power of seizure fell into disuse. The Children's Welfare and Public Relief Board (successor to the SCC from 1927) held to the view, until the 1950s, that Aboriginal and non-Aboriginal parents were to be subject to the same legal regime – that is, that a magistrate should review evidence of neglect before a child could be taken. Under this more limited authority, Aboriginal children were still removed, many of them growing up in the United Aborigines Mission Colebrook Home near Quorn.[24]

Victorian governments were confident that the Aboriginal population was rapidly declining through assimilation; they did not target Aboriginal children for removal or create special institutions for them. Nor did governments in Tasmania, as they simply assumed that the state's small and destitute population of Aboriginal descent was in the process of assimilating; an unknown number of Tasmanian Aboriginal children were removed on the grounds of neglect.[25] Victoria had been the first colony to legislate for managing Aboriginal people, with the *Aboriginal Protection Act* 1869. On the reserves of the 19th century, even those with dormitories, families stayed together.[26] However, in 1886 and 1890, the government had legislated and/or issued regulations to expel 'half-castes' from reserves. While the government had the power to remove children who were neglected, its preferred scenario was that whole families, denied residence on a reserve, would assimilate into settler-colonial society. As marginal workers in rural industries, many families fell on hard times. Broome reports that it is possible neither to quantify the number of children removed to institutions in Victoria nor to generalise about the extent and nature of their subsequent contact with their parents.[27] Haebich did not estimate the numbers of Victorian Aboriginal children removed; the theme of her account is the fate of whole families – either expelled from reserves or relocated to Lake Tyers.[28]

Queensland's legislation and institutional network enabled it to remove whole families from their country of origin to an institution. In their accounts of such 'removals', neither Thom Blake nor Raymond Evans has estimated the extent to which the 'removals' separated children from parents. In Blake's analysis, 'the removals program fulfilled a variety of objectives: removing the old and unemployable from station and fringe camps;

controlling behaviour in fringe camps, on settlements and labour relations; as means of extending prison sentences and punishment over and beyond the legal system'.[29] Evans reports that the policy distinguished between Aborigines who were useful to colonists and those who were useless and/or threatening in some way, targeting the latter.[30] Once these families were placed in an institution, many of the children were put into dormitories. To be so domiciled was to be 'separated' from parents, but in controlled contact with them.[31] According to Queensland government figures cited by Haebich, only 249 of 2024 children removed to institutions (12.3 per cent) were not accompanied by an adult. She reports that the government rejected most offers – often by employers – to adopt an Aboriginal child: the colony's 'protection' law had been devised to thwart abusive employers.[32] Queensland settlements attempted to school the children housed in dormitories, but Cherbourg's experience illustrates the poor standard: crude accommodation, the difficulty of recruiting competent teachers, the high pupil/teacher ratios (242 pupils taught by four teachers in 1939), the slow progress (eight years to get to fourth grade, in 1939), and the assumption that pupils would only ever be employed in manual labour.[33] Ruth Hegarty was excited to start school at Cherbourg, before she realised that this meant she would have to leave the dormitory of her mother (who soon left Cherbourg for work).[34] She recalls her misbehaviour as an emotional response to this separation; she was not 'the only naughty one, because we all suffered the trauma of separation and we were not old enough to know why'.[35] Isolated from the mainstream education system, she realised only much later 'that what we were being taught was substandard. Academically we would not have been able to compete in the school outside of the Settlement.'[36]

We do not know how many children were removed to church and government institutions in Western Australia. According to Haebich, that state's aim was 'to sunder forever ties with their Aboriginality and to mould them into docile rural and domestic workers or to render them invisible in a White Australia'.[37] Roth's 1905 report had painted a picture of Aboriginal childhood so miserable and endangered as to justify church and state intervention of some kind: their indenture, including on pearling boats, without payment or education; the arrest, neck-chaining and imprisonment of youths under sixteen years for cattle-killing; the failure to ensure that goods distributed as 'relief' got into the hands of intended beneficiaries, including children; the kidnapping of boys and girls by itinerant whites.[38] Roth predicted a future of 'vagabondage and harlotry' for the state's 500 'half-caste' children if the state did not intervene to ensure that they were educated and protected from exploitation.[39] He also recommended that institutions with child inmates be inspected and that the protector be made guardian of all Aboriginal and half-caste children up to eighteen years. Under the resulting *Aborigines Act* 1905, the Aborigines Department – usually with police as its agents – could remove an illegitimate Aboriginal child to one of the missions or government stations authorised to receive them. Because the criteria for removal were not specified in legislation, police judgment about the circumstances of children effectively determined the policy. Haebich reports that respect for pastoralists' need for a workforce affected police selection of children.[40]

From the reports of James Isdell, the Aborigines Department's travelling inspector in the Kimberley from 1907 to 1909, we can get some idea of the complexity of the judgments that had to be made and of the ambivalent relationship between authorised protectors and police. Isdell was critical of police who marched children to missions in much the same way that they had been marching them into gaols; they should be taken by vehicle, he proposed.[41] He believed that the moral risk from which he was removing children included their likely conviction on cattle-killing charges, followed by imprisonment. In Isdell's view, a mother's attachment mattered less than a removed child's benefit; the *Aborigines Act* was amended in 1911 to confirm, in law, that the protector did not need a mother's consent. Isdell also dismissed the pleas of pastoralists whom he judged to be exploiters of child labour.[42] For Isdell, and no doubt for other officials, removing a child to an institution that was, in theory, wholesome and accountable, was better than leaving it to a hazardous future on a predatory and harshly policed frontier. The decision to remove was easier if the child of mixed descent were more 'white' than 'black'.[43]

Although, from 1893, the government of Western Australia had made it compulsory for children to attend school, many white parents did not wish their children to share a classroom with Aboriginal children. The Aborigines Department, under A.O. Neville (protector from 1915 to 1940), saw a solution in founding Carrolup (in 1915) and Moore River (or Mogumber, in 1918) where children, housed in segregated dormitories, would train in occupations suited to their assumed intellectual limitations. Some children were fully separated from their parents; others had parents who camped within the institution, their contact with the children regulated by officials, including Aboriginal police. Tom Corbett, born in the Pilbara in 1910, spent much of his childhood, youth and early adulthood at Moore River. At first, fostered by Swiss refugees in Perth, he attended state primary schools; he was shy, taunted, but learning to speak English.

His foster parents returned to Switzerland when he was ten, by which time he had started grade three at North Perth. Sent to Moore River, he was put back into grade two. His education stalled: three years at Moore River did not progress him past grade three.[44] He was glad to leave school and start work at fourteen, at first doing tasks for the superintendent around the settlement. However, he wanted 'a real job' so 'I could earn my own money and be independent'.[45] At fifteen, he was offered work as a houseboy and water carrier at a hostel in Jitarning; he had a small room at the back of the hostel and was paid 10 shillings a week plus board. He earned a reputation as courteous and hard-working. After eighteen months, the hostel changed hands and Tom returned to Moore River. He stayed at the settlement until 1927, when he got a job protecting sheep from dingoes on a station near Welbungin; he worked there for eighteen months, learning how to protect, shear, crutch, kill and dress sheep, and to remove lambs' tails. His job ended when his employer fell on hard times and he returned for a brief spell at Moore River, before finding jobs ploughing fields, packing fruit and managing horses. The Great Depression threw Tom back into the care of Moore River for eighteen months. Even though conditions there were harsh, and a percentage of his wages went to the state's trust fund, Tom thinks that he was 'better off than a lot of white people at this time. I had the old Moore River Settlement's roof over my head, the meagre food that was given us, work when I could get it and a little bit of money in my pocket.'[46]

The oral history of Moore River reveals an institution run with austerity and with harsh punishments (flogging and incarceration in the infamous 'Boob'). However, to characterise it as a 'total institution' overlooks what Tom Corbett's life demonstrates: Moore River's permeability, its availability as a refuge from a demanding world, its possibilities of patronage for those residents who found the superintendent's favour.[47]

In the Northern Territory, Walter Baldwin Spencer recommended in 1912 that 'the children must be withdrawn from the camps at an early age'. Acknowledging that parents would find this a 'hardship', he insisted: 'if once the children are allowed to reach a certain age and have become accustomed to camp life, with its degrading environment and endless roaming about in the bush, it is almost useless to try and reclaim them'.[48] The Administration established two institutions: Kahlin Compound in Darwin, in 1913 and 'the Bungalow' in a series of locations in the Alice Springs district in 1914. Most children taken to these places were girls. Boys and girls were given little education beyond what was expected of a competent stockman or domestic servant. Both institutions were poorly resourced and became overcrowded, a problem that could not be concealed from the public. The Administration from time to time discussed with mission societies relocating many of the children to missions such as Goulburn Island, but Cecil Cook, Chief Protector of Aboriginals from 1927 to 1939, had no confidence in missions; and townsfolk valued the Darwin and Alice Springs institutions as sources of cheap labour and (in some cases) of casual sexual partners. Some Kahlin boys were moved to Pine Creek in 1931. These two institutions gave rise to a self-conscious and endogamous 'half-caste' minority.[49]

In early 21st-century Australian collective memory, the *invasion* of the domestic group and the child's *dispossession* of their Aboriginal heritage have made these 20th-century child protection regimes the epitome of colonial arrogance. In defence of these practices it might be argued that child removal policies focused on the 'half-caste' – typically born of an Aboriginal mother in a sexual relationship (casual or ongoing) with a non-Aboriginal man – and that 'half-castes' had no place in the Aboriginal social system. This view fails to allow for the ideological flexibility of 'descent' – a concept used in all societies to link people, as kin, through time. 'Descent' refers not only to a biological link. Recognised 'filiation' may attach less importance to biological descent than to who actually rears a child. For Aboriginal families to emphasise the social nature of 'descent' became particularly important when, as a consequence of the frontier's many sexually active non-Aboriginal men with Aboriginal women as sexual partners, many children were born to Aboriginal mothers who had little or no ongoing connection with the white men who had impregnated them. Were these children fatherless? From the point of view of the Aboriginal social system, this is an appalling possibility, a tear in the social fabric. The idea that an Aboriginal child could be without 'filiation' – descended from no father – made no sense in Aboriginal society. A child who was potentially anomalous in this way had to be rendered as 'normal' by applying the notion of descent to them. They could be understood as acquiring rights through the mother and/or through the Aboriginal men (such as the mother's brother) who, in association with that mother, took responsibility for the child's upbringing. The notions of descent and filiation had to be made to work, if there was to be any sense of an ongoing Aboriginal society. In handling one of the impacts of colonisation – many sexual encounters between Aboriginal and non-Aboriginal partners – Aboriginal notions of descent and filiation have been robust. They have had to be, as long as there were any heritable resources. To regard half-caste children as socially unbound and thus requiring removal was very much a white humanitarian view. Of course, there were (and are) children so ill-served by their kin that the state must remove them, if a better milieu can be found for them. That difficult judgment was for many years made on grounds saturated with whites' hopeless prognosis for Aboriginal society.

Past and recent censure of the cruelty and insensitivity of so much that was done by authorities in the interests of the child is justified, but it is important not to let 'Stolen Generations' be the summary image of what 'Protection' did. 'Removal' is an imprecise term and should not be used to refer to all the different ways that state and church authority compromised and shaped the parent–child relationship. As Jim Fletcher's study of New South Wales shows, many children who remained with their families were subject to an alternative regime of institutionalised inferior schooling, as governments tempered their mainstreaming ambitions to white parents' exclusionary wishes. In Queensland and Western Australia, where the transition to closer agricultural settlement highlighted Aborigines as noisome fringe-dwellers of rural towns, superfluous to employer requirements, governments developed institutions that separated without fully removing children from parents.

To officials, Aboriginal parents were visible usually as inadequate housekeepers, neglectful child-raisers and inconstant breadwinners, rather than as adults thoughtful of their children's futures. However, in the records of South Australia's 1913 Royal Commission we see Ngarrindjeri adults wrestling with the question of how to combine governmental and familial authority to secure a future for children and community. Standing before the commissioners, David Unaipon said that 'when the children leave school [that is, aged nine or ten] they should be taken in hand by some one and educated to some trade or other useful employment so that they can become independent and self-supporting'.[50] He was then asked if 'your people would be pleased to hand over the boys and girls to be apprenticed to trades?' He replied: 'As long as the parents know that the children were put into good hands, put in the hands of someone they could trust', they would not mind.[51] Unaipon's fellow resident, Philip Rigney, told the commissioners that children 'should be taught little jobs from the time they are able to do anything'. He complained that many 'are not under control, and when they are set to work they run away'. He suggested that children be 'taken away from here after they are about 12 or 14 years of age, provided they were put under some care. They could be taught to support themselves, and that would be better than living on the charity of the State.'[52] The next speaker, John Wilson, said that the children 'should be brought up on the mission station. They could leave the mission station when they reach manhood. The family tie is very strong among the natives.'[53] When Jacob Harris appeared, the commissioners probed parental feeling a little more:

> Do you think that the Government should take your young people at the age of about 14 years and teach them trades?—Yes.
>
> Do you think they should teach them here or take them away?—I should think they should take them away to teach them. I think they should be taken away from here, because you would have fuller control of them. There are too many chances here of their running about and playing.

> Do you not think that when it came to the point of sending your little boy away when he is 14 years old you would be reluctant to lose him?—If it were for his good I would let him go.[54]

Evidently, this issue was further debated at Point McLeay, after the commissioners had moved on, for the printed evidence includes 'Addenda'. One (dated 28 April 1913) is from Philip Rigney: 'if children were taken away from here for apprenticeship they should be allowed to return for, say, a fortnight or three weeks every year to see their relatives'.[55] Matthew Kropinyeri (6 May 1913) would 'embrace the opportunity of betterment for our children' but not if it meant 'complete alienation from our children'. He wanted the children 'taken in hand on leaving school by the state and taught to become useful and independent members of society', but they should be allowed to visit parents. 'On no account should any of our young people be allowed to be idle or be dependent on the Mission as many are at the present time.'[56]

To these Ngarrindjeri men the future of their community rested partly on how members participated in the wider economy, either as waged workers or as farmers granted land – so youths must acquire skills and a commitment to work. While some men referred to the training that they themselves had given their children, they each considered additional training, from an outside source, to be desirable, and so the issues arose: at what age, to what authority and with what provisos should they let their children go? The thoughts expressed orally and in the two addenda in 1913 show fathers seeking a path between the pain of disrupted family and the waste of idle, unskilled youth. In 1923 a delegation from Point McLeay strongly opposed the new *Aborigines (Training of Children) Act* that made the chief protector the guardian of all 'half-caste' children under eighteen: 'our children have never been state children and we don't want them to be'. They would 'rather give up their mission station than sacrifice their children'.[57]

Controlled miscegenation

It is odd that some Australian governments passed laws to enable them to regulate Aborigines' spouse selection. Should not the 'higher civilisation' of the colonists encourage individual choice of spouse among people whose primitive ways were known to have denied it? Legislators gave several reasons for regulating this most intimate and personal of choices.

By amendment in 1901, section 9 of Queensland's *Aboriginals Protection and Restriction of the Sale of Opium Act* said that 'no marriage of a female aboriginal with any person other than an aboriginal shall be celebrated without the permission, in writing, of a Protector authorised by the Minister to give such permission'. Queensland's Home Secretary had explained in 1899 that the power would close a loophole in the regulation of employment. 'Unscrupulous men'

> manage to evade the provisions of the Act by entering into a form of marriage with them ... If they do not marry them, the protector would take the women away and deal with them under the Act. If the women are legally married, as no doubt they are, the form of marriage under the Marriage Act is gone through – then unscrupulous employers can defy the Protector.[58]

Walter Roth, Queensland's first northern protector of Aboriginals, had alerted the government to this ruse. The home secretary explained in 1901 that the law's aim was not to prevent miscegenation; he 'did not see why a white man should not be allowed to marry an aboriginal woman if he was willing to maintain her and keep her properly as his wife and look after the children'.[59]

Western Australia's chief protector, Henry Prinsep (1844–1922), began soon after his appointment in 1898 to urge power over marriage. Walter Roth, as a Royal Commissioner 'on the Condition of the Natives' in 1904, endorsed Prinsep's efforts to make it more difficult for Aboriginal men to barter women for gin, tobacco, flour and rice. When questioning Prinsep as a witness, Roth highlighted the Asian interest in Aboriginal women of the north: 'Are Asiatics being legally married to aboriginal females?' Prinsep: 'I believe some are in the Broome district.'[60] The power over women's marriage could be used to prohibit such marriages or to make them rare events. When Western Australia legislated in 1905, the proposed marriage power (clause 42) was justified by James Isdell in the Assembly as curbing 'inter-marriages with aliens'. Aborigines should be allowed to marry only 'according to their own customs'. He proceeded to tell stories about problems in marriages of Aboriginal women with Chinese men and with 'Manilamen' (Filipinos). Isdell wanted White Australia, not 'piebald' Australia.[61] Without mentioning clause 42, the Assembly's Michael Troy implied that authority over marriage would prevent 'half-castes' from marrying the wrong type of person. 'Half-castes, if bred with white people, become in some respects almost as expert as the whites; but once they marry with aborigines, they become even more depraved than the aborigines themselves.' On the other hand, Troy wished to segregate half-castes on reserves. 'If we have reserves, we should try to put the half-castes on reserves by themselves.'[62] What chance would they have then to marry a white?

In 1910, the parliament of South Australia passed two Acts governing Aborigines: one for the Northern Territory (about to come under Commonwealth control in 1911) and one for South Australia itself. Clause 22 in the Bill for the Northern Territory replicated Queensland's and Western Australia's powers over the marriage choices of Aboriginal women, but over the Aboriginal people in South Australia there was to be no such power, as it had been that colony's policy to encourage miscegenation with a land grant to any white man marrying a 'lubra'. Donald Campbell asserted that the South Australian Bill 'dealt largely with a race which had come into close contact with civilisation, but [the Territory Aborigines Bill] dealt with the natives in their wild state', ignoring that, in the north-west of South Australia (not handed over to the Commonwealth in 1911), the Pitjantjatjara had scarcely begun their association with outsiders.[63] Another member said he saw no reason why a half-caste woman should not marry an Aboriginal man. He was told by one of the two members representing the Northern Territory 'that there would be no objection to such union'.[64] The attorney-general clarified that a half-caste woman who remained 'attached to aboriginal associations' was not to be prevented from marrying 'a full-blooded aborigine'.[65] He thus implied that those whose marital choices were to be regulated would be 'half-caste' Aboriginal women whose associations were primarily with non-Aborigines. John Newland said that he understood the purpose of clause 22 as preventing 'the forming of alliances between aboriginal and white or other races'.[66] Later Thomas Crush explained that the clause was 'for the protection of the females, and to prevent their marriage with undesirable people'.[67] Some MPs objected to the marriage power. James Moseley predicted that it 'would be impossible of exercise. The Act would fall of its own weight.' And William Blacker thought the measure amounted to an Aborigine Persecution Bill; he asked whether there would be an appeal from the decision of the protector.[68] In this short South Australian debate, there was no unanimity on the necessity, practicality or purpose of giving public servants authority over marriages by Aborigines.

Considering all three debates, it seems that legislators saw at least three reasons to regulate Aborigines' marriage choice: to remove a loophole in the regulation of employers; to discourage one kind of miscegenation (with 'Asiatics'); and to encourage other kinds of miscegenation (turning 'half-castes' away from 'aboriginal' partners towards white partners). However, in no state was the legislation written so as to bind officials to use their new power to further one or other of these objectives. Once the marriage power was legislated, its use would depend on what the empowered officials thought was important, and that person might be merely the local policeman.

In Queensland the chief protector of Aboriginals relied heavily on the police to administer the Act, including the marriage power. Mark Hannah's analysis of their exercise of this power from 1901 to 1934 found that the chief protector received approximately forty applications per year, initiated by either or both the parties to the intended marriage. Some applicants would attend a police station in the district in which they resided and ask to be married; others would write a letter or have one written for them by a literate person, such as an employer, a clergyman, a shopkeeper, or, in the case of men prosecuted for cohabitation, by their legal representatives. Some applications were forwarded directly to the chief protector. It was the duty of the local police to research the character and circumstances of both parties; in many cases, the police interviewed them at their residences. The police would also solicit character references from employers, neighbours and local notables; and they would comb their records for convictions of either party. Usually a two-page report would result from these enquiries, describing the physical appearance of the parties, their employment, their level of income and job security, the couple's dwelling, its fixtures and fittings, and the character traits of the parties. Some police reports speculated on the outcome of a marriage and offered an opinion about whether it should be approved. Evidently, many police and applicants were not sure who was subject to marriage regulation. The Act's definition of 'aborigine' called for judgment, as 'half-castes' were subject to it only if they lived with an Aboriginal person (as wife or husband or child) or if they habitually lived or associated with Aborigines. It was therefore possible to be of Aboriginal descent and not be subject to the Act.

From 1901 to 1934, according to Hannah, about three quarters of marriage applications in Queensland were approved. Most of those not approved were applications from men whose intended wife turned out, upon investigation, to be unwilling to marry the applicant. Some men were judged to be of bad character and/or to be unable to provide financially for the household: the chief protector was concerned that women left destitute would be a burden on the state. Some Aboriginal men wrote to the chief protector or to the superintendents of reserves and missions to seek out a bride. The demand for women of marriageable age on the reserves and missions exceeded the supply. In a small number of rejected applications, the female was deemed to be a 'sexual maniac' and morally incapable of maintaining a stable monogamous relationship. Such women were forcibly exiled to a mission or reserve. Few applications were rejected on explicit racial criteria. To prevent the proliferation of 'half-caste' children, the state usually forbade marriage of 'full-blood' Aboriginal women to non-Indigenous men. However, in order to legitimise such children, the state would permit such marriages if the man claimed paternity over children already born and if satisfied that the couple had been living as if married for many years. Aboriginal women were usually not permitted to marry Chinese or Japanese men. However, just as exceptions were made for 'full-blood' women with children, the state would protect a child born to an Aboriginal woman and an Asian man from the fate of being illegitimate.[69]

In the Northern Territory, the Commonwealth embraced from 1911 the power created in 1910 by the South Australian parliament. Baldwin Spencer recommended in 1913 that only in 'very exceptional circumstances' should a non-Aboriginal man be allowed to marry an 'aboriginal lubra'.[70] As protector in 1912 he had sometimes had to consider whether to permit an existing mixed couple to marry. 'In these instances the woman had become accustomed to the relative comfort of the white man's or Asiatic's camp and after many years absence had probably become quite unable and certainly unfitted to live the ordinary life in the native camp.'[71] To have refused permission would have forced the man and woman to separate, and the woman, with her children, to return to the native camp. 'To consign her to the latter would be a cruel thing to do and therefore in such exceptional cases permission to marry was given but, when proper provision for the aboriginals is made, such inter-racial marriages should not be permitted.'[72] Popular opinion would help to enforce such a policy, he implied, declaring that 'no white men, if white women are available, will marry a half-caste aboriginal'.[73] Half-castes should be 'encouraged' to marry among themselves. And, it was implied, the government should encourage white women to settle in the Territory.[74]

The Commonwealth's *Aboriginals Ordinance* 1918 clarified which 'half-castes' were not subject to its provisions. Effectively, the Ordinance allowed 'half-caste' men to exit controls upon their eighteenth birthday (raised to twenty-one in 1924), while 'half-caste' women would exit the controls by marrying and living with 'a person substantially of European descent'. The Ordinance thus gave the 'half-caste' woman an incentive to marry certain men, while obliging her (section 45) to get permission to do so. Among 'experts' advising the Commonwealth on Aboriginal policy in the Northern Territory there was still debate about how best to use this power over the choice exercised by women classed as 'half-caste'. Asked for his advice in 1929, the chief protector of Aboriginals in Queensland, J.W. Bleakley, said that there was much variation within the category 'half-caste'. He contrasted the 'uneducated' ones who 'are generally as much in need of protection as the full blood, in fact are frequently more exposed to temptation and abuse' with 'half castes showing the desire and capacity of raising themselves'.[75] Bleakley estimated that 'probably less than 10 per cent' of the 'half-caste' population were suited to marrying a non-Aboriginal man.[76] 'Some of the superior half-castes or quadroons may help to solve the sex question, by marrying men in the outback not able to get wives of their own colour.'[77] His advice implied that each proposed marriage should be assessed by the chief protector or his delegate.

Northern Territory Chief Protector of Aboriginals Dr C.E. Cook was optimistic about miscegenation. His annual reports show that he endorsed the spouse choice of sixty-nine women, from July 1929 to June 1938, thirty-eight of them marrying Europeans. This was a significant minority of the 'half-caste' female population of the Territory (237 in June 1938). Cook reported refusing ten applications, some of them from European men. Cook was thus a relatively liberal and integrationist 'protector' keen to assist 'half-castes' by permitting what he judged to be good unions. In 1929 and 1933 he introduced regulations to improve the training and remuneration of 'half-caste' employees. He initiated a low-cost housing estate for selected 'half-castes', resulting in twelve houses in Darwin by 1939. The social development of the so-called 'half-caste' was essential to Cook's vision of how White Australia could apply to northern development. As 'half-castes' were a rapidly growing segment of the Northern Territory population the government must help them attain the same standard of living as 'whites'. For Cook 'whiteness' was more a social than a biological status. He enumerated as 'European' the issue of the permitted marriages of 'half-caste' women. Darwin was small enough to allow Cook to keep an eye on those whom he had permitted to marry; he claimed in 1938 that 'with few exceptions the marriages of female half-castes with Europeans, which have been celebrated during the last six years, have proved eminently successful'.[78]

North and South in Western Australia

In Western Australia, the protectors differed in their use of the marriage power conferred by the *Aborigines Act* 1905, according to Haebich. Under Prinsep (chief protector in the period

1898–1907), 'applications from young white men were rejected out of hand'.[79] Prinsep approved some marriages of young Aboriginal women with Asian men, but his successors C.F. Gale (1907–15) and A.O. Neville (1915–40) disallowed such unions.[80] Some missionaries and parliamentarians criticised Neville's use of his power. Missions considered that guiding people into good marriages was an important element of their 'civilising' programs. Neville found that missionaries' criteria of a good marriage depended not on the couple's race but on their apparent adherence to the preached faith.[81] In 1917 Neville clashed with Father Creagh over marriages between 'Manilamen' and Aboriginal women raised by the Beagle Bay Mission. 'The humanist brand of Catholicism which had evolved in the North was totally opposed by governments with xenophobic anxieties about Asian-Aboriginal unions,' his biographer explains.[82]

By the 1920s, Neville was troubled by the Act's lack of clarity about which 'half-castes' were subject to his authority. His proposed amendments gave rise to two legislative debates (in 1929 and 1936) and a Royal Commission whose records afford our most extensive archive of Australians' thoughts about the regulation of Aboriginal marriage. When the Collier government in 1929 sought to widen the definition of 'Aboriginal' in the *Aborigines Act*, some parliamentarians saw an affront to people of Aboriginal descent who (in Sir James Mitchell's words) were living 'clean, decent lives'.[83] Mitchell asked: 'is the House prepared to agree to a proposal that all these people, civilised and uncivilised, shall be treated alike?'[84] Alexander Thomson wanted the Bill first to be discussed with 'half-castes', lest it curb their liberties.[85] Joseph Sleeman said that 'Quite a number of half castes, although they have black blood in their veins, are whites as regards their habits, but there are other half castes living practically the lives of blackfellows, and the Bill does not differentiate between the two.'[86]

This opposition to Neville was rooted in MPs' respect for the adjustment that many Aboriginal families of the agricultural regions of the state were making.[87] The Great Southern Region had been colonised in the 19th century by Europeans who grazed large herds; in the 20th century the region saw more mixed farming: wheat and sheep on family farms, among which small towns grew. Nyungar found work in this colonising system of land use – as domestics, as clearers of bush (to make open fields or paddocks), as fencers and as shearers of sheep. Sally Hodson has argued that in the social organisation of Indigenous labour, Nyungar customs of kinship persisted: they preferred to contract themselves as family teams. Kinship influenced 'where people worked, with whom they worked, the type of work that they did and how they shared the available resources'.[88] The composition of the Nyungar domestic unit varied, as it was accepted that children and youths would spend time with uncles, aunts and cousins and not only in the household of their natural parents. While women were expected to do cooking, washing and childcare, it was normal that they worked alongside their menfolk in team-based work, such as clearing bush to make paddocks. Children were also part of these teams (schooling for Aboriginal children in Western Australia was not compulsory until 1948). A farmer would negotiate a clearing contract with an individual who acted for a network of kin; these kin would then divide the tasks and the payments between the several domestic groups that made up the kinship network. Clearing work was done over several years, as it is a process with a sequence of tasks. Clearing could thus be fitted around the shearing season which takes place in

August–October or September–November. Shearing also lends itself to a team approach, with other family members doing work complementary to the skilled shearers. The working life of Nyungar was thus a predictable cycle. Wool-growers got to know certain shearers and their families, and it was possible (and for both sides desirable) for relationships of trust to develop.

Such familiarity between employers and employees allowed networks of kin to build on their customary sense that certain regions within the Great Southern Region belonged to them as their customary 'run'; as well, it enabled some MPs to question Neville's generalising account of feckless and morally vulnerable Aborigines. When the Minister for Agriculture Harold Millington defended the 1929 Bill he emphasised the government's wish to regulate marriage celebrants, such as clergy, rather than Aborigines themselves, to 'prevent marriages being solemnised by those who have not sufficient knowledge of the natives and their laws'.[89]

> It may be that a minister would propose to celebrate a marriage which from the point of view of the aboriginal would be undesirable and inadvisable. Such instances have occurred. Aboriginal women have been married to Asiatics … Marriages have been celebrated that have been objected to on tribal grounds … The whole object is to protect the aboriginal and not to dictate.[90]

William Kitson presented Neville as a man who, unlike missionaries, knew and respected the customs of Aboriginal marriage. When missionaries encouraged Aboriginal people to marry contrary to their own customs, 'the legal obligations of marriage may not be recognised, with the result that the offspring are left for the State to look after', and 'the probable result will be that one or other of the tribes concerned will take exception to the marriage, and that will lead to strife between the two tribes'.[91] These points referred more to the North than the South of the state, illustrating the difficulty of encompassing Western Australia's Aboriginal people in a single framework of law and policy.[92] While the government won the debate on the marriage clause in 1929, the parliament rejected the Bill as a whole because of provisions that would have criminalised miscegenation (punishing white men) and obliged employers to cover medical expenses of Aboriginal employees.

Neville did not give up seeking to extend his powers over Aborigines of mixed descent. At the Moseley Royal Commission in 1934 he presented himself as the state's expert on the mind of the 'half-caste'.

> The half caste is extremely difficult to handle. It requires years of experience to know him at all. He knows no gratitude at all. The man who today abuses you will calmly look for favours tomorrow. They are creatures of mood, and must be protected and disciplined in spite of themselves, for their sakes and ours.[93]

He evoked a rise in youthful sexual immorality: 'Unsuitable alliances are being contracted, incest is about and youthful depravity is general.'[94] Many of the proliferating 'half-castes' considered themselves not subject to the *Aborigines Act*, he lamented, 'yet they consort with natives. They run with the hare and hunt with the hounds as they please. No one can stop them.'[95] He regarded as 'unsuitable': 'marriages with Asiatics ... marriages between half caste girls and ... low-classed unemployed whites'.[96] It was essential that his oversight supply the moral judgment that, in his view, the young 'half-caste' woman lacked.[97]

Neville also reiterated his criticism of the missions' approach to marriage: 'curtailing the liberty of the subject, interfering with tribal customs, marrying against the wishes of the people, or consummating unsuitable marriages'.[98]

> The missionary does not always take cognisance of tribal laws, and breaches of these laws, or what seem breaches, to them do not appear to be breaches of any law. It is consequently necessary for someone with knowledge of the culture of the aborigines to safeguard these people in this way.[99]

Later, Neville acknowledged that he had been able to cooperate with one missionary, Schenk at Mount Margaret, who had suggested several marriages between 'half-caste' and 'full-blood'. Neville had 'visited the Mission, questioned the various couples and their relatives, and deferred consent to some of the marriages until the man to whom the girls had been promised in the first place could be consulted and asked to renounce their claims, if willing to do so'. The old man had stipulated 'that the couple must stay away from the Mission for about a year, which they did ... [I]f everyone was as careful as Mr. Schenk to avoid tribal complications matters would be more satisfactory.'[100] Neville's Royal Commission evidence showed that his respect for Aboriginal custom was selective. If granted the power to regulate marriages among Aborigines, he would use it to stop betrothal of young girls to old men and to stamp out polygyny. He believed that missionaries and feminists shared his opposition to these customs.

Neville was convinced of the naivety and moral vulnerability of all half-caste women, many of whom, he asserted, had ruined their lives by unions with Asians and disreputable whites. And no educated half-caste girl should, in his opinion, marry a 'full-blood'. The enforceable destiny of such women, he argued, should be marriage to a respectable white man. According to Neville, he had acquired much de facto power over marriages by persuading civil celebrants to refer to him before performing a ceremony that included an Aboriginal person. He now wanted church-based celebrants as well to be compelled to consult him. Pride in his powers and judgment led him to tell the story of his asking police to

> question a girl as to passing herself as a Maori and thereby inveigling a man into promising her marriage. In that case, when the man learned the girl was almost an aboriginal, he backed out. It is my desire that in these cases the man should know who the girl is before he takes the final step. I consider this preferable to any trouble occurring after marriage, probably leading to desertion of the girl. The department which advocates a natural progress towards the white for those girls is not likely to interfere with their aspirations in seeking marriage with white men, but it does desire to protect its charges as a father might protect his daughters against the wiles of wastrels.[101]

Expounding his diligent intervention into the intimate lives of young men and women, Neville revealed another reason for regulating Aboriginal marriage: it was more difficult to remove a child from a couple legally married.[102]

In 1936, the Willcock government sought to amend the Act – again to widen the category of 'native' persons under the protector's regulation. The population was said then to consist of 22 119 'full-bloods' and 4245 'half-castes' (those with 'any coloured blood in them').[103] As well, the Bill sought to make marriage celebrants (mostly missionary clergy) accountable to the protector. Again, Neville encountered resistance. Charles Latham argued that the state should have more respect for missionaries' judgment: 'We should say to the mission people, "the natives are your family and will remain your family while they are with you; we trust you and give you the right to say whether they should or should not get married".'[104] However, Aubrey Coverley thought that missionaries could make mistakes, 'when some person has been unfamiliar with the tribal customs of aborigines ... This would cause a general melée among the tribe itself.' Holding missionaries accountable would be 'a safeguard against cases of that description'.[105] Harrie Seward conceded that the chief protector should regulate half-caste marriages 'in certain instances'.[106] But Percy Ferguson objected to regulation of marriage by 'half-castes' and 'quadroons' in the South. 'Many of these people have just as much intelligence as the average white person. They have the same instincts.'[107] Later he protested that 'I know hundreds of half-castes who believe in the sanctity of marriage, and I believe no restriction should be placed on their laudable desire.'[108] The Minister for Agriculture (Frank Wise) replied that while most missionaries, like the chief protector, understood tribal marriage customs, there were instances in which 'the so-called marriages have been approved by the Chinese cook on a station'.[109] The 1936 Act was passed, with section 42 obliging marriage celebrants to notify the Commissioner for Native Affairs (as the chief protector was now to be called) and empowering the commissioner to object if: the marriage would contravene tribal custom; one of the parties was afflicted by disease; the ages of the parties were too disparate or for any other reason.

Conclusion

Between 1901 and 1940, Australian governments 'protected' Aboriginal people with laws, regulations and institutions that sought to determine how children grew up and how families formed. Non-Aboriginal opinion was sometimes divided about the extent and location of these powers, but generally it assented to laws and institutions whose segregating and stigmatising effect undermined the avowed long-term goal of absorbing well-conducted Aboriginal people into the wider society. Many Aboriginal families believed that children and youths had to be trained for work, to prevent the growth of a dependent and morally flawed population, but it was not easy for them to answer the question 'How do we train our children for the world they now have to survive in?' Some partnership between family and state was required, but a social contract between Australian governments and Aboriginal families seems to have eluded Australians whose vision of nationhood had not prepared them for a persistent and growing mixed-descent Aboriginal population. The exclusion of many Aboriginal children from mainstream compulsory schooling – so far fully studied in only one state (New South Wales) – was self-reinforcing. Deficiencies of education, health, housing and employment compounded and justified non-Aboriginal Australians in both their contemptuous unwillingness to associate with Aboriginal people and in their high-handed projects of 'protection' and 'advancement'.

From 1901 to 1911, three Australian jurisdictions introduced laws regulating the marriage choices of Aborigines. Among those who favoured such a power, however, there was no consensus as to its purpose. It was initially justified as part of the regulation of female employment, at a time when the labour movement and liberals were constructing a larger apparatus of protection for all employees in Australia. The eugenic relevance of the marriage power was also apparent. Some sought to prevent miscegenation or to limit it to cases in which it was necessary to legitimise children already born of multi-racial unions. Other advocates of the marriage power thought that it would best be used to encourage miscegenation, as long as suitable and willing non-Aboriginal partners could be found. However, there was no agreed eugenic purpose for the regulation of Aboriginal marriages; no national program to 'breed out the colour'.

Legislating the marriage power aroused debate about the liberty of the citizen and the status of 'half-castes' as members of the Australian community. Many Western Australian MPs were appalled that British subjects of good standing were being labelled as 'Aboriginal' and subjected to the legal restrictions applying to that class of person.

The defence of state authority – in the seizure of children and in the regulation of marriage – relied much on the public acceptance of stereotypes of Aboriginal Australians as feckless, immoral and childlike. The *milieux* to which 'protection' was addressed included some that were genuinely dangerous and others that were imagined to be dangerous. The fortunes of the rural economy shifted that boundary: during the Depression of the 1930s, many Aboriginal people who had been surviving in precarious independence found themselves turning to those ready to manage them. Writing in the late 1960s, Charles Rowley sought to explain the Aboriginal bitterness that continued to thwart Aboriginal advancement. It was not that 'indigenous culture' was so different from white Australian culture, he argued. Rather, the apparatus of 'protection' had exacerbated cultural difference by imparting 'insecurity and beliefs about injustice'. 'Present Aboriginal beliefs and attitudes, even were there no other causes, could be adequately accounted for by reference to the rigid controls which reached a climax in the depression years of the 1930s. The same systems of controls have been a factor in maintaining prejudices towards Aborigines.'[110]

4

Did 'protection' protect?

Even if one admired – from a respectful distance – the heritage of Aboriginal people, it took more to believe in their future. Whether 'protection' could save Aborigines from extinction was not clear. In his 1934 paper 'Anthropology and the future of the Australian Aborigines', Elkin, after a brief overview of Aboriginal society, concluded:

> [T]he aboriginal social, economic and religious organization is a very complex and delicate mechanism, and ... unwise interference, designed or unintended, mars its efficiency and causes social disintegration which is followed ... by depopulation. Of course, it may be that we cannot prevent this ultimate end.'[1]

To try to prevent Indigenous Australians from reaching their 'ultimate end' was a policy experiment which lacked an essential feature of experimentation: a clear empirical definition of success or failure. Two linked problems confront any answer to the question 'Did protection protect?' First, there were multiple meanings of phrases such as 'dying out' and 'extinction'. In the early decades of the 20th century, to refer to Aborigines as a 'dying race' could mean three things. Native people could die out or disappear through infertility and excessive mortality; they might cease to exist physically – death in its most literal sense. A second kind of 'death' did not involve excessive mortality, but had more to do with who impregnated native women: through procreation with a man who was not 'full-blood' the progeny of Aboriginal women would not be fully 'Aboriginal' genetically, but 'part-Aboriginal', and so a genetically distinct Aboriginal population would eventually dwindle to zero. The third imagined dying native scenario was the rapid attrition of the distinct economy, customs and beliefs of Aboriginal people: even were Aborigines to remain numerous and genetically pure ('full-blood'), they would 'die out' as a distinct way of life as they adopted the colonists' ways.

Second, the definition of 'Aboriginal population' was unresolved for almost seventy years after Federation. Australian authorities wavered between a narrow definition ('full-bloods only') and a broader definition in which those of mixed descent were added to the 'full-bloods'. This irresolution was an artefact of the federal compact. Management of Aboriginal and Torres Strait Islander people was not among the responsibilities of the Australian government commencing in January 1901. The six colonies that had agreed to confederate retained powers to decide land use and to manage Aboriginal people. Defining and enumerating Aborigines thus remained a state responsibility, and the 1901 Census of all humans in Australia was conducted not by a national agency but by each of the six colonies, whose data were then aggregated. In 1905 the national parliament legislated to establish a Commonwealth Bureau of Census and Statistics, but for many years this agency (the Bureau, henceforth) continued to draw on the expertise in each state for knowledge of the Aboriginal population. At the same time, there had to be a 'national' definition of 'Aboriginal native', for the term was used in Australia's Constitution. The six colonies had agreed that when the national government apportioned money and electoral representation between states it should be on a population basis; however, they agreed that in such 'reckoning', 'Aboriginal natives' could not be included in any state's recognised population. Section 127 said that 'in reckoning the numbers of the people, or of a state or other part of the Commonwealth, aboriginal natives shall not be counted'. The attorney-general, Alfred Deakin, clarified in 1901 that only 'full-bloods' were 'Aboriginal natives', so 'full-bloods' would be excluded from a state's population count when money and representation were apportioned by population.[2]

However, the Commonwealth's statisticians soon admitted that it was difficult to produce an Aboriginal population figure that was 'pure' ('full-blood' only). First, '"half-castes" living in the nomadic state are practically undistinguishable from aborigines'; thus Australia's first *Yearbook* included half-castes as 'Aborigines' if they were judged to be 'nomadic'. Second, 'up to the present it has not always been found practicable to make the distinction'. Third, 'no authoritative definition of "half-caste" has yet been given'.[3]

So, on the one hand, a rigorous distinction of 'full-bloods' from 'half-castes' was necessary if the regulation of intergovernmental dealings was to adhere to section 127 of the Constitution; while, on the other hand, the 'half-caste'/'full-blood' distinction was neither necessary nor possible in the administration of Indigenous Australians *within* each colony/state. When each state managed its own population, those known to be 'Aboriginal' were not only 'full-bloods': a 'half-caste' associated with 'full-bloods' was likely to be treated as 'Aboriginal' by police and other officials. This was so even in Victoria, whose policy from 1886 was to exclude 'half-castes' from reserves.[4] The 'Aboriginals' that each state managed were of various degrees of descent bound together by ties of kinship and community; they were known to authorities because of their dependency on state support: a local official – perhaps a policeman – had been issuing rations to them, or they were an institutional inmate.

To sum up, not only were there three visions – physical, genetic, cultural – of Aboriginal peoples' 'ultimate end', there were two usages of 'Aboriginal population' in the discourse of government. 'Aboriginal population' could refer either to a narrow ('full-bloods' only) 'Aboriginal population', relevant to constitutional regulation of interstate relations, or a broad ('full-bloods' *plus* those of mixed descent) 'Aboriginal population' relevant to each jurisdiction's managing of Aboriginal lives. The Commonwealth had a constitutional obligation to distinguish precisely by 'blood', but this was poorly supported by the established administrative practices of the states in which 'Aboriginal' was an ad hoc classification of people by skin colour, way of life, associations and dependency. Both the narrow and the broad 'Aboriginal populations' were objects of governmental knowledge, in different contexts. Australian governments collectively were not able to give a single clear answer to the question: 'What is the real Aboriginal population?' until the late 1960s. In a later chapter I will explain how that definitional dilemma was resolved.

Queensland's expertise

In its first statistical *Yearbook* (issued in 1908) the Bureau acknowledged that it could not count how many Aborigines lived according to their traditional way of life. Estimating a national total in 1901 of 150 000, it admitted that the states had enumerated only 41 389. The 'national' figure for the Aboriginal population in the 1901 Census was simply a summation of the estimates and enumerations made by each state's administration.

There were significant differences in both the method and the intensity of each state's administration of Aboriginal people. There were then two kinds of jurisdiction. The longer-colonised claimed exhaustive knowledge of their tiny Aboriginal remnants. 'The number of full-blooded aboriginals and nomadic half-castes living with those of full blood remaining in New South Wales was stated to be 4287, while in Victoria the total was only 271, and in Tasmania the last aboriginal native died in 1876.'[5] In New South Wales and Victoria, governments claimed that if there were any Aborigines within their borders they were under

TABLE 3 **The Australian Aboriginal population in the 1901 Census**

Persons, etc.	NSW	Vic	Qld	SA (including NT)	WA	Tas	Commonwealth (Australian total)
Males	2451	163	3089	14 076	2933	0	22 712
Females	1836	108	2048	12 357	2328	0	18 677
Totals	4287	271	5137	26 433	5261	0	41 389
Masculinity ratio	133.5	150.9	150.8	113.9	126.0	0	121.6

SOURCE *Yearbook Australia* no. 1 (1908), p. 145

the effective monitoring of a mission, employer or state official. In Tasmania the official view was that Aborigines were now extinct. In contrast, Queensland, South Australia and Western Australia were large states, with hinterlands still being occupied; the 'considerable numbers of natives still in the "savage" state' were for 'mere guessing'.[6]

Commonwealth officials looked to Queensland for expertise in counting and guessing. The Commonwealth's fifth *Yearbook* (published in 1912) published two 'Aboriginal population' figures, based on the 1911 Census: 19 939 for 'the number of full-blooded aboriginals who were employed by whites or were living in proximity to settlements of whites', and an estimated national total of between 100 000 and 150 000.[7] The Commonwealth statistician thanked Queensland officials for supplying the latter figure. To combine a low counted figure with Queensland experts' estimates was the best that the Commonwealth could come up with in the next eight editions of the *Yearbook*. By 1918, again citing Queensland's experts, the *Yearbook* estimated a national Aboriginal population of less than 100 000; in 1920, less than 80 000.[8]

The pride of Queensland's administration was thrown into relief by the confessed weakness of South Australia's. Since the 1860s, the South Australians had been estimating the Aboriginal population from the 'returns' (that is, local officers' reports) from as many as fifty-three ration depots (the number varied slightly from year to year). The sum of those returns was the best data that South Australia could submit in 1901 to Australia's first Census. However, in 1913, the state's protector of Aborigines, W.G. South, told the commissioners:

> I simply ignore the census. The number of half-castes is put down at 500 in the census and I have evidence to prove that they are over 800 ... The census is taken only in the settled districts. You cannot take a census of the natives who are in the wild bush.

At that time, South obtained monthly returns on rations issued from forty-two ration depots, but he was not sure whether only the old and infirm natives were getting rations, and whether 'quadroons' got rations.[9] He judged that

> there are hundreds of natives who were not included in the census ... By travelling through the country at different times, I have been pretty well all over the north and I know that wherever one goes one meets blacks. No census has ever touched the natives in the Gawler Ranges, and also in the country out from Oodnadatta ... I estimate that there is another 1000 or more in the districts that the census never reaches.[10]

Though uncertain in their data, South Australia's royal commissioners concluded in 1913: (1) 'that the aboriginal population of the state is gradually decreasing'; (2) that 'while the number of full-blood aborigines is certainly decreasing, the evidence clearly shows that the aboriginal half-castes are on the increase, so that the number of persons who would come within the scope of the law relating to aborigines is probably not less now than it was ten years ago';[11] (3) that now that South Australia settlement was beginning to enter into the country of the 'out-back blacks' in the state's north-west, it was necessary to know 'the best means ... to prevent the extinction of the aboriginal race'.[12] This was a cameo of the ambiguity of the 'dying native' scenario. On the one hand, the commissioners implied a narrow definition of 'aboriginal race': full-bloods would not have enough children of full blood to keep the race going. On the other hand, the trend in 'half-caste' numbers was increasing the number of people to be managed as 'Aborigines'.

The case of Queensland suggests that such conceptual confusion about the population to be 'protected' did not undermine the will to protect. The legislators of the *Aboriginal Protection and Restriction of the Sale of Opium Act* 1897 had assumed that state regulation was protective. 'In the emerging liberal democracies,' writes Mullins, the 1890s was marked not only by 'a hardening of racial attitudes in all the "settler" societies' but also by 'the expansion of progressive governmental intervention and social regulation. A confluence of these tendencies influenced Queensland government circles and resulted in a bipartisan approach to the "Aboriginal question" in the [Queensland Parliament] which expedited the framing and progress of the protectionist legislation.'[13] The controls were undoubtedly illiberal. However, Colin Tatz, a critic in the 1960s of the illiberal institutional legacy of Queensland's system, has recently described Queensland's 1897 Act as 'possibly the world's first specific anti-genocide statute'.[14]

South Australia's Royal Commissioners in 1913 thought so highly of Queensland's system that they convened a session in Brisbane. Perhaps the commissioners, arriving in Brisbane on 27 June, had a chance to read the most recent *Annual Report* for 1912, submitted 31 May 1913 by the chief protector in Queensland, Richard B. Howard. 'Table 2' listed thirty-one districts where a local protector (often a policeman, and many appointed in the previous four years) issued hundreds of licences to employ Aborigines (whose wages were then held in trust accounts).[15] Howard reported also on labour conditions on boats. His report quantified the issue of food and blankets to 'the indigent' and prosecutions of those who supplied alcohol or opium, who employed without a permit or who permitted females on their premises unlawfully. Listing removals of children and young women from 'unhealthy surroundings' to settlements and missions, the chief protector also referred to his permitting some women to marry.[16] He summarised health conditions and criminal prosecutions. A table quantified the Aborigines rationed at each of nine mission stations, by month, and the number of children in school at eight of those missions and in six schools in the Torres Strait. Reports from three missions/settlements in the agricultural regions (Deebing Creek, near Ipswich; Taroom; Barambah) and from seven in the remote north (St Paul's on Moa Island; Trubanaman, near Mitchell River; Aurukun, near Archer River; Weipa, near Embley River; Mapoon, near Batavia River; Yarrabah, near Cairns; Cape Bedford) took up the final pages of Howard's report.[17] Minister J.G. Appel boasted to the South Australian Royal Commissioners that through the network of police, 'we have tentacles like an octopus, and they stretch throughout the State. It is by that means that we have complete control over the aboriginal.'[18]

Comprehensive control, it seemed, enabled the government to save the race. When the commissioners asked if there was any 'possibility of the native race dying out', Howard replied, 'not for many years'.[19] The public servant who was about to succeed Howard as chief protector, J.W. Bleakley, told the commissioners that: 'I think that no matter what you do, the race will die out eventually. But that will take a good many years.'[20] Appel was more positive: 'the natives will not die out if they are cared for and receive good treatment'. He claimed: 'So far, we have been fairly successful in Queensland.'[21] Within a few years, Bleakley was agreeing. In 1922, as Queensland's chief protector, he claimed that his state's system of reserves was responsible for the Aborigines' 'improved vitality'.[22] The Queensland model demonstrated to other governments that a controlled population was a surviving and enumerable population.

As Appel claimed, the police were central to Queensland's 'protection'. Douglas and Finnane have argued that 'the Australian self-governing colonies were remarkable for their comprehensive policing arrangements, extending the reach of the state into the remotest parts of the continent' in order to exercise sovereignty in its most challenging form – enforcing a novel criminal law on peoples with thousands of years of their own law.[23] Until the 1890s, Queensland had deployed a native police force that had killed many Aborigines. After reviewing the native police in the mid-1890s, Queensland changed their instructions from intimidation to conciliation, and the native police remained active in Cape York Peninsula until 1914.[24] They thus became part of the wider police and public service apparatus that ensured that Aborigines and Torres Strait Islanders lived where the government authorised them to live, that invigilated their employment and marital choices and that prevented their consumption of alcohol and opium.

Did 'protection' protect?

Administrative coverage took a step forward in 1921, when Australian governments began to collaborate: on the fourth day of April 1921, each protector in each state other than Tasmania and in the Northern Territory produced a figure for 'full-bloods'.[25] For the previous ten years the Commonwealth *Yearbook* had cited

Queensland's estimates of 'full-bloods' in all states and the Northern Territory. As mentioned earlier, in 1918 the *Yearbook* had published an estimate of less than 100 000, and in 1920 less than 80 000. Now, in 1921, even with an estimated 10 000 Aborigines in Western Australia beyond administrative contact, the downward trend in those national estimates seemed to be confirmed.

TABLE 4 **Estimated 'full-blood' Australian Aboriginals, 4 April 1921**

Jurisdiction	Males	Females	Total
New South Wales	879	622	1501
Victoria	62	49	111
Queensland	7234	5380	12 614
South Australia	876	733	1609
Western Australia	13 611	11 976	25 587
Northern Territory	9466	7883	17 349
Commonwealth	32 128	26 643	58 771

SOURCE *Australia Yearbook* no. 14 (1921), p. 1128

In *Yearbook* no. 18 (1925) the table 'Census of Aboriginals 1924' included a column for 'full-blood' and a column for 'half-caste' – the first time that a *Yearbook* had made it possible to think of the 'Aboriginal population' as the sum of the two.[26] However, the *Yearbook*'s commentary on the table implied that only the 'full-blood' total mattered. Indeed, the 'full-blood figure' was interesting, as its rise from 58 771 in 1921 to 62 415 in 1924 might have challenged the view that the 'Aboriginal population' was diminishing. The Bureau argued that this apparent increase was the effect of underestimating, in 1921, the 'wild and unapproachable natives', for example those in South Australia, west of Oodnadatta.[27] The statistician presented a table showing diminishing 'full-bloods' in New South Wales and Victoria in the years 1891, 1901, 1911, 1921 and 1924 to substantiate that 'except in a few places where the blacks are under missionary influence, the numbers generally tend to decline, and the figures for New South Wales and Victoria, which are probably the most reliable, certainly evidence a rapid decline since the foundation of white settlement'.[28]

The period between the mid-1920s and the mid-1940s seems to be the nadir of official attention to Indigenous enumeration: there is no published evidence that Commonwealth statisticians were monitoring the success or failure of 'protection'. Population tables published in the *Yearbooks* of the late 1920s showed a rise in the ('full-blood') Aboriginal population (from 59 296 in 1926 to 60 663 in 1928), but these data did not upset the stated conclusion that the 'Aboriginal population' was falling.[29] In the two states where good administrative coverage made enumeration most plausible – New South Wales and Victoria – 'full-bloods' increased from 1086 in 1926 to 1250 in 1928. The *Yearbook* did not discuss these data. Administrative coverage of remote regions did not progress. The South Australian government gave up trying to estimate Aboriginal numbers in the northwest (Musgrave and Everard Ranges) between 1926 and 1938.[30] The Commonwealth statistician appeared to be interested in Aboriginal demography when, in *Yearbook* no. 23 (1930), the government published anthropologist A. Radcliffe-Brown's estimate of the minimum pre-colonial Aboriginal population of the continent (300 000). However, Radcliffe-Brown did not describe or speculate on current trends. Indeed, in *Yearbook* no. 23 and in the next three editions (nos 24, 25 and 26) the Commonwealth did not publish a table on the current 'Aboriginal population', devoting only two sentences to the topic in each *Yearbook*, recording the steady decline in 'full-bloods' and in those classed as 'nomadic', and the steady rise of the 'half-castes'. *Yearbook* no. 28 (1935) explained a dramatic fall in 'full-bloods' between 30 June 1933 and 30 June 1934 as reflecting improved administrative coverage and the greater accuracy of Western Australian and Northern Territory estimates.[31] *Yearbook*s nos 28–37 (1935–47) resumed the negligent practice of publishing a table without commentary.

Local regimes of protection and enumeration

The Bureau's slapdash monitoring is consistent with Russell McGregor's claim that in scientific and humanitarian commentary on Aboriginal population trends up to 1950 'the notion persisted that Aboriginal extinction was, if not inevitable, at least highly probable'.[32] He quotes writers in the 1930s who foresaw the 'extermination', 'doom' and 'dying' of the Australian native.[33] However, it was not only government officials who were trying to count: missionaries too were keeping records. 'More than anyone else,' McGregor explains, 'Christian missionaries had maintained some faith in Aboriginal prospects for survival, even when majority white opinion leaned heavily toward the doomed race theory.'[34] For example, at Beagle Bay Mission on the Dampier Peninsula 'mission records show the increase in live births and survival of children who were born under the mission influence … From the late 1930s, the rate of births and baptisms remained steady as young mission-raised men and women married and established their families.'[35]

In the Torres Strait an unusually effective combination of

Anglican Church and Queensland government efforts at registering births and deaths showed population recovery on Erub (Darnley Island). In Anna Shnukal's analysis, the Erub data show that after falling in the second half of the 19th century the population was in recovery by the first decade of the 20th century. One contributor to recovery was migration – from Papua, from the island of Mer, from Pacific Islands and South-East Asia (Malays and Filipinos). Migrants sometimes brought Aboriginal wives (from mainland Australia) but many married Erub women, so that the Erub families, in the period 1885–1928, became a mixture of immigrant-headed or Indigenous-headed families. Distinctions of origin rapidly became unimportant, as Erub Islanders conceived themselves to be a single people, various in origin but experiencing the same colonial transformations. In this period, an economy of commercial sea-harvesting displaced an economy of horticulture, people aggregated around church, school and store, and all were under the influence of Torres Strait and Pacific Island custom that had rapidly absorbed Christian norms. The new Islander outlook included ideas about sexuality and family, so that 'traditional practices of birth control were banned and ideal family size increased from the pre-contact two or at most three children to considerably more – eventually eight to ten children were not uncommon'.[36] Shnukal sees the Torres Strait Islanders as a hybrid people – transformed by regional migration, new economic institutions and their rapid taking up of Christianity; she also notes the strength of the Islanders' ideology of continuous identity and uncompromised custom. She suggests that what happened rapidly on Erub, in the 1880–1920 period, eventually happened all over the Torres Strait.

Immigration and intermarriage may also have been significant factors in maintaining an Indigenous population in other northern coastal regions such as the Kimberley. In regions where these factors were less significant, recovery probably owed more to better nutrition and healthcare, reduced violence, and regulated sexuality. The Tiwi, off the north coast of the Northern Territory, seem to be an example. Apart from the British government's brief attempt at a small military outpost on Tiwi country from 1824 to 1829, it was not until 1895 that the Tiwi came under sustained colonial influence. Catholic missionaries arrived in 1911. The Tiwi interested anthropologists: Herbert Basedow visited in 1911, and C.M.W. Hart worked among them in 1928 and 1929, conducting a comprehensive census that noted the age-group and sex of all Tiwi known to him – 1068 persons, of which 1010 were living on the islands. Hart distinguished Tiwi according to how much contact they had had with aliens of different kinds. His data show that families with most contact with the mission had more wives per man and more children per family than those influenced more by buffalo hunters or Japanese, or those with little contact with aliens of any kind.

In the 1990s, researchers Nicolas Peterson and John Taylor compared Hart's data with some postwar censuses (conducted in 1951, 1971 and 1996). They concluded that the Tiwi population had declined by about 1 per cent per year in the 1930s and 1940s and that it had become more concentrated around the poorly resourced Catholic Mission. Population recovery was evident in the late 1940s: a relatively high proportion of infants. This recovery was sustained over the following twenty-five years. The most likely reason for population recovery, in the judgment of Peterson and Taylor, was the mission's inception of a hospital in 1946. Bathurst Island Mission, like other northern missions, was better funded from 1941, when the Australian government began to pay 'maternity benefits' to missions servicing Aborigines.

The attracting power of the Bathurst Island Mission seems eventually to have created its own health problems, as sanitation failed to meet the needs of an unprecedentedly concentrated and growing Tiwi population: infectious diseases (intestinal and respiratory) menaced the infant population. Nonetheless, the high fertility of Tiwi women (instructed against contraception) sustained population growth. From the 1970s until the time of the Peterson and Taylor study, the Tiwi population grew steadily and quickly; a higher proportion of children surviving infancy offset the decline in the number of babies born, on average, to the Tiwi woman.[37]

In Queensland the chief protector, J.W. Bleakley, had spent the early part of his career in the Torres Strait at the time of the recovery traced by Shnukal. By 1922, he was asserting that the state-wide system of protection – involving church and state – was beginning to work. While the influenza pandemic had caused deaths to exceed births in the years 1918–20, in 1921 and 1922 births exceeded deaths. 'This improved vitality is particularly noticeable on self-contained reserves, where the native is segregated from the evils to which, if the popular prophecy is to be fulfilled, their extinction will be due.'[38] Gordon Briscoe's study of official population data from Queensland and Western Australia in the period 1900–40 supports Bleakley's claim, by showing stable and climbing numbers of both 'full-bloods' and 'half-castes' and normalisation of sex and age ratios. Briscoe's study is largely a description of these two states' recognition of infectious diseases as a problem, of their efforts to regulate unhygienic living (by creating settlements and transferring people into them), and of the protectors' attempts to work with Commonwealth health surveys (about hookworm, tuberculosis, leprosy). The study contains hardly any causal analysis, but Briscoe's data are open to the inference that, somehow, government actions contributed to better health and reduced mortality. Policies of institutionalisation – though harshly coercive and unhealthy by modern standards – probably secured basic nutrition, improved the detection and treatment of infectious diseases and helped to mitigate infective sexual contacts that had reduced the fertility of women. At the same time, both states were developing their public health and regional hospital networks, and the 'protectors' in each state urged hospitals to accept Aboriginal patients. Briscoe conveys the mingling of compassion, apprehension and physical disgust in the growing governmental and church concern, in the period 1900–40, for these stricken people.[39] He notes also that strategies that aggregated people created some health problems, as well as alleviating others.[40]

Blake's study of the Queensland settlement Barambah confirms this story. He begins by noting that in the period 1905–25 recorded deaths were more than twice the number of births. In these years Barambah received many dispirited and impoverished inmates removed by the government from – for example – south-west Queensland.[41] This high death period also included the influenza pandemic, when 200 inmates died, 'almost one-fifth of the settlement population'.[42] By the late 1920s, however, the Barambah birth rate began to exceed its death rate. The date of Barambah's recovery thus coincides with that reported by Briscoe for the Queensland system as a whole and Blake agrees that this institutionalised population was, eventually, a recovering population.[43] The health of these survivors was poor, however, partly because the high birth rate and the decreasing infant mortality rate put pressure on the institution's meagre resources.[44] The infectious diseases tuberculosis, pneumonia, influenza, whooping cough, typhoid and measles, arriving as epidemics, continued to be prominent causes of death. Non-fatal infectious diseases, such as ophthalmia (trachoma) remained prevalent. Blake acknowledges that the government took episodic measures against these assaults, such as closing the school temporarily, quarantining the settlement, deploying more nurses and arranging visits by the Australian Hookworm Campaign.[45] Against the official view – then expressed – that the government was dealing relatively effectively with a sick and disheartened Aboriginal population, Blake cites the government's own reports about Barambah to argue that 'the quality of the water supply, sanitation, diet [quantity and quality] and, to a lesser extent, overcrowding and migration' made Barambah a difficult place to stay healthy and that by encouraging residents to work off the reserve, the government opened the settlement to infection.[46]

Blake claims that 'the health of the Aborigines did not improve when they were removed to Barambah'.[47] To evaluate this claim we would need data that we do not possess: on the health of Aborigines before removal and data on the morbidity and mortality of 'the total Aboriginal population of Australia' and of those remaining in 'bush camps'. While it is clear that Barambah inmates sickened and died from many preventable disorders, the government's positive claim that it was making a difference to *mortality* is not undermined by Blake's illustrations of Barambah residents' *morbidity*. If we agree with Blake that the 'key determinants in the health of the settlement were the government's policies and administrative practices', then we must credit the diminishing mortality of the Barambah inmates and their recovery as a population from the late 1920s to government action.[48]

Because the regimentation of Aboriginal life has become so offensive to liberal sensibilities, historians have characterised 'protection' as a moral failure by government. However, without disputing that government management was heavy-handed, we must not ignore the demographic history of 'protection'. Recent studies show that Victoria's institutions of protection, initiated forty years before Queensland's, were effective. In 1853, the new colony of Victoria had counted only 1907 surviving Aborigines; it soon began to manage their lives on seven small supervised reserves and in twenty-three camping places. About half of the known Victorian Aboriginal population began to live under legislation and policy that sought to define and to protect a population that was expected to die out soon – either by failing to produce sufficient descendants or by blending with the wider immigrant population. To encourage such blending, from 1886, the government no longer permitted Aboriginal people of mixed descent to live on reserves or to receive the government's material support. However, people of Aboriginal descent strove to stick together and to make the best communities that they could on the reserve lands that the government conceded to them.

Meanwhile, notwithstanding some sexual unions with Aborigines, the non-Aboriginal people of Victoria tended not to accommodate Aborigines as employees, workmates, neighbours or spouses. In Victoria, a sense of racial distinction, on both sides, was robust, and the government's continuing legislative and administrative recognition of 'Aboriginal' status contributed to its persistence as a population. By the 1920s, the Victorian government had reduced its reserves from seven to two; the resident 'Aboriginal' population by then consisted largely of people of mixed descent whom the authorities would have preferred to think were not under 'Aboriginal protection': in theory, fewer and fewer people of mixed descent should have lived on reserves as 'Aboriginal' clients of the government. However, the government was not able to guarantee a secure place in non-Aboriginal society for those who were of mixed descent, and some Aborigines regarded the reserves as their home and the government as responsible for them. When the Victorian government reviewed its laws and administration in 1956–57, it accepted advice to take responsibility for any person who claimed any degree of Aboriginal descent. In this sense the 'Aborigines of Victoria' did not disappear into the wider community but remained a self-conscious and conspicuous responsibility.

Genealogical analysis of the currently acknowledged Aboriginal population of Victoria shows lines of descent only from those who were known and institutionalised as 'Aborigines' in the middle of the 19th century. Smith and his colleagues have argued that in the hundred years (1850s to 1950s) of Victorian government intervention, the demographic history of Victorians of Aboriginal descent amounted to three distinguishable stories. One division of the population consisted of those, alive in the 1850s, not subjected to the colony's Aboriginal protection administration and not recorded as 'Aboriginal' in any subsequent population counts. The researchers speculate that 'they were killed by settlers, or they died because they lost access to their traditional economic resources'.[49] If it is possible that some of them survived, intermarried and had children, neither they nor their descendants have ever presented themselves as persons of Aboriginal descent to any researcher or official enumerator. The other two divisions of the Victorian Aboriginal population descended from those who were under institutional 'protection'; they did survive, but in two different ways. Some of them remained constantly visible, as 'Aborigines', to the authorities whose job it was to count such people. The other descendants of the 'protected' became temporarily invisible, in the sense that they were not labelled and enumerated as 'Aborigines' – either because they did not wish to be known as 'Aborigines' (when that category was racially stigmatised and carried significant legal disabilities) or because assimilation policy, from 1886, compelled government officials to recognise as few remaining 'Aborigines' as possible. Their invisibility encouraged governments to report that 'assimilation' was working: recognised Victorian Aborigines ('full-blood' plus 'half-castes') fell to between 500 and 600 in the 1920s, living on government reserves. People of Aboriginal descent who were not counted officially as 'Aboriginal' were presumed to be 'assimilated'. However, the family traditions of many such people kept their Aboriginal genealogy in memory and maintained associations with known kin. These once 'invisible' Aborigines have become visible since the 1960s and they and their descendants now constitute a large proportion of the known Aboriginal population of Victoria.

Thus, according to Smith and his colleagues, what we now call 'the Aboriginal population' of Victoria owes its survival to two factors: to the institutionalisation of about half of those known as Aborigines in 1853, and to the persistence and revival of Aboriginal identity among the descendants of those then institutionalised. While Victoria's practices were coercive and patronising to their subjects, and while for much of the 20th century many Victorian Aborigines neither presented themselves nor were recognised as 'Aboriginal', the consequence of 'protection' policies initiated around 1860 is that an Aboriginal population has persisted, not died out.[50]

In South Australia, the Christian mission at Point McLeay seems also to have had protective effects. The Ngarrindjeri people – living on the lower reaches of the Murray River and on Encounter Bay – had come under sustained European colonial influence (South Australia) by the middle of the 19th century. To ameliorate their destitution and to aid their physical recovery and spiritual renewal, the Aborigines' Friends' Association funded George Taplin's mission at Point McLeay (also known as Raukkan), on Lake Alexandrina, from 1859. Taplin established a dormitory for children but did not prevent parental access.[51] He arranged for annual vaccinations, though his infirmary, erected in 1871, was unstaffed.[52] He recorded Ngarrindjeri births and deaths. Fay Gale's analysis of the births and deaths of 2336 persons from 1870 to 1964 yields a narrative of survival. From 1870 to 1894, the population declined: death rates exceeded birth rates. Gale infers that this decline continued a trend that had begun when Aborigines in that region first came into contact with colonists, around 1838. From 1895, the birth rate rose. More and more of the births were the result of sex between an Aboriginal and a non-Aboriginal person, but the Raukkan people deemed these babies to be no less 'Aboriginal' for that. Though epidemics of respiratory illness threatened this population recovery between 1905 and 1909, birth rates continued to exceed death rates, as the death rate slowly declined. This population recovery accelerated between 1910 and 1940, and continued in the period 1940 to 1964. Though the birth rate declined after 1940, so too did the death rate. Eventually population pressure encouraged a steady stream of migration away from Raukkan. Gale speculates that to be sedentary on a settlement was, for the first generation that attempted it, an unhealthy way of life.[53] But that adjustment also contributed eventually to reduced mortality because of reduced contact with non-Aborigines (other than those allowed by mission authorities) and because of medical attention that reduced rates of infant and child mortality. After the high toll on the first generation of people exposed to new diseases, the immediately following generations would have enjoyed acquired immunity to 'European' diseases. That the proliferating 'mixed-blood' people were recognised – officially and by Ngarrindjeri – as 'Aboriginal' was an essential part of the story of recovery.

These analyses of local population histories all point to the same conclusion: that in the first half of the 20th century, the intervention of church and state into the lives of Aborigines – imposed or negotiated, in various degrees – created conditions conducive to population growth. Ian Crawford, considering the Kimberley region, has summarised possible explanations.

> It has been argued ... that the breakdown of traditional marriage patterns enabled younger men to marry younger women and thus the population as a whole achieved a greater level of fertility. Alternatively the introduction of effective medicines, particularly of antibiotics, helped combat diseases which had earlier proved fatal. Others have seen the introduction of social service benefits [maternity payments to missions from 1941] providing an economic incentive to parents. The late Albert Barunga explained the change by reference to the psychological state of Aborigines: 'We were worried people, and worried people do not have children.'[54]

The localised success of these interventions, recorded in the archives of missions and interested academics, was not widely understood at the time because of a poor national database and because of persistent unclarity about who was included in 'Aboriginal population' and what 'survival' meant. The weakness of demographic knowledge at mid-century is illustrated by Cleland's presidential address to the Anthropology Section of ANZAAS 1949. Throughout the 1930s and 1940s Cleland had been preoccupied by the possibility of Aboriginal extinction, in both the first sense of biological catastrophe and the third sense of cultural loss. As he recounted in 1949, he had gathered information on Aboriginal births and deaths from missionaries at Hermannsburg, Ooldea and Ernabella, the hinterland that the South Australian Royal Commissioners in 1913 had admitted was beyond administrative knowledge. He had come to the conclusion that 'when the full-blood native forsakes his nomadic life and becomes more or less Europeanised the birth-rate decreases ... and [this] may be attributed in part to loss of interest in life and in part to vitamin deficiencies in the food'. He added that when 'full-bloods' become attached to the pastoral industry, they were unlikely to die from starvation but were 'almost certain to suffer from latent if not manifest vitamin deficiencies and be little able to resist infectious diseases when exposed to them'. Though he advocated government intervention to relieve such dire conditions, Cleland's dismal tales from the frontier offered no evidence that such interventions were working.[55]

Cleland's pessimism was not without reason. Young anthropologists Ronald and Catherine Berndt reported how destructive the frontier could be when neither missions nor governments were present to counter the worst effects of pastoralists' self-interest. During World War II, a pastoral company concerned about its future supply of Aboriginal labour commissioned them to investigate conditions on pastoral leases in the Victoria River district. Only a brief summary of their 1946 report was published at the time. However, when published in full in 1987, their data on births, childlessness and child survival showed the steady attrition of groups of Aborigines on or attracted into eight pastoral leases (Birrundudu, Limbunya, Waterloo, Wave Hill, Manbulloo, Willeroo, Delamere and Berrimah) and two buffalo hunter camps (Marrakai, Woolner). A catastrophic combination of poor diet, insecurity, abortion and disease (causing infertility and child mortality) made it necessary for employers to attract fresh stocks of Aborigines from the bush; among the incentives for 'bush' Aborigines to 'come in' and work was the diet that seemed so fatal. The Berndts described their findings across a number of contact sites as 'uniformly depressing'.[56]

As I will show in a later chapter, during and after World War II, the Commonwealth government took steps to better the conditions of Aborigines in the Northern Territory: lump sum payment to missions of the 'maternity benefits' to which Aboriginal mothers were entitled from 1941; the recruiting of Aborigines into 'native labour camps' administered to high material standards by the Army; negotiations with pastoralists about new regulations covering postwar employment conditions; and the formation of new ration depots that became, in time, 'welfare settlements' in zones of relatively recent and meagre colonial occupation. A journalist's account of a scientific expedition to Arnhem Land in 1948 challenged the public to stop assuming that 'full-blood' Aborigines were doomed to die out: 'the aborigines are here to stay'. Citing the recovery of Maori and North American Indian numbers, the Australian Broadcasting Commission's Colin Simpson predicted that the Census would soon show Aboriginal increases.[57]

Officials in the Welfare Branch of the Northern Territory Administration gathered evidence in the mid-1950s that confirmed that hope. In August 1956, Gordon Sweeney, a former lay missionary (Methodist) with experience in Arnhem Land in the late 1930s, and a Commonwealth patrol officer since 1940, circulated within the Northern Territory Administration some graphs of populations in four northern districts: Arnhem

Land Reserve, Darwin (very broadly defined as a 'district' east of Daly River, north of Katherine and west of the East Alligator River), the Barkly Tableland/Borroloola and Kimberley/Hooker Creek. Using information compiled by patrol officers up to the end of 1955, Sweeney divided the Aboriginal population into age groups and then inferred from the age structure of each region whether each population was growing, through a combination of high numbers of births and the survival of those born.

In the Arnhem Land Reserve, there were 3501 Aborigines, with a high proportion of young; nearly all lived under the influence of mission programs in 'health, education and industry', and their 'tribal and family and community life are still largely intact'.[58] The high proportion of children and youth on the reserve reflected 'mother and infant welfare activities, increased medical facilities and the suppression of war and vendettas'; the small proportions of people in the age groups 30–39, 40–49 and 50–59 reflected how recently war, vendettas and epidemics had been suppressed by the missions. In the Darwin district there were now 1756 Aborigines; for several generations they had been living under the influence of a town, of the north–south road and rail corridor, of buffalo camps, and of mining, agriculture and pastoral activity. From the low proportion of children and youth, Sweeney inferred a low birth rate (though a high rate of infant and child mortality would also explain this age structure). In the two pastoral districts (which patrol officers had begun to visit regularly since World War II) there were 2143 (1076 in Barkly/Borroloola, 1067 in Kimberley/Hooker Creek); their 'detribalisation was advanced' through contact with the pastoral industry. The pastoral districts' age structure pointed to an increasing birth rate and reduced child mortality 'due to better nutrition for women and children following the implementing of the Aboriginals (Pastoral Industry) Regulations 1949, and improved medical facilities' in the late 1940s. Sweeney concluded that mission and government efforts were protecting 'the natives from destructive white contacts and maintain[ing] a developing family and social pattern'.[59] Sweeney's colleague, E.C. (Ted) Evans, commented that the memorandum showed 'the advantage of Missions, the benefits of medical and dietary aids, the disabilities of town areas and the importance of control of pastoral areas'.[60]

There is some evidence that the extension of the welfare frontier into the Western Desert was by then having a similar effect. Shielded from colonial penetration by being dry, hot and far from cities and towns, the Western Desert — roughly 2.6 million square kilometres, across Central Australia, eastern Western Australia, the north-western corner of South Australia and the south-western corner of the Northern Territory — was home to people who made exploratory journeys to missions and pastoral leases on the periphery of their homeland from the 1910s. Some stayed on in the places they visited, but those who went back or who had never ventured out became a concern of welfare authorities, particularly Commonwealth officials, in the 1950s. West of Alice Springs, the Commonwealth and the Lutheran missionaries at Hermannsburg had established ration depots at Haasts Bluff in 1940, at Areyonga in 1943 and then at Papunya in 1957. The authorities hoped that by administering to the physical needs of Western Desert people at Haasts Bluff and Papunya they might induce them not to venture any further east to potentially destructive contact on pastoral leases and in Alice Springs. Rations and the promise of renewed contact with kin attracted several hundred Western Desert people, known as Pitjantjatjara, Warlpiri and Pintubi, to settlements west of Alice

Springs. Public servant Jeremy Long was among those responsible for managing and monitoring their welfare and for encouraging the immigration of more of their relatives from the desert. Long's 1960 analysis of the birth and death records at Haasts Bluff compared the late 1940s with the late 1950s, finding 'a dramatic increase in the birth rate and a corresponding decline in the death rate'. As he explained,

> The Aborigines congregated and became increasingly sedentary. Exposed to a variety of epidemic diseases and respiratory infections, many died, especially the very old and very young, and there was no equivalent rise in birth rate. Normally, these processes have continued to, or almost to, the point of extinction. Here, however, an improving diet and medical care have checked the death rate and permitted immunities to be built up. At the same time there appears to have been a large increase in the number of babies born ... The reasons for limiting family size no longer hold good, and infant mortality has been reduced, especially at the crucial weaning period, when, in the bush, malnutrition was a normal condition.[61]

Long believed that a change in the way of life of Western Desert people, if carefully managed and well resourced, could result in a rise in population. Infant and child deaths at Papunya in the years immediately after Long wrote his report revealed that short-term success created a new horizon of problems. The concentration of Western Desert people around a reliable food source, with a rising ratio of children to supervising adults, formed a problematic ecology of sanitation and social order, to which government expenditure (on staff and infrastructure) and

Aborigines' slowly changing domestic routines and governance were not immediately equal.

By 1960, through such analyses by Symonds and Long, the Australian government was beginning to confirm that government and mission action was averting the physical extinction of the continent's remote Aboriginal population. At the 1961 Native Welfare Conference (a meeting of the states with the Commonwealth government), under the agenda item 'Progress in health', the Commonwealth claimed that expenditure on settlements and missions in the Northern Territory had arrested infant mortality, increased female fecundity and controlled endemic diseases; 'and the health of the people generally appears to be improving'.[62] Nonetheless, in 1964, Elkin's judgment was that 'protection policies not only failed to ensure the survival of the Aborigines; they also failed to protect them from harsh treatment'.[63] While the second assertion can be amply illustrated, the first is wrong. Perhaps his error could be excused by conceding that as late as the early 1960s national Aboriginal population data were uncertain in that they still included estimates for remote Western Australia; and perhaps Elkin had yet to resolve his own definitions of 'Aboriginal population' and 'survival'. In addition, Elkin never ceased to promote 'assimilation' by dismissing 'protection', the preceding policy. However, within a few years Charles Rowley could remark that the 'destruction of Aboriginal populations was eventually arrested, partly by the efforts of missions on the large reserves'.[64]

The unresolved significance of the 'half-caste'

In the 1960s, the Australian government did not offer a clear public narrative of saving the 'Aboriginal race' from extinction. Rather, until the 1971 Census, the Australian discourse on native population was plagued by a combination of administrative weakness and the lack of agreement about whether 'part-Aborigines' should be included in the total Aboriginal population. Complete administrative reach was apparently achieved in the 1966 Census: the Bureau claimed that with the help of missions every Aboriginal person could be individually identified and counted.[65] The issue of how to define 'Aboriginal population' was less easy to resolve, as each of the two possible definitions ('full-bloods' only, and 'full-bloods' plus 'half-castes') was embedded in concurrent government practices and public comments about 'the Aboriginal problem'.

The Commonwealth statistician had long published tables on 'half-castes', even though they were not in constitutional law 'Aboriginal natives', because of two Australian concerns. One was whether 'White Australia' would be compromised by the continuing presence of non-white races. The Australian government used 'half-caste' data not to monitor whether 'protection' was averting 'extinction' but to consider the size of non-European minorities in 'White Australia'. *Yearbook* no. 15 (1922) included 10 113 'half-caste' Aborigines in a table comparing the quantities of certain 'non-European races'. *Yearbook* no. 16 (1923) revised the figure to 11 406 and disaggregated them by jurisdiction. *Yearbook* no. 17 (1924) published a table comparing their numbers, by jurisdiction, in 1911 and 1921.[66] These data showed that in Queensland, South Australia, Western Australia and the Northern Territory 'half-castes' were growing in number – 'a matter of grave concern'.[67] A table published in *Yearbook* no. 28 (1935), comparing the Censuses of 1921 and 1933, continued to portray 'half-castes' as a non-white minority. Australians who believed that their nation was fundamentally 'European' would have been pleased to see in that table that the 'full-blood European' population grew by 22 per cent (an additional 1 192 847 persons) between 1921 and 1933, while 'full-blood non-Europeans' fell by 26 per cent (8157 persons fewer). However, they would have been displeased to see that this latter change in the nation's racial stock was more than offset by a 53 per cent rise in the number of 'half-caste non-Europeans'. Nearly all of these additions (9073 out of 9415) to the non-white population were 'Australian Aboriginal half-castes'.[68] This obstacle to national homogeneity could not be dealt with by a restrictive immigration policy.

The other concern sustaining attention to 'half-caste' Aboriginal numbers was: are 'hybrids' assimilating or remaining dependent on government agencies that deal with 'Aborigines'? In *Yearbook* no. 17 (1924), data from New South Wales compared sub-populations classified by their proportion of Aboriginal descent. The table showed that the less 'Aboriginal' a person was in their descent, the less likely he/she was to be 'receiving aid'. The table confirmed the belief that interbreeding was one way to end the dependency that had made 'half-castes' – like 'full-bloods' – a responsibility of governments.

The neglected question to which data on 'half-caste' Aborigines would have been relevant was: is Australia protecting its Aboriginal minority from extinction? Two answers were possible. On the one hand, as McGregor points out, for many observers 'the prediction of extinction pertained to full-bloods only' and 'full-blood' numbers were (in most years) falling.[69] On this view Australia was slowly but steadily losing its tiny 'Aboriginal population'. Totalling state and territory Censuses 1921 to 1939 into national figures showed that 'full-bloods' had diminished (from 58 771 in 1921 to 51 557 in 1939). On the other hand, if 'Aboriginal population' included 'half-castes', it would have been relevant that 'half-castes' had risen from 12 630 in 1921 to 25 712 in 1939. That is, adding 'full-bloods' to 'half-castes' showed the 'Aboriginal population' in the broader sense to have increased from 71 401 in 1921 to 77 629 in 1939 – due largely to rising 'half-caste' numbers. As a proportion of the broadly defined 'Aboriginal population', 'half-castes' increased from 17.69 per cent in 1921 to 33.28 per cent in 1939. Discounting 'half-castes' – as many did – 'the foundations of the doomed race idea were in no way shaken'.[70] A.P. Elkin in 1937 still considered it possible (but not certain) that Aborigines would be unable to adapt and, 'like the dinosaur in the face of a glacial epoch', would become extinct.[71] Fellow anthropologist W.E.H. Stanner asserted that 'the aborigines are dying out'.[72] These gloomy readings did not count as truly 'Aboriginal' the proliferating people who were descended from Aborigines and 'other races'.

In the 1950s, the definition of 'Aboriginal population' remained unresolved. *Yearbook* presentations of 'the Aboriginal population' could easily be read as confirming that Aborigines were 'dying out': published figures showed the estimated 'full-blood' population diminishing. The 1951 *Yearbook* (no. 38) published 47 014 as the total full-blood population, using state governments' estimates made at various times during World War II. Yearbooks from 1952 to 1959 (nos 39–45) published the 1947 Census estimate of 'full-bloods' (46 638). Yearbooks from 1960 to 1962 (nos 46–48) published the 1954 Census estimate of 'full-bloods': lower still at 39 319. This downward trend ended with the 1961 Census, which estimated full-bloods at 40 081 (*Yearbook* no. 49, 1963) – a slight rise. This moment in Australia's colonial history could have been marked with a cautious announcement that the Aboriginal population (narrowly defined) was recovering. However, incomplete administrative penetration meant that the 'full-blood' figure in the 1961 Census included an estimated 2000 Western Australian nomads.[73]

The idea that 'half-castes' were part of the 'Aboriginal population' had remained available since the *Yearbook*s of the mid-1920s had published tables that placed 'half-castes' and 'full-bloods' within the same table for 'Aboriginal population'. As well, from the point of view of welfare administration, it was not only 'full-bloods' that mattered: for example, 'full-bloods' and 'half-castes' were combined in what Commonwealth official Jeremy Long in 1964 called the 'problem population – the numbers of people who consider themselves Aboriginals and who live in conspicuously Aboriginal groups'.[74] This broader notion of 'Aboriginal population' was also supported by field research showing that 'half-caste' men were being initiated into traditional culture and that they saw themselves, and were seen by others, as part of the kinship system and thus as part of 'Aboriginal society'.[75]

Obliging the constitutional imperative to enumerate 'full-bloods' distinctly (as 'aboriginal natives') became a technical burden on a Bureau that had no clear definition of 'half-caste'. After analysing the 1954 Census data and comparing them with recent state and territory Administration figures, the Bureau concluded that there was no reliable way to enumerate 'half-castes'. Bureau officers were frustrated that state and territory authorities, when supplying population data, were not applying 'caste' definitions rigorously and consistently. As well, there was growing suspicion that Aboriginal respondents to the Census, refusing the very idea that they could be fractionally 'Aboriginal', were giving technically unsound answers when asked to classify themselves as either 'full-blood' or 'half-caste'. The Bureau published no data on the latter category in *Yearbook*s 46–48 (1960–62). Lacking confidence in 'half-caste' enumeration, the Bureau advised that it would be technically unsound to publish a total 'Aboriginal' population figure that simply added all 'full-bloods' to all 'half-castes': some persons would probably be counted twice. In the seventh decade after Federation, the nation had no measure of a 'total Aboriginal population'.

Conclusion

Reflecting on a career dedicated to averting Aboriginal extinction, J.W. Bleakley acknowledged in 1961 that Aborigines 'often resented the measures designed for their welfare, because these naturally imposed certain controls and restrictions on their liberty'.[76] Protection, under his comprehensive system, had constituted the police and missionaries as 'protectors', empowering them to manage closely the lives of people whom many Australians pitied and despised. Although the illiberal laws and procedures of 'protection' have earned the regime a bad reputation, we should not overlook that one purpose of 'protection' – to prevent Aborigines' physical extinction – was fulfilled. By the narrowest definition – only 'full-bloods' – the nadir of the 'Aboriginal population' may have occurred in the 1950s. Using a more pragmatic definition of 'Aboriginal population' – people of various degrees of descent, recognisable to officials and to themselves as 'Aboriginal' – the 'Aboriginal population' seems to have begun its recovery by the 1920s. Government and mission interventions since the late 19th century contributed to this recovery.

A government narrative of Aboriginal demographic recovery did not emerge, however, because officials lacked an unquestionable database. Administrative under-reach until 1966, and the difficulty of deciding the relevance of 'caste', meant that the presentation of the 'Aboriginal population' in official publications from 1911 to 1966 could neither clearly confirm nor decisively refute the idea that 'Aborigines' were dying out. As well, there was more than one meaning to 'dying out'. Thus the 'dying Aborigine' scenario lingered as a humanitarian trope. In a paper published in 1970 (but written in 1960) Kimberley missionary Father E.A. Worms referred to Aborigines as a 'slowly dying race'.[77] The melancholy appeal of the 'dying native' persisted because there has always been more than one way that the story could be 'true' and useful.

5
Global awareness and the recession of race

Between the World Wars, Australians who were thoughtful about the colonial situation within Australia – not least, emerging Aboriginal intellectuals – drew on globally circulating ideas about the history, present condition and likely future of 'native' people under colonial authority. Although a language of universal human rights was soon to emerge as the terminology of global political institutions, what is more striking in the 1920s and 1930s is the historical imagining of native peoples: they were understood as being on trajectories – whether of decline, development, absorption, disappearance, detribalisation … Crosscutting these narrative imaginings of people were typologies based on racial science – in particular the distinction between purity of racial descent and hybridity. A struggle was taking place between older intellectual schemes which saw significance in race and biological descent and an emerging focus on the malleability of human destinies whatever the 'descent' of the people in question. While there was no single 'Australian' approach to this interplay and contest between racial and cultural understandings of difference, the distinction between 'full-blood'/'primitive'/'tribal' and 'half-caste'/'detribalised' was prominent, a refraction of the imagined geography of North and South.

Imagining Aborigines in art and literature

In the period between the two World Wars, some Australians began to appreciate the 'primitive' human history of their land. An Aboriginal artistic heritage had been acknowledged by the end of the 19th century, when Adelaide's town clerk Thomas Worsnop compiled *Prehistoric Arts, Manufactures, Works, Weapons, etc. of the Aborigines of Australia* in 1897. The civilised should judge primitive art 'leniently', he suggested.[1] When Worsnop included Aboriginal prisoners' pencil drawings, he classed them as artefacts of the prehistory of Australia – not of its colonial history. To recognise Aboriginal art as a living strand of Australian art was difficult for colonists who thought that Aboriginal people were exemplary of humankind in its infancy, destined to die out: Aboriginal modernity was a contradiction in terms.

Field research in South Australia's northern territory soon deepened thoughtful Australians' knowledge of their colony's Aboriginal past. Drawing on the globally admired writings of Walter Baldwin Spencer and Francis Gillen, Bernard O'Dowd's epic poem 'The Bush' (1912) twice used 'Alcheringa', an Arrernte word reported by Spencer and Gillen to refer both to Arrernte cosmology and to the incised stones and boards that signified the travels of mythic ancestors and thus each Arrernte clan's connection with its *pmere* ('country'). 'And Spencer sails from Alcheringa, bringing / Intaglios, totems and Books of the Dead', O'Dowd wrote. Spencer's cargo splendidly endowed the National Museum of Victoria, and in 1929 the museum exhibited bark paintings that Spencer had collected at Oenpelli in

1912. The exhibition presented such work as 'primitive' – a category then understood 'as distinct from European fine art as the art of children'.[2]

A global archive of 'primitive art' had by then begun to inspire modernist painting and sculpture in Europe, North America and Australia. Margaret Preston had discovered the Primitive in Europe in 1904–1906 and 1912–19; in December 1924 she commended the study of Aboriginal art as an antidote to the derivative 'South Kensington dullness' that inhibited a truly national art.[3] By the 1940s Preston was incorporating Aboriginal motifs and organising her picture plane in a way that echoed collected specimens of Aboriginal visual expression. In her view, art that drew on Aboriginal Australian art in this way was both modern and authentic to this continent.

European Romantic sensibility, a constituent of the 19th-century nationalism that contributed to the Federation movement, held that it was the duty of literary, musical and visual artists to express the spirit of place. If Anglophone Australians felt that they were not yet transplanted to this continent – their imaginations compromised by imported diction and visual conventions – they could find in Aboriginal Australian art a source of national authenticity. Learned study of a culture assumed to be fast-vanishing was shifting artists' sense of the continent's heritage. The Ngarrindjeri David Unaipon, after writing down 'Legendary Tales of the Australian Aborigines' in 1924–25, suggested: 'Perhaps some day Australian writers will use Aboriginal myths and weave literature from them, the same as other writers have done with the Roman, Greek, Norse, and Arthurian legends.'[4] However, the first appreciative moves were limited by a conception of Aboriginal 'tradition' that rendered it anonymous and outside of history. The anomalously modern Unaipon (a Christian, an inventor) was effaced from the tales' publication by William Ramsay Smith – medical practitioner, coroner and author of an 'expert' article on Aborigines in the third *Yearbook* (1909). Smith obtained the copyright of 'Legendary Tales', and his 1930 edition *Myths & Legends of the Australian Aborigines* omitted Unaipon's preface and referred to him only as a 'narrator'.[5] Smith thus enacted the idea that the 'primitive heritage' that he published no longer had Aboriginal people to sustain it, just as the National Museum of Victoria had thought it unnecessary, in its 1929 exhibition catalogue, to name the living painters from whom Spencer had collected barks at Oenpelli. Similarly, Preston was ambivalent about whether her appreciation of Aboriginal motifs depended on Aboriginal explanation of their totemic significance. For modernists, the formal beauty of Primitive expression was inspiration enough.[6]

The premise of Rex Ingamells' national cultural manifesto *Conditional Culture* (1938) was that Aboriginal civilisation was all but gone. The nation must remember its predecessors; their lost heritage could be known by gathering legends from the few thousand Aboriginal people who remained in remote and inaccessible regions of Australia. To read such gleanings was to experience 'the fertility of the Aboriginal mind in imagination and poetry based on the realities and mysteries of environment'. Ingamells referred to the recent research of Theodor Strehlow – collector of Arrernte songs – who in a September 1935 letter to Ingamells had wished that 'White Australia would soon wake up to the richness of its heritage, & preserve it and honour it, instead of treading it down ignorantly under its feet'.[7] Ingamells was also inspired by the stories that a north Queensland teacher, James Devaney, had published in 1929 as *The Vanished Tribes*.[8] Now was the moment for a 'transplanted European culture' to take stock of its predecessors, Ingamells urged, and to acknowledge that it had yet to acquire the Aborigines' profound understanding of Australia's physical environment. To be 'honest' with themselves, Australians must learn from the study of Aboriginal culture how to live in the land they now possessed. He commended the label 'Jindyworobak' – said to mean 'annex' or 'join' in an Aboriginal language that Ingamells did not name – for those who agreed with him that Australian culture required: '1. A clear recognition of environmental values. 2. The debunking of much nonsense. 3. An understanding of Australia's history and traditions, primaeval, colonial and modern.'[9]

Thus were Aboriginal Australians historicised by some thoughtful Australians between the World Wars. The still tribal people would remain tribal only if sequestered beyond destructive contact with modernity; their collectively and anonymously authored culture must be recorded respectfully while it remained possible to preserve it. Once tribal Aborigines came under colonial influence they rapidly detribalised: their entry into world history was their spoiling, loss, adulteration. Consigning Indigenous Australia respectfully to the 'primaeval', the obituarising Ingamells imagined the actual modernity of the Aborigines around him as a welfare problem. 'The blacks that remain are a degenerate, puppet people, mere parodies of what their race once was.'[10] This aesthetic and historical distinction was all the more persuasive for being mapped onto the legal–constitutional distinction asserted by Attorney-General Deakin in 1901 that 'half-castes' were not 'Aboriginal natives'. That distinction pervaded much progressive thinking.

Aborigines and the Communist International

In the 1930s, the Communist Party of Australia (CPA) was active in the wool industry, organising both black and white shearers and encouraging denunciation of the New South Wales Aboriginal Protection Board; it also campaigned against imposing the death sentence on Northern Territory Aborigines convicted of murder.[11] In 1931, the CPA's *Fight for Aborigines: Draft Programme of Struggle against Slavery* demanded:

> (1) Full and equal rights of all aborigines – economically, socially, and politically – with white races.
>
> (2) Absolute political freedom for *aborigines and half-castes*; right to membership in, and right to organise, political, economic and cultural organisations, 'mixed,' or aboriginal. Right to participate in demonstrations and public affairs. Right to leave Australia as full citizens.
>
> (3) Removal of all color restrictions on *aborigines or half-castes*, in professions, sports, etc. Aboriginal intellectuals, school teachers, etc., not to be prevented from practising because of the 'color line.'
>
> (4) Cancellation of all licenses to employ aborigines without pay. Cancellation of all indentures and forced labor conditions from aborigines, and payment at full wages for all time worked.
>
> (5) Prohibition of slave and forced labor, whether through the A.P.B. [Aborigines Protection Board], police,

indentures, missions, or otherwise, and compensation for all previously employed.

(6) Unconditional release from gaol of all *aborigines or half-castes*, and no further arrests until aboriginal juries can hear and decide cases.

(7) Abolition of Aborigines Protection Boards – Capitalism's slave recruiting agencies and terror organisations against *aborigines and half-castes*.

(8) Absolute prohibition of the kidnapping of aboriginal children by the A.P.B., whether to hire them out as slaves, place them in 'missions,' gaols or 'correction' homes.

(9) Full and unrestricted right of *aboriginal and half-caste* parents to their children, without living in constant fear that the A.P.B. or mission stations will kidnap them to send into slavery.

(10) Aboriginal children to be permitted to attend public and high schools and to sit for all examinations.

(11) Liquidation of all missions and so-called homes for aborigines, as these are part of the weapons being used to exterminate the aboriginal race by segregating the sexes and sending the young girls into slavery.

(12) Full right of the aborigines to develop native culture. Right to establish their own schools, train their own teachers, for the children of the *aborigines and half-castes*.

The Australian Government to make available sums of money for such purposes, to be paid into and controlled by committees comprised solely of aborigines and half-castes.

(13) Unemployed aborigines to be paid sums not less than other workers as unemployment allowance. Employed workers to have the 7-hour day, 5-day week, with pay at the same rates as other races.

(14) The handing over to the aborigines of large tracts of watered and fertile country, with towns, seaports, railways, roads, etc., to become one or more independent aboriginal states or republics. The handing back to the aborigines of all Central, Northern, and North West Australia to enable the aborigines to develop their native pursuits. These aboriginal republics to be independent of Australian or other foreign powers. To have the right to make treaties with foreign powers, including Australia, establish their own army, governments, industries, and in every way be independent of imperialism.[12]

The phrase 'aborigines and half castes' occurred six times. The distinction between the two became important to the most prolific Communist theorist of Indigenous liberation, Tom Wright, of the Sheet Metal Workers' Union and the NSW Trades and Labour Council. An active correspondent with contemporary non-Communist activists on Aboriginal issues, Wright promoted the view that the terms 'Aborigines', 'natives' and 'Aboriginals' should be defined so as to exclude 'half castes and others of mixed blood'. The latter were better considered as coloured workers who suffered racial discrimination (including from the white labour movement itself). Their struggle for social advancement was as part of Australia's working class, but they had no future as a distinct nation or people.[13]

The CPA's influence in the NSW Trades and Labour Council contributed to that council's 1933 resolution supporting Aboriginal control over 'tribal sanctuaries'. According to Wright's 1938 booklet *A New Deal for Aborigines*, the rights of 'Aborigines proper' who lived on 'tribal sanctuaries' were those of a 'national minority', in the jargon of international communism; their future rested on their strict territorial and cultural segregation from Australian society. On their behalf, Wright demanded absolutely inviolable reserves, with tribal ownership of mineral resources. Only secular organisations (and not missions) were to be allowed to interact with these sovereign reserve-owners. Communist doctrine projected that they would develop economically, but instruction for such advance must be in their own languages, as well as in English. A new Commonwealth department should be established, Wright recommended, with powers to police alien contact with the reserve dwellers. Re-issuing *A New Deal for Aborigines* in 1944, Wright reviewed the war-time militarisation of remote Australia (described in the next chapter).

> Changes due to the war, particularly in North Australia, have further reduced the opportunities for effective remedial measures to ensure their survival as a race. A comparatively large number have been organised virtually as slave workers in connection with construction work in N. Australia and the remnants of tribal life further disrupted.[14]

To rescue 'the remnants of the aboriginal race', he wrote, it would be necessary to exclude 'mixed blood' people from inviolable reserves. People who were of Aboriginal descent but who were no longer 'Aborigines proper' should play no part in the development of reserve residents 'because of the danger of providing focal points for disintegration'.[15] Wright thought it a mistake to combine people of mixed descent and 'full-bloods' in the one organised movement with a single program, as some Aboriginal organisations were beginning to do. As he explained to the Australian Aborigines' League in 1948, the social development of Aboriginal people would proceed along two lines. Some would survive within an evolving tribal organisation; others had lost tribal organisation and thus were a racially oppressed section of the wider Australian working class.[16]

Though he often used the racial terms 'full-blood' and 'half-caste', Wright's intended meaning was to distinguish social organisation and political capacity. The central question for him was whether the 'tribal organisation' of Aborigines still worked effectively: where it did, Aborigines had a possible future as a distinct people with their own territory; where it did not, their destiny was as members of the working class. So, when Aboriginal people took militant industrial action against Pilbara pastoralists in 1946, it raised an important question for Wright: what was the basis of their cohesion?

The question was not easy to answer, for there had been more than one pathway of Indigenous adaptation in the Pilbara. Yandying for tin around Nullagine required only a flattened 'yandy' dish, and Aborigines and Europeans participated in tin mining in this region from the 1890s. For Aborigines this was an alternative to working for pastoralists, and by 1906 there had been about 300 Aborigines on the Nullagine tin fields. On pastoral stations there had remained 'uneasy paternalism on the part of managers' and a continuing attachment to homelands on the part of the resident Aborigines, sustained by their seasonal release from working for the pastoralist.[17] By the 1920s, some had been getting cash wages. In the 1930s the Western Australian government had relied upon the pastoralist to look after all Aborigines on their property; they could pay low wages and were assured that police would discourage station hands from leaving pastoral employment. Some Aboriginal people had emerged as roving contractors, possessing their own equipment: fencing, well-sinking, carting, mustering. There were no missions in the Pilbara until the Apostolic Church of Australia founded Jigalong Mission in 1945. In the coastal towns of the Pilbara were people of mixed race, some in skilled occupations, who were beginning to organise themselves, for example the Euralia Association, a funeral benefit society. Meanwhile, migration from the Western Desert repopulated the Pilbara's pastoral fringe, creating some instability in the politics of religious seniority. By World War II 'much diffuse dissatisfaction' had developed among the Pilbara's Aborigines, 'but it was not organised and found its expression in stubbornness, laziness, fighting amongst themselves, and in specific disputes between station managers and "trouble-makers"'.[18]

Aboriginal restlessness was accentuated in the disturbed social conditions during World War II, when troops were stationed in the area. Some Europeans had left Port Hedland and Broome under threat of Japanese bombing. Military authority regulated sexual contact between white soldiers and Aboriginal women; it exposed Aborigines to servicemen whose manners were more egalitarian, and it paid better wages.[19] The Army decided who could remain in Port Hedland, and the Euralia Association represented the interests of Port Hedland Aborigines; some white townspeople expressed solidarity with the 'coloureds'. Increasingly aware of their importance as labour, some Aborigines reached out to a white contractor, Don McLeod. He had employed Aborigines, and was known to be sympathetic to their position as exploited labour. They invited him to a meeting at Skull Springs where they showed him their rituals and discussed their political options; he soon understood himself to be their trusted representative, and he acquired two collaborators, Clancy McKenna, a contractor from a tin-mining Aboriginal family and Dooley Bin-Bin. As their delegate, McLeod told the Commissioner for Native Affairs in June 1943 that Aborigines in the Pilbara wanted their own station near Port Hedland. The alarmed authorities cancelled McLeod's licence to employ Aborigines; they restored it upon his appeal – a stoush that consolidated local support for McLeod.

When the war ended, the committee of local Aborigines associated with McLeod called a strike of pastoral workers, beginning on May Day 1946, to demand higher pay in the shearing season. Nine committee men spread the word, seeking coordinated action. Meanwhile, negotiations over pay rates began, and although some stations agreed to higher rates in late April, the strike went ahead. The police saw things from the employers' perspective and arrested Dooley Bin-Bin, Clancy McKenna and Don McLeod for enticing Aborigines from a place of employment. By the end of May, a Committee for the Defence of Native Rights had formed in Perth, gathering support from churches, academics, unions, welfare organisations and the Communist Party of Australia. Pilbara Aborigines were heartened by such support and by the legal steps that soon led to the prisoners' release. The systems of local control – police and employers deciding where and when people could get rations – were proving ineffective, once people felt the potency of collective action. Against police orders, Aborigines formed a large camp outside Port Hedland; McLeod was arrested when he tried to meet with them, but when the campers marched into Port Hedland, the police released him. The state government was not sympathetic to the strikers, but certain trade unions were: in 1948, the Seamen's Union banned loading wool from stations that refused to pay what the strikers had been demanding.

Looking on from Sydney, Tom Wright welcomed the strike, but he needed to know how his theory related to the strikers' practice: were they to be understood as militant black workers or as self-organising tribes? In a schematic rendering of Wright's theory, the Pilbara mob could be either 'full-blood' (Aborigines) or 'mixed descent' (coloured working class). Thus, Wright asked Don McLeod in May 1946: 'Are the "natives" on De Grey Station full-blood Aborigines or persons of mixed blood?' Wright then spelled out what he understood to be the possibilities. 'If of full blood, do they belong to the same aboriginal tribe or are they drawn from different tribes? If of mixed blood together with full blood Aborigines, what are the proportions?'[20] McLeod told him that 'with a few exceptions the natives on De Grey are full blood aboriginal most of them from the original tribe with a sprinkling of near neighbours included as the result of the break-up of the old family organisations'.[21] On the one hand, the strikers' demands were what one would expect from members of the working class: better wages and conditions. On the other hand, their subsequent self-organising actions – cooperative ventures in mining – illustrated Wright's hopes of tribal resilience and alternatives to wage labour.

Notwithstanding the difficulty of applying his categories to this outstanding instance of Aboriginal militancy, Wright persisted in his belief that there were two distinct Aboriginal struggles: tribal autonomy for some and workers' rights for others. In September 1951 he wrote to the honorary secretary of the Council for Aboriginal Rights (Melbourne) giving the 'half-caste'/'full-blood' distinction geographical expression. New South Wales and Victoria were historically different from the Northern Territory and adjacent areas: 'there is no Aborigine question in Victoria or N.S.W. where few if any aborigines have survived', and the terms 'native', 'Aboriginal' or 'Aborigine' should not 'refer to persons of mixed blood'. [22]

Feminist internationalism and the Aboriginal woman as slave

The 'international' in which some Australian feminists were active was not the Moscow-centred Comintern but the London-centred British Commonwealth of Nations, and it too had an historical vision of native peoples' struggles. When speaking to the British Commonwealth League (BCL) in 1929 Ruby Rich described the British Commonwealth as 'a gigantic experiment in international racial co-operation'.[23] The BCL was formed in 1925 'to deal with issues of Equal Citizenship within the countries ruled under the British flag' and its third conference, in 1927, tackled the social and industrial position of women subjects of British rule but not of British race.[24] White Australian women activists joined this discussion. Through membership of bodies such as the Australian Federation of Women's Societies for Equal Citizenship and several state-based women's associations, Australian women such as Mary Bennett, Bessie Rischbieth, Constance Mary Cooke, Edith Jones and Helen Baillie were affiliated with the BCL and attended its conferences in London. Publicising the Aboriginal question from the centre of the Empire, their views were reported in London's press and thus attracted notice in

Australia. They also participated in the London-based Anti-Slavery and Aborigines' Protection Society, whose cause resonated with the campaigns against unfree labour pursued in the League of Nations by the International Labour Organization.

These women activists took seriously the multi-racialism of the Commonwealth. The *British Nationality and Status of Aliens Act 1914* had created a common status for the Empire's British subjects, regardless of race. Imperial ideals of formal equality across races did not displace the underlying conviction that the British race had a duty to teach the world's lesser races how better to live; rather, the ideal of formal equality helped to define that tutelary relationship as the obligation of the 'British race' to guide, assist and advance other races within the Commonwealth. If whites in some Dominions enslaved rather than advanced natives, and if Dominion laws qualified or denied native citizenship (as Australia's did), there were grounds for Imperial reproach. Australia's Imperial feminists 'applied equality of rights between men and women to the question of just relations between white and black', and they were 'concerned to improve the lives of native women and girls, in whom the inequities resulting from being not-white and women combined'.[25] In particular, these women criticised policies that supposed the Aboriginal woman and mother to be defenceless and morally incompetent, and that mandated supervision of her marital choices and the removal of her children. The feminists upheld the Aboriginal woman as a human with rights, a vulnerable individual to be empowered (as a woman) against sexually predatory, enslaving men and (as a mother and a woman) against crushingly 'protective' bureaucracy.

The feminists wished to 'uplift' all lives, to promote all 'women's transition from tribal to modern society', but they distinguished the frontier from the longer-colonised regions. At the

1933 BCL meeting Mary Bennett explained her view that 'the study of the Aboriginal mother falls into two parts: (1) dealing with the Aboriginal mother living the wild life uncontaminated by whites; and (2) dealing with the Aboriginal mother living in touch with civilisation'. Women in the first situation are property of men. In the second situation (that included but was not confined to the situation of 'half-caste' women) that property had become traded merchandise: women were prostituting themselves, driven by hunger. Bennett recommended that Aboriginal people be given fifty territories across Western Australia, where they would not be molested by whites and where they could grow food.[26]

These feminists' aims and suggested methods of protection overlapped with those of the state and territory Administrations. In their policy demands they shared ground with other humanitarian groups in the 1920s and 1930s, such as the Aborigines' Friends' Association and the Association for the Protection of Native Races: more reserves, better education and health services and access to citizenship. However, according to Marilyn Lake, their 'focus on the violated woman and grieving mother as paradigmatic of the oppressed condition of Aboriginal people ... distinguished feminist discourse from the other Christian and humanitarian discourses current at the time'.[27] In particular they demanded the appointment of women like themselves as protectors. The anthropologist Olive Pink advocated 'secular sanctuaries' for remote Aborigines, some of them administered by a woman.[28] Such female protectors would take aim at 'domestic slavery in their own cultures'. As Alison Holland explains,

> The international feminist movement utilised the new definition of slavery promoted by the League of Nations as,

'the status of a person over whom all or any of the powers attaching to the right of ownership are exercised', to press for the abolition of 'tribal' marriage practices such as polygamy, infant betrothal and purchase of girls by dowry. Furthermore, they argued that the slavery of Indigenous women in their own cultures made them particularly vulnerable to exploitation in contact situations.[29]

It is not clear how the female protectors were to confront the male power exercised as customary polygyny. As no Australian government appointed female protectors, we do not know what such women would have done to help girls 'foredoomed to give their clean little bodies to dirty old men in the bush who can claim them by native right' (to quote Edith Jones).[30]

To champion the rights of Aboriginal women was also to raise the issue of child removal. Some such as Mary Bennett criticised government and mission authorities that removed children from their mothers. Aboriginal mothering, she said, was noble and beneficial and must be defended by providing Aboriginal women with '"independence" through guidance and uplift'.[31] Bennett's defence of the Aboriginal woman as mother entailed defending her as wife: she advocated that polygamy be banned, and it is possible that some Aboriginal women agreed with her.[32] Other activists with whom Bennett collaborated – sharing her horror of polygamy – accepted that some children were being removed and institutionalised and called on authorities to accommodate them better and – capitalising on their 'white blood' – to train them for absorption into the wider Australian society.[33]

Like others at this time, the feminists attached significance to the 'half-caste'/'full-blood' distinction: the former should be assimilated, the latter protected by a high degree of segregation.

That is, on the one hand, they 'opposed the exclusion from citizenship of mixed-descent Aborigines living in contact with whites', as such persons 'were likely to be already sufficiently educated and politically aware to participate in Australian national life'.[34] On the other hand, they supported institutions of the frontier, such as missions located on large isolated reserves that limited Aboriginal contact with settler society to interactions with a few carefully selected whites. Thus in a 1932 letter to Bessie Rischbieth, Bennett distinguished the task of the mission to 'wild natives', such as could be found in the Kimberley, from the task of the mission serving those who had been '"civilised" or contaminated' by contact with settler society, such as could be found on the edges of pastoral settlement.[35]

The word 'contaminated' sometimes occurred in 1930s discourse to refer to those affected by colonial contact. For example, when the anatomist Frederick Wood Jones told ABC Radio listeners in 1934 that 'the aborigine is essentially of a pure race', he used the word 'uncontaminated' to refer to those still living tribally whom he presumed to be 'full-blood'.[36] In Australians' language about the colonial situation, a biological term often functioned metaphorically: the progeny of frontier miscegenation were not 'full-blood', so they were also compromised in behaviour and outlook, detribalised, characterised by cultural loss, demoralised – contaminated.[37] The terminology of descent – 'full'/'half' – summarised a sociological distinction: the contrast between 'tribal' and 'detribalised'. The currency of the language of descent should not be taken as evidence that Wright, Jones, Bennett and the other feminist critics were racial determinists who believed that Aboriginal behaviour and outlooks were the effect of genetic admixture. On Fiona Paisley's reading these feminists understood differences of race and gender to be 'cultural as well as biological'.[38] However, there is no doubt that some feminists saw racial distinctions as determinant to some degree. As Constance Cooke explained to the BCL in 1927, Aborigines' 'blood-grouping is the same as that of the Caucasian races, and quite distinct from that of the negro. This is an important point, for where their blood mingles with ours the white blood is dominant.'[39] For Cooke, this was a genetic basis for hopeful engagement with the products of miscegenation.

On the position of women – whether 'full-blood' or mixed – feminists criticised customary authority: Keen's 'reproductive power'. Others who valued tribal cohesion (Tom Wright and Donald Thomson) were not inclined to question tribal authority. The distinct feminist contribution to humanitarian thought was to focus on female personhood and thus to take aim at tribal patriarchs, frontier ruffians and high-minded protectors who presumed, in different ways, to take masculine charge of women's bodies and minds. To promote female personhood presumed to speak on behalf of the Aboriginal woman. In the case of Mary Bennett the presumption was confirmed by her experience of working with Aboriginal women at Mount Margaret Mission, with Mysie and Rod Schenk. With the exception of Helen Baillie, who was associated with William Cooper and was an honorary life member of the group that he founded, the Australian Aborigines' League, and Mary Bennett, who was thanked by 'the coloured people of the Collie district' for her testimony to the Moseley Royal Commission in 1933–34, the feminist women joined their activities not with Aboriginal activists, but with global networks of women like themselves.[40]

The Garvey-ites of New South Wales

A black ('Negro') international inspired the Hunter Valley–born Koori Fred Maynard. The Universal Negro Improvement Association (UNIA), led by the Jamaican Marcus Garvey, flourished in the United States after World War I among African Americans for whom post–Civil War Reconstruction had failed. From 1920 Garvey presided over the first of several international conventions of the UNIA. The UNIA promoted the global solidarity of black people against white oppression, to end Imperialist rule and to create modern societies in Africa. Through the newspaper *Negro World* the UNIA projected these aspirations to black communities everywhere. While appealing to working-class blacks, Garveyism also promoted business formation: the Black Star Line, an international shipping company formed in 1922 to provide transportation and trade among the black businesses of Africa and the Americas. Garvey also founded the Negro Factories Corporation.

Hearing Garvey's call for global black solidarity, some Aboriginal Australians formed a chapter of UNIA in Sydney in 1920. The ground for this initiative had been laid before World War I through contact, in the port of Sydney, between Aboriginal workers and black seamen. A Coloured Progressive Association was founded in Sydney around 1903; made up mainly of African Americans and West Indians, it may have included Aborigines. The Sydney visits of the champion African-American boxer Jack Johnson in 1907 and 1908 were occasions for the city's 'blacks' – including wharf labourer Fred Maynard – joyously to gather. John Maynard suggests that this milieu contributed to the confidence with which Aborigines – angered by the NSW government's handing over of much of their reserve lands to returned non-Aboriginal servicemen after World War I – formed a chapter of UNIA. Those putting their time into the Sydney chapter of UNIA then established the Australian Aboriginal Progressive Association (AAPA) in 1924, building their platform 'around Garvey's call for pride in culture, solid economic base, and strong association to land of birth'.[41] AAPA referred to Aborigines as 'Australians', and its motto 'Australia for Australians' repeated the Garvey-ite motif 'Africa for Africans'. *Negro World* reported frequently on 'enslaved and brutalised' Aborigines in the mid-1920s, pointing to the parallel with the 'Red Men' of North America.

AAPA campaigned for four years (1925 to 1929), establishing eleven branches, holding four conferences, and demanding: good land in 'fee simple sufficient … to maintain a family', a 'family life free from invasion', government reserves for 'the incapables of the Aboriginal community', and delegation to 'educated aboriginals' of the supervision of 'Homes, Hostels or Reserve'. Sick of the bullying of the Aborigines Protection Board, AAPA asked that it be replaced by a 'board of management comprised of capable educated aboriginals under a chairman to be appointed by the Government'.[42] The distinction 'capable/incapable' also appeared in a petition presented by AAPA to NSW Premier Jack Lang in July 1927. According to a press report of a meeting between Maynard and the chair of the Australian Board of Missions (Reverend J.S. Needham) in November 1927, Maynard envisaged that 'native communities' would be supervised not by white officials of state and church but by 'educated and capable aborigines'.[43] John Maynard has pointed to parallels with what Aborigines in South Australia and Western Australia were saying to governments at this time: demanding that governments acknowledge 'capable' Aborigines as leaders.[44]

Unlike communist and feminist internationalists, AAPA did not use the language of 'caste' or 'blood' when making distinctions among Aboriginal Australians. The contrast between full-blood/uncontaminated/tribal and half-caste/contaminated/detribalised was useless (and quite possibly offensive) to many emerging Aboriginal intellectuals, because in that way of dichotomising the Indigenous situation, the emerging Aboriginal intellectuals would be numbered among the impure, the contaminated, the detribalised. The articulate urban and rural Aborigines of the south-east and south-west of the continent could hardly take up a language that disqualified them for leadership, as pitifully damaged and estranged from their authentic being. They were more conscious of what they had achieved than of what they had lost; they were proud, not regretful, of their cultural distance from those Aboriginal people who needed protection, and they sought recognition for it.

British Aborigines

Whereas Maynard and his Garvey-inspired associates could look to 'Negros' as the exemplars of the global advance of black people, other Aboriginal people were inspired by the advance of certain native peoples under proper 'British' tuition. This was the perspective of the Yorta Yorta William Cooper, founder of the Australian Aborigines' League (AAL) in 1936. Cooper, like other Aboriginal intellectuals of his time, believed that the 'half-caste'/'full-blood' distinction was a misleading and harmful way to differentiate the needs, achievements and entitlements of Aboriginal people; he insisted that there was a single path of progress along which Aboriginal Australians were advancing and that 'blood' was neither a determinant nor an index of how far any person had advanced.

When Cooper differentiated among Aborigines, he invoked the criteria of 'civilisation'. He suggested to Prime Minister Joseph Lyons that 'the aboriginal population shall be grouped into classes determined by the stage of their progress and that the policy of the [Northern Territory] Administration shall be the progressive elevation from one class to an [sic] higher one till the whole race is fully civilized and cultured'.[45] Cooper classified his Aboriginal contemporaries under three headings: 'primitive aborigines' who needed reserves, rations and special courts based on customary law; 'semi-civilised and detribalised natives' who needed help to turn their land to agricultural use, 'the right to work for adequate remuneration or the provision of full rations and housing' and access to schools and to pensions; and 'civilised natives' (he included all NSW Aborigines) who were entitled to what the 'semi-civilised' should have and, in addition, to vote and to receive the 'maternity bonus'.[46] The 'civilised' – including Cooper himself – had a duty to defend the 'primitive' and to 'uplift them morally, socially, intellectually and spiritually'.[47]

In Cooper's understanding of history each race advances through stages, from primitive to civilised. 'The British were once where we are now,' he reminded the Commonwealth Minister for the Interior in June 1937. 'The conquering power of Rome, whatever else it did, lifted the British to culture and civilisation. We want the same uplift. Are we unreasonable?'[48] Fijians under British tuition had moved on quickly from being cannibals; were Aborigines to be denied advancement?[49] Both Aborigines and whites were creatures of the Christian God and both were inheritors of British civilisation and 'subjects of the Realm'.[50] Aborigines were becoming 'not merely European in culture but British in sentiment', and 'the aboriginal is more British often than the white'.[51] 'We ask the right to be fully British.'[52] Governments oblivious to Aboriginal potential were failing in their duty of care, and 'many of our civilized Aborigines have not been given the status of citizens of the Commonwealth'.[53] Native advancement in Australia had been thwarted by 'contact with the worst side of Civilisation that has brought them Corruption and Diseases'.[54] Cooper made specific demands: seats in parliament, such as Maoris had in New Zealand's parliament, and the dole for the 'dark unemployed', who could be 'taught to be self-reliant and industrious and to win his rights by sheer worthiness'.[55] The states should cede to the Commonwealth their powers over Aborigines. Aboriginal people should enjoy inalienable title to their land.[56] Reserves for Aborigines should be managed in an accountable way, and they should be open to Aborigines 'of full or part blood' who could develop the land.[57] Improvement in Aborigines' standard of living need not extinguish that which made them a different people. 'The ultimate object of the League shall be the conservation of special features of Aboriginal culture and the removal of all disabilities, political, social or economic, now or in future borne by aboriginals and to secure their uplift to the full culture of the British race.'[58] The 'special features' of Aboriginal culture that were worthy of 'conservation' excluded 'the undesirable practices which will retard their uplift'.[59] Whereas Maynard and AAPA focused on New South Wales, Cooper's vision was continental; commenting on 'northern development', he saw a special role for Aborigines in the settlement of northern Australia.[60] Aborigines were more suited than Italian migrants to developing the tropical north.[61]

Different distinctions

Although all informed observers in the 1930s agreed that the situations and outlooks of Aboriginal Australians were differentiated, the terms in which differences were described and the policy significance of such distinctions were in dispute. The 'half-caste'/'full-blood' distinction was entrenched in official statistics and in law, and some policy reformers thought that people's character and outlook were closely correlated with, and substantially determined by, their genetic make-up. Others whose thinking was not so determinist used the terminology of 'blood' and 'caste' as shorthand for sociological distinctions: a 'full-blood' was, in most cases, not yet 'detribalised', and a 'half-caste' definitely was.

The most important issue in this discourse between the World Wars was whether there were two pathways forward for the colonised people, or one way. Generally speaking, those who used the 'full-blood'/'half-caste' distinction believed that there were two paths of advancement: 'half-castes' should be enabled as individual citizens and absorbed as quickly as possible into the wider society, while 'full-bloods' should be enabled as tribal groups to defer indefinitely their engagement with Australian institutions and to develop themselves, with carefully chosen assistance, along a path that maintained their culture, at their own pace, in remote regions. In contrast, many Aborigines of south-eastern and south-western agricultural Australia who saw themselves as relatively 'civilised' saw a single line of advance along which all Aboriginal people were moving and must move. Some Aboriginal people, they said, had travelled further than others along that path. Those who saw themselves as more advanced said that they merited distinct entitlements and responsibilities, as a consequence not of their mixed 'blood' but of their cultural attainments. Some Aboriginal people who claimed this distinction of capability presented themselves as guardians and guides of their less advanced fellows.

Australian political forums did not enable a reasoned confrontation between what I have described here as the two-path and one-path scenarios; on particular issues at particular times, the two sides were in agreement – for example, on the right of remote Aboriginal people to live undisturbed on large reserves. However, there was a deep, undebated tension between the two perspectives: the role assigned to the 'advanced'/'detribalised'/ 'half-caste'/'contaminated' Aborigines. Wright advocated that 'detribalised' Aborigines should play no part in the remote people's future; enlightened government officials should guide the remote, tribal people, he suggested in 1939 and in 1944. The feminists also rested their hopes on appointing a better kind of official (though, in their scheme, the female protector might be on the staff of a mission, not necessarily a government employee). The Aboriginal woman needed the empathy that only a female protector could offer. Contrast these reform schemes with Maynard's view: the NSW government officials were to move aside so that 'capable' Aborigines could supervise the 'incapable' – a term broad enough to include many different ways of not (yet) engaging effectively with modern Australia. In Cooper's view,

> the proper method of dealing with the primitive people would be to send educated and cultured Aborigines to their own uncivilized people. These men, of the same blood, would understand their people and would be able to suggest to the government means whereby the hardships and sufferings of these people could be alleviated or removed.[62]

Commonwealth government discourse, 1937–52

Australian governments in the 1930s evidently saw the 'full-blood'/'half-caste' distinction as important. The first resolution to issue from the Initial Conference of Commonwealth and State Authorities (to which neither Victoria nor Tasmania sent delegates) in 1937 was 'that the destiny of the natives of aboriginal origin, *but not of the full blood*, lies in their ultimate absorption by the people of the Commonwealth'.[63] However, the conference resolutions were not strictly racially determinist as they made sociological distinctions among 'full-bloods': 'the detribalised living near centres of white population' (whose children should be educated for employment); the 'semi-civilized' (to be supervised 'in their own tribal areas' on reserves); and the 'uncivilized natives' (to be kept apart on inviolable reserves, possibly with mission contact).[64] The 'semi-civilized' on reserves would eventually become as educable as the 'detribalised living near centres of white population', who were to be educated to the white standard. The 1937 conference was silent on the future of the 'uncivilized native'. Within two years, the Commonwealth Minister for the Interior, John McEwen, declared in a fresh statement of Commonwealth policy (not binding on any state) that even those of a 'tribal nomadic state' were to be transformed – over 'many generations' – so they could 'take their place in a civilized community'. However, he had no immediate intention to change 'their ancient tribal life'.[65]

World War II, as we will see in the next chapter, put the most remote Aboriginal people in contact with civil and military administrations. Their increasing proximity made it more difficult to omit them from the governmental imagining of Aboriginal futures. To bring them within reach was to gather them into universal human history, not as timeless 'primitives' (soon to be gone) but as incipient members of Australian community imagined in continental terms. Racial categories lost their relevance to government thinking not only because of changes in scientific thought (the decline of racial determinism) and not only because of the growing influence of a discourse of universal human rights through the League of Nations, but also because, in Australia, the increasing proximity of remote Aboriginal people meant that they could more readily be imagined in cultural and historical terms — that is, as having futures open to the contingencies of government programs. As the terms in which officials differentiated within the Aboriginal population became less racial/genetic and more social, cultural and geographical, the sociological connotations of 'full-blood' — that is, that they were 'tribal' — became more relevant than their genetic status. Their proximities to non-Aboriginal people and the length and type of their exposure to non-Aboriginal influence were what mattered, not their 'blood'. The fruit of this intellectual shift — from biology to history, one might say — can be seen in Hasluck's five speeches between June 1950 and August 1952, published as *Native Welfare in Australia*. In this manifesto for a post-racial program of 'assimilation', Hasluck avoided terms such as 'half-caste' and 'full-blood' (except when he had no choice, reporting population sizes). Instead, like Maynard and Cooper, he presented Aboriginal variety as a single scale of acculturation.

> At the end of the scale is the primitive tribesman, a nomad who wanders naked in his tribal territory, hunting and gathering food, wholly bound by tribal custom and belief. Ascending the scale will be found people in all stages of contact with civilisation and of progress in education …

'[A]ll persons of aboriginal blood or mixed blood in Australia will live like white Australians do', he predicted, though they would differ in their 'rate of progress' towards that ideal.[66] There was no prospect of isolating the most remote Aborigines from this process, in 'some sort of anthropological zoo'.[67]

Hasluck's vision of Indigenous advance drew on the same progressive narrative – from incapacity to capacity – that AAPA and AAL had voiced. However, assimilationists such as Hasluck did not express confidence that 'advanced' Aboriginal people had the right and the destiny to be entrusted with guiding their people's advancement. Assimilationist thought was unresolved on the issue of whether, as an Aboriginal 'advanced', he or she became less 'Aboriginal'. The AAPA and AAL activists assumed that it was their advanced condition that qualified them for leadership as Aborigines: who better than acculturated Aborigines to guide their people to modernity? In the 1930s, their bid for a trustee role in assimilation failed; defensive governments saw the agitation of 'advanced' Aborigines as a threat, not as an opportunity. Only with the revision of assimilation in the period 1965–75 and the inception of 'self-determination' did governments confer on 'advanced' Indigenous people the trusteeship that they had begun to request in the late 1920s.

6

World Wars and the Cold War

Recent historical scholarship has shown that a tradition of Imperial and Australian patriotism prompted Aboriginal people in some regions to enlist in Australian forces under British command in the Boer War and in World War I.[1] While the Boer War numbers are unknown (and probably small), estimates of 1000 Aboriginal persons enlisted in World War I are now plausible.[2] Horton points out that 'in Victoria, joining the military was one of the few acts Aboriginal men living under the Protection Acts could undertake without asking the Board's permission'.[3] She profiles the Gunditjmara man James Arden, attributing to him a strong feeling of 'Aboriginal equality with other Australian "Britishers" … founded in imperial loyalty, national service, personal sacrifice and masculine prowess. He sought inclusion in a white institution by claiming his status as a British subject, but he did so on behalf of the Aboriginal people of "Condah station" [which the Victorian government was planning to close].'[4]

Their patriotism was not rewarded. On the contrary, governments that thanked non-Aboriginal returned soldiers by granting them farm land now had another reason to revoke the reserves that Aborigines in New South Wales and Victoria had learned to call home. Between the two World Wars, Aboriginal people commented that governments bent on 'protection' were ignoring the capacities and the loyalty that they had demonstrated by enlistment and by supporting the war from the home front. Protesting the Victorian government's sale of the reserves, John Egan, an Aboriginal man, reminded readers of the *Portland Guardian* in 1925 'that these Mission Stations have all given their loved ones to serve in the Great War ... Do the traditions of the British race condone such an action as forcibly making exiles of us?'[5] In 1925 the Noongar William Harris argued that 'half-castes' should get the vote; he noted that 'many of that despised class fought in the Great War'.[6] Because Aborigines had enlisted, said William Cooper in March 1933, 'it is our duty to protect the remainder of their race from inhuman treatment'.[7] War service, Cooper told Prime Minister Lyons in 1938, had turned out to be 'thankless'.[8] The 'half-castes of Broome' suggested in 1934 that Australia had been acting like 'the Hun' towards those who had enlisted to defeat 'the Hun'.[9] Queenslander Tom Blackman wrote to a sympathetic white researcher in 1935: 'Think of all the half caste soldiers who were killed at war. What thanks have the half caste soldiers got for going to war. We were good men at war but looked down on now the war is over.'[10]

World War I did not transform relationships between Indigenous and non-Indigenous Australians because the apparatus of 'protection' was deeply entrenched and still being consolidated; as well, and more important, the hostilities were far from Australia. World War II was transformative because the war economy made huge demands for labour and because the threat of Japanese invasion changed the North/South relationship; settled Australia (cities and their mining and agricultural hinterlands) were forced to pay unprecedented attention to vulnerable northern Australia, to invest material and to deploy people there. From the perspective of the geography of Australia's colonial nationhood, World War II must therefore be bracketed with its Cold War sequel. Through World War II and the Cold War, the remote spaces in which many Aborigines and all Torres Strait Islanders had been protected, managed and left at the margins of Australians' attention became strategically important as sites for the deployment of personnel and weaponry, and for weapons testing.

However, war-time changes in Indigenous/non-Indigenous relationships were not reflected, at first, in policy debate or in legislation. 'During the war years,' Paul Hasluck recalled in 1988, 'aboriginal affairs faded into the background.'[11] For example, 'Aboriginal affairs' was marginal to the war-time debate about the shape of the federal compact. The national government proposed to increase its constitutional power to effect postwar reconstruction. Had the 1944 'powers' referendum been carried, the Commonwealth would have determined Aboriginal affairs policy, after consultation with the states and with others experienced in administration; the Commonwealth would have passed legislation, formulated regulations, employed all staff and paid all costs.[12] Opposition leader R.G. Menzies supported this change, but he vigorously opposed giving the Commonwealth the other proposed thirteen heads of power. Fifty-four per cent of voters refused to transfer the fourteen powers to the Commonwealth, and Queensland, New South Wales, Victoria and Tasmania voted 'No'. This was not a popular verdict on whether Aboriginal affairs should be a national government responsibility, for in the state parliaments, in the press and in campaign advertising the debate on the Aboriginal 'power' was 'muted or non-existent', except in Western Australia, where the state government wanted the Commonwealth's financial support but not its control.[13]

Revaluing Indigenous labour

In 'North' Australia, up until 1939, Aboriginal labour had become important to the livestock industries, as cheap and immobile labour. The rapid construction of a war machine in the North launched the public sector's competing bid for that labour – as soldiers and as support workers. The Army's anthropologist W.E.H. Stanner pointed out in December 1942: 'the present search for organized native labour is a radical outside intervention in NT native policy, and may well be all to the good'.[14] Not welcoming Indigenous enlistment at first, the Australian military had 3000 Aborigines and Torres Strait Islanders in uniform by the end of the war, with 150–200 serving more informally in various roles on the northern coast, and 3000 as civilian labourers.[15] In the Northern Territory by May 1943, at 'Native Labour' compounds along the Stuart Highway between Alice Springs and Darwin, the Army employed over 700 men and women (mostly men) in a variety of unskilled and semi-skilled tasks; that number halved by February 1946, as these people returned to their homelands on reserves, missions and pastoral leases.[16] In the Torres Strait, over 700 Islanders served, most of them in the Torres Strait Light Infantry Battalion or the Torres Strait Pioneer Company, along with forty-one Aborigines (in the Second Australian Water Transport Group).[17] Coastal missions became Royal Australian Air Force (RAAF) bases and/or radar posts: Lombadina, Drysdale River (Kalumburu), Port Keats, Bathurst Island, Croker Island, Goulburn Island, Milingimbi, Yirrkala, Groote Eylandt, Mitchell River, Mornington Island, Edward River, Aurukun, Weipa, Mapoon, Cowal Creek.[18] At least seventeen northern airstrips were built by Aborigines during the war.[19] By 1944, there were sixteen stations from Groote Eylandt to Kimberley, each with its own contingent of Aborigines under a novel mix of mission, military and civilian authority.

Military authority was a new and sudden arrival in remote regions where the contest between mission authority, civil authority, pastoralists' authority and customary Indigenous authority was not yet decided; indeed, in many of the places just mentioned, Aborigines had begun to adapt to alien authority only in the last eight to twenty years. The state challenge to mission authority was shockingly explicit when police arrested Pallottine missionaries at Beagle Bay and Lombadina. After an appeal by Archbishop Mannix, some were paroled and allowed to remain at these missions, while others were confined to a Roman Catholic institution in Melbourne. The government appointed observers to live at Beagle Bay and at the Finke River Mission in Central Australia. The Lutheran Mission at Cape Bedford (north Queensland) was closed, its residents trucked south to the government settlement Woorabinda. Missionaries not displaced had to accommodate military authority. Drawing on Kalumburu's Benedictine diarists, Hall has suggested that RAAF employment challenged mission authority by offering labouring Aborigines goods 'without the accompanying religious instruction that many missionaries insisted upon'.[20] As well, servicemen tended to conduct themselves with less formality and social distance than many missionaries.[21] Hall generalises that most servicemen stationed in the Northern Territory brought 'new attitudes fashioned from the liberalism of the big cities'; they were 'free from any preconceived ideas about Aborigines, had no long term commitment to the Territory and no economic dependence on the exploitation of Aboriginal labour'.[22] Hall nonetheless gives several instances of dictatorial responses, and even killing, when Aborigines dared to assert themselves.[23]

Some missions were empowered by the sudden proximity of a well-financed RAAF that urgently needed labour; missionaries were practised in the marshalling of Aboriginal workers, and missions functioned as, in effect, labour brokers and advocates.[24] The RAAF's employment policy deferred to mission norms – 'natives should not be forced to work, but called on' – and, in the Northern Territory, to Native Affairs Branch standards of remuneration.[25]

While it is difficult to generalise about the degree to which authority in Native Labour camps broke with or continued established colonial authority, there is no doubt that many Aboriginal people experienced novel routines of care and command. Some labourers had not been employed before; others had been employed by civilian bosses (the Native Affairs Branch, pastoralists, private contractors) or by missions. The military concern for hygienic order and for adequate nutrition, particularly after the inception of centralised feeding in July 1943, lifted these compounds to levels of domestic discipline unknown in Territory institutions with Aboriginal residents.[26]

Some missionaries felt a loss of control as these labourers took to the new amenities. The Lutherans at Finke River Mission had been trying, since 1938, to limit the access of Arrernte to the pleasures of Alice Springs; cooperating with the Army, they helped recruit some Arrernte men and women to the Native Labour compound, even advising their rates of pay, while seeking to limit the Army's access to men and women less used to town pleasures. Pastor Albrecht later regretted that 'our natives, as a whole, were not prepared' for the cultural changes that labour camp residence stimulated; gambling, venereal disease, swearing and mixed messages about equality were among the effects of Army administration.[27] At Oenpelli in 1939 the Reverend Dick Harris, after explaining to the new Director of Native Affairs, E.W.P. Chinnery, his objections to paying for labour with tobacco (effects of sharing on health, induced dependency leading to prostitution), announced a 'no tobacco' policy. He gave Oenpelli residents three months' warning.[28] The visiting Anglican priest and linguist Arthur Capell hailed the no-tobacco policy as 'courageous', while Chinnery greeted this 'experiment' with interest, and the Oenpelli people met it with 'silence'. The policy was undermined during the war when Army and Air Force recreational visitors made free with tobacco. In response, the Oenpelli missionaries decided to issue tobacco, in the hope that they could determine the quantity in circulation.[29]

Pastoralists also had to reassess their hold over the men and women on whose country they ran their stock; the militarisation of the North made these workers less a captive labour force. Working for Harry Bloomfield on Love's Creek Station (east of Alice Springs) had become hard for Alec Kruger to endure by 1942; he looked to the army. 'The idea of getting equal pay was a shock for us all', he recalls in *Alone on the Soaks*. 'The local station owners and bosses were not happy about it.'[30] To get to the recruiting office, Kruger had to evade Bloomfield's oversight; local officials with little regard for Bloomfield were pleased to sign up Kruger. According to Kruger, Bloomfield began to pay his remaining workers better.[31] On Mornington Island, when war broke out, some young men at the Presbyterian Mission were restless and hoped for work and money on the mainland. Dick Roughsey and his friends borrowed a dugout canoe and paddled to a point on the mainland whence they could walk to Burketown. The police told them there were no jobs and put them on the first boat back to Mornington Island. Roughsey and his friends then killed a bullock. Recently the Aboriginal protector had punished such actions by expelling the culprits to Palm Island – a penalty that worried the mission's women but promised much to the men who observed it. 'They had to be fed while in jail,' Roughsey recalls thinking, 'and when they got out they had a chance of getting a job on cattle stations out from Townsville and Burketown.'[32] Perhaps the same exit to a wider world would open for him and his mates? He was disappointed. Even though the mission authorities reported the cattle killing to the Department of Native Affairs, no action was taken against the miscreants. Apparently, the demands of war-time administration were giving the department more to think about than a few purloined bullocks. Fortunately for Roughsey, the war was also luring white workers out of the beef industry. The Burketown police were soon approaching the mission, asking for young men to move to the mainland to work the cattle. Roughsey found employment that required him to learn to ride a horse: 'I had money in my pocket for the first time in my life.'[33]

With the disbanding of the Native Labour camps in 1946, Ronald and Catherine Berndt observed two contradictory emotions: Aboriginal people wished to return to their home country to be with kin, but they wondered whether they could fit back into the old working and living conditions. Some expressed attachment to the Army that had treated them with dignity, and they were proud of contributing to Australia's war victory. Many white people in the Northern Territory thought that the Army camps had undermined the authority of whites generally. In a letter to the Minister for the Interior, Archie Cameron MHR warned in January 1944 that station owners now feared that Aboriginal men would come back 'in an arrogant and insolent mood'.[34] The Berndts saw such apprehension in 'the overwhelming majority of European residents in the Northern Territory.'[35]

In the Southern regions of Australia, the demand for labour brought both opportunities and coercion. Opportunity came from movement into the cities, where employment and entertainment could be found. Official statistics do not allow a precise description of urban relocation in the 1940s, but one indicator is James Bell's account of the population of the Sydney suburban reserve La Perouse: from 1880 to 1930, it increased on average by 2.3 per cent per year; from 1931 to 1956, the average annual increase was 15.9 per cent.[36] Redfern's Aboriginal population also grew at this time. In Melbourne the Aboriginal population doubled during the war: some were wives accompanying enlisted husbands, others were job-seekers. One child at George Street (Fitzroy) Primary School recalls 100 Aboriginal children enrolled at that time. When their parents used Collingwood's Manchester Unity Hall for dances, it was affectionately renamed 'EMU Hall'.[37] Some Fitzroy councillors worried that the influx was concentrated in their neighbourhood.[38] Other cities seem not to have experienced war-time migration from rural regions. In Western Australia, the government discouraged such movement. To keep Aborigines in agricultural occupations that were losing white workers to enlistment or to other kinds of work, the government instructed police to monitor Aborigines and to send to Carrolup (a government institution opened in 1940 ostensibly to educate children) any person found in Perth without a job. The government discouraged enlistment because it deprived rural industries of Aboriginal labour and put unprecedented amounts of money into Aboriginal pockets.[39]

Enlistment and entitlement

Both Aborigines and governments were ambivalent – at least initially – about Aboriginal enlistment: it enacted community and signified entitlement, perturbing a racially stratified society. On the government side, in 1939 and for part of 1940, there was not a clear policy of exclusion. The *Defence Act* 1910 exempted from combat service persons not 'substantially of European origin or descent', but it permitted voluntary enlistment of non-Europeans. Some Aboriginal people who tried to enlist were rejected as illiterate or physically incapable. The authorities were also worried that white Australians would not like to serve alongside Aborigines. They recognised nonetheless that if the war's demands increased, Aborigines would have to be considered. In the RAAF, these high demands for men – even Aboriginal men – were felt first, but getting Aborigines into the Army and the Navy was much more difficult. From 1940, the position of the government was clarified, though not made public: no Aboriginal people were supposed to be recruited to the Army and the Navy.[40]

That there were already some obviously Aboriginal soldiers (and possibly sailors?) presented an opportunity to champion their citizenship. The prominent New South Wales activist Pearl Gibbs claimed in her radio broadcast, 8 June 1941: 'I want you to remember that men of my race served in the Boer War. More so in the 1914–18 War and today hundreds of full-bloods, near full-bloods and half-castes are overseas with the AIF.'[41] The government found itself in a contradiction: were not *all* Australians both eligible and obliged to serve that cause? It became evident (even without official records of 'race') that a steady trickle of Aboriginal Australians was joining up. When the

Army discharged Aborigines, those in sympathy with Aboriginal enlistment suspected that these men were 'unfit' only in being Aboriginal. By mid-1941, Aboriginal people and their supporters were realising that the path to citizenship that ran through military service was being blocked. The Army agreed that some 'part-Aborigines' would be permitted to enlist, if the medical inspectors and recruitment officers judged an individual to be suited to living on close terms with whites – but not 'full-bloods'. These revised regulations were classified as 'secret'. Not only was the public not told of them, but some civilians working in recruitment centres were not allowed to know either. The most threatening period of the war, for Australia, was from December 1941 until June 1942, when the Japanese advanced through the south-west Pacific and South-East Asia with frightening speed and ease (until they lost a decisive naval battle against the United States in June 1942). Could Australia afford a racially selective defence policy? Torres Strait Islanders – on the northern frontline – were treated with more respect. In June 1941 the Army began to recruit an all-Islander unit to help garrison the Strait.[42]

Those advocating segregated Aboriginal units thought that making the military service of Aborigines conspicuous would spread acceptance of Aborigines. In 1940, William Ferguson, president of the Aborigines Progressive Association, wrote to the prime minister asking for 'an Aboriginal Division, composed entirely of men with Aboriginal blood, and the nurses be the same, and trained only by white officers'.[43] In 1942, the Association for the Protection of Native Races, of which A.P. Elkin was president, lobbied for the 'formation of a battalion entirely composed of aborigines, so that all of them who desired to enlist would be enabled to do so, even if difficulties do occur when black men and white are in the same camps'.[44] Although an all-Aboriginal unit of large numbers was never assembled, the AIF did create a small 'all Aboriginal squad', which, as Elkin and others predicted, received press attention. A war-time newsreel featuring the squad declared: 'ABORIGINES ARE THE TRUE SOLDIERS OF THE KING! ... They come from Australia's oldest family. They've got a fighting tradition thousands of years old. In the battle dress of the soldier of 1941 ...With bayonets instead of the spears their forefathers carried.'[45]

The Melbourne *Herald* noted that Aborigines matched whites not only in loyalty but also in ability; war was lifting them 'to the standard of his white brethren'.[46] In the Northern Territory, any 'half-caste' who enlisted was exempted from the *Aboriginals Ordinance*.

A war of democrats against Nazis and Fascists created a space for revaluation of Australia's racial hierarchy. In 1940, the Commonwealth Department of Information was 'unable to ascertain' whether there was any truth to the rumour that Hitler himself had 'taunted Great Britain as to her treatment of minorities in the case of Australian Aborigines'.[47] The Committee for Aboriginal Citizenship reasoned that 'as we are at war to uphold democracy we do consider that democracy should begin at home in Australia'.[48] In October 1941 a trade union that included staff of hotel bars presented Western Australia's chief protector with a dilemma: should they serve alcohol to Aboriginal servicemen? If they did, they broke the law; if they did not, then they faced violent challenge from the white mates of the Aboriginal soldiers.[49]

The experiences of the Victorian Banjo Clarke (born 1922) illustrate the new possibilities of fraternity. At the outbreak of war, a recruiting officer in Fitzroy persuaded him and his mate Herb to join the Allied Works Council, instead of the Army.

They found themselves in Brisbane, where black American soldiers welcomed their company. Posted to a road-building camp, Clarke soon was unjustly accused by his overseer of creating a drunken row that had kept many men awake overnight. When he was told he must transfer to another gang (dismissal was not an option), his workmates offered to strike. Clarke declined their offer, only later reflecting on 'how momentous it was'. Had he stayed and enabled the strike, he rued, 'It might have taught the people of Australia not to do whatever they liked to someone just because they was [sic] Aboriginal.'[50] Clarke found Queensland pubs unwelcoming at first, though he was served on the basis that, as a Victorian Aborigine, he was not covered by Queensland laws. The publican who explained that nice legal point to him became his friend. At a dance in Woolooga he was accosted and pushed down some stairs by a white American soldier. Clarke replied with fists and was pleasantly surprised that the dance crowd seemed to back him. Queensland might have been racist, he reflected, but it included 'people what [sic] will side with you if you do the same work as they do'.[51]

The war compelled unprecedented mobility across Australia. The Northern Territory's 'half-caste' children were sent to Southern regions of Australia, to Otford and Mulgoa (NSW), Carrieton and Balaklava (SA) – a transformative upheaval. Adult 'half-castes' such as Hilda Jarman Muir were also on the move. With her three children she left Darwin and arrived in Brisbane in January 1942, a month before the bombing of Darwin. Before the war, Muir had lived in Darwin for eleven years, having been removed from the Borroloola area at the age of eight to live in the Kahlin Compound. Aged sixteen, she had her first child. She and her husband, Billy, were among the many 'coloured people' living in makeshift housing at 'Police Paddock' (now the suburb of Stuart Park) when war started. Billy had been a member of a 'half-caste' delegation to the Administration in 1936, claiming citizenship for 'half-castes'; the Administration had amended the *Aboriginals Ordinance* to allow exemption of selected 'half-castes'. Having joined the Citizen Military Force before the war, he was called into the AIF to guard Darwin's infrastructure; he became a platoon leader.[52] But Hilda had to leave; she went to Brisbane because Billy's foster mother, Sarah, was already there.

Brisbane's size and material abundance exhilarated Hilda. 'In Brisbane I had to go into the world,' she recalls.[53] 'Like a fairy godmother', Sarah showed Hilda the city.[54] At her hostel accommodation in Wynnum/Manly, she felt too shy, at first, to mix with other evacuees. Sarah soon found a house in Bowen Hills that was large enough for two mothers and their children, and the children went to school in Fortitude Valley. Later, they moved to Milton 'with lovely old Aboriginal people'.[55] Hilda's account of Brisbane is a story of her emergence as a confident young woman. For some of that Brisbane time, she was joined by her sister Bridget, whose ship voyage from Darwin had been traumatic. Hilda mentored Bridget in city life, as Sarah had mentored her. Their Bowen Hills household was increased by the arrival of two old Filipino people: 'I don't know where they turned up from, but … Sarah hated to see anyone left out.'[56] Hilda and her evacuee network, receiving letters in Brisbane, knew more than officials were allowing them to know about the bombing of Darwin: 'in Brisbane we were cut off. We were safe living there, but the War still scared us.'[57]

At the end of the war, with Billy Muir demobbed, Hilda found that she was 'a city slicker now and I liked the big city with good shops, trams and buses'.

It was such a good life with the shops, people I knew, and my new friends. The kids were doing well at school and they had friends there, too. After the freedom of the big city, I didn't like the idea of a small place. But I had no choice: my husband wanted me back in Darwin.[58]

Because her husband's work postings took them to rural parts of the Top End (Billy worked for the Department of Native Affairs at the Aboriginal settlement Delissaville), the children had to be left in the care of Darwin's Retta Dixon Home, to receive schooling. Hilda recalls being restless, 'lonely and missing my children'.[59] Billy Muir arranged for her to have domestic help – 'a beautiful old Larrakia woman'. That this helper was deaf and dumb limited her companionship. Hilda eventually persuaded her husband to get a transfer closer to town, but their home was not in Darwin, where she wanted to be, but at Berrimah. Whereas Billy worked outside the home and had plenty of male companionship in the evenings, Hilda found herself repeatedly pregnant and living in substandard accommodation on Darwin's periphery. Her demobilisation, so to speak, was her disappointment. 'The evacuation had shown me that I could live in a big city.'[60] Hilda Muir was not the only person for whom return to the North was not a straightforward transition. The return of the evacuated children also became an issue, as some newspapers questioned whether remote missions were fit to train them for joining the wider community.[61]

From World War to Cold War

The ideals of the victorious Allies' Atlantic Charter, elaborated in the formation of the United Nations and in the writing of the

Universal Declaration of Human Rights (1948), implicitly reproached Australia's colonial hierarchy. Commenting on lobbying by the United Nations Association of Australia in 1949, the Administrator of the Northern Territory, A.R. Driver, acknowledged the recent and growing influence of United Nations ideals on 'Australian consciousness' and, he claimed, on government practice.[62] Driver's internal briefing points to intra-governmental anxiety not to be caught out as white Australia adjusted to the demands of liberal capitalism's global triumph. As Australia moved from victory over the Axis powers to Cold War with Soviets, uneasy responses to liberal reproach could quickly turn into suspicion that the champions of the human rights of Aborigines were dupes of Communists and even, perhaps, Communists themselves. The magistrate F.E.A. Bateman – asked to review Western Australia's Aboriginal affairs in 1948 – attributed the unexpected persistence of the Pilbara Aborigines' mobilisation to Communist influence. However, he also conceded grounds for grievance: low wages, and poor food and accommodation. He had heard that the strikers' restlessness was spreading to Derby. To counter Communist influence among Aborigines, he argued, the state must set and enforce standards for employers (minimum wage, with margins for better workers, clothes, accommodation and amenities).[63]

The Cold War, like World War II, altered the way that Australians considered the remote homelands of Indigenous Australians. In November 1946, the Chifley government made an agreement with Great Britain to host the testing of experimental guided projectiles and pilotless supersonic aircraft. A sector of Australia's Western Desert, stretching north-west from the centre of South Australia to the Pilbara coast, would become a 'rocket range'. To observe the projectiles' trajectory, it would be necessary to grade roads through the Western Desert and to build and staff depots within the Central Australian reserves.[64] This proposal fuelled discussion of the rationale of remote reserves.

Inviolable reserves had their champions. In 1941, Norman Tindale, ethnologist at the South Australian Museum, had argued that Western Desert people should retain the option of having little or no contact with outsiders.

> Isolation of desert aborigines would favour their survival; the whole of the desert steppe should be set apart for them. The desert folk need only intermittent care of an itinerant medical missioner; the formation of fixed settlements and rationing depots among them disrupts their economy.[65]

Tindale had imagined, reasonably, that pastoralism was the land use that was most likely to encroach on the desert reserves, but now the Cold War spawned another: weapons testing. The scientists and defence chiefs who advocated this new use for the Western Desert knew that the originating ideal of the reserve as an inviolable sanctuary had lost credibility – in part because of actions by reserve residents themselves. Seeking access to the colonists' goods, some Aborigines had moved from northwest South Australia south to Ooldea soakage, from 1917, after the construction of the transcontinental railway. Daisy Bates had rationed and dispensed medicines to 300–400 people at Ooldea between 1919 and 1935; the United Aborigines Mission had commenced there in 1934, an evangelism that sought to extinguish Aboriginal ways.[66] In the 1920s, some people from the southern parts of the Central Reserves had moved west to Laverton, Mount Margaret, Kalgoorlie and Wiluna; others had gone east to Oodnadatta. Such migrations justified asking: can reserves protect if people emigrate from them?

Those who thought that reserves must be continued were quick to respond to government's first acknowledgment, in November 1945, that a Western Desert rocket range was under discussion.[67] By August 1946, one of the founders of Ernabella mission, Dr Charles Duguid, was pointing to the range's most intrusive feature – not falling projectiles but three planned observation stations. He proposed an alternative firing point – Mt Eba – so that the range would extend to the west of the reserves, not through them. Critics of the rocket range included the Australian Government Workers' Association (SA Branch); the National Missionary Council; the Bishop of Newcastle; the Australian Women's Charter; the Intervarsity Fellowship of Evangelical Unions, the Women's Christian Temperance Union; Sir Gilbert Murray (who wrote a letter to the London *Times*); and the Communist Party of Australia (CPA). The *Argus* suspected the CPA of being the orchestrator of this alliance.[68] Jean Blackburn, an independent Victorian member of the House of Representatives, was a lone parliamentary critic of the rocket range; she cited emerging international codes of social justice.[69] Anthropologist Donald Thomson, while conceding the need for weapons testing, argued that the rocket range would be a fatal invasion, repeating the 'fate of the Tasmanians' and the attrition of the Victorian Aboriginal population.[70] On the other side, the Aborigines' Friends' Association claimed that Aborigines would welcome continued association with the military, and some argued that Aborigines, like other Australians, would be more secure if research on weapons went ahead.[71]

It was not possible to insist that the reserves be totally inviolable. Duguid himself saw reserves as a way to manage and limit contact: Ernabella Mission was intended as a buffer, on the eastern edge of the Central Australian Reserve, where hunter-gatherers exchanged dingo scalps for western goods, to sustain their hunting economy, 'the first white contact with the [Pitjantjatjara] natives'.[72] During World War II, when Duguid was unable to visit, the mission was sometimes said to be intervening too little. The residents, albeit transient, were judged by some observers to be unclean and underfed, and some observers questioned whether teachers should instruct children only in their own tongue, failing to equip them for the increasing contact with whites occasioned by their parents' ventures east.[73] Such carefully moderated contact had kept the Pitjantjatjara 'fully tribal' – a good thing, in Duguid's view.[74] He complained that the rocket range's graded roads and staffed observation posts would detribalise reserve dwellers.

Keen to show that it had Aborigines' interests at heart, the government's Guided Projectiles Committee co-opted native welfare officials (from South Australia, W.R. Penhall; Western Australia, A.O. Neville; Northern Territory, F.H. Moy) and Professor A.P. Elkin. The committee also invited Duguid and Thomson to the committee's meeting on 31 January 1947. Elkin proved invaluable to the committee and to Dedman. To placate critics, Elkin advised, Dedman should promise that there would be no roads through reserves, a minimal labour force to construct air strips, no warheads on the rockets (unless 'useless sandhills' were the target), no atomic testing, no forced relocation of Aborigines, minimal staffing of observation posts (by persons of 'reliability and good character'), patrol officers to keep Aborigines from contact with non-Aborigines, and no interference with sacred places.[75]

Elkin's willingness to accept the rocket range was consistent with his wider revisionist argument, initiated in 1932, that 'protection' had been, effectively, a policy of neglect.[76] Reserves were not preventing detribalisation because curious Aborigines were leaving them. In 1944, he wrote that 'the preservation of Aboriginal culture in its pre-European form, even in the isolated regions, is impossible, and policies which emphasize segregation with this end in view are one hundred and fifty-six years out of date'. Reserves could help only to control 'the rate of contact and change ... they must not be places of protection; they must be training and preparation places'.[77] Throughout the 1940s Elkin was developing the concept 'intelligent parasitism' to describe the Aboriginal tendency to access non-Aborigines' material culture without allowing themselves to be affected by the ideals, habits, outlook and morality of the providers of those goods. A constructive policy would treat intelligent parasitism as a problem to be overcome rather than accept it as a mutually convenient accommodation, he argued in January 1947. The Army had modelled constructive engagement with Northern Territory Aborigines, he wrote. '[T]he war has changed the whole aboriginal situation. All aborigines have been in contact with us and we cannot keep them as they were. Any policy that savours of segregation is doomed by the aborigines themselves.'[78]

Elkin's historical perspective on reserves was conducive to the position taken by the Guided Projectiles Committee after hearing Duguid and Thomson express their views on 31 January 1947; the reserves were failing to prevent Aborigines' detribalisation; the intrusion of rocket range personnel could be managed by appointing patrol officers. The impact of the rocket range would be only 'the putting forward of the clock regarding the detribalization by possibly a generation ... the acceleration of the detribalization which is now taking place'.[79]

In considering how 'reserves' could continue to be a tool of humane policy, Elkin, Duguid and Thomson shared more ground than is apparent from their opposed views on the rocket range.[80] Like Duguid, Elkin thought that reserve intrusion should be limited to small numbers of carefully chosen people; and, like Elkin, Thomson was not opposed to involving Aboriginal land and labour in the defence of the nation. Although Thomson had advised the Commonwealth government in 1939 to continue to treat Arnhem Land as an 'inviolable' reserve, conceding missions to be a 'buffer', only on the reserve's edge, the perceived threat of Japanese invasion had persuaded Thomson to undertake his own militarising intervention into a reserve.[81] Thomson had joined the RAAF and spent part of 1940 organising Pacific Island coast watchers in the Solomon Islands. Confident that he had good relationships with Yolngu, he had soon advocated a similar force in their reserve, and the Australian Army gave him permission in September 1941. In 1941–43, he had led the Northern Territory Special Reconnaissance Unit (NTSRU), training the residents of Arnhem Land Reserve (Yolngu) to observe and perhaps kill any Japanese who set foot in Arnhem Land. Thomson had wanted the NTSRU not 'to interfere drastically with Yolngu cultural development'.[82] He had formally enlisted only one Yolngu – Raiwalla, his guide in his earlier Arnhem Land trips. He had rewarded his corps with gifts, not service pay.[83] Like the local missionaries, Thomson had not taken Yolngu loyalty for granted, and there was much to explain to Yolngu. Their relatives had been gaoled, ten years before, for killing Japanese; now it would be the duty of Yolngu to kill any Japanese they found.[84] Thomson had appealed not to their patriotism – for Yolngu had no conception of Australia as a nation to which they belonged as British subjects – but to their prudent calculation that Australia was much stronger than Japan and thus that Yolngu would in future have to deal with white not 'yellow' men.[85] To quell the enmities among the warriors themselves, he had required them to perform *makarrata* – ritual combat (sometimes bloody) to extinguish grievances. His squad's drills were basic and minimal, each warrior's weapons simple: 'one spear thrower, three fighting spears, one wire fish spear, and – whenever possible for hunting – tomahawks, fish lines, and hooks'.[86] His one concession to modern armoury had been the Molotov cocktail. In 1942 and early 1943, the NTSRU had constructed two observation posts – one at the entrance to Roper River, the other in Caledon Bay; they had also patrolled the coast in the *Aroetta*.

Thomson later reported to the Army that with the support of the older men he had established a 'sense of pride in service' and 'shame in the idea of breaking faith in the undertaking that they had agreed to complete'.[87] When he had discovered pilfering of supplies from one of the depots, he had told the Yolngu that such acts had humiliated him, and he had thus persuaded his most trusting supporters to help him punish those who had stolen: 'hard labour in the garden' and 'a payment of a large number of fish', a canoe, spears, and no hunting for a while.[88] Thomson's authority had derived not only from his understanding of Yolngu norms of shame and restitution, but also from his mobile clinics using medicines that the Army had supplied, as 'many people, especially the children, suffered from yaws and from many other tropical diseases'.[89] The treatments for yaws had worked quickly, cultivating 'the faith of the people'.[90] Drawing on Thomson's account, Riseman has concluded that, in his militarisation of the Yolngu, Thomson had 'work[ed] within the Yolngu customary framework'.[91] Thomson's practice in Arnhem Land foreshadowed thoughtful militarisation of remote Aboriginal homelands, and the debate over the rocket range was won by those who argued that thoughtful intervention, not segregation, was the humane way to use Aboriginal reserves.

The rocket range itself turned out to be a relatively minor source of harm to Western Desert Aborigines: only one projectile fragmented in flight into debris landing within the reserve, and only one observation post was built – Giles Weather Station, in Western Australia, and not until 1956. The greater intrusion on the Western Desert was what Elkin had advised Dedman, in 1946–47, to rule out if he wished to win the debate on the rocket range: the explosion of nuclear bombs. The British government exploded two devices on Aboriginal homelands at Emu Field in 1953 and seven at Maralinga in 1956–57. The purpose of the Giles Weather Station, commencing in August 1956, was to gauge upper atmospheric wind directions and speeds, to predict the pathway of the explosions' radioactive plumes.

Just as mission intervention in the remote 'North' had brought into Southern view the fishing, pearling and pastoral frontiers of remote Australia, so the rocket range brought witnesses to the Western Desert. Patrol Officer Walter MacDougall, formerly a mission worker at Kunmunya and Ernabella, was appointed by the Commonwealth in November 1947, working under the direction of the Western Australian and South Australian governments. Ron Macaulay was appointed in 1956, to add to MacDougall's efforts. Their surveillance focused on the numbers, location and health of people whose country was in the Central Reserves and in the 'open spaces' not designated 'reserve' but now zoned for nuclear fallout. MacDougall's reports in 1951–52 pointed out to his employers the physical limits of his surveillance. What he did *not* know mattered: in 1952, when the government was deciding on the 'Emu' test site for the 'Totem' series of explosions, he could not completely account for the numbers and whereabouts of those between Ooldea and the Northern Territory border.[92]

It took many years for the Australian public to learn what the Cold War had demanded of the Western Desert Aborigines. The 1985 Royal Commission into the British nuclear tests in Australia concluded that the region of the Emu test site was 'not adequately monitored'.[93] It further concluded that Aboriginal people at Wallatinna Station (not within the reserve) had experienced radioactive fallout from the Emu site explosion 'Totem 1', in the form of a 'black mist'. Subsequent tests ('Buffalo' series) at the Maralinga site had affected Western Desert people who nomadically occupied the country between Ooldea (no longer a mission/reserve since 1952) and the Central Reserves: the tests poisoned the land surface, making it dangerous, for thousands of years, to roam the country for food. Perhaps there were even worse effects. We do not know. According to the Royal Commission, 'the attempts to ensure Aboriginal safety during the Buffalo series demonstrate ignorance, incompetence and cynicism on the part of those responsible for [their] safety … [I]f Aborigines were not injured or killed as a result of the explosions, this was a matter of luck.'[94]

At the time of the tests, however, there was controversy about whether the people of the Western Desert were receiving due care. The Western Australian state parliamentarian William Grayden, having visited the Western Australian portion of the Central Reserves in 1953 and 1955, persuaded his parliament in 1956 to appoint a committee to investigate reserve residents' conditions of life. In February 1957, with the Yorta Yorta pastor Doug Nicholls, Grayden made a documentary that included shocking images of malnourished Aboriginal people in the vicinity of Warburton Mission. The film (*Their Darkest Hour*, also screened as *Manslaughter*) circulated at the same time as his book *Adam and Atoms* (1957), though the book included reports not only from the Grayden Committee but also from investigators who disputed whether Western Desert people were as badly off as the film portrayed.[95] The interventions recommended by the Grayden Report included: investment in pastoral production; a road connecting Giles Weather Station and Warburton Mission; assisting mothers to look after multiple births; increase government subsidy to the mission; bi-annual medical and dental surveys; more resources for pre-school and primary education.[96] The Commonwealth, having contributed to the disruption of Western Desert people's lives, was obliged to assist Western Australia financially, Grayden argued.

Militarisation and assimilation

Australia's mobilisation for World War II and then for the Cold War provoked a revaluation of remote Aborigines and their lands and added impetus to the trend in policy thinking away from 'protection' (was it not neglect, denial of citizenship?) and towards 'assimilation' (the nation's responsibility, the Aborigines' right). While Hasluck was right to recall the war years as a 'hiatus' in Aboriginal affairs debate, Australia's war against the Axis powers and Cold War against the Communists contributed to a rethinking of the future of remote regions that were still effectively under Indigenous governance. The remote Aborigines entered into the consciousness of the wider Australian public as an inescapable responsibility, in a series of steps in the twenty-five years 1934–59. First, in response to the Caledon Bay affair, there was public debate about the reach of law and order, followed by government-backed scientific investigation (by

Donald Thomson) into Arnhem Land 1934–39: how to extend effective government control into that region in order to minimise destructive exposure to the world outside? Second, the perceived threat of Japanese invasion brought the people native to the entire North coast into focus: were they loyal to Australia? How could they be useful in defence? In the final step, the militarisation of the Western Desert brought attention to the people of the desert interior: was not intervention into (if not 'violation' of) their reserve a national responsibility? In this sequence of confrontations with the 'remote', the tension between protective segregation and benevolent intervention animated debate among concerned non-Indigenous Australians. Respectful distance began to seem more like heartless neglect.

The mandate to 'assimilate' was easy to promote when the imagined 'Aborigine' was close to the Southern public, a mixed-descent figure on the edge of town, so to speak, who had proved himself or herself as a loyal and capable citizen in the military and in the war economy. A mandate to assimilate the remote people was more elusive: were they perishing from our neglect or, by their own standards, surviving through our considerate distance? Was welfare to be their saviour or their well-intentioned destroyer?

The public seems to have been divided about how to deal with those labelled 'remote' and 'tribal'. The first public opinion poll ever taken on an issue of Aboriginal policy was conducted in February 1947, by the Australian Gallup Poll. When asked to consider those Aborigines who were still 'living in their native state' or 'tribal', respondents were divided evenly about whether government responsibility lay in 'helping Aborigines to live their tribal lives' (47 per cent) or in 'educating them towards white standards' (46 per cent). Ten years later, in February 1957, the pollster asked an almost identical question: 'In your opinion, should we help the aboriginals in Central Australia live their tribal lives, or educate them to live like white men?' The word 'tribal' linked this question to its predecessor. Again, opinion was evenly divided, 47 per cent preferring that Aborigines be left in their 'tribal' condition, and 45 per cent wanting them educated to live like 'white men'. It seems that notwithstanding the humanitarian plea that even the remotest nomad was Australia's responsibility, one in two Australians said that 'assimilation' should not (or could not?) apply to a certain category of Aborigine – 'tribal' people.[97] The two polls can be interpreted as indicating the persistence, in the face of arguments for 'assimilation', of an older understanding that remote regions (including 'reserves') should continue as inviolable 'sanctuaries' for tribal people.

7

Towards racial equality

The constitutional referendum conducted on 27 May 1967 was a popular expression of inclusive egalitarianism. Over 90 per cent of voters agreed to change two clauses of the Constitution that were understood to discriminate against Aborigines and Torres Strait Islanders. Section 51(xxvi) prohibited the Australian parliament making laws for '[t]he people of any race, *other than the aboriginal race*'. Deleting the words in italics gave the Commonwealth power to intervene in the 'Aboriginal affairs' policies of any state. Though the campaign for a 'Yes' vote projected that the Commonwealth would use this power to overcome the many disadvantages suffered by Indigenous Australians, it did not seek a mandate for any specific laws or policies. The Australian government has seldom used this power, wary of state political backlash against interference by 'Canberra'; it has even used the power to Indigenous Australians' disadvantage.[1] The Commonwealth has influenced state policies less by exercising the 'concurrent power' conferred in 1967 and more by its specific purpose grants to state governments, under powers possessed before 1967. The referendum also deleted section 127: '[I]n reckoning the numbers of people of the Commonwealth ... aboriginal natives shall not be counted.' Deleting these words did not enable the Census to count 'aboriginal natives': Aborigines had been enumerated or estimated since the first Commonwealth Census in 1901. Removing section 127 allowed Census data on 'full-bloods' to be taken into account when the 'reckoning' of what each state is entitled to relies on a comparison of state populations: House of Representative electorates; shares in federal finance.

Much of the legislation that denied rights to Aborigines and Torres Strait Islanders was under state powers; state governments had repealed or substantially amended most of these laws by 1967. For example, four states had amended their laws restricting access to alcohol: New South Wales and South Australia in 1963, Western Australia in 1964 and Queensland in 1965. The constitutional changes of 1967 did not grant citizenship to Aborigines and Torres Strait Islanders, as the *Nationality and Citizenship Act* 1948 had made citizens of all born in Australia after 26 January 1949. The false memory that the 1967 referendum extinguished racial discrimination by making citizens of Aborigines and Torres Strait Islanders has obscured the fact that, before 1967, the Commonwealth government had dealt three blows against formal racial inequality: entitling Indigenous Australians to vote (1962), to receive welfare payments (1941–59) and to be paid at the same minimum wage rates as applied to other employees (1966).

Social security – the states lobby for change

When passing the *Invalid and Old Aged Pensions Act* in 1908, the Australian parliament refused pensions to 'Asiatics and natives of Australia, New Zealand, Africa and the Pacific Islands'. In 1959, amendments to the *Social Services Act* 1959 modified restrictions on the eligibility of Aborigines for old age, widow and invalid pensions, for unemployment and sickness benefits, for maternity allowances and child endowment; from that date, only 'nomadic or primitive' Aborigines were ineligible, because they could not be identified or because they had no fixed address.[2] These impediments ceased to be effective by 1975. Indigenous Australians gradually became entitled to welfare, with very little public debate.

Welfare payments to Indigenous Australians had become a topic of discussion among Australian governments by the late 1930s. Indigenous activists in 1940 asked 'that Aborigines who have lived and worked all their lives among the white people be granted the same social services, pensions and maternity bonuses as the white citizen'.[3] Under Commonwealth policy at that time, a person was not entitled to welfare payments if he or she were supported by a state or territory 'native welfare' or mission administration. However, from the 1920s states' support for Indigenous Australians began to take two forms: as well as issuing goods in kind (rations and houses, on a supervised settlement) to Aborigines or Torres Strait Islanders, states began to pay some people benefits as if they were part of the wider population of deserving people. The Lang government in New South Wales had not excluded Aborigines from the state widows' pension (in 1925) and family endowment (in 1927). Family endowment in New South Wales went directly to Aboriginal mothers.[4] When Queensland established compulsory unemployment insurance for seasonal workers, with contributions from workers, employers and the state, exclusions applied only to those 'native of Asia, Africa, or the Pacific Islands'.[5] Accordingly, by the late 1920s, some Aboriginal people in New South Wales or Queensland were entitled to receive not only the institutional support of the state government in which they lived (rations, housing) but also mainstream welfare benefits. During the Depression, unemployed Aboriginal people had 'uneven' access to sustenance payments (administered by the states) and were not as 'explicitly excluded' as they had been from aged pensions and maternity allowances (administered by the Commonwealth).[6]

The states saw the national welfare system as a potential source of money to buttress their straitened budgets for native welfare. Although the Australian Constitution did not forbid Commonwealth expenditure on Indigenous Australians who lived under state government supervision, the Commonwealth wished to limit spending on pensions, and public servants upheld the convention that a client of a state native welfare bureaucracy could not be paid social security by the Commonwealth. While it was arguably in the states' financial interest to question this exclusion, it was not possible for 'protectors' to present Indigenous Australians as entitled to cash welfare payments as long as state governments assumed that Indigenous Australians were incompetent in the use of cash, even cash they earned as employees. That is, the governments of Queensland, New South Wales, Western Australia and South Australia compelled employers of 'protected' persons to pay all or some of their wages into government-run trust funds, so that protectors could regulate individual spending. Even those pressing for Indigenous people's citizenship rights agreed that (in the words of William Cooper to Robert Menzies in 1939) 'many are not able to understand these matters and [are] as little able to benefit from them'.[7] William Ferguson distinguished between the entitlements of 'wild' and 'educated' Aborigines.[8] The trust funds were based on the reasonable fear that those new to money would be tricked and exploited in their unsupervised use of it.[9]

If Australian governments were to consider which Indigenous Australians – if any – might be paid a pension, they needed a criterion of social advancement. In 1939, E.W.P. Chinnery, a recognised expert in 'native affairs', advised the Commonwealth that a worthy Indigenous recipient should be 'capable of exercising the privileges and of fulfilling the obligations of citizenship'; 'of proved good character, vouched for by a reputable and responsible European'; 'capable of earning his own living ... he should not be a permanent dependent inmate of an Aboriginal institution. He should also be living in the manner of a European'; and 'he should have the capacity for education ... [and] be reasonably intelligent and able to read and write if possible', though literacy was not essential.[10] In 1940, Sir Frederick Stewart (a minister in the Menzies government) told the acting Commissioner for Pensions, T.A. Maguire, to consider ways to give maternity allowance and old age pensions to Aborigines 'living the complete European life'.[11] In response, Maguire drew in part on the idea of genetic determination of capacity: pensioned Aborigines would have to be less than 50 per cent Aboriginal descent and not living on a pastoral station, mission or state reserve. Maguire added that they would also have to be eligible to enrol to vote in Commonwealth elections. To apply these criteria would limit the charge on the Australian government while continuing states' rights to judge Indigenous capacities; the *Commonwealth Franchise Act* 1902 denied the vote to any 'aboriginal native of Australia, Africa, Asia or the Islands of the Pacific except New Zealand' *unless they were enfranchised by the State in which they lived*.

However, states could choose to relax their protective grip on Indigenous Australians: their criteria for judging capacity could put less emphasis on a person's 'blood' (or descent) and more on a person's perceived level of social development. As I have argued, the relative significance of 'blood' and 'culture' was an unstable part of official thinking, as all native welfare administrations were learning from experience that people's needs and behaviour could not be predicted merely by calculating their degree of Aboriginal descent. A Commonwealth welfare benefit might be awarded if the person (or her husband) had militarily served his country; refusing such claim on the basis of 'caste' could seem embarrassingly unfair. Even without a war service record, a person's social development — that is, their perceived ability to benefit from deciding for themselves how to spend money — was becoming more salient in official thinking, as governments acknowledged that Aboriginal people were not dying out but were, indeed, a proliferating charge on state governments.

The rapid reformation of the Australian welfare state in the 1940s further undermined the convention that a national government should not pay social security benefits to a person 'protected' by a state government. After considering a contributory national insurance scheme in the late 1930s, the Menzies government and then the Curtin and Chifley governments introduced a series of tax-funded benefits: child endowment in 1941, widow pension in 1942, maternity allowance and funeral benefits in 1943, unemployment and sickness benefits in 1945, and pharmaceutical, hospital and tuberculosis benefits in 1944–45. When the Australian government introduced a child endowment payment in 1941, its primary motive was to dampen wages growth in a war-time economy. However, Aboriginal mothers were eligible because, politically, a national child endowment scheme could not be less supportive than the most supportive of the state policies that it subsumed, and New South Wales had been paying family endowment to Aboriginal mothers on reserves. 'Ignored and included by default in family allowances in New South Wales', Murphy has pointed out, 'this was the first time Aboriginal Australians were positively included in welfare benefits.'[12] Murphy quotes the New South Wales and Western Australian premiers pushing the Commonwealth in 1941 to agree that only mothers classed as 'nomadic' – that is, beyond any white authority's supervision – should be ineligible for child endowment.[13] The *Child Endowment Act* 1941 empowered institutions to receive 'child endowment' payments in respect of the children that they were feeding and housing (whether or not those children had their mothers with them).

However, some Aboriginal mothers and children were not living on a mission or supervised reserve. Their applications for child endowment raised the question: who will supervise the recipient mother? Should it be a post office official, a policeman, a pastoralist, a state's trust fund? In New Zealand, where the same question had arisen after the introduction of a family allowance in 1939, storekeepers were the state's first choice of supervisor of the Maori mother, but by 1945 the *Maori Social and Economic Advancement Act* 1945 formalised the supervisory role of the Maori welfare officers who had proven themselves worthy of that role by their contribution to the Maori war effort.[14] The Commonwealth saw New South Wales' practice as the model: state officials would decide whether a mother should receive child endowment in cash or as goods purchased for her by the state. In May 1942, the Labor government led by John Curtin allowed missions to receive child endowment – effectively a state subsidy for church-governed 'native welfare'.[15]

Labor also amended the invalid and old age pensions and maternity allowances legislation so that these benefits could go to 'aboriginal natives of Australia who are living under civilized conditions, and whose character and intelligence qualify them to receive pensions' – words implying a judgment against standards set by some local authority (welfare official, missionary, local police) who could advise the Commissioner for Pensions.[16] In June 1942, the government set eligibility for the new widows' pension in the same terms. The judgment that a person was entitled to a pension paralleled the judgment that an 'Aboriginal native' could be exempt from the laws of 'protection'. Exemption was available to those deemed worthy in Queensland (since 1901), in Western Australia (since 1936), in the Northern Territory (since 1936), in South Australia (since 1939); New South Wales introduced 'exemption' in 1943 and Western Australia revised procedures and criteria of exemption in 1944. Tasmania did not then recognise an 'Aboriginal' population.

The war economy and postwar reconstruction policies of the 1940s increased the national government's share of taxation revenue. States thus had even more reason to agitate for Commonwealth financial support. A.P. Elkin backed the states' and the missions' lobbying for Aborigines and Torres Strait Islanders to get social security. At the 1948 conference of Commonwealth and state welfare authorities, governments agreed that among residents of institutions there were people of different levels of social development and that the more competent should not have to leave their community to become eligible for a pension or unemployment benefit.[17] As Elkin remarked in support of this view, 'they cannot help being Aborigines at the same time as they become citizens'.[18] From 1951, annual meetings of a Native Welfare Council (all governments except Tasmania) continued to discuss eligibility for welfare payments. In May 1955 and May 1957 the National Health and Medical Research Council recommended that the Commonwealth Departments of Health, Territories and Social Services combine to review Aboriginal people's eligibility for Commonwealth benefits.[19] By the late 1950s some critics were arguing that to deny these entitlements breached Australia's human rights obligations.[20]

The Menzies government amended the *Social Services Act* in 1959, giving pensions and maternity allowances to Aboriginal people other than 'those who are nomadic and primitive'.[21] This reform added £1 million per year to the incomes of Indigenous Australians. The Minister for Social Services Hugh Roberton's cabinet submission had advocated a national approach to assessing eligibility, pointing out that no change in the Constitution was required for such 'a bold step – but not a rash step'.[22] However, we should note that the parliament did not discuss this reform as a major step in assimilation. Hasluck did not participate in the debate on the amendment, and those who did speak did not mention Aboriginal people – until Labor MP Gordon Bryant noted at the Bill's third reading (conventionally, a brief formality) that, by enlarging the discretion of the Director-General of Social Services 'to pay social services for aborigines to someone other than the aboriginal himself', the Act empowered the Commonwealth to begin treating Aboriginal people as individuals. Bryant continued: 'I hope that there will be a more vigorous application of the principle that the aboriginal should have his individual rights protected and be treated in the same way as we ourselves expect to be treated by such bodies as repatriation tribunals and the courts.'[23]

At first, many eligible Indigenous Australians may not have experienced their new status as anything more than a small cash payment from a missionary, state official or pastoralist. For example, in South Australia, the Aborigines Department received the pensions as a block grant from the Commonwealth and then disbursed money through individual trust accounts to which reserve superintendents also had access, to charge residents for food, electricity and firewood.[24] However, Bryant had discerned a significant change in the relationship of Indigenous individuals to government authority. In subsequent years, the *Annual Reports* of the Director-General of Social Services saw no reason to mention Aborigines as a category of recipient, other than a brief paragraph in 1966–67 saying that three references to 'aboriginal natives' that had remained in the Act after 1959 had been deleted lest the Act seem 'discriminatory'.[25] 'Nomads' were still outside the welfare net, but by 1975 decisions delegated to the Director-General (that is, not requiring further legislation) meant that the category 'nomad' no longer disqualified anyone. Including Aboriginal and Torres Strait Islander people in the welfare state was assimilation's quietest achievement.

Indigenous enfranchisement

Granting Indigenous Australians the right to vote aroused much more attention. In 1949, the Commonwealth had amended the *Commonwealth Electoral Act* to extend eligibility to an Aboriginal adult who 'is or has been a member of the Defence Force'. As well, the amendments allowed 'an aboriginal native of Australia' to enrol to vote if that person were 'entitled under the law of the State in which he resides to be enrolled as an elector of that State and, upon enrolment, to vote at elections for the more numerous House of the Parliament of that State (or, if there is only one House of the Parliament of that State, for that House)'. That is, the interaction of Commonwealth and some state legislation excluded certain Aboriginal people from voting in Commonwealth elections. Aborigines classed as 'wards' under the 1953 *Welfare Ordinance* were disqualified from voting in Northern Territory elections. There were 17 000 'wards' (not all of voting age). In practice, they were Aborigines classified as 'full-blood'; those of 'part aboriginal descent', exempt from wardship since 1953, were allowed to vote (but were not necessarily enrolled). In Queensland, the *Elections Act* 1915–59 disqualified those 'protected' as Aborigines and Torres Strait Islanders; a 'half-caste' was disqualified if he or she were 'an inmate of any institution for aboriginals, or an inmate of any mission station or like institution, or whether hired out for employment with an employer, and who, notwithstanding such hiring out, is still under the control and general supervision of the Protector of Aboriginals'.[26] In Western Australia, the *Electoral Act* 1907 had disqualified 'natives' as part of a wider exclusion of non-white people from the franchise. Subsequent laws had defined 'native' to include 'half-castes', while setting out an exemption procedure in the *Native (Citizenship Rights) Act* 1944–58. In all, the Select Committee estimated, 26 000 people of 'full-blood' and 4000 adults 'of preponderantly Aboriginal descent' were prohibited from voting in these three jurisdictions and so they were disqualified from voting in Commonwealth elections.[27]

To escape international criticism that Australian democracy was racially discriminatory the Commonwealth could have amended the Act to put Aboriginal people on the same footing as other Australians. This would have made their enrolment and voting compulsory, as voting had been compulsory for those entitled to vote in Commonwealth elections since 1924 and in all states after 1941. This solution to racial discrimination would have risked criminalising Indigenous Australians who were unprepared to exercise their rights to enrol and vote.

After canvassing scores of Aboriginal and Islander communities on the issue of compulsion, the Select Committee recommended that enrolment not be compulsory for 'aboriginal natives'. The Australian parliament amended the *Commonwealth Franchise Act* in 1962 to allow but not compel adults disqualified as 'aboriginal natives' to enrol to vote in Commonwealth elections.

Many of the 120 Indigenous Australians who spoke to the Select Committee approached the prospect of voting rights cautiously because 'citizenship' had become linked in their minds to certain models of behaviour and outlook about which they were ambivalent. Some revealed a lingering appreciation of ways of life afforded by 'protection'. Ruth Fink, an anthropologist working with Yamatji people (near Geraldton, WA), in 1955–57, had interviewed fifty-two people living in town camps or in stations; she had discovered such ambivalence. To qualify for the standard rights of citizenship, Western Australian 'natives' were obliged to supply two references from 'reputable citizens' and to convince a magistrate that, among other things, they had 'adopted the manner and habits of civilised life' over the previous two years; were not suffering from 'active leprosy, syphilis, granuloma or yaws'; and were persons 'of industrious habits', of 'good behaviour' and of 'good reputation'.[28] Because many applications had been refused, these people perceived exemption as difficult to obtain.

Of Fink's fifty-two interviewees, only three had citizenship rights. Of the remaining forty-nine, thirty-five said that they were not interested in pursuing citizenship rights, mostly because the law demanded that they dissolve 'tribal and native association except with respect to lineal descendants or native relations of the first degree'.[29] Fink asked people whether they would rather be white. The thirty-eight who said they'd prefer to be 'native' listed characteristics of their life that they valued: as natives they had fewer responsibilities ('white people are the boss'), could go where they liked in the bush, belonged to this country and felt free in the bush, were happier and had more fun than white people, were more easily satisfied than white people, got out of trouble more easily than whites, and didn't pay taxes. Some said that they preferred their own law.[30] Their 'native' freedoms might strike white authority as feckless, but from the perspective of these Yamatji, getting the vote via the *Natives (Citizenship Rights) Act* 1944 had come to seem an insignificant gain for a large price. Fink's fourteen interviewees who were in favour of pursuing exemption mentioned rights that would be their reward: freedom to drink beer; full wages; being 'like white people'; and 'for the sake of my children'. To be able to vote, Fink found, was not a prominent aspiration. Feelings about voting were overdetermined by negative feelings about the process of exemption.

Freddy Johnstone (not enrolled), speaking to the Select Committee in Derby, where he worked on the wharves, said that he would like to vote, but not if he had to 'move away from the native' and 'to be with the white'.[31] Agnes Coyne of Gnowangerup was not concerned that she was not enrolled. Her husband also did not desire citizenship and voting rights: 'My husband feels that he does not want his citizenship rights. Why? I don't know. He said he would not have it and we live happy without it. We can always get on.'[32] At Borden (WA), the committee heard Sybil Roberts (not enrolled) say that voting rights would help advance Aboriginal people. However, her interest in other citizenship rights went beyond her interest in voting: she aspired to take her children to the cinema and to travel with more ease. The committee prompted: '[Exemption] gives more opportunities?' 'Yes,' she replied, 'when travelling. We cannot go into a hotel and put up for the night. They won't have you unless you have that ... I want a home for my children.' She answered 'Yes' to the question 'Would that be more important than having the vote?'[33]

In Queensland, where the philosophy and practice of institutional 'protection' remained strong, the committee found that Aborigines and Torres Strait Islanders and officials shared the assumption that Indigenous Australians faced a choice: lots of 'protection' but not full rights, or full rights but living unprotected. This dichotomy was another expression of the convention that had blocked Indigenous Australians under state 'protection' from receiving Commonwealth welfare payments. Notwithstanding the 1959 amendment to the *Social Services Act* 1959, the distinction between being dependent on government and enjoying full rights of citizenship was still, for many Queenslanders, common sense. Queensland's Director of Native Affairs Cornelius O'Leary explained, 'the hallmark of eligibility for voting rights is the ability of a person to care for himself, maintain himself and take his place in the general community ... Until such time as they are willing to measure up to the responsibilities of full citizenship, I say they have not the right to vote.'[34] One Country Party committee member, Charles Barnes, posed questions that presented witnesses with a choice between enfranchisement and continuing government support. 'We can bring hardship to a lot of people if we come in and give full citizenship rights,' he remarked.[35] Labor's Kim Beazley (senior) questioned anthropologist Ronald Berndt in such a way as to elicit Berndt's firm contradiction of this view: for Berndt, there was no reason enfranchised Aborigines should not receive special services from the government. Under questioning by Beazley, Mr G. Sturges, the superintendent of Cherbourg, agreed that the right to vote should not depend on whether or not people lived on a settlement. However, he argued that 'the thing that is keeping them [on Cherbourg] is that they have not got the security of employment, housing and other amenities, away from the settlement that they have here', and that 'if a person is concerned completely and totally with the economics of his family life, he has no available time to devote to the study of exercising the vote'.[36]

Some Aborigines under his supervision shared this view. Vincent Law, an enrolled voter himself through his war service, said that the unenfranchised residents of Cherbourg were not concerned about voting rights and would be reluctant to leave the settlement. With full citizenship rights, Law explained, 'we would not be much better off than we are here because we have all the amenities here around the settlement'.[37] Fellow resident Jeffrey Doolah told the committee that 'I don't think I like voting while I am on the settlement … We have got everything here that other men get outside. We get help.'[38] He said that he had never heard people in Cherbourg express a desire to vote. The committee found Torres Strait Islanders also who assumed that they faced a choice between the entitlement to state support and the entitlements of citizenship. Lui Bon (not enrolled) said that he would like to vote, and that he had tried to enrol. He judged that the Murray Islanders would want voting rights, even if this meant forsaking government support: 'I think the people would look after themselves.'[39] Gordon Coolwell, speaking from Palm Island, thought people wanted the vote, and would be willing to give up the security of the settlement to get it.[40] Leslie Foster, also speaking from Palm Island, told the committee that he had tried living on the mainland, working in a sugar mill, but had not found housing, so his family had not been able to join him.

He had returned to Palm Island. He hoped that his children, with better education than he, would be able to live on the mainland. Voting rights should be extended to Aboriginal people who are in the general community, he said, but not to those on the settlement unless they could be assured of continuing to receive government support. He worried about Palm Island's many pensioners who, unlike the better-educated younger generation, would not survive in the mainstream.

> You find that a lot of people here want to vote, but their problem is leaving here. As far as I know, this place, Palm Island, has been selected by the Government to be a reservation or a home for the Aborigines. To the Aboriginal people, the first Australian, Australia is not a home. This is our home here. It has been selected by the Government and all through the years the Government has looked after us. In a way the Government has spoilt us by spoon-feeding and all that.[41]

Not only Queenslanders assumed a dichotomy between being protected and having rights. At Port Hedland, Peter Coffin, an illiterate prospector and director of the Pindan Aboriginal cooperative, was not enrolled to vote; he said that voting should be compulsory for all Aboriginal people, even for those living on reserves. He also assented to the proposition that, if given citizenship rights, Aboriginal people should not be able to live on government-funded reserves but should live like white Australians.[42] His own independence – as a member of that highly independent fellowship, the 'Pindan Mob' – had taught him not to fear release from government 'protection'.

The Select Committee found ignorance of the Australian political system. Holder Adams, a contract worker and trade unionist with a family in Snake Bay (Northern Territory), told the committee that 'there will not be many interested in [the vote]. It is not quite understood at the moment.'[43] At Roper River and on Groote Eylandt, the committee met people who had been trained in mission schools and who held responsibilities within their mission's institutions (school, clinic, council) but who did not know what parliament or the Legislative Council did.[44] The Bathurst Island Mission authorities had staged a mock election the night before the committee arrived, awakening the interest of Benedict Munkara, Edmund Johnson, Barney Tipuamantumirri and Albert Crocker.[45] Witnesses at that mission admitted freely that they knew nothing about the government, though they knew it paid their pensions, and they expressed confidence that they could learn about voting. The committee got the same admission of ignorance from other Tiwi, at Snake Bay, though Billy Hetherington said that he had heard parliament mentioned on the radio.[46] In Katherine, the committee spoke to Aboriginal employees of CSIRO, the local council and the hospital who were already aware of the possibility of Aboriginal people voting. However, when the committee headed west to Victoria River Downs it met people who seemed unable to comprehend their questions.[47] Men and women at Hooker Creek Settlement admitted that they did not know voting and that they would have to be taught it.[48] When the committee asked them if voting should be compulsory the elicited 'Yes' probably expressed politeness, not informed conviction. When Smiler Major told the committee, at Tennant Creek, that few Aborigines in the Northern Territory were educated enough to vote, they had good reason to agree.[49] Others who spoke to the committee that day (2 August 1961) and the next day in Papunya further illustrated this point, though some witnesses recognised a member of the committee, their representative in parliament, Jock Nelson.⁵⁰ Throughout these outback visits, however, the committee heard people say that they wanted to learn and wanted jobs. Edwin 'Paperultja' (a misspelling of Pareroultja) said he wanted formal ownership of his land.⁵¹

Pastoral colonisation in remote Australia

These least informed men (and a few women) of the Northern Territory's hinterlands were among the thousands isolated from contemporary Australia by their participation in the pastoral industry. To enable them to enrol to vote did little, in the short term, to change their way of life. Far more consequential was the introduction of 'equal wages', when assimilation policy required that Indigenous employees be included in industrial awards. The move to 'equal wages' between 1966 and 1968 was part of a wave of changes in Australian pastoral industries that extinguished the customary industrial order formed by Aborigines' adjustment to pastoralists' authority. Charles and Elsa Chauvel, who had spent much of the 1950s making films and TV documentaries about Australia's 'Outback', described the situation in 1959.

> Although station men of the far north will say that one good white stockman is worth ten aborigines, such good white stockmen are hard to come by, so the stations must depend on the aborigine for his labour. Today the white man and the black man are interdependent. The white man, having taken the aborigine [sic] water supplies as well as his natural hunting grounds when he came with

the first herds, now provides water by bores or pipelines, and keeps the abo in beef, flour sugar and tobacco. In return the aborigines will work well, for they like the free-and-easy life with the cattle: they can live in their tribal grounds with their families, and at certain times take 'walkabout' and go hunting on their own.[52]

This portrait applies better to Western Australia and the Northern Territory than to Queensland, where, by 1965, 36 per cent of Aboriginal employees on cattle stations were recruited from town camps, 56 per cent from missions and only 8 per cent from station camps.[53] The Chauvels' words omitted also that pastoralists' occupation had occasioned bloodshed on both sides, securing for whites continuing discretion about how to discipline and reward Aboriginal people. Nonetheless, the Chauvels' description has been substantiated by scholarship on an enduring 'pastoral system' that 'provided an essentially stable domain' in which settlers 'accessed inexpensive labor and were keyed into a much wider network of knowledge regarding available resources in the environment. Indigenous people were provided with a colonial period enclave, in which they had access to rations and opportunities to maintain connections to their land and to other members of Aboriginal society positioned "outside" of the pastoral system.'[54] Thalia Anthony has persuasively described the pastoral order until 1968 as a 'feudal' jurisdiction, in that the 'working relationship was based on rights and obligations on both sides' (especially after employee rights were made explicit and enforceable in the 1930s); their common interest was the land, 'albeit for very different reasons'.[55]

Research using Aborigines' oral history has revealed the reciprocities of this relationship.[56] Notwithstanding that, in some regions, Aborigines' destruction of stock and threats to pastoralists had forced them to withdraw their herds and to abandon their primitive homesteads, Aboriginal people had adapted to pastoralists' authority. Pioneers had guns and horses and the backing of the police; some were poor and desperate men – including veterans of World War I – prepared to crush threats to the one economic opportunity that they were likely to see in their lives. The Aboriginal people had nowhere to go: this was their country, and if it was not possible to evict alien intruders then it was necessary to coexist with them. Pastoral leases were initially unfenced, making it necessary to use Aboriginal labour for shepherding and mustering. Far from slaughterhouses and markets, the pastoralists needed someone to drove the cattle. The newcomers were sources of goods that Aboriginal people found prestigious, useful or simply addictive (tobacco). As governments later recognised, the pastoralists learned that it was best to issue these goods not only to those who worked but also to their families. Sharing country was possible if Aboriginal people refrained from eating stock without the pastoralist's permission; astute pastoralists soon learned how much beef to issue, to secure the rest of the herd.

Pastoralists without spouses who were lonely and wanted sexual comfort found that some women – perhaps at the instigation or with the permission of their menfolk – were available. Some liaisons developed into lasting intimate relationships. The male adults associated with these women (brothers, husband) were entitled – as 'in-laws' – to some of the consideration shown to the woman herself. Indeed, Aboriginal men in the Kimberley may have been puzzled by colonists who declined their offers of sexual hospitality. One American visitor travelling to the Kimberley by boat in 1929 recalled that when his party came ashore in search of water and was offered women their refusal seemed to insult the old man making the gesture. The visitor and his companions thought it prudent to return to their boat, and he reflected: 'They had merely adopted the usual way to cement friendship with strangers, and to have their hospitality treated so contemptuously was a deep affront.'[57] The Afghan and Scots-born pastoralists who arrived in northern Kimberley in the 1920s not only dispersed herds on the land but also took up with women, which drew in the women's relatives and thus constituted a pool of labour. The women were from Ngarinyin-speaking clans whose country the pastoralists were occupying. These ongoing sexual liaisons were illegal and so could not be acknowledged. Redmond reports, from recent fieldwork, that the Ngarinyin people explain the relationship as a version of the customary reciprocities between certain categories of kin (known in Aboriginal English as the 'owners' and 'managers') who exercise complementary responsibilities over knowledge and ceremonies. Whites may well have understood themselves as the superior party, but the Ngarinyin now recall them as complementary actors in the management of shared country.[58] As well, the Kimberley stations were on land that had long been criss-crossed by customary trading routes in a system of ceremonial exchange across the region – the *wurnan*. Station camps became the nodes on this network, and the exotic and useful goods obtained from white settlers became traded items. Karunjie Station, near Wyndham, was the location of one of the biggest exchange centres in the region, drawing in sometimes hundreds of participants to its *wurnan* ceremonies, where bolts of red cloth from the Chinese stores in Wyndham port, as well as spear-tips, bamboo, shells and ochres, were traded. By the early 1920s it had become a ration depot, to induce some of those who were there for ceremony to stay for longer periods and to work at the station.[59]

Pastoral colonisation developed a typical spatial order – a distinction of camps from households. Doug Abbott grew up under the influence of both Hermannsburg Mission and the pastoral leases of the west MacDonnell Ranges. He recalls of the 1950s and 1960s:

> We didn't like it in the whiteman's house, because it was a no-go area for us. 'Don't speak language in front of people' – Mum told me that, my great-grandmother told me that. 'Don't talk loud language in front of the whitefellers. Just whisper.' Just thought it would be rude. Just frightened. In the early days people were flogged for speaking language. Not the Lutherans, I'm talking about station people I worked with. They were kind people but they never invited us into their house for a cup of tea, put it that way. Henbury's [a pastoral lease on Doug Abbott's country] the only one. The early station owner, Woody Pierce, he was a really kind man.[60]

The seasonality of beef production afforded a temporal order: intense work of mustering and branding in the cooler/dryer months (April to September), leaving some time (usually December to January) for what the Chauvels knew as 'walkabout' ('holiday' in Aboriginal English), when the Aboriginal camp would roam the country, engaging in ceremonies. Pastoral regions that developed a tradition of annual picnic races also helped to stage, in a new way, the social life of wider Aboriginal networks.

Not all pastoral lessees allowed large rationed camps. Geoff Shaw recalls that

> No-one was allowed to live at Utopia Station. Only people who were employed at Utopia Station were allowed to live there, like the stockmen and the housemaids. So you had a couple of hundred people living across the [Sandover] river on Mount Skinner Station. Jock Nelson had empathy for Aboriginal people, and he let them stay there. He got rations for them, so maybe him and Peg were the protectors of Aboriginal people there. I think he might have got paid for making sure people were fed ... Years later I found out that those people who were living there were traditional owners of Utopia Station and weren't allowed to live in their own country. They were allowed to go hunting. Jock Nelson never stopped them from going hunting.[61]

Thus Aboriginal people learned to distinguish within the range of pastoralists' approaches, between 'empathy' and exclusion. Some pastoral lessees were companies, using managers whose styles of authority might vary, while other leases were run by families who stayed for generations. Mount Doreen, on Warlpiri country, was leased by the Braitling family from the 1930s, and Eddie Robertson Jampijinpa remembers

> Bill Braitling was a lovely man to some people. Us children, he really wanted us to go to school, but we just kept moving back bush everywhere. But he looked after us. If we wanted breakfast, we used to just go up the hill, Mount Doreen hill, from the camp, with milk tins. We used to earn it. Fill up a milk tin with wolfram [tungsten] and take it to old Bill. He was a Jangala [Warlpiri kinship term]. If we stayed around the station, then we had to earn it, breakfast. People who didn't want breakfast, they

just stayed home. Life was very hard for some, easy for some.[62]

To survive by working was to be valued as a worker, and pride in work was central to finding honour within the pastoral colonial order. Aboriginal memories point to their efforts, as workers, to maintain self-respect in the face of self-interested white authority. Jimmy Wave Hill recalls that

> Vesteys [British lessees of Wave Hill] sometimes they didn't like blackfellas. They used to give us hard time. But it don't matter that they used to give us hard time. In the work, out in the bush, we used to do a good job for them and that. In that day we used to work hard and we used to make money for kartiya [white] people. And after work we used to holiday and go back to camp and we used to get a bag and go out in the shop there [the pastoralist's store] and get flour, sugar, tea, stick of tobacco, that is all. They bin use us just like a slave, working hard for them. We used to do more work than all the kartiya used to do.[63]

Bruce Breaden recalls a manager who trusted him: 'You have got to be a good man to be trusted.'[64] This boss paid him in stock and in money.

> He was good with wages. He didn't give me a salary but when we would come into town he'd ask me, 'How much do you want?' He'd give me big money. The next morning he'd ask me again, 'Do you want more?' If I had some left, then alright, but if nothing, then he'd give me another lot. He was good.[65]

The training of boys to be useful men – central to the reproduction of Aboriginal society before the colonists arrived – was adapted to meet the requirements of their pastoralist patrons. Lease-holders knew that men would train their sons. Morndi Munro recalls that he was selected as a promising worker, as a teenager, and given certain responsibilities, just as his brother and his father had been. This meant that his father mediated the rough discipline of pastoralist Harry Bannon of Napier Downs: 'Oh Christ, my father was rough too. I used to get more experience from my father and more hammerings too … My father chained me one time. He was a rough man.'[66] 'Rough' treatment aligned the training requirements of coloniser and colonised: it was what men had to do to produce men – obedient men – fit for country. Morndi Munro told Mary Anne Jebb that this demanding process had made black people 'sensible'.[67]

Aboriginal subjects of pastoral rule over much of remote Australia incorporated the pastoralists and their goods into their own systems of action and understanding, as if the pastoralists were 'strange relatives'. Strangeness made humour possible. An old woman staged a performance for visiting psychologist Stanley Porteus on Gogo Station in 1929. She sat in the boss's truck,

> hands on the wheel, while [her companions] gave vent to an extraordinary series of grunts, squeaks, and rattles, ending in a most realistic splutter of an imaginary engine. When silence fell, the mock driver fiddled with all the knobs on the dashboard, gave a signal to her companions, who then repeated the performance with great enthusiasm. When this failed to start the car, the old woman descended, walked to the front of the station wagon, kicked the front tire viciously,

and then in the exact tones of Millard's voice said loudly, 'I wonder what's wrong with the bloody bastard now!' The response of the native onlookers was uninhibited.[68]

Complementary to state and mission institutions, this hierarchical, often cruel accommodation of land-owners to lease-holders shaped colonial authority over much of remote Australia and over thousands of Aboriginal people, for much of the 20th century. Pastoralists' demands on Aboriginal people altered, but did not extinguish, the Indigenous economy and moral order. Aboriginal beliefs in a spirit world were robust, and the performance of that belief – ceremony on country – was scheduled and located so as to fit the pastoralists' seasonal labour process. From the 1930s, the Commonwealth and Western Australian governments began cautiously to demand more of pastoralists as custodians of Aboriginal lives. In 1947, the Labor government of Ben Chifley negotiated with the Territory's pastoralists to set the minimum wage for Aboriginal stock workers at about one-fifth the minimum for other workers, with the pastoralists covering the costs of the employee's wife and child; the Administration would subsidise the pastoralist to meet the costs of rationing all other dependants of the employee. From 1949, the Northern Territory's patrol officers began to inspect the conditions of employment on pastoral leases. They were lenient not only because governments saw the beef industry as economically significant but also because the pastoralist, if too much were demanded by the state, could unload his lease's Aboriginal residents into the government settlements and missions, overcrowding them.[69] Frank Stevens reported that in his discussions with pastoralists in the 1960s, the Northern Territory Administrations' 'attempts at assimilation and the numerous failures associated therewith were the source of much mirth'.[70] Pastoralists across remote Australia were confident that they knew 'the blacks' better than any well-intentioned civiliser. In Western Australia, according to the 1958 *Report of the Special Committee on Native Matters* (by Frank Gare), pastoralists were largely unaccountable to state regulation. Indeed, the Western Australian government had reduced its direct influence on Aboriginal employment in the Kimberley in 1955 when it closed Moola Bulla cattle station (because it was now seen as state-sponsored segregation, contrary to 'assimilation'). Ronald and Catherine Berndt, in their submission to Gare, described the wide discretion enjoyed by pastoralists as 'reminiscent of a feudal situation'.[71]

In Queensland, typically, the government had by then been more assertive; its systematic approach to supervision of Indigenous Australians complemented a labour movement determined to prevent competition from underpriced and state-supervised Aboriginal labour. Dawn May argues that 'the lifestyle of Aborigines on Queensland cattle stations' changed from around 1920. The Australian Workers' Union's (AWU) agitation for equal pay in 1918–19, according to May, was intended to boost the demand for white labour, which the union assumed to be more skilful.[72] The government, the employers (United Graziers' Association) and the AWU compromised on an Aboriginal rate of two-thirds the minimum pay for white workers in the pastoral industry. The closer to 'normal' wages and conditions the Aboriginal workers approached, however, the less willing the employers were to support the workers' dependants – a situation favouring the single Aboriginal man or the married man whose wife and children could be looked after on a mission or government settlement. According to May, in Queensland, 'increasingly from the 1920s the nexus between Aborigines and traditional land was broken', and workers and their families had to live in towns (or on their fringes) during the cattle industry's seasonal lay-offs or when beef prices were low.[73] Having to pay more for Aboriginal labour in a world of volatile beef prices, the pastoralists' defence of their interests 'seriously destabilised the Aboriginal workforce and damaged the Aboriginal ability to retain some pre-industrial traits which had been essential to the industry' and to the reproduction of Aboriginal custom.[74]

The greater influence of the state in Queensland from the 1920s prefigured what happened in Western Australia and the Northern Territory when the state and the labour movement combined, in the 1960s, to force pastoral feudalism to conform to what Justice H.B. Higgins had once called 'the new province of law and order'. Whether and how the decisions of the Commonwealth Conciliation and Arbitration Commission (established in 1904) affected Indigenous workers depended largely on what material was presented to it by the trade union movement. With the exception of the North Australian Workers' Union (which included white and 'half-caste' workers in Darwin), the trade unions covering industries in which most Aboriginal employees worked – the wool and beef industries – were not active on Aborigines' behalf until the 1960s. The North Australian Workers' Union applied to the Commonwealth Conciliation and Arbitration Commission in 1965 to include Aborigines in the *Cattle Station Industry (Northern Territory) Award*. The Commonwealth was a major employer of Northern Territory Aborigines on settlements, at lower rates of pay, but it did not oppose the union's application, as it accorded with the government's overall policy of assimilation. 'The field of labour relations,' said the Commonwealth's submission, was 'the last major area requiring attention'.[75] The Commission ruled in 1966 that equality of entitlement be granted gradually, so that by 1 December 1968, all male Aboriginal employees would be entitled to the award rate or more, unless they were classified as 'slow' workers.[76] Some Aboriginal workers objected to the three-year phasing in of 'equal wages'; they took industrial action at Newcastle Waters and Wave Hill stations.

Knowing that wage rises would further weaken demand for Aboriginal labour across Northern and Central Australia, the commission anticipated that missions and settlements would accommodate people who found themselves no longer welcome on pastoral leases. Residents of missions and settlements were given 'training allowances', while the Commonwealth rapidly dismantled the remaining barriers to remote Indigenous Australians' access to cash welfare, over the years 1968 to 1975. Seeking a less isolated and supervised life, and enabled by cash social security benefits, Aboriginal people in Northern and Central Australia moved into towns.[77]

State and civil society

Assimilation was pursued not only as public policy, but also in steps taken by individuals, households and organisations. In 1959, Paul Hasluck, Minister for Territories, had pleaded for 'community' action on assimilation: 'it is not governments but the community that touches the feelings of these outcasts about the way they live'.[78] In his understanding, 'assimilation' was a responsibility not only of the state but also of 'civil society' – private, public-spirited organisations and well-to-do families.

Insofar as non-Indigenous Australians reached out to Indigenous Australians, they built on a colonial tradition of private action to induct Aboriginal people into colonial ways. According to Shirleene Robinson, since the first half of the 19th century, colonists had incorporated children – some orphaned by frontier violence – within their households; such children would thus find a place in a superior civilisation.[79] William Cooper's boyhood service in a white household had increased his understanding of white society. Usually, these unofficially adopted children did domestic work, thus meeting two needs of colonial households: to ease domestic drudgery and to do good. In the 20th century, under 'protection' legislation, the domestic grooming of Aboriginal girls became more systematic. Voluntary charitable and religious agencies were prominent in their recruitment; William Cooper's closest white collaborator, the Christian (Church of Christ) trade unionist Arthur Burdeu, once argued against recruiting domestic servants from Asia by asserting: 'We have all the domestic labour needed, but waiting for organisation, in Aboriginal girls.'[80] A study of NSW Administration by Inara Walden uses files on 570 girls apprenticed in the 1910s, 1920s and 1930s. Trained for domestic service at the Cootamundra Girls Training Institution, they went on to work for 1200 employers.[81] Aboriginal girls made up about 1.5 per cent of the domestic service workforce in New South Wales in the years circa 1910–40. Walden argues that these young women were less able than white domestic workers to change employers if they did not like their conditions, because they were apprenticed and legally bound.[82] Typically, their work included not only cleaning and cooking (if taught to prepare what their employers wanted) but also minding children. In the memories of many women, they were worked hard, treated as social inferiors, and sometimes not given enough to eat; some had to sleep in their workplace (for example, the laundry). They were also at risk of social isolation: the main persons in their life were the householders they served; friends and family were generally inaccessible to them.

According to Victoria Haskins, in this pre–World War II partnership between state and private homes

> authorities set the conditions of employment and wage rates, the latter typically artificially low, with a significant proportion being withheld 'in trust' by the authorities. Placements were organised by the administration, and girls placed in service could be moved about and transferred as officials directed, with minimal consultation with the young women themselves or their families. Those who were forthright enough to complain about their wages or conditions were usually encouraged to bear the situation with fortitude or, if they persisted, treated as troublemakers.

Licensed employers were subject to inspection by police or other officials. Some types of people were refused licences: hotel-keepers, Asian Australians.

> The ideal employer was a married, middle-class, white woman with a salaried husband and several young children ... [D]emanding mistresses were disliked by the authorities and if they complained about the worker and sought a replacement they could not presume they would be so supplied.

Authorities could withdraw permission and remove the servant.[83]

Oral histories of Aboriginal women in domestic service include some accounts of white households that were kind to their black servants. Haskins has argued that, for white women who aspired to better the lives of Aboriginal women, becoming the mistress of an Aboriginal maid was a privatised alternative to the 'female protector' role that feminists had recommended without success to Australian governments. She gives the example of Ida McKay, a champion of Aboriginal interests in Adelaide, whose social network included Adelaide households that received 'half-caste' girls from the Alice Springs Bungalow. Noticing that in Adelaide the girls were lonely and unwelcome, McKay soon ceased to support this practice.[84] Elizabeth McKenzie-Hatton and Joanna Kingsley-Strack saw Aboriginal women's domestic service as their opportunity to be upwardly mobile. Such middle-class patrons were critical of the careless ways that young Aboriginal women were sent out to work as domestics, far from their region of origin and at risk of the male employer's sexual harassment and even rape. 'Strack called for the appointment of a woman on the NSW administrative board, because "all the employees handled by the Bd. in Sydney, are girls, poor little human flotsam".'[85] Walden reports that 8.5 per cent of the NSW records that she examined reported pregnancy during apprenticeship. A male employer was not always to blame: prostitution has long been the recourse of the female poor. A girl who conceived in service was unlikely to be allowed by the Protection Board to keep her baby. A young woman could be in domestic service not only in a white household but also in 'the commercialized sector of domestic service'; in the 1966 Census, Aboriginal women were five times more likely than other Australian women to be in 'domestic service' in this wider sense.[86] The Cootamundra Home for Girls closed in 1968.

Aboriginal women's domestic competence, in looking after *her own* family, was a central concern of governments committed to assimilation. If the effective Aboriginal household was the key to the 'advancement' of Aboriginal people, governments had to provide houses for people who would otherwise camp on the edges of towns. The Victorian government, for example, constructed two 'transitional housing' communities at Rumbalara and Manatunga, to accommodate and to train Aboriginal families.[87] The flaw in governments' efforts to uplift Aboriginal domesticity, argues Anna Haebich, was that the Aboriginal housewife lacked houses and domestic goods that other Australian women had come to expect.[88]

One widely respected voluntary association, the Country Women's Association (CWA), sought to help such impoverished Aboriginal women. Between 1956 and 1972, concerned at the persistent 'colour bar' in rural Australia, several CWA branches in New South Wales and Queensland helped 'coloured' women to set up branches on reserves. Beginning on Toomelah Reserve, the CWA aimed to encourage Aboriginal women's domestic arts and to enable their ladylike behaviour, so that they would conduct themselves acceptably in rural society. The Aboriginal women who took up this opportunity saw themselves as already worthy of respect; they not only displayed their respectability, they expressed dissatisfaction with the buildings that the Aboriginal Welfare Board provided, particularly the under-equipped kitchens. Asking the postmaster-general to install a public telephone on reserves, so that residents did not have to ask the manager for the privilege of using his phone, they enlisted CWA support. At Kempsey the CWA practice of conducting competitive baby shows combined with agitation for better access to infant health services. When the CWA held beauty contests, it was a chance for Aboriginal women to represent themselves as admirably feminine. At Purfleet Reserve, the CWA branch opened the Gillawarra Gift Shop in 1962, selling handicrafts made by reserve residents. The social activities of the CWA became a platform for Aboriginal women to show that they could meet the standards that assimilation prescribed. Respectability and social connections made the CWA a powerful ally for reserve residents demanding more material support from a complacent state government.[89] For A.P. Elkin, CWA member Ella Simon embodied the anti-racist potential of assimilation policy: a respectable, determined Aboriginal woman who 'blazed a trail through this maze of prejudice and fear'.[90]

Relations were sometimes uneasy between government Aboriginal welfare bureaucracies and private organisations that sought to 'advance' Aboriginal people and to overcome race prejudice. The 'community' summoned by Hasluck to reach out to Aborigines could be a discomfiting critic of governments. During the Cold War some in the 'community' were Communist Party members, or were suspected of Communist sympathies. Radical university students, attracted to the 'civil rights' agenda of assimilation policy, sometimes divided public opinion with newsworthy and courageous confrontations of community racism.[91] Politically conservative Australians, both white and black, had to consider how offensively they could confront community prejudice and how publicly they should criticise government. White Queenslanders with goodwill towards Aborigines faced a particularly confident state paternalism. Disturbed by certain criticisms of the state's administration of Aboriginal and Islander affairs, some Queenslanders formed the One People for Australia League (OPAL) in 1961, accepting the minister's invitation to form 'a body that would cooperate' with his department 'rather than harry it'.[92] In July 1961 representatives of churches (Anglican, Catholic, Congregational, Methodist, Presbyterian), Rotary, the YWCA, the Women's Christian Temperance Union and Toc H met and agreed on three aims: 'solve aborigine [sic] problems by influence and example in Brisbane and thence throughout Queensland'; 'seek as members, organisations and persons of repute'; 'weld dark and light elements in Australia into one people'.[93] Other church-based organisations soon joined. By 1967 OPAL had about 300 individual members and thirty member organisations. They were united not only by the three stated aims but also by their perception that the Federal Council for Aboriginal Advancement (founded in 1958, renamed FCAATSI – the Federal Council for the Advancement of Aborigines and Torres Strait Islanders – in 1964) was under Communist influence. As a matter of policy, OPAL did not cooperate with FCAA(TSI). W.E. Tomasetti presents OPAL and FCAATSI as complementary, FCAATSI dealing 'largely with the policy and legislative aspects of civil rights, including wage matters, whereas ... OPAL's efforts are devoted largely to helping individuals (or families) with social service matters'.[94] OPAL aimed to provide services to Aboriginal and Torres Strait Islander people not formally under the government's care (on a mission or settlement), with housing, transit hostels, a medical clinic, bursaries and accommodation for school pupils, handcraft workshops, children's town holidays and seaside camps. OPAL also advocated job-seeking Aborigines to employers. Annually it ran a Miss OPAL contest. OPAL aspired to form local branches 'wherever aggregations of aborigines make them necessary' and each branch sought to involve local Aborigines.

OPAL and the government were in a relationship of 'reciprocal obligation'.

> Vulnerable because its policies were outdated, bewildered because the necessity to change clashed with its inertia, and given the choice of OPAL or the other bodies, the

Government breathed a sigh of relief and chose OPAL, and has therefore had its tail twisted less painfully and less publicly than otherwise would have been the case.

Two Department of Aboriginal and Islander Affairs (DAIA) officers were directors of OPAL in 1967, and the president was an employee of the DAIA. This made OPAL an effective lobbyist and a discrete 'inside' commentator and partner. In May 1963 the Minister for Education agreed to an OPAL request that the title of a department textbook be changed from 'The Australian Black' to 'The Australian Aborigine'. OPAL sometimes persuaded the police to investigate complaints by Aborigines about police, and OPAL requested the Police Pipe Band to play at the opening of its production of *Uncle Tom's Cabin* – 'a public affirmation of good OPAL/Police relations'.[95]

Conclusion

That 91 per cent of voters agreed to remove evident 'racial discrimination' from the Constitution in May 1967 seemed to confirm the openness and decency of Australian political culture. The 1967 'Yes' vote has become a necessary memory for a nation unsure, since 2000, about what to do. Assimilation was a partnership between the state (reforms in law, administration, programs) and civil society (white private organisations and families reaching out to help Aborigines 'advance', blacks welcoming the opportunity to meet white expectations). However, assimilation was more successful politically than socially, in that formal equality did not vanquish prejudice. From the few studies of public opinion available at the time of the 1967 referendum, we can draw three conclusions about the inclusiveness that was expressed by voting 'Yes'. First, by a slight margin, many respondents to surveys saw a difference between 'part-Aborigines' and 'full-bloods'; they expressed greater acceptance of the former. Second, by substantial majorities, respondents rejected the idea of an Aboriginal person ('part' or 'full') marrying into their family. Third, they overwhelmingly accepted the idea of associating with Aborigines in less intimate ways. The bigger distinction that respondents to surveys and polls made in the 1960s was not between their degrees of acceptance of 'full-bloods' and 'part-Aborigines', but between more intimate and less intimate forms of acceptance. To have an Aboriginal person ('full-blood' or 'half-caste') marry into one's family was more widely rejected than having an Aboriginal person ('full-blood' or 'half-caste') as a friend, neighbour, work colleague, café/restaurant worker or shop assistant.[96] This greater white tolerance of less intimate association made Aboriginal people acceptable as fellow citizens. While respondents told pollsters that they agreed with negative statements about Aborigines, and a large proportion said that they would not welcome a close relative marrying an Aboriginal person, a relatively low proportion said that Aboriginal people should be denied the vote. Excluding Aboriginal people from family did not entail excluding them from polity through equality of franchise and of wages; the nation hardly noticed when Indigenous Australians became equally eligible for welfare payments.

8

From the referendum to 'self-determination'

William Stanner, appointed to advise the Commonwealth government on what policies to pursue after the May 1967 referendum, was puzzled by the 91 per cent 'Yes' vote: 'No one knows or can say exactly what message that signal sent.'[1] If there was one unmistakable message to the Holt government it was that the Australian government should improve the lives of Aboriginal and Torres Strait Islander people. The 1966 Census – the first that enabled comparison of the education and employment status of the total non-Aboriginal and Aboriginal populations – measured some ways that their lives were lacking. When publishing these data, the Bureau defined 'Aboriginal' as those who reported themselves (or were reported by institutions) as of 50 per cent or more Aboriginal ancestry; this amounted to about 80 000 people. Data on 16 000 to 17 000 'identifiable Aborigines of less than 50 per cent' were not available for analysis. Had they been included in the 'Aboriginal population', the contrast between 'Aborigines' and 'non-Aborigines' would not have been so stark, sociologist Leonard Broom speculated.[2]

Broom's 1970 paper showed the political legacy of the

exclusion or underservicing of Aboriginal people from the education systems of Australia since Federation (respondents to the 1966 Census included people born in the 1890s): 'they enter school later, progress slower, quit sooner, and terminate at a lower level', with resulting high rates of illiteracy.[3]

> The constraining and inhibitory effects of illiteracy and the sense of vulnerability before the authority of the printed word, the official document, the price list, or the column of numbers is an inherent part of the life experience of most adult Aborigines ... [Aboriginal people are] often dependent upon the honesty, generosity, forbearance, and friendliness of strangers, at best a poor substitute for self-defence.[4]

Broom's next paper showed that because children (age 0–14) comprised a relatively large proportion of the Aboriginal population a smaller proportion of the Aboriginal population was available for paid employment, so that the average Aboriginal employee supported more dependants than the average non-Aboriginal employee.[5] As well, an Aboriginal employee was much more likely to be in a low-paid, low-technology job and much more likely to experience seasonal unemployment.

Broom's pioneering use of the 1966 Census data to show the extent of 'racial inequality' – cultural, economic and political – described the problems to be overcome. In May 1967, the Commonwealth had gained power, concurrent with the states, to legislate about 'the aboriginal race', but the 'Yes' campaign had neither spelled out nor given a name to the policies that the Commonwealth was now mandated to adopt. Was 'assimilation' still the objective? If not, then what?

Integration?

The term 'self-determination' had surfaced briefly in discussions of Indigenous affairs when newspaper reports had used the phrase to describe the program of the Australian Aboriginal Progressive Association (AAPA) in 1925.[6] The word then seems to have disappeared from Australian discussions until forty years later, when criticism of 'assimilation' as both coercive and ineffective raised the question of whether Australia should adopt a new approach. At first, 'integration' circulated as the name for such a change of direction. After close study of many uses of 'integration' in the 1960s, McGregor has drawn two conclusions: that it was used to mean 'modes of national inclusion on a group basis, respectful of minority heritage and identity'; and that some considered 'assimilation' already to have this possible inflection.[7] Was 'integration' an alternative policy to 'assimilation' or did 'integration' merely name a more tolerant approach to 'assimilation'?

Hasluck himself had illustrated how 'assimilation' could assume that all Aboriginal ways were impediments to their advancement when he referred in 1959 to Aboriginal people being 'tangled in their own distressed situation like flies on sticky paper. They could fly if only they could get clear of their surroundings, lift themselves free of their past, leaving behind them their present life.'[8] Programs of advancement that seemed comprehensively to denigrate extant Aboriginal ways aroused Aboriginal scorn for assimilation (and for governments' selective exemption of those deemed assimilated) and distrust for white authorities. The NSW Aboriginal activist Bert Groves stated his ambivalence about 'assimilation' to the first federal conference of Aboriginal organisations in Adelaide in 1958. He could accept 'citizenship and equal status', but he would resist 'the disappearance of the Aboriginals as a separate cultural group, and ultimately their physical absorption by the European part of the population'.[9] Some officials with responsibility for assimilation policy thought that programs should not be 'dependent upon individuals subjecting themselves to a humiliating investigation and turning their back on their identity, family, and culture' – the words of the Commissioner for Native Affairs in Western Australia (1948–62) Stanley Middleton in 1952.[10]

The term 'integration' gained currency when thoughtful ministers and officials were sensitive to the distinction made by Groves and Middleton between the right to formal equality and the pressure to forfeit all Aboriginal distinction. They wanted Indigenous Australians to choose the pace and the terms of their adaptation to the ways of other Australians. In 1965 the Aboriginal Welfare Council (a meeting of ministers responsible for Aboriginal affairs in each Australian jurisdiction) discussed reformulating 'assimilation' to include words proposed by the South Australian government: 'It is recognised that the existence of distinctively Aboriginal groups at their wish is not inconsistent with [assimilation] policy' and 'The participation by persons of Aboriginal descent in formulating plans for their future is inherent in this policy.'[11] The ministers did not agree to include these words but they conceded that attaining 'a similar manner and standard of living to that of other Australians' would be for Aboriginal people to 'choose'.[12] The South Australian minister Len King, in 1971, explained that his government's intention, in 1965 and since, had been to recognise 'the right of Aboriginal people to live in our community on fully equal terms but retaining, if they so desire, a separate and identifiable Aboriginal heritage and culture'; he called this approach 'integration'.[13] He gave examples: not putting pressure on people to leave reserves;

encouraging people to learn about their traditions; enabling them to be schooled in their own language; allowing people to live 'in a way which is different from the way of life of the white community'.[14] King's counterpart in the Commonwealth government, the special minister of state William Charles Wentworth, declared in 1969 that 'assimilation' referred to some Aboriginal aspirations and 'integration' to others; government should concede that Aboriginal people could 'choose' the manner and pace of their attachment to Australian society. He hoped that Australia was becoming a 'pluralistic society where people are not all the same, although they have the same rights privileges and responsibilities', a society in which Aborigines may 'maintain for themselves, inside their own group, the characteristics of that group'.[15] Coercive approaches had been 'quick and easy', he remarked, but removing children from their parents had undermined heritage and produced 'a depressed class and a depressed people'.[16] In January 1972, Liberal Prime Minister William McMahon expressed support for Aborigines 'increasingly to manage their own affairs – as individuals, as groups, and as communities at the local level' at the same time as they 'preserve and develop their own culture, languages, traditions and arts'.[17]

In this mood of liberal reassessment, in which 'integration' seemed to name a less demanding approach to improving Indigenous Australians, the term 'self-determination' began to rival 'integration' as the possible name of a better policy. In 1970, the Aboriginal writer Kath Walker (Oodgeroo Noonuccal) commended academic Henry Schapper, the University of Western Australia's Reader in Agricultural Economics, for using 'self-determination'. Speaking at the same Perth Summer School in which Wentworth had spoken, Schapper had diagnosed Western Australian Aborigines as suffering from 'dependent poverty', which he contrasted with the desired condition of 'self-determination'. For self-determination, society must permit individual choices and individuals must have the capacity to make them; as well, 'indigenous ethnic minorities' must be 'involved in government'. Citing the psychologist Erich Fromm, Schapper described the social fabric – family and community – necessary for effective individuality. Aborigines in Western Australia lacked powers of self-expression; a sense of identity; the right and opportunity to be influential in Australian society; and a 'frame of social orientation' in which their actions seemed rational and meaningful. Aboriginal people were being trained to be useful, but not to be self-determining, he asserted. Non-Aboriginal Australians had acquired low expectations of Aborigines, he continued; they had invested little in Aboriginal advancement and, in effect, practised 'apartheid' while professing assimilation. Walker warmly praised Schapper for seeing 'the subject from the Aboriginal side of the social, economic and political barrier'. 'Self-determination is the key to the Aboriginal dilemma.'[18] The emergence of 'successful' and sharply articulate Aboriginal activists such as Charles Perkins in the 1960s had presented the public with plausible models of Aboriginal capacity and initiative, and Schapper probably had them in mind when he called for Aborigines to 'belong to all relevant committees in government, short of Cabinets'.[19]

Walker went beyond Schapper, however, in that she presented such Aborigines' success as a possible problem. Governments had groomed spurious pride in some Aborigines, who satisfied material needs while spurning their own kind; 'a policy of self-determination would bring these black white parrots to their senses'. Self-determination 'would unite the Aborigines and, instead of working to protect the white race or administrations, such Aborigines would be put to work in their own community helping their own people overcome their difficulty'.[20]

Schapper and Walker gave striking emphasis to the social and psychological dimensions of 'self-determination', but Walker pointed as well to a political effect of assimilation: alienation of the assimilated Aborigine from those whom assimilation had failed.

'Self-determination' acquired currency in the early 1970s. The Council for Aboriginal Affairs (CAA, made up of H.C. Coombs, Barrie Dexter and W.E.H. Stanner), appointed in late 1967 to advise Commonwealth policy innovations, had not given the label 'self-determination' to the reforms they proposed to non-Labor ministers William Charles Wentworth and Peter Howson. Nor did the staff of the ALP leader Edward Gough Whitlam include that term in his November 1972 campaign speech.[21] However, once elected in December 1972, the Whitlam government accepted CAA advice to use 'self-determination' to distinguish Labor policies from their predecessors' 'assimilation' policies. At the April 1973 meeting of the Aboriginal Welfare Council, the Commonwealth committed 'to restore to the Aboriginal people of Australia their lost power of self-determination'.[22]

As an ideal, 'self-determination' won acceptance as an essentially liberal critique of heavy-handed government policies that were understood to have diminished and even destroyed Indigenous 'selves'; the critique imagined, plausibly, that these trammelled selves – individuals, families and communities – could be revived and released from crippling supervision so that their potential – human and 'Aboriginal' – could be realised, their integration achieved.[23] That there were features of 'Aboriginal culture' to admire and preserve had begun to inform debates about whether 'Australian culture' could be more than a provincial Anglophone formation. Esteem for 'Aboriginal culture' grew in the 1960s as major art galleries (for example the Art Gallery of New South Wales, acquiring bark paintings from Arnhem Land) and performing arts entrepreneurs (the Australian Elizabethan Theatre Trust touring Mornington Island dancers in southern capital cities) developed urban Australia's taste for expressive arts from remote communities. Critics of assimilation blamed government and mission actions for drying up the springs of such creativity and beauty.

Before describing what Australian governments did in the name of self-determination, we should note that 'self-determination' already had other meanings that did not immediately resonate in Australian policy debates. After being promoted during World War I by both Woodrow Wilson and Vladimir Lenin, the term 'self-determination' had been given legitimacy by the League of Nations; it then proliferated after World War II in the United Nations, as Europe's empires disintegrated – sometimes violently – into independent nations. However, although anti-colonial nationalism was beginning to appeal to some Aboriginal intellectuals in the 1960s, this was not what 'self-determination' meant to Australia's political elite in 1973. Their public policy endorsement of 'self-determination' emerged from a rethinking of Australian tactics of citizenship, not from any conception of Aborigines and Torres Strait Islanders as potentially self-governing peoples. If global anti-colonialism and Australian liberalism shared any ground, it was hostility to racial discrimination.

The global campaign for Indigenous rights gained much from the rise of critical international attention to racial discrimination. In 1965 the United Nations (UN) adopted the

International Convention on the Elimination of All Forms of Racial Discrimination (ICERD). South Australia was the first Australian jurisdiction to put these principles into its laws: the *Prohibition of Discrimination Act* was passed in 1966, the same year that it gave Aborigines title to their reserves.[24] In 1970, when the Victorian Aborigines Advancement League (VAAL) invited the United Nations to censure Australia's lack of land rights legislation, the AAL presented the issue as a problem of racial discrimination.[25] Notwithstanding Hasluck's belief that 'assimilation' was essentially a liberal assault on protection policy's racist exclusions, some practices of assimilation could be criticised as failing a global standard of racial equality.

While it was possible, in the early 1970s, to present 'self-determination' as a corrective to racial discrimination, the concept of self-determination included possibilities beyond the liberal program of outlawing racial discrimination. 'Self-determination' came to mean – to some – that Aborigines and Torres Strait Islanders were 'peoples' with distinct rights such as the rights to land, to political representation and self-government – that is, rights to degrees of sovereignty within the nation-state. By hosting the World Council of Indigenous People meeting in Canberra in 1981 (on a grant from the Fraser government) Indigenous Australians facilitated an intermittent global forum in which Indigenous 'self-determination' was acquiring such connotations of 'sovereignty'.

Over the next three decades, some Aboriginal intellectuals would participate in the UN and other global forums to develop the idea that 'self-determination' meant not only freedom from racial discrimination but also the right to land and to institutions of self-government within the framework of a nation-state.[26] In this quest for Indigenous autonomy they were following a strand of international human rights discourse initiated by the Latin American members of the International Labour Organization (ILO) in the 1940s.[27] The ILO had produced the first formulation of 'Indigenous' rights in 1957 – Convention 107 'Concerning Indigenous and Tribal Populations'. This Convention's words about tribal ownership of reserves were echoed in the 1958 manifesto of the Federal Council for Aboriginal Advancement.[28] However, advocates of Indigenous rights in the 1970s came to see this Convention's vision of 'rights' as still conceding too much to assimilationist thinking. Their continuing diplomacy replaced 107 with Convention 169 'Indigenous and Tribal Peoples' in 1989, in which the ILO used 'peoples' instead of 'populations' in order to reflect the continuing 'distinctive identity' of 'these population groups'. The ILO also expressed caution about where this line of thought could go, declining 'to interpret the political concept of self-determination': 'The use of the term "people" in this Convention shall not be construed as having any implications as regards the rights which may attach to the term under international law.'[29] Not until the UN Declaration on the Rights of Indigenous Peoples (UNDRIP) in 2007 did an international instrument identify indigenous people as 'peoples' with the right to self-determination.

> Article 3: Indigenous peoples have the right to self-determination. By virtue of that right they freely determine their political status and freely pursue their economic, social and cultural development.
>
> Article 4: Indigenous peoples, in exercising their right to self-determination, have the right to autonomy or self-government in matters relating to their internal and local

affairs, as well as ways and means for financing their autonomous functions.[30]

In the early 1970s, Australian discussion of these possible implications of 'self-determination' had barely begun, and so a properly historical answer to the question 'What was "self-determination"?' must not attribute to Australian governments any intention to recognise Aborigines and Torres Strait Islanders as 'peoples' who would 'freely determine their political status'. That politicians would find confronting such an implication of 'self-determination' became clear in 1979 when the Fraser (Coalition) government's Minister for Aboriginal Affairs, Senator Fred Chaney, explained why a treaty between Australia and Indigenous Australians was not desirable: 'one is in some way talking about more than one Australia or more than one nation within Australia'.[31] The policy thinking of Australian governments in the early 1970s was more cautious: it went no further than allowing that Aborigines and Torres Strait Islanders would have more responsibilities than previously. As individual citizens and as publicly funded corporations, they would be accountable to governments in their 'free' use of the funds granted to them.

The five strands of 'self-determination'

The ensemble of programs that came to be called 'self-determination' can be understood as five strands of revised government practice; initiated from 1967 to 1977, each built on assimilation's achievements and responded to its dilemmas.

First, in the Census enumeration of the Aboriginal population the Bureau changed the terms in which it asked respondents to report their 'race'. Kath Walker had suggested in 1964 that the Bureau drop 'this caste business ... Surely we can identify the Aborigine as one who identifies himself as an Aborigine.'[32] The Bureau did not immediately do so: in the 1966 Census respondents who saw themselves as 'Aboriginal' were supposed to say whether they were one quarter, half or three quarters 'aboriginal'. The change to 'self-determination' came in the 1971 Census, whose 'race' question allowed only singular 'racial origin', no fractions:

> 5. What is this person's racial origin? (If of mixed origin indicate the one to which he considers himself to belong) (Tick one box only or give one origin only): 1. European origin, 2. Aboriginal origin, 3. Torres Strait Islander origin, 4. Other origin (give one only).

This reform was not necessitated by the 1967 referendum vote to delete section 127 of the Constitution. Section 127 had merely restricted how enumerations of 'Aboriginal natives' could be used to make certain decisions, not whether or how 'Aboriginal natives' were enumerated. For reasons that had nothing to do with constitutional change, the Bureau changed the terms in which it counted; it abandoned fractional terms of racial classification as a step towards a more accurate Census. Examination of Census returns in 1954, 1961 and 1966 had revealed that many respondents to the Census who were 'half-caste' were declaring themselves to be 'full-blood', and people who were less than 'half-caste' were claiming to be 'half' Aboriginal.[33] That is, people showed little respect for the fractional conceptions of racial heritage that were supposed to enable precise measurement of the biological absorption of coloured people and to distinguish the Constitution's 'Aboriginal native' from those of various degrees of Aboriginal descent. Accordingly, 'reporting by persons with Aboriginal blood in the 1966 census was insufficiently precise to determine whether a person was a "full-blood" or a "half-caste"'.[34] By replacing a fractional with a unitary concept of 'Aboriginal', the Commonwealth shifted from a biological to a social concept of identity: people could no longer misrepresent their 'caste', as they were no longer being asked about it. By valuing Aborigines' and Torres Strait Islanders' subjective identity, their feelings and self-knowledge, the change meant a lot to many Indigenous Australians, particularly those who had children with non-Indigenous partners, for it allowed them to report their offspring as 'Aboriginal' or 'Torres Strait Islander' without reference to the child's genetic admixture. In 2003, the ANU Professor Mick Dodson (Aboriginal and Torres Strait Islander Social Justice Commissioner 1993–98) praised this as a concession to Indigenous rights to 'self-determination and self-identification'.[35] The change had the additional effect of enlarging the Indigenous population.

Second, remote communities would continue to evolve into municipalities consisting mainly of Aboriginal and Torres Strait Islander residents. Wherever Aboriginal and Torres Strait Islander people lived in institutions established to house, train and employ them – missions and government settlements in regions far from Australian cities – the residents would be encouraged to form governing councils; superintendents and missionaries would become advisors. As well as drawing on Australian government experience in the formation of village authorities in Papua New Guinea, this encouragement of Aborigines' local collective responsibility aligned with recent innovations in social work theory and practice: community development would empower clients of the welfare state.[36] South Australia had legislated to form reserve councils in 1967, under 'assimilation' policy, and the Commonwealth, by the late 1960s, was training Aboriginal residents of Northern Territory welfare settlements to be councillors.[37] A seminar of Northern Territory officials in Batchelor in March 1973 endorsed devolution to councils and gave it new impetus as 'self-determination'.[38] Granted funds under government programs, such councils, employing administrative staff, were to take responsibility for delivering essential services. Since then, the state governments of Queensland, Western Australia and South Australia and the Northern Territory government (self-governing from 1978) have gradually absorbed the former missions and welfare settlements into their local government apparatus (without necessarily labelling this process as 'self-determination'). A national review of local government finance in 1985 led to the recognition of ninety-nine new Indigenous local governments by 1994: sixty in the Northern Territory, thirty-three in Queensland, five in South Australia and one in Western Australia. In the Torres Strait, this process of municipalisation has resulted in the Torres Strait Regional Authority, established in 1994.

Third, the state endowed Aborigines with capital in the form of finance and land title in order to relieve poverty and unemployment. In 1968–69, the Commonwealth allocated $5 million to a new Commonwealth Capital Fund for Aboriginal Enterprises, to give loans to individual or cooperative businesses to achieve economic independence, complementing 'welfare' and employment programs. Borrowers had to put in at least 5 per cent of the capital requirement of their enterprise. By June 1975, loans for 542 projects amounted to just under $8 million.[39] This initiative continued under successor bodies: the Aboriginal Development Commission (1980–89) and the

Aboriginal and Torres Strait Islander Commercial Development Corporation (1989–2005). Some of this money was spent on land, and I will deal with the growth of the 'Indigenous Estate' in the next chapter.[40] When forming an Aboriginal and Torres Strait Islander asset base, governments were responding to the 'surplus population' revealed wherever the demand for manual rural workers was declining through structural change in the economy, in particular the beef industry's long-term replacement of labour with capital (fences, beef-roads, helicopter mustering).[41] Aboriginal people moved from pastoral leases to regional towns, where many of them languished: unemployed, poor, unhealthy and in trouble with police. To accommodate the displaced, governments encouraged enterprises, secured land titles over former reserves and purchased pastoral leases in the hope that land-based enterprise would constitute these people as communities. Aboriginal people with some education to whom pastoralists, missionaries and settlements had delegated some managerial authority were now expected to emerge as the leaders and organisers of these communities.[42] In a complementary program starting in 1977, the Commonwealth administered unemployment benefits as a block grant (including a capital component) to communities that chose to be funded in this way – the Community Development Employment Projects (CDEP) scheme. CDEP spread from 'remote' communities to towns and cities with high rates of Aboriginal unemployment. Popular with newly empowered local Indigenous leaders, the CDEP scheme would prove vulnerable to criticisms that it perpetuated the marginal socio-economic status of Indigenous Australians and that it was a cheap way for governments to provide community infrastructure.

Fourth, self-determination encouraged Indigenous Australians to act collectively as corporations. In the second half of the 20th century urbanisation had spawned Indigenous welfare associations. Aborigines and (especially) Torres Strait Islanders were attracted to cities and large towns by the possibility of better housing, healthcare, schooling, employment and consumption. They may also have experienced less racism in the suburbs than in many country towns. To make it easier to adjust to town, whether as resident or visitor, white people of goodwill combined with Aborigines and Torres Strait Islanders in welfare organisations. State and Commonwealth welfare bureaucracies either tolerated or encouraged these bodies as assisting assimilation. Examples of such associations that helped with jobs, accommodation and loneliness were: in Brisbane (and regional centres), the One People of Australia League (founded in 1961 – see Chapter 7); in Sydney, the Foundation for Aboriginal Affairs (1963); in Melbourne, VAAL (1957); in Adelaide, the Aborigines' Progress Association (1954) and the Council of Aboriginal Women of South Australia (1963); and in Perth, the Coolbaroo Club (1946, reconstituted in 1950), the Youth Club (1957) and the Native Welfare Council (1952). In the late 1960s, as Aboriginal political identity firmed, white members and/or patrons of such organisations were under increasing pressure to justify the roles that they had assumed. The Northern Territory Council for Aboriginal Rights, founded on 24 December 1961, had led the way with constitutional requirements that at least 75 per cent of its governing committee be of Aboriginal descent and that Aboriginal members be in the majority at all meetings.[43] 'Activists' were sometimes warned that if their advocacy became 'political', funding for 'welfare' would cease.[44] Although 'Black Power' rhetoric in the late 1960s attracted the scrutiny of ASIO, governments' pragmatic assessment of Indigenous associations' helpful programs assured continuity of funding.

The VAAL illustrates an organisation's ability to mediate changing conceptions of Aboriginal interests and white responsibilities, while retaining a core of services that governments and the white public recognised as 'welfare' to urbanising folk. From the beginning in 1957 the VAAL harboured white and black sceptics of assimilation, people who affirmed the Aboriginal right to decide how much of their heritage they wished to maintain. In 1959, the VAAL dropped the word 'assimilation' from its statement of goals, and was one of the first organisations to espouse 'integration'. It convened three two-day Aboriginal congresses, with 'Aborigines-only' sessions, in the years 1964–66. One strand of anti-white feeling was directed at communists (and their suspected dupes), but the stronger strand was a renewed pride in Aboriginal tradition and in international black solidarity.[45] In 1968, the VAAL added to its five principles (which had always included the right of Aborigines to own reserves) a sixth that affirmed the right to language, identity and heritage. In 1969 people began to refer publicly to themselves as 'Koories' and to profess admiration for Afro-American Black Power.

In New South Wales, Gary Foley has pointed out that Redfern's Koori political activists grew up in rural districts and migrated to Sydney in the 1960s. Inspired by the 'Freedom Rides' of 1965, which had drawn city people's attention to racial discrimination in several country towns, the young migrants congregated at the Foundation for Aboriginal Affairs (810 George Street, near Central Railway Station), learning from seasoned older activists of the 1967 referendum and other campaigns: Ken Brindle, Charles Perkins, Shirley Smith, Faith Bandler, Bert Groves, Chicka Dixon and Dulcie Flower. They also met African-American servicemen (on leave from fighting in Vietnam) who introduced them to the political literature of US campaigns against racism, including the racism of law enforcement. Foley and his inner-city companions had direct experience of police brutality, and through annual FCAATSI conferences they met Aborigines from Melbourne and Brisbane with similar stories of uniformed racism. The Oakland (California) 'Black Power' model of a 'Pig Patrol' – monitoring police activity – appealed to them. Their strategy of using legal processes to put pressure on police found favour with Sydney lawyers, including the Dean of Law at the University of New South Wales, Hal Wootten. On 29 December 1970, the Australian government granted $20 000 to start the Redfern Aboriginal Legal Service in a shop front. As Foley recalls, a surge of pan-Aboriginal nationalism made the service an icon, boosting the confidence of Sydney Aborigines.[46]

Policy intellectuals who formulated 'self-determination' referred in hopeful terms to the Aboriginal tendency to 'group'. Charles Rowley, leader of a large multi-volume study of 'Aborigines in Australian Society', urged governments to focus less on changing individuals, and to encourage Aborigines to formalise collective action, as corporations.

> [T]he Aboriginal company is as important as an *objective* as for what it may achieve. Such an objective completely re-orients the whole approach of the government and the public service to Aboriginal affairs. Instead of a disappearing liability, as in 'assimilation', the Aboriginal group is re-sited in policy as an asset, to be endowed, by its own efforts, with enduring legal personality. The fringe group is the raw material for a corporation in perpetuity.[47]

Publicly funded voluntary organisations, supervised by men and women proud to call themselves 'black' and denouncing Australian society as racist, gave concrete form to what Rowley envisaged. The Fraser government's *Aboriginal Councils and Associations Act* 1976 encouraged Indigenous Australians to form corporations. The Howard government replaced this statute in 2006 with the *Corporations (Aboriginal and Torres Strait Islander) Act*. These laws have both facilitated 'group' action and prescribed the forms that groups should take. They have thus continued the underlying task of 'assimilation': to train colonised people to function within an imposed political order. Recognising that Aboriginal and Torres Strait Islanders are new to these modes of association, the Office of the Registrar of Indigenous Corporations seeks to train people in accountability to governments and to members and clients of the organisations.

In the fifth strand of 'self-determination', the Whitlam government experimented in national political representation. In 1973 Gordon Bryant (Minister for Aboriginal Affairs 1973–74) selected eighty-one Aboriginal and Torres Strait Islanders as an Interim National Aboriginal Consultative Committee (NACC), replacing it by November 1973 with an assembly elected from forty-one electorates by an 80 per cent turnout of the 37 000 Indigenous persons who voluntarily enrolled to vote. The NACC ran from 1973 to 1977, when the Fraser government replaced it with the National Aboriginal Congress (NAC); the NAC's first election (of thirty-five members, from an Indigenous electoral roll) was in November 1977. The Hawke government terminated the NAC in 1985, replacing it in 1989 with the Aboriginal and Torres Strait Islander Commission (ATSIC). The NACC and the NAC were merely advisory, but ATSIC was given programs that had formerly been the responsibility of the

Department of Aboriginal Affairs (DAA). The Howard government extinguished ATSIC in 2005.

In this series of experiments in Indigenous representation over a thirty-year period, Australian governments solicited the emergence of a national Indigenous leadership with a mandate to speak for all Aborigines and Torres Strait Islanders. To conceive of themselves as a national constituency was an unprecedented experiment in the scale of Indigenous politics. While aggregating Indigenous concerns into a 'national' view, each of these bodies had also to recognise and respect the local and particular, because there were significant regional differences in Indigenous circumstances and because most Aboriginal and Torres Strait Islander people find more tangible and legitimate the forums, personalities and issues of their region. Local and regional Indigenous politics were in these years becoming more lively, animated by the local corporations that formed to deal with local needs, including land councils set up as part of land rights legislation in the Northern Territory, New South Wales and Queensland. The electors of the NACC, NAC and ATSIC thus had increasing reason to focus on the vitality of local and regional politics, and the relevance of 'national' Aboriginal politics to their lives was open to doubt. The members elected to the NACC and to the NAC represented regional electorates, as members of the lower houses of Australian legislatures do, but it was not clear to such men and women how they were to consult with those who elected them, unless the elected member were prominent in the incorporated Indigenous organisations of their region, as many were. The architects of ATSIC learned how to articulate national with local political activity; ATSIC's national commissioners were elected from a tier of elected regional councils, though the discretion of regional councils in program administration was restricted by program design at the national level.

The Aboriginal and Torres Strait Islander politicians who invested time and hope in this series of national bodies thus faced an ongoing crisis of their legitimacy, called to account by local forums, jostled by competing Indigenous political platforms, often ignored by governments and – in the case of ATSIC – subject to intense scrutiny of their administration of what conservative populists called 'taxpayers' dollars'. It is reported that some sceptics of ATSIC quipped that the acronym stood for 'Aboriginals Talking Shit in Canberra'.[48]

Indigenous uncertainties

In July 1967, Neville Bonner, vice-president of OPAL, reflected on the large 'Yes' vote of May 27 by asking whether he and other Aboriginal people were yet 'fully equipped' for equality. Bonner was exemplary of the traits that the Queensland system aimed to encourage. He had been in and out of the Queensland reserve system and – at his wife, Mona's, insistence – he had spent the years 1945–60 living on Palm Island. His moderate stance during a 1957 dispute between Palm Island residents and the administration had attracted the favourable attention of the government, which rewarded Bonner with the very public role of managing the Department of Aboriginal and Islander Affairs' art and craft exhibition room in Brisbane. In 1967, acknowledging that 'my European brothers have gone to the polls full of confidence in his coloured kin ... [showing] full acceptance of me as a fellow citizen', Bonner asked 'Am I quite ready? Am I fully equipped? Is it too soon? Has the cart been put before the horse?' Equal citizenship imposed responsibilities on people who were 'untrained and untried', he suggested, when compared with 'our lighter brothers and sisters'. He asked the 'Yes'-voting Australian public to be 'tolerant' and 'patient': 'don't expect us to change overnight'.[49]

Compare Bonner with fellow Queenslander Kath Walker, an active member of the Queensland State Council for Advancement of Aborigines and Torres Strait Islanders. In December 1964 she had warned an audience of academics, clergy and public servants not to expect formal racial equality to deliver uniform happiness for Indigenous Australians. Drawing on personal experience of Queensland Aborigines who had 'got out from under the Act' and had made the transition to citizenship, she observed that when suddenly promoted from 'child' to 'adult', some misused their money before they 'levelled off'.[50] She had explained:

> There are some who will never ever make the grade, but the average are not any different from any other society or any other race. You all have your rejects. We are no different. We too are quite well aware of the fact that some of our people will not make the grade and we are not as naïve as to think that all of us can be rescued. Some of us will be left behind, as you yourselves have left some of your own people behind.[51]

Walker was herself soon to publish a book of poems that sold well to white Australians. Included was 'Civilisation', expressing ambivalence about entering into Australia's modern social order. The poem lists puzzling features of modernity ('Your strange cult of uniformity/This mass obedience to clocks, timetables.') before concluding:

> Suddenly caught up in white man's ways,
> Gladly and gratefully we accept,
> And this is necessity.
> But remember, white man, if life is for happiness,
> You too, surely, have much to change.[52]

The campaign to vote 'Yes' in the 1967 referendum had solicited a massive affirmation of racial equality, but some Indigenous Australians predicted that 'equality' would challenge them. The Whitlam government's commitment to self-determination in 1973 elicited Kevin Gilbert's searching inquiry into the Aboriginal 'self' that policy now required. Gilbert was a Wiradjuri man, raised in an orphanage from the age of seven. Finishing school after grade five, he worked as a rural labourer. Convicted of murder in 1957, he spent fourteen years in gaol, learning that prisoners enjoyed better material conditions than 'Aboriginal people, on the outside'.[53] In 1971, he became editor of (and almost sole contributor to) *Alchuringa*, the short-lived (four issues) organ of the National Aboriginal Theatre Foundation and the Aboriginal Tourist and Economic Development Association, covering the position of NSW Aborigines. Gilbert penned 'Of black patriots and a black intelligentsia', in which he complained of the ineffectiveness of 'respectable' Aborigines and the insincerity of 'verbally aggressive black radicals'.[54] While the inception of the Whitlam government in December 1972 seemed to him 'the best thing that has happened to blacks for a long time', he continued to warn in *Because a White Man'll Never Do It* (1973) that Aboriginal leadership remained flawed.[55] Redfern's young radicals would have to learn to be self-disciplined 'or the movement will never get out to where it is really needed – the Aboriginal reserves'.[56] He welcomed the recent overseas travels of several of his peers, for 'the average reserve black has the mental horizons of a Tennessee hillbilly'.[57]

However, he warned that young, educated and travelled Aborigines would have to contend with conservatives such as Neville Bonner, by then a Queensland Liberal senator. Aborigines such as Bonner were ambivalent about Aboriginal culture and even contemptuous of it, Gilbert alleged. They were too afraid of losing the acceptance of whites. Gilbert saw such people in OPAL, and he quoted the Wiradjuri student Paul Coe's observation that such blacks had also become comfortable in FCAATSI and in the Foundation for Aboriginal Affairs.[58] Like Kath Walker's strictures on 'black white parrots', Gilbert's book evinced much distrust of the leaders – at least those in New South Wales – who were within the milieu of the Minister for Aboriginal Affairs Gordon Bryant, a long-serving and high-ranking member of FCAATSI. Probably on legal advice, Gilbert was restrained in his comments on Charles Perkins, a rising public servant in Bryant's Department of Aboriginal Affairs, who had been a central figure in the Foundation for Aboriginal Affairs.[59]

Extensively quoting young NSW Aborigines, Gilbert demanded that 'self-determination' be more than a new platform for established and respectable Aborigines who had learned how to work with whites of goodwill. He questioned whether such an old guard, more empowered than ever by Labor, could be credible to the new militant generation that observed, from an admiring distance, the militancy of African-American 'Black Power'. As Labor policies opened fresh horizons of Aboriginal choice and initiative, Aboriginal leadership would be unstable, as people exposed each other's weaknesses: 'this honesty is going to hurt', he wrote, for the black community was psychologically 'far

... from a realization of the need not only to face and cease condoning its own gutlessness, but from a realization of the need for community self-discipline and total community organisation'.[60] He was not speaking for an idealised 'grass roots', he wrote, for he had no illusions about the quality of life on reserves where 'all hell breaks out on Friday night' and only police provide order.[61] Gilbert's mordant portrait of 'what Aborigines have become, at all levels' was motivated by his sense that at last Aborigines were being given a chance: 'there has been more growth for black people in the last two or three years than in almost two hundred years of previous white rule'.[62] However, he argued that without a program of self-reform, Aborigines would lack the capacity for self-determination.

Thus there was a tension within the transition from 'assimilation' to 'self-determination', in the 1970s. On the one hand, building on the more liberal and anti-racist inflections of assimilation policy, the transition conceded choice to Indigenous Australians about their involvement in what was referred to as the 'Australian way of life'. Self-determination afforded new modes of collective action and self-representation, and it solicited and valorised certain differences of heritage. On the other hand, the people best able to seize and operate the characteristic instruments of 'self-determination' were those most familiar with Australian institutions, those who had gained most from assimilation. Regional and generational differences became apparent in the ways that new opportunities were seen and grasped; the new sense of purpose and opportunity was laced with self-doubt and mutual recrimination. Self-determination changed political relationships among Indigenous Australians.

9

The Indigenous Estate in Land and Sea

In the last third of the 20th century, nearly one-fifth of the Australian land mass was transferred to Indigenous Australians' ownership. By 2013, Indigenous interests had been recognised over more than half of Australia – a combination of land rights, native title, and Indigenous Land Use Agreements enabled by the assertion of native title.[1] To this estate, hectares will be added every year through purchases by the Indigenous Land Corporation (ILC), a statutory authority set up by the Keating government in June 1995. As long as the ILC's endowment yields an annual purchase fund, there is no limit to the acreage that can be, to some degree, Indigenous land.[2]

This 'land titling revolution' (Altman's term) was inconceivable in the 1960s, when Indigenous people and their allies first used the phrase 'land rights'.[3] However, whether Indigenous Australians had a right to land and seas had ceased to be an issue of politics or jurisprudence by 1998. By amending the *Native Title Act* 1993 the Howard government sealed bipartisan acceptance of 'native title'; in the same year the Federal Court ruled that the Croker Island community had rights to the sea and seabed adjacent to the island: by customary right, they could travel through it, gather its food products (non-commercially), visit its sacred places and protect their knowledge of these places.[4]

The rise of the Indigenous estate has rested on the political condition that non-Indigenous land interests are not dispossessed. In 1983, the Wran government made this explicit. Under pressure from 40 000 NSW Aborigines and their supporters to allow Aborigines to claim even privately held, leased or public land, Attorney-General Frank Walker explained that such claims would arouse 'unnecessary political and social antagonism in the community, squander enormous amounts in drawn out legal battles to obtain resumption orders on private land' and oblige the government to pay 'just compensation at market value to the owners'.[5] His political judgment was soon mirrored by the common law: the High Court's 1992 Mabo judgment, while questioning the morality of the Crown's past indifference to Indigenous peoples' pre-existing ownership, reaffirmed Australian governments' sovereign right to extinguish native title.[6] Land rights are what a legislature chooses to grant; native title rights are what remains after sovereign Australia has decided what it does not want. The defining asymmetry of Australian law is that while settler-colonial right can extinguish native title right, the reverse does not apply. The Indigenous Estate does not require Australian law to surrender colonial prerogative; it results from fairer exercise of that authority.

Four processes have assembled the Indigenous Estate. First, governments have legislated to *convert former reserve lands* to Indigenous title; this has yielded much Indigenous Estate in the Northern Territory, Queensland, South Australia and Western Australia. Second, governments have legislated procedures for *assessing Indigenous claims* to certain lands; some procedures (in

MAP 2 **The Indigenous Land and Sea Estate (2017) and the Aboriginal and Torres Strait Islander Population (2016), by jurisdiction**

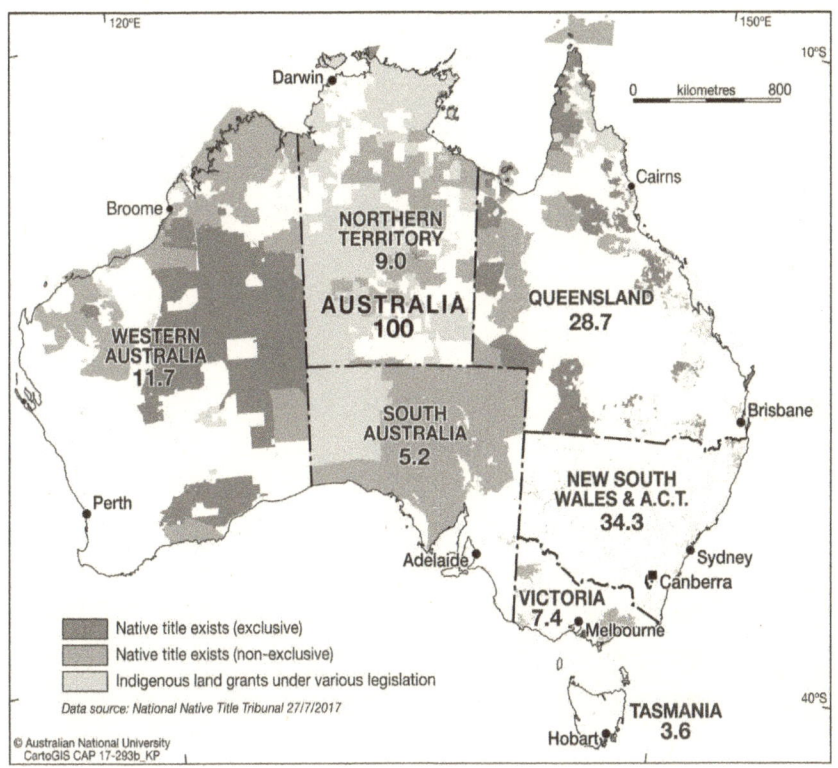

This map shows the extent of the Indigenous Land and Sea Estate in July 2017. The map includes tenures of different kinds and strengths. (More detail on kinds of title and their legislative basis is available on the website of the National Native Title Tribunal.) The map also shows the proportion of the total Australian Indigenous population living in each State or Territory, according to the 2016 Census. Thus the map shows that Indigenous Land and Sea Estate has accumulated largely in the hinterlands of Western Australia, Queensland, Northern Territory and South Australia – jurisdictions inhabited by a relatively small proportion of the Australian Indigenous population. Whereas the Indigenous Land and Sea Estate is mostly in 'remote' and 'very remote' Australia, the Indigenous population is more like the non-Indigenous population – that is, heavily urbanised. In 2006, 32 per cent of Indigenous Australians lived in major cities, 21 per cent in 'inner regional' areas, 22 per cent in 'outer regional' areas, 9 per cent in remote areas and 15 per cent in very remote areas.

Queensland and the Northern Territory land rights law and in native title proceedings in the Federal Court) involve the adjudication of evidence of customary association with the land claimed and the weighing of non-claimant objections. Third, government agencies and endowed Indigenous organisations, using public funds, have *purchased land* on the market and have vested ownership in Indigenous entities. Fourth, in response to some groups' assertions of native title, governments and natural resource corporations have *negotiated land use agreements* that effectively recognise specific 'native title' interests.

Reserves

Reserves were strategies to ameliorate the destructive effects of dispossession; authorities judged how much land to allow for Aborigines to occupy under supervision. As the colonists advanced into the remoter parts of the continent, humanitarians persuaded governments to declare as 'reserves' large areas unsuited to colonial enterprise. Governments conceived reserves not as their residents' property but as protective sanctuaries and later as sites of training; assimilation policy envisaged that residents, once trained, would leave reserves. Governments in Tasmania, Victoria and New South Wales were well advanced, by the 1960s, in extinguishing the reserves (a tiny proportion of each state's area), thus ending the racial segregation of those they purported to train. To revoke reserves was to declare their residents sufficiently uplifted to enter the mainstream of Australian life. The more recently declared reserves in the remote regions of the North and Centre were larger and their residents would take longer to train: to revoke these large remote reserves was not in immediate prospect. Indeed, as recently as 1959, the Australian and Western Australian governments jointly declared the region that includes Lake Mackay and Lake Macdonald to be a reserve for Western Desert Aborigines.

Incidents on Cape York, in eastern Victoria and in Arnhem Land aroused public demands in the 1950s and 1960s that governments recognise reserves as residents' property. In Queensland, by the early 1950s, Presbyterian missionaries who had formed communities on Cape York early in the 20th century were ambivalent about the state government request to the Presbyterian Board of Missions to merge the Mapoon and Weipa populations (by closing Mapoon) and the Mornington Island and Aurukun populations (by closing the mission on Mornington Island). Yielding reluctantly to the wish of the Lardil people and missionaries to maintain Mornington Island Mission, Queensland then ignored further representations of the Presbyterian missionaries. In 1957 Queensland leased 5780 square kilometres of the reserve land around Mapoon and Weipa Missions to Comalco, a bauxite miner. The government hoped that reserve residents would become employees of Comalco. When these Aboriginal people spurned inducements to leave Mapoon, the government forcibly removed them in November 1963, burning their dwellings.[7]

The Mapoon assault was a critical moment in state–church relations. Christian churches had begun, in the 1940s, to debate how to discharge their responsibility to Aboriginal people on missions. Should they collaborate with government programs of development, or should they respect residents' customary attachment to country on which missions stood? When Anglicans considered this question, they were painfully aware of the material and cultural inadequacies of their Queensland missions: perhaps handing responsibility to state governments was the best course?[8]

In Victoria, the government did not have to confront mission authorities when it sought to complete the settlement closures that it had initiated in 1917 (closing Lake Condah) and had continued with Coranderrk's closure in 1923. Framlingham and Lake Tyers remained, their populations diminishing in the years following World War II. In 1956, Lake Tyers resident Laurie Moffatt told the Melbourne *Sun* that the remaining residents wanted to stay and to manage the reserve, including farming the land. However, in 1963 the government said it would close Lake Tyers and assist the dispersion of its residents. A public campaign in which Aboriginal Christians such as Church of Christ Pastor Douglas Nicholls were prominent persuaded the government to reverse this decision: in May 1965 Lake Tyers became a 'Permanent Reserve'.[9]

In the Northern Territory, the residents of Yirrkala Mission were astounded to learn in 1963 that their estate had been excised from the Arnhem Land Reserve to enable bauxite mining. Encouraged by their Methodist missionaries, Edgar and Anne Wells, they submitted two petitions, on bark, to the Australian parliament. A select committee of inquiry in 1963 criticised the government's failure to consult, but it did not declare the reserve to be the property of the Yolngu.

Each of these cases made the Australian public aware that Aboriginal people were resisting assimilation scenarios that cost them their homelands. Pleas such as the Yirrkala petitions made it necessary to consider how to reconcile Indigenous entitlement with the imperative to 'develop' land and to enable residents' employment.[10] Missionaries with a sense of trusteeship had to evaluate the secular model of Aboriginal development presented by governments and, in Northern Australia, by mining companies.[11] According to John Harris, 'the modern land rights movement and the involvement of the churches can be said to have begun with the Methodists in the 1960s'.[12] At the same time, the new human rights idea of 'indigenous rights' presented reserves as tribal homelands. In 1957, ILO Convention 107 affirmed 'the rights of ownership, collective or individual' over lands that Indigenous people 'traditionally occupy' (article 11) in member states. Australia did not ratify this convention, but in 1958 the Federal Council for Aboriginal Advancement (FCAA) included in its foundational platform the words 'Absolute retention of all remaining native reserves, with native communal or individual ownership'.[13] In the year that the Yirrkala Aborigines submitted their petitions, there were still 353 separate reserves for Indigenous Australians, totalling 48 500 hectares (119 846 acres), with 53 000 residents. A growing portion of the Australian public began to question whether 'development' had to entail what Aboriginal people considered to be dispossession.[14]

However, 'land rights' was an awkward innovation within Australian liberalism. Those promoting the civil rights of Indigenous Australians did not present the 1967 referendum on the Australian government's constitutional power as a plebiscite on land rights; sticking to safer ideological ground, they projected equality, citizenship and inclusiveness as their goals. The 'civil rights' slogans of the referendum campaign were not easy to reconcile with 'land rights' that were specific to Indigenous Australians: 'similarity, not difference, was emphasised in the referendum campaign'.[15] Popular support for 'land rights' nonetheless grew quickly in the second half of the 1960s. In 1966–67, the Gurindji people on Wave Hill pastoral lease, with the help of Communist trade unions, FCAATSI and church groups, campaigned nationally for the right to better conditions of employment and for title to a portion of their homeland.

Public perceptions proved to be more labile than the law, which held that reserves were not the customary property of residents but merely the Crown's act of grace. From 1968 to 1971, the residents of Yirrkala Mission, encouraged by Methodist clergy, tested this presumption by litigating the Commonwealth government's permission to mine the reserve. Until this case, no judge had been obliged to state the common law doctrine on which Aborigines' dispossession rested, simply because no Aboriginal people had briefed counsel to present their customs of ownership for adjudication. Responding to the Yolngu in 1971, Justice Richard Blackburn invoked a judgment from 1889 – not a case involving Aboriginal interests – that Australia is a 'settled' colony, meaning that there was no law in Australia until the colonists introduced British law and then passed their own laws. Conventional narratives of Australian history had so marginalised Aborigines' prior occupation and resistance to invasion that they offered scarcely no factual challenge to this legal fiction. By forcing a judge to spell out the fiction, the Yirrkala plaintiffs drew attention to its moral and factual weaknesses. Many Australians thought it unfair that Yolngu wishes could be doctrinally dismissed. If there were no Aboriginal property rights unless they were created by British-Australian law-makers, then law-makers had a choice: tell the plaintiffs to reconcile themselves to dispossession as the price of their improvement, or legislate Aboriginal title in Arnhem Land.

The public was learning to appreciate Aboriginal traditions. The Yolngu had presented their title deeds, in 1963, as painted images referring to their connections with their homelands, inviting Australians to interpret their art as an expression of spiritual connection with place.¹⁶ That land rights was being championed by some missionaries helped to alienate Christian opinion from governments whose secular schemes of assimilation made light of Aborigines' spiritual connection to land. Prime Minister William McMahon conceded, in a speech released for Australia Day 1972, that Aboriginal people had an affinity with the reserve land. His government would award Yolngu a general purpose lease, but only if 'they have the intention and ability to make reasonable economic and social use of the land applied for'. His government would not concede that Yolngu held a customary right, fearing 'uncertainty and possible challenge in relation to land titles elsewhere in Australia which are at present unquestioned and secure'.¹⁷

The Australian Labor Party was by then proposing an alternative. The 1967 ALP national conference had resolved to make 'special provisions for aborigines to reside in reservations where they prefer' and to investigate 'forms of titles and land ownership'.¹⁸ In 1969, the conference had resolved:

> All Aboriginal lands to be vested in a public trust or trusts composed of Aborigines or Islanders as appropriate. That exclusive corporate land rights be granted to Aboriginal communities which retain a strong tribal structure or demonstrate a potential for corporate action in regard to land at present reserved for the use of Aborigines, or where traditional occupancy according to tribal custom can be established from anthropological or other evidence. No Aboriginal lands shall be alienated except with the approval both of the trust and of Parliament. Aboriginal land rights shall carry with them full rights to minerals in those lands.¹⁹

The Whitlam government elected on 2 December 1972 thus claimed a mandate to legislate Aboriginal title to reserves, and it sought advice from Royal Commissioner Edward Woodward (who had pleaded for the Yirrkala litigants before Blackburn). A Bill based on Woodward's reports was before the Australian parliament in November 1975 when the governor-general John Kerr dismissed the Whitlam government. However, land rights was confirmed as bipartisan when the Fraser government (1975–83) passed the *Aboriginal Land Rights (Northern Territory) Act* 1976 (a revision of Whitlam's Bill). The Act gave Aborigines in the Territory title to reserves, and it established an Aboriginal Land Commissioner to assess claims to land that the Crown had not yet alienated.

South Australia and Victoria had preceded the Commonwealth. In 1966, South Australia vested the reserves in a Lands Trust, and in 1970, Victoria granted freehold title to the residents of Framlingham and Lake Tyers Reserves. However, these two states' laws did not recognise a *customary right* to reserves. The assumptions behind 'assimilation' policy remained strong; these two states' concessions of title arose from the belief that Aborigines would take more responsibility for their futures if the Crown empowered them as trustees of reserves. In a similar spirit, as one of a series of reforms flowing from a 1965 parliamentary inquiry into Aboriginal policy, New South Wales in 1973 created an Aboriginal Land Trust to hold title to all reserves. The Western Australian government in 1972 began to vest reserves in an advisory trust whose members it appointed and supervised.[20] In the Northern Territory the Commonwealth went further – not only by recognising the customary basis of the Aboriginal property right but also by creating strong structures of Aboriginal representation – statutory land councils to advise and to act for Traditional Owners. The Territory land councils were financed by government payments equal to mining royalties on Aboriginal land, giving Traditional Owners an incentive not to refuse minerals exploration. The Australian Mining Industry Council (AMIC) objected that Traditional Owners should not have a choice about mining. Under executive director James Strong, the AMIC argued in the early 1980s that since minerals belonged to the Crown and thus to all Australians, Aborigines should not have the right to block development of shared wealth. The Commonwealth's model of land rights, argued the AMIC, undermined the legal 'equality' of all title-holders and thus jeopardised racial harmony.[21]

This critique of land rights revealed that the liberal political culture of Australia allowed two opposed notions of fairness. On the one hand, fairness to Indigenous Australians compelled respect for their customary right to determine land use; on the other hand, the nation, imagined as a community of equals, had a right to access all of the continent's natural endowment, without impediment from particular interests.

The Commonwealth's land rights law put pressure on the states to reconsider their approaches. Under South Australia's 1966 Act, the Pitjantjatjara of the North-West Reserve ('Anangu') had been encouraged to send delegates to a state-wide land trust established by the Dunstan government, but Anangu found it hard to identify with the Aborigines from the south of the state who were implementing the trust, and they were dissatisfied that the minister's powers over the trust did not give them the final say about who could visit their country. As well, the Anangu homelands straddled three jurisdictions: they knew that South Australian law did not secure their land across the border in Western Australia, and they were aware of what Woodward's Royal Commission was recommending in the Northern Territory.

In 1976, Anangu established the Pitjantjatjara Council. Though its members were bonded by song-lines that cut across state/territory borders, they heeded advice that they be good federalists and assert their claims severally, in three jurisdictions. The South Australian government was sympathetic to the council's request for a distinct Pitjantjatjara Land Trust, and the idea enjoyed the support of both sides of parliament. To demonstrate their determination to city folk, the people of the North-West Reserve camped on Victoria Park Racecourse in February 1980. South Australia passed the *Pitjantjatjara Land Rights Act* in 1981.[22] This encouraged Anangu to the south of the reserve to assert their customary right to the 'Maralinga lands' – the site of nuclear tests in the 1950s. Premier Thomas Playford had promised the return of these blighted lands in 1962, and when the government granted a mining lease to Aquitaine, the company was obliged to consult southern Pitjantjatjara – mostly then living at Yalata – in order to avoid damaging sacred sites. The miners' road-building and archaeological research encouraged more visits by Anangu who had continued – despite up to three generations' absence – to regard the land as theirs by customary right. Negotiations with the government took place on the lands, at Oak Valley. There were no political costs in giving Anangu title to radioactive dirt, and the media and the public found the astutely led and well-advised southern Pitjantjatjara convincing. The parliament passed the *Maralinga Tjarutja Land Rights Act* in March 1984.[23] The owners of these former reserves or weapons-testing lands have the right to negotiate with miners, and a judge must arbitrate unresolved negotiations.

In Victoria, after transferring Framlingham and Lake Tyers

Reserves to Aboriginal ownership (*Aboriginal Land Act* 1970), the state government provided for funded corporations to govern these lands in the *Aboriginal Land (Lake Condah and Framlingham Forest) Act* 1987, in which rights to negotiate over mining follow the South Australian model.

Facing a public with much sympathy for Aboriginal land claims, Queensland at first would give no more than fifty-year leases, to two reserves, in 1978. Queensland warned the Fraser government not to use the power conferred by the 1967 referendum. The Australian government declined to confront, with land rights, the potent political sentiment of 'states' rights'. The Bjelke-Petersen government vested deeds of grant in trust to reserve councils (*Land Act (Aboriginal and Islander Land Grants) Amendment Act* 1982), making them part of the state's local government system, with significantly weaker powers over land use compared to titles conceded to Aboriginal owners in the Northern Territory, Victoria and South Australia. In Western Australia, the government led by Charles Court saw mining as central to economic development. When the Bunuba Traditional Owners of Noonkanbah pastoral lease blocked the access of geologists testing for oil near a sacred site in 1979, Court despatched police to eject their blockade. The Court government's 1980 amendments to the *Aboriginal Heritage Act* weakened the only legal recourse of Aboriginal customary law.

Noonkanbah polarised Australian views about what Aboriginal people required and deserved. Portraying 'land rights' as Canberra's economically ruinous imposition on their states, Premiers Court and Bjelke-Petersen won significant popular support, kept alive the hopes of the mining industry's leaders, and humiliated the more liberal MPs in the conservative parties. The Hawke Labor government, succeeding the Fraser government in

1983, promised to use the Commonwealth's concurrent powers to impose national land rights legislation. However, the Minister for Aboriginal Affairs, Clyde Holding, proposed a 'national model' that would satisfy the mining industry; he thus infuriated the Northern Territory's Aboriginal Land Councils by trying to persuade them to give up the Traditional Owners' mining veto, for the sake of national uniformity. Meanwhile, the mining industry strengthened its bargaining position by enlisting the Western Australian government led by Brian Burke. In 1984–85, the Burke government was considering vesting the state's reserves and pastoral leases held by the trust (an advisory body) more fully in Aboriginal title-holding bodies – freeing Traditional Owners from the authority that the Minister (for Community Welfare and Aboriginal Affairs) exercised over trust lands under the *Aboriginal Affairs Planning Authority Act* 1972. The Western Australia Chamber of Mines ran advertisements warning that such land rights would surrender that state's future wealth to a black minority. By increasing measured public opinion against land rights, the chamber's campaign persuaded the Burke government to agitate against land rights within the Labor Party. In 1986, the Hawke government abandoned national land rights, citing (and leaking) an Australian National Opinion Poll (ANOP) study that showed (on Labor's reading) a weakened mandate for land rights.[24]

Notwithstanding this defeat, urban and reserve-dwelling Aboriginal people (increasingly in touch with each other) persisted, with significant public support. Changes in the policy of the National Party government of Queensland in the 1980s illustrate the increasing political difficulty of conservative resistance to their demand for land title. Opponents of land rights must have sensed their weakening purchase on Queensland opinion when, on 10 March 1983, the leaders of the Anglican and Roman Catholic communities of Queensland publicly rejected the Nationals' claim that the 1982 Deeds of Grant in Trust were assuring reserve residents 'security and stability'.[25] Appointed Minister for Aboriginal Affairs from October 1983, Robert Katter embodied the ideological flexibility that embattled conservatives now needed. His lifetime association with Aborigines in northern Queensland and his unquestioning belief in the long-term soundness of Queensland's native policy made him confident that 'land rights' did not have to be 'apartheid' (as some of his colleagues had said); it could be the next step in the normalisation of reserve residents, their integration in Queensland's local government system. Thus Katter's *Aborigines and Torres Strait Islanders (Land Holding) Act* 1985, complemented by community services legislation, granted private ownership of homes on reserves and encouraged lease-holding for small businesses. He contrasted this with the Commonwealth's Northern Territory model where, he said, inalienable collective title over reserves and claimed lands inhibited development.

> Neither the federal nor state government has the financial
> resources required to develop these remote and already
> heavily subsidised areas [in Queensland]. The people
> themselves, however, will be able to develop their blocks
> individually ... Aboriginal and Islander people ...
> should enjoy the same rights and privileges and bear
> the same responsibilities and obligations as every other
> Queenslander.[26]

Katter believed that he had Indigenous support; he certainly had the mute acceptance of the Hawke government (whose polling indicated the wider public's acceptance of Katter's approach).²⁷ In Katter's ceremonial bestowal of title deeds over the next few years, he was repeatedly celebrated as the champion of Queensland's reserve populations. The National Party government soon found itself on better terms with the Aboriginal Coordinating Council – the reserve community leaders empowered by Katter's laws. Their dialogue led to agreement, in 1987, that community councils should have more say over mining on reserves than Queensland law allowed to anyone holding freehold title. This was a blow, from an unexpected quarter, against the AMIC's cherished notion of fairness as formal legal equality (equal vulnerability to the demands of miners), and it became a benchmark against which to measure subsequent 'land rights' laws in Queensland.²⁸ In 1991, the Goss Labor government built on Katter's achievements with the *Aboriginal Land Act* 1991 and the *Torres Strait Islander Land Act* 1991. These Acts added 20 000 square kilometres of vacant Crown land (1.16 per cent of the state) to 34 000 square kilometres of land held by Aboriginals and Torres Strait Islanders. Goss's laws transferred Deed of Grant in Trust (DOGIT) reserve lands, including the Aurukun and Mornington Island shire leases, to Aboriginal trust ownership, and they established a land tribunal to hear claims for vacant Crown land (except in towns and cities), which was gazetted as claimable land.²⁹

In all mainland states other than New South Wales, the reserve system – large or small – was well defined, and so participants in debate about land rights knew what was at stake; the issue for politics was how to formulate a compromise between the security of reserve owners' tenure and the nation's right to realise the land's wealth. In New South Wales, however, the existence of reserves themselves became a legal and thus a political issue. Consultations by the government in the period 1979–83 aroused Aboriginal expectations that Labor would legislate title to New South Wales reserves; Aborigines were beginning to assert claims. However, a review of seventy years of land administration revealed that New South Wales governments, since Federation, had illegally given away or assigned to other public uses 15 000 hectares of reserves. Only 4378 hectares had been preserved from such loose dealing, having been transferred to the Aboriginal Land Trust since 1974. While the latter 'reserves' would become Aboriginal land, it was not clear who now owned the illegally revoked acreage. If Aborigines claimed such lands, the absence of clear title deeds would threaten the interests of those non-Aborigines who now considered themselves owners; their protest would erode assurance that no member of the public would lose land under land rights policy. The Wran government therefore decided to pair the *Aboriginal Land Rights Act* 1983 with legislation 'to validate the theft of many thousands of hectares' retrospectively, confirming Aborigines' 'deep-seated suspicion and fear of deception by governments'.[30] The NSW law is unique in the history of Australian land rights for the Aboriginal antipathy that it aroused. Aborigines in New South Wales had cherished reserves as material links to a pre-colonial past and as the sites of surviving community; white authorities' years of careless disposal, validated legally by the Crown in 1983, left a deep wound. New South Wales made steps towards healing by setting up a land purchase fund and by allowing that Aboriginal freehold title included ownership of minerals – other than gold, silver, coal and petroleum, which continue to belong to the Crown.

The attrition of population and of reserve land in Tasmania might well have pre-empted any conversation about land rights. The government of Tasmania had legislated Cape Barren Island as a reserve in 1912, conceding it to be the residents' 'moral' but not legal right.[31] Although Tasmanian Aborigines have maintained a sense of Cape Barren Island as a homeland, the Tasmanian reserve heritage, from the government's point of view, was too broken and discontinuous to enable the smooth political and legal transition from 'reserve' to 'Aboriginal land' that occurred in mainland Australia. When the *Cape Barren Reserve Act* expired in 1951, the government thought that there were no longer any 'Tasmanian Aborigines'. However, after the government recognised the Aboriginal community by the late 1980s and early 1990s, it commenced land title negotiations. Tasmanian legislation in 1995 and 1999 granted the elected eight-member Aboriginal Land Council of Tasmania title to small areas at Risdon Cove, Oyster Cove and Wybalenna, where Aboriginal people had lost their lives in the 19th century – either through combat or through heartless and incompetent administration. In 1995, Premier Ray Groom evoked Risdon Cove as a site of recent ceremonies commemorating soldiers and Aborigines who had clashed fatally in 1804. As well, he welcomed the site's 'clear heritage and cultural tourism potential.[32] Premier Jim Bacon in 1999 referred to Risdon Cove, Oyster Cove and Wybalenna as 'sacred sites' in the memories of Tasmania's Aborigines.[33] By invoking a narrative of violence and dispossession, Tasmania's negotiators innovated in the rationales for Aboriginal title. The government narrative of conquest and resistance added Aboriginal themes to older 'convict' heritage themes, while borrowing and augmenting the mainland Aboriginal idea of 'sacred site'.

Land purchases

On the recommendation of Royal Commissioner Woodward in 1974, the Whitlam government initiated land purchases. The Aboriginal Land Fund Commission (ALFC, 1975–80) was succeeded by the purchasing programs of the Aboriginal Development Commission (1980–89), of the commercial arm of ATSIC (1989–95) and, since 1995, of the Indigenous Land Corporation. Each has operated on a national basis. The ALFC chair Charles Rowley declared in 1980 that Aborigines' 'orderly human living' depended on their control over 'land, water, shelter, etc'.[34]

The ALFC's purchases – fifty-nine properties, for $6 million – provoked resistance from the governments of Western Australia and Queensland who feared that under Aboriginal ownership land would not be productive. The Queensland government opposed the purchase of land 'for development by Aborigines or Aboriginal groups in isolation' and so would not transfer the lease to Archer River Station, purchased by ALFC in February 1976.[35] The ALFC sought to reassure Queensland that the lease would be run as a beef business, but Queensland wanted another buyer – perhaps the mining company Comalco. The stand-off led John Koowarta – one of the intended lease-holders – to bring an action in the Queensland Supreme Court, arguing that, by refusing the lease transfer, the state government was discriminating against him, in violation of the Commonwealth *Racial Discrimination Act* 1975 (RDA). When the court ruled in Koowarta's favour, Queensland (with support from Victoria and Western Australia) challenged the constitutional validity of the RDA. The High Court of Australia ruled that the RDA expressed Australia's commitment to the international community to oppose racial discrimination; it was thus a valid Act under the constitutional power of the national government to make agreements with other nations.[36]

The ALFC's land-buying duty passed to the Aboriginal Development Commission (ADC), steered by an appointed Indigenous board, in 1980. By the time the ADC terminated in 1989, 148 properties had been purchased since 1975 (the figure included the fifty-nine purchased by ALFC).[37] Land-buying then became one of the programs of the Aboriginal and Torres Strait Islander Commission (ATSIC): from 1990 to 1997, ATSIC acquired approximately 200 properties.[38] In 1997, the Indigenous Land Corporation (ILC) took this program over; it had purchased 250 properties by the end of June 2014.[39]

Among the rationales for these purchases (many have been pastoral leases), 'cultural significance' ranked high, though some properties were for commercial and/or administrative use. The purchasing agencies have vested titles in incorporated community bodies, when they judged the recipient capable of holding title. In 1980, Rowley reflected that to gain control over land through the ALFC process was, at first, disruptive for people long dispossessed; it required the new owners to form leadership and to come to agreement on the distribution of surpluses, and it obliged the ALFC to help them devise development plans.[40] As the implications of full legal ownership sank in, Indigenous proprietors might choose to sell, lease or borrow against their land rather than to develop it. This was extremely unlikely when the land was of 'cultural significance'. However, all agencies considered land also as a base for commercial activity, imagining the new owners as not only spiritual but also entrepreneurial folk.

Not only Commonwealth agencies have purchased land for Aboriginal groups; so too has the New South Wales Aboriginal Land Council, using a fund created by siphoning 7.5 per cent of land tax over fifteen years (1984–99). Half was for land purchase. Local land councils, established by the Act, have purchased properties in their region – such as 'Weinteriga', on the Darling River, for the Wilcannia Local Aboriginal Land Council, and a cattle station renamed 'Barooga Karrai' (warrior lands) by the Wiradjuri Land Council.

Land claiming

Some Australian jurisdictions set up adjudicative processes through which Aboriginal people could claim Crown land. In New South Wales, the *Lands Rights Act* 1983 appointed the Minister for Crown Lands as the ultimate judge of such claims, once they had been formulated by the Office of the Registrar (an office created by the Act) and reviewed by the Crown Lands Office. Ministers have discretion to judge whether the claim is pre-empted by the government having already intended a public purpose (other than satisfying Aboriginal aspirations) for the land. Non-Aboriginal interests have often lobbied the government to refuse claims; ministers have varied in their sympathies for one or other side of the argument. Of the 17 600 claims made by May 2009, only 2325 had been granted by 2013.[41] In the western third of New South Wales, non-Indigenous lease-holders persuaded the NSW government to restrict Aboriginal grants to lease-hold.[42]

Under the Northern Territory *Aboriginal Land Rights Act* (ALRA) the claimants were obliged, in the years 1977 to 1997, to submit to a land commissioner evidence of their 'spiritual' attachment to lands (other than the reserves that automatically came into their hands with the passing of the ALRA). In Queensland, under the *Aboriginal Land Act* 1991 and the *Torres Strait Islander Land Act* 1991, a land tribunal heard claims to non-reserve land based on customary and historical associations and on evidence of economic and cultural viability. In both jurisdictions, these processes have necessitated ethnographic reports that have enlarged our knowledge of how customary law regulates who can credibly (in the eyes of Aboriginal people themselves) claim ownership of land.

Until the 1960s – before Australian law took any interest in Aboriginal customary law – anthropologists had inherited from the University of Sydney anthropologist A. Radcliffe-Brown a model of the land-owning group as patrilineal – what Radcliffe-Brown most often called the localised exogamous patrilineal horde. That is, a person's rights were determined by his or her descent from an acknowledged male ancestor, and the right of ownership passed down through the male line. The network of blood relatives defined by this shared inheritance was sometimes known to anthropologists as a clan. Radcliffe-Brown used the terms 'clan' and 'horde', presenting the 'horde' as combining people from more than one clan.

> The horde ... as an existing group at any moment, consists of (1) male members of all ages whose fathers and father's [sic] fathers belonged to the horde, (2) unmarried girls who are the sisters or daughters of the male members, (3) married women, all of whom, in some regions, and most of whom, in others, belong originally to other hordes, and have become attached to the horde by marriage.[43]

That is, a woman belonged to her father's clan (because she had been born into it) and until married participated in the life of the horde in which her clan was the core; she then became part of her husband's horde, and as a member of his horde she was in day-to-day association with people from the clan into which she had married. Research in Arnhem Land and the Western Desert in the late 1950s and early 1960s made more of this clan/horde distinction (to which Radcliffe-Brown had attached little importance). The people with whom one resided and hunted from day to day came to be known as the 'band' or, in some accounts, the 'community'. Like Radcliffe-Brown's 'horde', in any 'band' there would be persons drawn (by in-marriage or friendship) from more than one clan. Notwithstanding this increased attention to the band as a social unit, the revised model of Aboriginal social organisation continued to present patrilineal inheritance as the way that customary rights of ownership and use were passed on; thus the 'clan' was seen as the fundamental political unit.

Beginning with Justice Blackburn's testing of this model in the hearing of the Yirrkala plaintiffs in 1968–69, and proceeding through hearings of land claims under the Northern Territory and Queensland laws, this model gave way to a greater appreciation of the sensitivity of 'customary law' to practical exigency, in two ways. First, it had already become clear from ethnographic research since the late 1950s that Aboriginal custom accorded land *usage* rights more widely and flexibly than the model of *inherited ownership* seemed to allow. Inheritance was not the only consideration in the minds of Aboriginal people as they considered degrees of 'ownership'; prolonged associations between people – living together, hunting together – were also relevant when people considered ways that land belonged to them. Rights to use country could be negotiated among band or community associates, without compromising the more restricted allocation, through descent, of rights and responsibilities in the ceremonies that performed custody (or 'ownership') of country. This willingness to negotiate rights of usage was particularly important as

Aboriginal people came to reside in larger aggregates such as missions, settlements and pastoral stations. The more exclusive sense of 'ownership' remained; it applied especially to those valued areas that were coming to be known as 'sacred sites'.[44]

At the same time, it became clear to researchers that there was more than one way that a person could claim descent as the basis of a proprietary interest in country. Evidence presented at the first few land claims in the Northern Territory showed that a person inherited rights not only from his or her father (and grandfather), but also from his/her mother (and grandmother). A person could inherit rights to more than one place; custody of country and ceremony, it emerged, was a process of cooperation (sometimes tense) between sets of persons with complementary duties inherited down the male line and down the female line. Female anthropologists (more numerous and influential in the 1980s than ever before) pointed out that a male-centred account of Aboriginal society had reflected the social character of anthropology as a disciplinary community: men talking to other men about the business of men. The training of more female anthropologists and the law's forensic fieldwork in land claims hearings combined to transform 'expert' knowledge of the inheritance of rights and the formation of land-holding groups.

The revision of scholarly knowledge of Aboriginal law has made it easier to imagine Aboriginal people as historical actors – that is, as people using the flexibility built into their customary law to adapt to the pressures of colonial occupation in the regulation of their own affairs and in the transmission of entitlements. Marcia Langton, an Aboriginal anthropologist who has worked on land claims in the Northern Territory and in Cape York, has argued that colonisation, in some regions, has affected men and women differently. As the ranks of older males were thinned by violence, disease, arrest, alcoholism and employment, some communities cohered around a 'female gerontocracy'. To the extent that men have figured less in the oral transmission of who belonged where, it has become important to know mothers' and grandmothers' stories of belonging to country, to hear women's accounts of the links between generations that pass from mother to children, and to note the links, within generations, between sisters.[45] The pressure of land rights law has encouraged the elaboration of such accounts of relatedness among Aboriginal people themselves. These accounts have been repeated by land claimants, incorporated as evidence into anthropologists' and lawyers' revised models of land-owning corporations, and legitimised by judges' and commissioners' findings. The presentation of land claims evidence has in this sense vivified Aboriginal custom.[46] If the revealed flexibility of custom made it difficult for an outsider to draw a clear line around an owning group and to codify variations in rights among those with some entitlement, the difficulty was not significant to those who made the system work; they sorted things out, peacefully or not, in a pragmatic way.

Indigenous Land Use Agreements

In the 1990s, Australia created a new proprietary interest – the Indigenous Land Use Agreement (ILUA) – whose substance is largely determined by negotiation. The opportunity to negotiate is grounded in the legislative formulation of 'native title'. So how did Australia come to recognise 'native title'?

In 1981 the Melbourne barrister Barbara Hocking asked a conference at James Cook University: 'Will Australia ever join with her fellow members of the British Commonwealth and uphold the customary traditional ownership of the Indigenous

Aboriginal people?'[47] Solicitor Greg McIntyre spoke next, arguing that what recent statutes had encoded as 'land rights' did not fully realise the possible scope of Indigenous rights. Having studied common law judgments in British and US courts that recognised 'native title', he predicted that the judicial recognition of 'native title' might 'spur' legislative action.[48] McIntyre recruited Torres Strait Islander plaintiffs. With over 100 years of contact, Islanders were Christian and loyal (they had formed the Torres Strait Infantry Battalion in World War II). As residents of reserves, they had long assumed that the Strait's islands remained their legal possession. The Queensland government had encouraged this belief (not wanting Islanders to move to the mainland) and had institutionalised limited Islander authority in councils. However, with the politicising of 'land rights' in the 1970s, the Queensland government thought it prudent to formalise tenures in the Strait. Astonished to be offered thirty-year leases over land they saw as immemorially their own, the Island Coordinating Council had demanded inalienable freehold title.[49] They were poised to listen carefully to McIntyre.

Approaching the Islanders had not been McIntyre's first thought. The Western Desert Ngaanyatjara and Ngaatatjara people had seemed promising plaintiffs. Only recently (some as recent as the 1960s) in contact with colonial institutions, they could have exemplified surviving Indigenous custom more vividly than the acculturated people of the Torres Strait. However, anthropological research showed that it would be difficult to codify, for a court, Western Desert land tenure custom. The Murray Islanders would be good litigants because their proprietary customs – as horticulturalists – better resembled the proprietary notions familiar to Australian judges. As well, a century's subaltern experience had taught the Islanders that colonial authority (both church and state) was amenable to pressure, to reason and (it follows) to litigation. The Western Desert people would have required more tuition in colonial law's possibilities and in what law expected of litigants. McIntyre thus turned away from the Western Desert and began to work with Eddie Mabo, the Anglican priest Father David Passi, Celuia Salee (Mabo's father's sister) and James Rice in 1982.

Eddie Mabo, though born and raised on the island of Mer, had long been politically active in a black community school in Townsville. Speaking on the day before Hocking and McIntyre, his paper to the Townsville land rights conference had mentioned land tenure, but had not proposed litigation. Rather, Mabo had reiterated a proposal that he had been making for several years about Australia's maritime border with Papua New Guinea (PNG). Before and after gaining independence in 1975, PNG leaders had been trying to persuade Islanders that they had more in common with black PNG than with white Australia. In 1976, Mabo had responded that Torres Strait Islanders were a distinct people who were better off under Australian rule, as long as the Torres Strait could become an autonomous region within the Commonwealth, with a right of secession. Mabo's Townsville paper had continued this proposal: he likened potential Torres Strait autonomy to Norfolk Island's special status.[50] When McIntyre approached Mabo, he tapped into a well-informed and evolving vision of Torres Strait Islander autonomy.

Working with McIntyre, the plaintiffs asked the High Court of Australia to declare that when the Queensland government took over the islands of the Torres Strait in 1879, it was subject to the inhabitants' customary rights of ownership and use. To thwart this claim, Queensland passed the *Queensland Coast Island*

Declaratory Act 1985 to extinguish all native title rights. The plaintiffs challenged this law in the High Court. By a four to three majority, the High Court ruled in 1989 that Queensland's 1985 law had violated the *Racial Discrimination Act* 1975 in that it had discriminated between those on the Murray Islands whose right to own and inherit property was rooted in custom and those whose property rights were rooted in Queensland law. Having defeated Queensland's tactic, the case of Mabo and his associates could proceed. The High Court directed the Supreme Court of Queensland, under Justice Moynihan, to determine questions of fact about the Murray Islands – its customs and modern tenure history. By the time that inquiry concluded in November 1990, Moynihan had rejected Eddie Mabo's assertions of ownership but accepted that other plaintiffs were owners in customary law. The question of whether such customary law mattered could now be heard by the High Court (Mabo No. 2). In June 1992, a 6–1 majority ruled that the common law of Australia must recognise Murray Island (Meriam) custom as 'native title'. To ignore customary law, the court argued, would be to perpetuate 'terra nullius', the doctrine that said that the British Crown had brought law to a land without law.

Barrister Bryan Keon-Cohen has written that 'without Eddie Mabo there was no case', such was Mabo's faith that Australia's common law could be remade to deal justly with customary law.[51] However, not only Moynihan but some of Mabo's adoptive family had disputed most of Mabo's evidence about his own inheritance of property. Moynihan relied more on Father David Passi, assessing him as an 'essentially honest' guide to custom. Passi, speaking a few years later at a Sydney conference, laid out a cosmology that robustly synthesised Australian law, the law of his priestly ancestor Zogo Le and the law of Jesus as explained by St Paul. He praised the High Court judgment and subsequent legislation for aligning these three sources of right.[52]

The High Court's recognition of native title created a crisis in Australian property law. Since the *Racial Discrimination Act 1975* (RDA) came into force (31 October 1975), Australian governments had been obliged to compensate native title holders whenever it created a tenure that extinguished native title. In granting (for example) mining rights, governments had unknowingly extinguished native title, without compensation. The validity of all such tenures was now in doubt, and the mining industry, in particular, felt exposed. Indigenous leaders, noting the desire for urgent return to legal certainty, on 27 April 1993 offered to support legislation that would validate mineral titles issued from 31 October 1975 to 3 June 1992, provided that miners and the Commonwealth negotiated to protect sacred sites, to compensate for disturbance, to protect the environment, and to pay Traditional Owners some of the value of the minerals extracted. This 'Aboriginal Peace Plan' made such validation conditional on proposed principles of a Commonwealth *Native Title Act*.

The Keating government's response in June 1993 was that the Australian parliament would legislate to validate all titles issued between 31 October 1975 and 30 June 1993, with compensation of all who could be identified as the native title holders. However, the government did not commit to negotiating the Aboriginal Peace Plan.[53] Indigenous leader Noel Pearson labelled this response 'slimy' and 'bureaucratic real estate management'.[54] By seeming to give priority to assuring title-holders that their investments were secure, Keating failed to satisfy many Australians who saw the Mabo judgment as a moral turning point for Australia as a nation – a perception Keating himself had encouraged in his December 1992 'Redfern Park Speech'. Keating nonetheless felt obliged, politically and constitutionally, to negotiate with state and territory governments that tended to champion the natural resource industries. To satisfy Indigenous aspirations, the Commonwealth sought state and territory commitment to updating their laws to take account of native title and to establish non-adversarial tribunals to decide 'who has native title and where'. Keating pledged 'standard setting national legislation ... a new framework for recognition, protection and management of native title ... including how future grants [of title] are to be validly made'.[55] During negotiations on the standards to be encoded in a Commonwealth 'native title' Bill, Indigenous leaders appealed to the Australian public, boosted by knowing that the March 1993 general election had made Labor a minority in the Senate. Keating could expect no support for his native title policy from Liberal and National Party senators; though conservative MPs conceded that 'native title' was now a common law right, Opposition leader John Hewson scorned Keating's Native Title Bill as 'a millstone around our country's prosperity and our kids' future'.[56] His stance gave the government no alternative to combining with the Democrats and Green senators, and they were sympathetic to Indigenous demands.

A difficult issue in the design of a law of native title was the relationship between lease-hold and native title. Did a lease (to do specified things on the land) fully extinguish all native title rights? If it did not, how should the two sets of rights coexist and what should happen when a lease expires? To appease the AMIC and the National Farmers' Federation, the Keating government had proposed that on land subject to native title, pastoral and mining leases could be renewed upon expiry without negotiation with Aboriginal interests. However, Liberal and most National senators (as unyielding spoilers of the Bill) combined with Greens and Democrats (as promoters of Indigenous rights) to defeat this part of the Bill. This left the legislation silent on the relationship between lease-hold rights and native title rights. The relationship of lease-hold to native title would be for the High Court to decide, were a relevant case ever brought before it. The High Court got its chance in the 1996 'Wik' case, ruling that some Cape York tenures did not fully extinguish native title: Indigenous interests and others' interests might coexist on some land. Lease-holders were alarmed that they were now obliged to negotiate with Aboriginal people who asserted native title, during their lease and at its termination. Pastoralists were especially vocal about the 'uncertainty' of their lease-hold rights.

Their complaints gave the Howard government, elected in March 1996, a reason to redesign native title law. The ten points of amending legislation in 1998 made it easier for native title to be extinguished, reassuring pastoralists. They imposed a more demanding test for registering a claim to native title, encouraging Indigenous Australians to combine, deliberate and carefully prepare their assertions of native title, to make them more credible. The amendments also increased the incentives to negotiate land use agreements, even when registered native title claims were yet to be tested in court. Many Indigenous and non-Indigenous parties were keen to try negotiation, as if native title did exist, rather than wait for a court to decide whether it really did. Section 21 of the Act as passed in 1993 had framed a negotiated agreement process, requiring a judge as mediator, but it proved cumbersome and was little used. Howard's amendments made a judge unnecessary by giving legislative protection to the outcomes of agreements not mediated by a judge of the Federal Court: an Indigenous Land Use Agreement (ILUA) would be enforceable, as a contract, under the *Native Title Act*. This amendment was consistent with what the National Indigenous Working Group and over-stretched Federal Court judges had been recommending.[57] Government did not have to be a party to the contract, unless the ILUA fully extinguished native title. ILUAs quickly proliferated: by October 2002, fifty-four had been registered – thirty-two dealing with land in Queensland. In 2002, Fred Chaney (former Minister for Aboriginal Affairs in the Fraser government) hailed a 'new culture of negotiation'.[58] An academic review observed in 2003 that 'in a context of denial of Aboriginal self-government', agreements regulated relationships among 'Aboriginal polities' and gave 'Indigenous people a real decision-making role in a range of issues affecting their lives and their country'.[59] By August 2015 the tribunal had registered 1005 ILUAs.

ILUAs have challenged Indigenous people to develop their political capacity to stabilise coalitions of local groups within regions. In 2017, it became even easier to produce an ILUA when the Australian parliament clarified the decision-making powers of those negotiating ILUAs, weakening the bargaining power of Indigenous dissenters from proposed ILUAs.

ILUAs have also enabled corporate learning about how to work in a land that respects native title. In the 1980s, Conzinc Rio Tinto Australia (CRA), had been expensively taught by the militant people of Bougainville that prudent project design included consideration of native people's wishes. By 1995, under the leadership of Leon Davis, CRA had brought this lesson to its Australian operations. Committed to identifying and negotiating with Indigenous Australians, CRA profit-seeking was guided by 'pragmatic desire for rights-based recognition of customary land connections, on-going mining approval, transparent governance and a sustainable relationship'.⁶⁰ Two cases demonstrated this commitment.

To get access to diamonds in the East Kimberley in 1979, CRA had benefited from the pro-mining stance of Western Australia's Court government. After initially ignoring Aboriginal objections, in 1980 CRA (as the Argyle Diamond Mine) negotiated a 'Good Neighbour Policy' with some local families whose legal counsel it had paid for; the Western Australian government soon recognised their secret agreement in a special Act in 1983. As elements of the agreement were implemented, it became clear that, in both process and substance, it fell short of standards being set by Traditional Owners, just across the border, under the Northern Territory Land Rights Act. The Good Neighbour Agreement became exemplary of how not to take Aboriginal interests seriously. Subsequent research has shown how the Aboriginal parties approached this agreement: they saw the company as bound into the *wirnan* – a tradition of exchange between neighbouring groups in the region. *Wirnan* had long served Kimberley people as a way to understand their relationship with the pastoralist. More open-ended than most commercial contracts, *wirnan* is an ongoing practice of demanding and giving, building mutual obligation whose scope cannot be delimited or predicted. The company learned that much was expected of the Good Neighbour Policy, and it responded pragmatically, consulting anthropologists from 2000. In 2001, it seemed prudent to look at the entire agreement afresh – this time welcoming and funding the participation of the Kimberley Land Council. The company accepted that the *Native Title Act* had created new standards and processes for 'community relations'. The persistence of *wirnan*, as an Indigenous model of relatedness, must also be credited. The Argyle

Participation Agreement was registered as an ILUA in 2004.[61]

Natural resource corporations were learning from experience to be wary of the 'support' of state governments hungry for revenue from mining. CRA thought it wise to decline the Queensland government's offer in 1997 to legislate a way around the native title claims of Aboriginal people in the Carpentaria Gulf region, where CRA wished to mine zinc (the Century mine). Instead, the company negotiated what became known as the Gulf Communities Agreement with native title claimants whose claim had met the National Native Title Tribunal's registration test. While constructing the Century mine, however, CRA sold it to Pasminco. Pasminco's learning experience intensified in 2002, when fifty to eighty Aboriginal people, frustrated by obstacles to the agreement's implementation, occupied the mine site kitchen, non-violently, for nine days.[62]

Mining and Indigenous well-being

When the mining industry leaders of the 1980s attacked the exploration veto given to Traditional Owners in the Northern Territory, defenders of the *Land Rights Act* came up with the slogan 'Land rights not mining'. Well intended, the slogan overlooked that Northern Territory Traditional Owners were using the right to veto exploration as, effectively, a property right, enabling them to negotiate deals with mining companies that would pay monies in addition to the statutory royalties that flow from miners, through government, to land councils and to Aborigines affected by the mine. Northern Land Council Chair Galarrwuy Yunupingu, marking the ALRA (NT)'s 20th anniversary in 1996, said that entitled owners and mining companies were more likely to be friends than enemies: 'most of the land under mining exploration is Aboriginal land ... land rights are good for business, if both sides act in good faith and keep their legal rights intact'.[63]

Aboriginal people could benefit in two ways by hosting mines on their land: royalty payments and employment (by the mining company or by enterprises stimulated by the company's presence). Methods for measuring well-being are crude and imply non-Indigenous ways of thinking about how to live that Indigenous Australians do not necessarily share. Nonetheless, one statistical analysis, using 2001 Census data, compared Indigenous income, education and employment status and home ownership in 'mining areas' (eight remote regions with large mines) with the same measures of well-being for Indigenous populations in other regions and for the Indigenous population as a whole. The comparison showed that people near a mine had higher rates of employment and home ownership, and better education status than was found, at that time, among Indigenous people in remote regions that lacked a mine. However, the communities near large mines were still poor when compared with the Indigenous population as a whole.[64] Proximity to mining was having a small effect in ameliorating the socio-economic disadvantage – as the Census measures it – of the remote Indigenous Australians. The effect on their incomes was not uniform: those in Arnhem Land, Borroloola and western Cape York had lower median incomes than those in the East Kimberley, the Gulf and the Pilbara.[65] Remote Indigenous people tend to lack the skills that an employer values. NAPLAN test results in remote and very remote regions in 2010 showed that Indigenous literacy and numeracy, years 3–9, were far below that of non-Indigenous children in the same regions.[66] Low engagement with the education system has two sources: under-investment by governments and the relatively low priority that many Indigenous families have given to the schooling that is available. By the second decade of the 21st century, there was much debate about how to direct the wealth of mining back into services (including schools) for the people of the mined regions. How was responsibility to be allocated between governments (Australian and state), corporations (who might deserve tax breaks for their social programs) and Indigenous organisations (whose capacities were determined partly by the resources received from governments and corporations)?[67]

Rationales for the Indigenous Estate

How has it been possible for a settler colonial-society to concede the Indigenous Estate? It would be a true and important history to tell the rise of Australia's Indigenous Land and Sea Estate as a story of non-Indigenous resistance against Indigenous insistence on just dealings. However, to answer my question I will develop a theme no less truthful: the positive disposition of settler-colonial and global liberal-capitalist culture towards the Indigenous demand for property rights. Four influential and enduring stories about the pasts and futures of Australia and its peoples have contributed to public acceptance of the Indigenous Land and Sea Estate: the 'dying native'; detribalisation as alienation; the right to human development; and the imperilled human species.

Dying natives
Responding to the evident physical vulnerability of the Aboriginal population in the 19th century, the colonists declared reserves as a way to slow down or avert the extinction of Aborigines and Torres Strait Islanders. These reserves now form a large part of the Indigenous Estate. Reserves were populated either by taking

people to them, or by declaring them where people already were (in the hope that they would stay there, unharmed). Some of Archibald Meston's 1896 recommendations were adopted in the *Aboriginals' Protection and Restriction of the Sale of Opium Act* 1897. Colonial access to remote parts of Queensland should be restricted, he argued, so that Aboriginal people not yet degraded by colonial contact would not be disturbed. '[I]solation on reserves and the total exclusion of whites has long been adopted by the Canadian and American governments towards the Indians.' Reserves where people would be fed and taught gardening and farming were 'the only possible method of saving any part of the race from extinction'.[68]

Queensland established large reserves, mostly in Cape York. In 1904, the government of Western Australia asked Meston's colleague Walter Roth for advice. Roth recommended for Western Australia 'that large areas be resumed in the northern unsettled districts for the sole benefit of the natives'. As he explained, 'The poor wretches must be allowed the wherewithal to live – their main hunting grounds and water supplies. They dare not voluntarily migrate elsewhere, as such action, according to tribal law, would constitute a trespass, punishable by death.'[69] Walter Baldwin Spencer recommended reserves in the Northern Territory in 1912, and Donald Thomson reinforced his advice in 1937. Paul Hasluck supported reserves, while foreseeing that eventually residents would not need them to be inviolable. He decided in 1952 that reserves could be mined, but to ensure Aborigines benefited, he created the 'Aborigines (Benefits From Mining) Trust' fund.[70] This concession was not represented as conceding 'land rights' to reserves, but the trust was adapted to be included in the Fraser government's *Aboriginal Land Rights Act* 1976 as the Aboriginal Benefits Trust Fund. Initiated as 'protection', 'reserves' were repurposed as the land portions that governments could most easily include in 'land rights' and 'native title' policies from 1966.

Detribalisation

While one version of the 'dying native' story lost credibility, with population recovery, by the 1960s, another version – the detribalisation story – remained influential as a way to make sense of the Indigenous situation: people of Aboriginal descent were physically surviving, but they were less and less 'Aboriginal' in their way of life. Assimilation policy was grounded in the evident certainty of detribalisation. The collapse of Aboriginal society was thought to have gone further in some regions of Australia than in others, but detribalisation was sure to continue, necessitating assimilation and justifying the revocation of reserves.

However, confidence in the methods of assimilation faltered when it became clear that many 'detribalised' Aboriginal people were, at best, ambivalent about the demands and opportunities of assimilation. Astute observers began to understand that if upward social mobility meant the dispersion of reserve communities and the revocation of reserves, Aboriginal people would dread 'advancement' as a loss of security. In 1966, Don Dunstan justified the setting up of South Australia's Aboriginal Land Trust as a way to assure people that assimilation would not cost them their security of tenure. Promoters of the South Australian legislation in 1966 imagined that as the people of the North-West Reserve 'detribalised' they would acquire the will and capacity to form councils, like the Aboriginal people in longer-colonised parts of the state. However, when Dunstan imagined the North-West Reserve residents committing to economic development, his projection was shadowed by the knowledge that on the southern reserves residents had remained resentfully dependent. They had acquired a 'chip on the shoulder'.[71] Security of land tenure was intended to remove or diminish this 'chip on the shoulder', making the residents of southern reserves receptive to the message that they should seek 'gainful employment' – either on or off the reserve – rather than rely on the state government. For the residents of the North-West Reserve, the Dunstan government anticipated that, if they got land rights now, before they grasped that their homelands were not theirs in legal title, they would avoid the 'chip on the shoulder' and not follow the southern Aborigines in their bitterness towards advancement. Their outlook not clouded by insecurity, they would not recoil from government programs but develop economically by harnessing their artistic abilities, making craft such as clothing, pottery and jewellery for sale. Mining, should the legislation grant mineral rights, would add to the reserve owners' income.

That is, the South Australian legislators amended the detribalisation story in the light of governmental observation that the detribalised, if not secure in their homes, could be unreceptive to assimilation. That granting secure tenure of reserves would ameliorate the insecurity of advancement occurred also to those considering land rights in New South Wales. In 1979, after an unprecedented program of consultation with Aboriginal people, a Select Committee of the New South Wales parliament chaired by Maurie Keane wrote one report recommending land rights and another documenting socio-economic inequality and recommending changes in the delivery of state government services. Keane explained in a foreword that 'the implementation of the Committee's recommendations on Land Rights is an essential pre-requisite for the resolution of the other complex socio-economic issues affecting the Aboriginal people'.[72] Convinced that dispossession was the leading cause of poverty and ill-health among Aboriginal people, Keane also drew on a paper written for the Australian Labor Party by Charles Rowley that touched on the psychology of Aboriginal poverty. It differed from white poverty because 'in the general population insecurity of tenure of the home is a deviation from the average. In Aboriginal society it is the norm.'[73] Rowley continued:

> Without security family ties and organization break down. Planning and saving are almost impossible. Discrimination and insecure homes are the root causes of alcoholism, petrol sniffing, mental and physical ill-health, the despair and lack of incentive, which are typical of the so-called 'culture of poverty' anywhere. No medical patching or family advising or skilful social work can reverse the downward spiral of welfare until these groups acquire a minimum of basic property.[74]

Whether or not title-holders used their land as an economic asset, Rowley suggested, title was vital to their psychological security. He imagined that once people felt more secure they would escape the 'culture of poverty' and plan and save, as families should.

The 'detribalisation' story has remained a credible narrative about Indigenous Australia, and it has cost some Indigenous Australians 'native title'. Justice Olney denied native title to the Yorta Yorta in 1998 because he judged that their heritage was too discontinuous with the practices and beliefs of their ancestors at the time the British assumed sovereignty. Since the High Court endorsed Olney's decision in 2002, 'the degree of legally tolerable interruption to the observance of law and custom and to societal continuity, and the degree of tolerable adaptation and change to the content of law and custom have become key legal issues for Indigenous groups, respondents and the Federal Court'.[75] Judges differ in their understanding of 'detribalisation' and continuity of custom. Hearing the Noongar native title claim in 2005, Justice Murray Wilcox was able to find that Noongar had title to land portions in the south-west of Western Australia because he relied on historical and ethnographic research that presented Noongar as a continuous community, with customs evolving since colonisation. On appeal, three Federal Court judges ruled that Wilcox had paid too little attention to the question of continuity of Noongar custom; they reassigned the case to a fresh hearing by another Federal Court judge.

What happened next helps to demonstrate the persistence of the idea – evident to Dunstan and Rowley – that 'detribalisation', if not handled carefully by authorities, might result not in a readiness to participate in the wider society but in bitter alienation from its demands. The Western Australian government settled the Noongar claim out of court, through negotiation, resulting in a package featuring land, political recognition and a future fund. According to Noongar leader Glen Kelly, one motive for the Western Australian government to negotiate was that it was worried by the alienation of many Noongar from Western Australian society. Noongar leaders suggested that the high rates of criminal incarceration, particularly among youth, and the young age structure of the region's Aboriginal population spelled continuing trouble for the state; the security of a negotiated settlement would ameliorate Noongar alienation. Though the Noongar had little native title land in the region to bargain with, Noongar advocates could remobilise the narrative of detribalisation as a scenario of risk; in this way they framed the issue of Noongar need and entitlement in wider than legal terms.[76]

Thus a positive disposition towards 'land rights' does not rest solely on the recognition of customary law. In some political deliberation, a version of the detribalisation story has created narrative contexts for concessions of title. It has remained plausible to say that a 'culture of poverty' or a 'chip on the shoulder' or criminality – if not ameliorated by measures of security – will hinder the advancement and integration of the 'detribalised'.

Development as modernity

The 'human development' narrative has become powerful in Australia because it has become globally influential, propagated within and by the agencies of the United Nations.[77] During the Cold War, Soviet and liberal-capitalist schemes of development competed, but by 1989 the Soviet model was discredited, enabling the liberal-capitalist model to become the common sense of global governance, including the governance of rights. In the context of this modernist grand narrative a proprietary interest is supposed to be the basis of economic and social development, as conventionally measured. This perspective imagines Indigenous Australians according to an assumed story of inevitable modernisation: they are destined to become more disposed to value their land as income-generating property. The Darkinjung Local Aboriginal Land Council (NSW) demonstrated this possibility when it sold prime coastal land (a former garbage tip) in 2000 for $40 million. Justice Paul Finn's judgment in the *Akiba* native title case in 2010 and the High Court's endorsement of it in 2013 have shown that native title can be formulated as a property right more consistent with, and recognisable to, the property rights transacted by financiers and investors.[78]

However, Heidi Norman reports that, among Kooris (and presumably other Australians), the practices of native title as 'property' will be controversial to the extent that they make land an income-generating asset – even more so if that means treating title as alienable.[79] To imagine Indigenous Australians transacting land and sea rights clashes with a widespread conception of indigeneity in which land is sacred patrimony, the ground of personal and collective identity, the means of cultural and spiritual recovery. Anthropologist Erich Kolig has predicted that Aboriginal Australians will mediate the tension between these two ways of being Indigenous by learning 'to think in terms of sacred enclaves in an increasingly non-sacred environment; they will come to see sacredness clearly separated, physically, spatially and temporally, from a predominantly secular, mundane world and its demands'.[80]

In 1984, Paul Seaman QC reflected on this tension among land's meanings when he considered land rights law in Western Australia. Although the Burke government did not enact Seaman's recommendations, they are significant as a thoughtful attempt to combine two ways to think of land rights. On the one hand, Seaman recommended that land should be an inalienable 'base upon which to re-build Aboriginal society and culture'; he hoped that this would 'overcome their anxieties about security'.[81] On the other hand, he envisaged that Aboriginal people would like freedom to deal in their land in ways that went beyond their customary responsibilities for it. In recommending the right of owners to prosecute trespassers, Seaman said it was 'to give security', but also that 'it is an important element in their freedom to negotiate and contract'.[82] To qualify inalienability, Seaman recommended that title include the power to transfer title or to grant a lease to the Crown or to a public authority, or to another 'qualified incorporated Aboriginal organisation'; he also wanted land-owners to be allowed to create 'any lease or licence for up to five years' and to grant a lease or licence 'which is a necessary part of an agreement which relates to exploration or mining or oil extraction'.[83] He proposed a tribunal that would be empowered 'to grant a lease or licence not otherwise permitted' and to permit, with conditions, Aboriginal land-owners to sell.[84] In an earlier 'Discussion Paper' (January 1984) Seaman had noted that 'Aboriginal people in nearly every part of the State are poor, that their organisations have pressing financial needs and that mining negotiations may be the only opportunity which they have to redress an almost complete lack of economic power.'[85]

Rival imaginings of Aborigines and their feelings about land were evident when the Senate in 1995 debated the ATSIC Amendment (Indigenous Land Corporation and Land Fund) Bill. The Keating government intended the fund to remove 'structural and institutional barriers to full participation in Australian economic life by its indigenous peoples'. However, the Bill's aims included 'safeguarding and developing indigenous culture' implying limits on how the land could be used and to whom it could be sold.[86] Clauses 191S and 191T in the Bill would have empowered the Indigenous Land Corporation (ILC) to set conditions on a grant: the title-holders would not be allowed to dispose of or enter into an agreement to make a charge against their property without first consulting the ILC. Green and Coalition senators objected that the liberty of title-holders should not be so restricted: the two clauses would make the land effectively an asset of a public agency. One senator quoted unnamed Aboriginal people saying: 'don't let this ILC become a quasi black government, a quasi big brother to say "We know what is best for you"'.[87] Senator Chamarette put the argument for 'full possession with no strings attached': the Indigenous title-holder should have the same rights to sell as other title-holders.[88] The government countered that if dealings by title-holders were not subject to ILC approval, Indigenous owners of land purchased for them might get a private benefit from selling a publicly funded good. Senator Collins warned senators not to presume that Aboriginal people were too virtuous to behave in such a self-interested way: 'there are some Aboriginal people ... who do misappropriate money'.[89] In the debate, this imagined opportunistic figure – the dreaded prototype of Indigenous modernity? – was referred to as 'Flash Harry'. Senator Kernot backed the government, while admitting that she found 'horrid' the choice between 'self-determination' (including 'the right to make a mistake') and 'the ownership of the resource by the many'. She quoted an unnamed 'black woman' warning against 'greedy blackfellas'.[90] The senate voted to omit 191S and 191T.

In May 2015 Indigenous leaders met in Broome to discuss the Indigenous Estate, hosted by two government-appointed guardians of Australian liberalism: the Aboriginal and Torres Strait Islander Social Justice Commissioner Mick Gooda and the Human Rights Commissioner Tim Wilson. Wilson is reported to have said that 'Property rights are actually the forgotten human right. Without property rights you don't get security, you don't get people being able to materialise the efforts of their labour, and in the end, without property rights you don't have economic development.'[91] Such language evoked the human need and right to develop through the exercise of property rights. The implementation of land rights has encouraged many Indigenous Australians to consider their rights in terms of a human story, wider than the story of decolonisation in which they also figure – as I will further illustrate in my final chapter.

The human species

The fourth story that has offered sympathetic grounds for Australians' thoughts about the Indigenous Estate is a relatively new story about the human relationship to the non-human world. Humans once lived within the limits of the earth's natural endowments; then humanity developed technologies so powerful that we have begun to change the earth's natural systems, to our potential detriment. The possible future evoked by that story is grim: the human species might destroy or severely damage the physical and biological bases of its existence. In this story, the early 21st century is imagined as a moment of choice, a potential turning point, in which humanity might adopt new ethics and new technologies for relating to the non-human world, re-establishing the material possibility of human existence. Through this increasingly important narrative, the Indigenous Land and Sea Estate is imaginable as one means to repair the human engagement with the non-human world. In the words of legal scholar Lee Godden, there has developed 'a greater appreciation of the inherent tie between Indigenous cultural identity, and connections to land and waters within a prevailing western ecological conservation paradigm'.[92]

An early initiative in Indigenous land management was taken by the residents of a Queensland reserve, Palm Island, in 1983: the first independent Aboriginal ranger service in Australia. A co-management agreement for Kakadu National Park soon followed. Since then, land and sea management strategies have been increasingly among the matters negotiated as ILUAs and when title-holders sign Indigenous Protected Area (IPA) agreements with the Australian government; there were sixty-five IPAs by mid-2014, comprising over 36 million hectares. The political struggle over Queensland's 'Wild Rivers' legislation showed that Aboriginal people in some regions remain wary that their interests could be subordinated to conservation agendas.[93] As environmental services become commercial – for example when carbon sequestration becomes a valued commodity – there is potential for Indigenous Australians to find market value for their land and for their labour 'caring for country'.[94]

Now that Australia has created a massive Indigenous Land and Sea Estate, for whatever reasons, there is a cultural and political struggle over how its owners should imagine its future use. In Chapter 12, I will describe a recent skirmish in that contest.

10

Asserting 'Southern' Aboriginality

Extinguishing the 'part-Aboriginal'

As government thinking – in the Census and in other ways – paid less attention to genetic distinctions within the Aboriginal 'race', Indigenous Australians affirmed the shared historical fates of Aborigines and Torres Strait Islanders. Historians have illustrated the rise of 'Aboriginal nationalism' in the late 1960s and early 1970s, in public statements by Aboriginal people born since World War II.[1] Aboriginal nationalism has taken two forms. In one, Indigenous Australia is many 'nations', each with its own customary territory as well as distinct heritage of language and myth.[2] In the other, all people of Aboriginal descent are encompassed within a pan-Aboriginal identity. Pan-Aboriginalism was fuelled by increased contact among Indigenous Australians as laws regulating their movement were repealed; it was the product also of federalised political mobilisation – most importantly, FCAATSI – developing a shared sense of grievance across all Australian jurisdictions; and it was reinforced by the Commonwealth's adoption of the unitary category 'Aboriginal' in the 1971 Census. Distinctions of 'blood' nonetheless remained in popular usage. A conference of Indigenous Australians in 1994 lamented the persistence of 'racist and derogatory terminology' such as 'coloured', 'half-caste' and 'full-blood'; it urged 'all Aboriginal and non-Aboriginal people to stop using such language now'.[3] And the geography and policy history of each state/territory continued to differentiate the opportunities and obstacles facing activists.

How the experience of Torres Strait Islanders could be fitted into a shared sense of 'Aboriginality' was little discussed, except in regions where Aborigines and Torres Strait Islanders were in daily association. Queensland since 1939 had distinguished laws about Aborigines from laws about Islanders, while keeping the two statutes similar in content.[4] However, apart from distinguishing 'Aboriginal' from 'Torres Strait Islander' in the 'race' question in the 1971 Census, the Commonwealth government still used 'Aboriginal' to refer to all Indigenous Australians; the Department of Aboriginal Affairs (established in 1973) was supposed to deal with Islanders too, and the Australia Council made sure that the Aboriginal Arts Board (founded in 1973) included a Torres Strait Islander. In 1984 the Commonwealth renamed the Australian Institute of Aboriginal Studies (AIAS) the Australian Institute of Aboriginal and Torres Strait Islander Studies (AIATSIS).

It was important to Torres Strait Islanders that they were not 'Aboriginal'. Eddie Mabo told Noel Loos in 1984 that it was 'traditional' for Islanders to regard Aborigines as not 'culturally advanced' and as 'lesser beings mainly because they don't know the art of cultivation and they don't live in central villages like we did, and they don't have a religion'. Mabo thought that while 'the idea is going out now' through intermarriage between the two peoples, it was being kept alive in Townsville because of competition between Islanders and Aborigines for housing and jobs.⁵ Mabo's critical view of such racial typing was encouraged by his activism in a trade union and in the Aboriginal Advancement League – milieux of ideas of a global 'black' struggle that included Aborigines and Islanders equally. In 1970, he became president of the 'all-black' Council for the Rights of Indigenous People which supported Townsville's Aboriginal Legal Aid Service, its Aboriginal Medical Service and its 'Black Community School'; he came to see himself as a 'black' activist.

'Black' came to convey a distinct historical entitlement to redress for those (of different heritage) oppressed by 'white' colonisation. Many outspoken Indigenous Australians knew that non-European peoples were asserting self-determination, and that African Americans were demanding not only civil equality but respect for their distinct heritage.⁶ The least 'black' in skin pigment (such as Tasmanian Aborigines) were becoming 'black' in this political and historical sense. Tasmanian governments had refused to use the category 'Aboriginal'; until 1968, they had stayed away from inter-governmental forums on 'Aboriginal policy'. But popular views were more complex. Ida West recalls how her 'black' identity was sensitive to shifting regimes of recognition. Born in 1919, West grew up among families of Aboriginal descent on Cape Barren and Flinders Islands and worked in manual occupations. Her community was Christian, believing in human equality in the sight of God. However, to be 'black' in 20th-century Tasmania was to be spurned by many whites. Her parents trained her and her siblings 'to fight our own battles. We got a hammering if we came home and said someone called us black. We stuck up for ourselves and weren't allowed to come home and tell tales. We had to get back in and fight.'⁷ To be called 'black', as a child, was a taunting, but to call oneself 'black' became an awakening, for West and others in Tasmania

– a new way to assert entitlement. As an adult, West joined the movement through which Tasmanian Aborigines encouraged each other to be 'black'.

> It wasn't an easy job, knocking at doors and asking who had dark blood in them, but on a whole they were all very good ... They helped us as much as they could, but it wasn't very easy just the same to knock on the door and ask them have they got a dab with the tar brush.[8]

Some 'experts' sympathetic to Indigenous aspirations were nonetheless perplexed by the 'black' Aboriginal identity of mixed-descent people. Ronald Berndt, in a 1968 lecture, noted 'an upsurge of Aboriginality throughout the southern regions of this continent, among people who know little or nothing of traditional Aboriginal life but are vocal about their Aboriginal identity'. This 'Aboriginal "professionalization"' was both an effect of white society's barriers to their entry (barriers now being removed) and a 'healthy pride in their Aboriginal background' (which he hoped would become an 'informed pride'). Berndt acknowledged the potency of a sense of shared history among people of Aboriginal descent.[9] However, in this perspective, it was assumed that there would be regional differences in the Indigenous claims on the colonial conscience. An early champion of land rights, the federal MP Kim E. Beazley, had heard Yolngu speak their 'deeply felt attachment' to the Arnhem Land Reserve in 1963. He distinguished their palpable desire for land from the feelings of 'the de-tribalised people of Victoria and New South Wales'.[10]

Pan-Aboriginal self-assertion invited Australians to reimagine what 'detribalisation' meant to the 'detribalised'. In his 1988 memoir *Shades of Darkness* Hasluck recalled that while assuming that black Australians were willing to make themselves more 'socially acceptable' to whites, his policy had not 'required the abandonment of all aboriginal tradition and custom', as long as there was 'conformity to the minimum standard' that other Australians demanded. Looking back, he regretted that he had not paused 'as long as I would do now' over the question of what Aboriginal people wished.[11] It had been easier for concerned non-Indigenous Australians to see Aborigines' material distress, social disorganisation and abjection than to appreciate their resilience, the pride beneath their reserve. The young activist Marcia Langton, in a 1981 critique of experts' writing about Aboriginal Australians, scorned 'the insidious ideology of tribal and detribalized' that presumed to measure people such as herself against a standard of 'real' Aboriginal life and to find them lacking in 'Aboriginality'. Recently graduated in anthropology, the Queenslander complained that as the distinction 'urban-rural-tribal' acquired credibility among social scientists, it reinforced an older distinction between 'half-castes' and 'full-bloods' that had disqualified, as not fully Aboriginal, those of mixed ancestry such as herself. An educated woman of rural background, urban by her own choice, Langton demanded recognition that she and others like her were now 'exploring our own Aboriginality'.[12]

Urban and rural Aborigines' 'ethnogenesis' – their accentuation of a common Aboriginal heritage distinct from the heritages of immigrant Australia – challenged liberal assumptions that 'civil rights' would be associated with a decreasing consciousness of 'colour'. FCAATSI had not only protested race discrimination, its procedures had embodied the civilities of race equality, a conscientious playing down of racial identity. However, between 1968 and 1970 FCAATSI became a forum for the assertion of Black Power. At the annual conference of 1968, when (black) Dulcie Flower beat (white) Stan Davey in the vote to elect the general secretary, the delegate Philip Roberts (an Aboriginal activist from the Northern Territory) is reported to have said: 'Stan Davey was a real gentleman, he worked hard and he gave a deal of his life for us, but HE IS WHITE! ... If we could have an all-black executive we would be extremely happy.'[13] To some members, this way of thinking was 'racial discrimination' – the enemy FCAATSI had been founded to fight. Over the next two years FCAATSI debated whether and how to ensure that it expressed 'Black' aspirations. The 1970 annual conference rejected a constitutional change that would have restricted membership of the executive to Aboriginal people and voting rights to Aboriginal members.[14] Disappointed promoters of black self-representation immediately formed the National Tribal Council; its manifesto included a call for 'programmes, seminars, and courses which aim at the re-acculturation of Aborigines and Islanders'.

These words acknowledged Southern Aborigines' sense of cultural loss.[15] Some were already turning to anthropology for a remedy. 'Whenever the subject of the former culture arose,' reported anthropologist of La Perouse Jim Bell in 1961, 'informants were always interested enough to discuss it and to learn anything that I knew about it.' The Aborigines that he worked with had migrated from the Illawarra region, settled at La Perouse and had been selling 'curios' to Sydney people since the late 19th century.[16]

> As tourists inspect their curios, these Aborigines offer them information or answer their questions on different features of the past life to encourage sales. Informants asked me to

get them 'real blackfeller' designs to copy on to their curios to make them look more authentic, and wanted full details as to their meaning. I also supplied photographs of 'real blackfellers' which they wanted to lend atmosphere to their curio stalls.[17]

Cultural loss was real. In 1983 it was estimated that only about 30 000 people were still speaking traditional Aboriginal languages and that for over 100 of these languages there were fewer than 100 speakers.[18] On the other hand, Aboriginal people who had 'lost' their 'tribal culture' had acquired much new knowledge: they had learned to communicate in English or in Kriol (estimated in 1983 at 15 000 speakers) or in Torres Strait Creole (15 000). They had become familiar with items of Euro-Australian material culture such as houses and motor vehicles. However, the sense of loss – of language, of rituals, of how to make things, of rules of marriage and etiquette, of a sense of the sacred – was strong. 'We want to relearn and relive … the wisdom of our ancestors if possible, learn the cultural, the spiritual values of the Aboriginal people – our ancestors,' the young Wiradjuri Paul Coe told ABC viewers in 1972.[19] To be unfavourably compared with 'tribal' Aborigines was the risk that urban and rural Aboriginal people ran whenever, in the name of black solidarity or at the invitation of governments, they presented themselves as 'Aboriginal'. As Kevin Gilbert wrote in 1973, 'the northern full-bloods do not consider that the southern blacks are Aborigines, though a Pan-Aboriginal feeling is on the move'.[20] A 'Workshop on Aboriginal culture and identity' in 1973 recommended that 'the tribal Aboriginals should help those Aboriginals who have lost their culture to find out more about the Aboriginal way of life and customs'.[21]

Black Theatre

Any such restorative project had to find a place for a lively urban Aboriginal culture such as the 'Black Theatre' that had recently emerged in Sydney and Melbourne. The earliest performances of 'Black Theatre' were in the cities – Melbourne, Sydney, Perth – whose black communities, such as Redfern (NSW), had grown largely by migration from rural regions. There were precedents to Black Theatre but they were too sparse to amount to a tradition. In 1951, the Australian Aborigines League had presented 'An Aboriginal Moomba: out of the dark in Melbourne', with an all-Indigenous cast. In two parts, 'The Past' dramatised traditional myths followed by 'The Present', which included 'tableaux, cabaret and sketches' showing 'that Indigenous Australians had survived with vibrant and ongoing identities and cultures'.[22] In the 1960s, Kath Walker submitted play scripts to radio stations and competitions, but these were not performed. It is understandable that in 1969 Stefan Haag, an advocate of Australian theatrical writing and performance, could not imagine an urban Aboriginal theatre: 'We must accept that pure ethnic Aboriginal culture ... can only exist in traditional tribal living and is therefore doomed ... the individual is therefore faced with either a void or the complete adoption of an alien culture – our culture.'[23]

Kevin Gilbert is unlikely to have agreed that his *The Cherry Pickers*, written in prison in 1968 and partly performed in 1971 at Sydney's Mews Theatre after Gilbert's release, was a 'complete adoption' of Haag's culture. The theme of the play is the possibility (or not) of a small group of 'fringe-dwellers' living out elements of the ancient, sacred culture: the characters' speech features much 'Aboriginal English'. *The Cherry Pickers* was performed in full in 1973 in Melbourne by Nindethana

Theatre Company. Nindethana arose partly from the interest of anti-racist white performers in dramatising antagonistic global relationships between whites and blacks, plays such as Lorraine Hansberry's *A Raisin in the Sun* (performed in 1964 in Melbourne with an all-Aboriginal cast), and *Blood Knot* by Athol Fugard, about South African apartheid. An Aboriginal actor from Victoria, Jack Charles, was an important figure in this milieu of radical and socially relevant theatre; in the Pram Factory production of a British play *If There Weren't Any Blacks You'd Have to Invent Them*, Charles, in 'white face', played a white bigot. Out of these collaborations grew the Nindethana Theatre Company in 1971. *Jack Charles Is Up and Fighting* was its first production, in 1972. The play's subtitle 'It's tough for us boongs in Australia today' mocks (in effect) Haag's restriction of Aboriginal options to either 'traditional tribal living' or 'our [white] culture': while 'boongs' is a term of white Australian bigotry, 'us boongs' seizes the term for black use. The phrase epitomised the ability of 'Black Theatre' to address white and black audience members in terms that defy classification as either 'our [European] culture' or 'pure ethnic Aboriginal culture'.

The Australia Council for the Arts (ACFTA), founded in November 1967 and including an Aboriginal Arts Advisory Committee since February 1970, was interested in funding Nindethana if it were controlled exclusively by Aboriginal members, such as Jack Charles and fellow actor Bob Maza. Maza had acted in television and was recognised as a professional; he had recently returned from North America inspired by the African-American National Black Theatre in Harlem (New York) and by First Nations theatres in Canada. He soon left Nindethana, at the suggestion of Sydney Aborigines such as Gerry Bostock, who wished to start a Black Theatre. Sydney's

Kooris had recently performed political theatre by intervening in that city's Cook Bicentenary celebrations (throwing wreaths into Botany Bay) and by staging street theatre in demonstrations asserting land rights, including, in the summer and autumn of 1972, at the Aboriginal Tent Embassy in Canberra. In Bostock's view, colonial history made all Aborigines actors.

> It is the experience of living as a black person in the general Australian society, wearing two faces – that is political theatre, because kids, when they grow up on missions and then move to the city, they have to 'wear' two faces. They have to present one face to European society and one face to their black brothers and sisters.[24]

However, the Sydney activists knew that they must present a professional face – Maza's – to the ACFTA. With Maza's help the nascent 'National Black Theatre' (NBT) was granted $5500 from the ACFTA and began to conduct acting workshops in Redfern in 1972. In partnership with the Nimrod Street Theatre, the NBT staged *Basically Black* in October 1972, incorporating material from *Jack Charles Is Up and Fighting*. The cast was all-Aboriginal, and both whites and blacks authored satirical sketches. Audience responses convinced author Gary Foley that theatre written from an Aboriginal point of view and performed by Aborigines was 'getting through' to both whites and blacks.[25] The final night of *Basically Black* was 2 December 1972, the day that the Whitlam government was elected.

The Aboriginal Arts Board

By reconstructing the agencies of arts patronage, the Whitlam government created a national forum in which 'urban' and 'traditional' cultural activists could compete for funding while also exchanging ideas about what 'Aboriginal culture' was becoming. The Whitlam government turned the ACFTA into the Australia Council, meeting first on 16 February 1973. An all-Indigenous Aboriginal Arts Board (AAB) under the Australia Council took over the work of the ACFTA's Aboriginal Arts Advisory Committee. The appointed AAB members were 'an equitable distribution amongst states, a balance of tribal and urban interests and a representation of both sexes'.[26] The chair was Dick Roughsey (Mornington Island), and the members (with their postal addresses) were: Raphael Apuatimi (Darwin), Mick Miller (Edge Hill, Queensland), Vai Stanton (Darwin), Albert Lennon (Alice Springs), Kitty Dick (Weipa South), Wandjuk Marika (Nhulunbuy), Harold Blair (Doncaster, Victoria), Eric Koo'oila (Cairns), Terry Widders (Brickfield Hill, Sydney), Chicka Dixon (Darlinghurst, New South Wales), Ken Colbung (Nollamara, Western Australia), Ruby Hammond (Angle Park, South Australia), and Tim Leura Tjapaltjarri (Alice Springs). The board soon adopted a seven point policy:

> To strengthen and revive traditional Aboriginal arts.
>
> To encourage a pride in and knowledge of Aboriginal arts both amongst the wider Australian community and overseas.

To formulate programmes to teach Aboriginal children traditional arts.

To arrange cultural exchanges of Aboriginal art and the arts of the wider community.

To stimulate developments in the arts where the traditional culture has been lost.

To assist the best of professional work to emerge in theatre, dance, music, painting, craft and all other arts amongst Aboriginal people.

To educate the wider community in the value and quality of all aspects of Aboriginal arts through exhibitions, performances, publications and films.[27]

While the AAB was committed to developing 'contemporary non-traditional art skills in depressed Aboriginal communities as a means of promoting social aspirations', it also understood 'the view of many Aboriginals' to be that maintaining traditional culture is 'an essential element in preserving self-respect and a sense of identity among Aboriginal people'.[28] In maintaining 'traditional culture' the AAB had the support of the AIAS, the Commonwealth agency founded in 1964 to record heritage that was being destroyed by 'detribalisation'. The AAB and the AIAS overlapped in the key figures of Dr Robert Edwards (a specialist in rock art who was director of the AAB and a member of several committees within AIAS) and Dick Roughsey (founding chairman of the AAB and a member of the AIAS's Aboriginal Advisory Committee). But what was the AAB to do about 'non-traditional art skills in depressed Aboriginal communities'?

The AAB's first meeting was part of a five-day 'seminar' in Canberra where the urban black thespians, in a series of conference resolutions, warned the AAB not to privilege the Aboriginal culture of 'tribal' regions at the expense of the resurgent culture of 'detribalised', urban Aborigines. Resolutions recognised Black Theatre: one called for the setting up of a Central Aboriginal Theatre Company in each state, another for a salaried 'talent agent to look after the interests of Aboriginal actors and actresses, and other performers, and to help them with negotiations, financial arrangements, and legal rights'.[29] The seminar passed a resolution deploring the failure to fund Nindethana's production of *The Cherry Pickers*; another warned the Minister for Aboriginal Affairs, Gordon Bryant, that 'he cannot impose on Aboriginal Theatre activity the same standards and principles that have been applied to white theatre groups', and another resolution demanded 'that Black Theatre be more heavily subsidised than white theatre as it has been totally neglected for over 200 years'.[30]

Some seminar participants (the movers and seconders are not named in the seminar report) also took aim at an institution – the Aboriginal Theatre Foundation (ATF) – that seemed to reek of white patronage. One resolution called on the AAB 'to investigate the Aboriginal Theatre Foundation's constitution and activities over the past three years with a view to proposing a scheme which would better serve the needs of Aboriginal Theatre on a planned basis'; the other asked the AAB to pass 'control and direction of the Aboriginal Theatre Foundation to the hands of people of Aboriginal descent, while retaining non-Aboriginal advisors and technical staff where necessary'.[31] However, many at this conference did not share such suspicion of the ATF. One statement 'by Aboriginal participants' endorsed the ATF.

> Some white people we know can help us. We don't want them to pull out. We want the Aboriginal Theatre Foundation to keep working like before. We don't want people to kill the Foundation. We want the Foundation to stand.[32]

Another resolution questioned some participants' evident suspicion of white helpers.

> White and black can stand together as one and work together to keep the culture strong. We do not want people to have hard feelings in their hearts about the colour of a man's skin. We all have red blood in our bodies and we believe you should judge a man by his heart and by his feelings and how hard he works instead of talking hard words about skin colour. This skin colour argument must stop. Bad things have been done to us tribal people in the past but we have no hate in our hearts.[33]

The ATF had commenced at the end of 1969 to promote traditional Aboriginal performance arts. The founding director, Lance Bennett, travelled through the Kimberley, the Northern Territory and north Queensland to document 'the remaining Aboriginal dance resources' and to fund their performance from a grant bestowed by the ACFTA. That is, the ATF project was to defend – with money and recognition – what was left of a tradition that was evidently being lost, with the hope 'to reawaken racial pride among Aborigines as a whole, including those of mixed blood whose tribal background has been long since submerged by the tide of white settlement but who have so far failed to find a satisfactory identity in the new economy'.[34] By the end of 1971, the ATF claimed 250 Aboriginal and sixty-six non-Aboriginal members.[35] The ATF enjoyed non-Aboriginal endorsement of Aboriginal tradition. The ATF president was Justice R.A. Blackburn (who in the years 1969-71 was hearing evidence in the NT Supreme Court on whether the people of Arnhem Land had a customary right to decide whether mining could take place on the Arnhem Land Reserve), and Harry Giese (Director of Welfare, Northern Territory) was its vice-president. The governor-general, Sir Paul Hasluck, was 'patron'; and Mary Durack – heir to the Kimberley 'Kings in Grass Castles' – penned an early statement of the ATF's purpose. Among the other welfare and mission officials and anthropologists that made up the ATF's 'Top Committee' was the Northern Territory Administration's Ted Evans, who, in the early 1960s, had initiated a competitive Darwin Eisteddfod for dancers from Top End Aboriginal communities.

The contrasting perspectives on the ATF that emerged in the May 1973 AAB seminar dramatised North/South differences in Indigenous Australians' experiences of colonial authority and differences in understandings of the obstacles to Aboriginal cultural expression. The ATF *Newsletter* (presumably written by Bennett) saw the threat to the Aboriginal culture as coming from the indifference and disrespect of young Aboriginal people, not from non-Aboriginal hostility. The ATF formed regional branches that solicited Aborigines' involvement, and the resources of the ATF rewarded Aborigines' participation.

The ATF's cultural restoration project became an experiment in political reformation by remote Aborigines, led by two members of the 'Top Committee', Albert Barunga (Worora, Mowanjum Mission) and George Winunguj (Maung, Goulburn Island). Because the ATF publicised and celebrated the performances that it funded, it had to ensure communication between branches, as it had found that images classified as 'public' by the custodians of Law in one region were sometimes classified as 'secret' by the custodians of Law in other regions. The ATF thus became 'anxious to organise meetings of elders from different, widely-separated areas so that such difficulties can be thrashed out in their own terms'.[36] At the Darwin Eisteddfod in 1972, a meeting of elders from Kimberley, the Top End and Queensland decided to hold a non-competitive, unjudged festival at Winnellie Showground – for Aboriginal people, but with interested non-Aborigines allowed to watch. On 14–18 March 1974, 'ceremony leaders' met in Darwin to reconsider the way that the ATF functioned. The ATF report of that gathering, making no mention of the 'Top Committee', presented decisions about issues arising from Indigenous political mobilisation: how to delineate the roles of local, regional and interregional forums, how to encourage the participation of women, how to regulate alcohol use. The meeting also asserted rights to site protection, to repossess 'ceremonial gear' in museums, and to regulate the recording and reproduction of images and sounds.[37]

Non-Aboriginal patrons of 'tradition' could not prevent (and perhaps did not wish to prevent) the ATF developing a political momentum of its own as an interregional network of Law leaders; for such active members the ATF's principal concern was the public declaration of continuing Aboriginal Law through dance and music. Describing the work of the Mowanjum Dancers (Barunga's local concern) Ronald Berndt and E.S. Phillips (Education Department, Western Australia) noted a shift in the terms of self-expression and recognition between the old patronage and the new. Having grown up under Presbyterian supervision, young people at Mowanjum did not know the old dances, or did not know their meaning. Sensing the danger, Barunga had renewed efforts to teach dances, songs and myths. In January 1971, the Mowanjum dancers performed in Perth (Parkerville Amphitheatre) to an audience furnished with interpretive notes. In November 1971 the ATF took young dancers from Yirrkala to several Kimberley communities, including Mowanjum, 'to show how the old culture can be and has been held onto in some parts of Australia'.[38] This had introduced the didgeridoo to Kimberley dancing. In 1973, the Mowanjum dancers performed again in Perth, at the Cottesloe Civic Centre. According to Berndt and Phillips, these shows by Mowanjum were 'not as "polished"' as the Arnhem Land dancers whose tours south had long been sponsored by the Australian Elizabethan Theatre Trust (AETT); the Arnhem Landers' performances had been more varied in content, with more attention to stage craft and to the influence of ballet. For the Mowanjum dancers, the performance had required more of a revival of disused skills. They were 'attempting to restore their pride, and to communicate the significance of this to their audience'.[39] Whereas the AETT had 'polished' extant tradition to show southern audiences what classic culture had been, the ATF was using these pockets of strong and strengthening tradition to restore pride in Law whose transmission had been faltering.

Thus some of the motions passed at the AAB's founding seminar in Canberra in May 1973 revealed conflicting ways to read the politics of the ATF. White patronage of the ATF aroused some delegates' suspicion that the radical culture of the 'detribalised' would be discounted in favour of the northern communities' 'authentic' dancing. Should the ATF become exemplary of government patronage of 'Aboriginal culture', patronage would marginalise them in the AAB's constituency and in national politics. Those who had 'lost their culture' asserted a heritage that must be nurtured for what it was – a tradition of struggle, resistance, survival as Aboriginal; a tradition of critique that was as likely to be expressed in humour as in bitter denunciation and in demands for justice. These Southern Aborigines were fed up with white authority; their oral histories were of the revocation of reserves, the petty tyranny of superintendents, the seizure and institutional abuse of children, the humiliation of adults, the racism of violent police. At the AAB's Canberra seminar, people with these bitter histories faced Aboriginal elders from the North with a different colonial history.

In many Northern communities, there were elders who could recall the missions negotiating a form of colonial authority that did not take land and whose intervention into family life and the world of the spirit had often been respectful and cautious. Gwen Baker's oral history work with Yolngu has revealed this memory tradition. Baker has discerned two kinds of narrative of the missionaries' arrival: 'invasion' and 'invitation'. Invasion is common in the writings of historians and some Aborigines and missionaries endorse that theme, highlighting the initiative of Europeans and the difficulties and adversity – at least in the short term – of the missions' inception. The alternative theme of memory is 'invitation and negotiation', with emphasis on the agency of Aborigines in permitting and assisting the settlement of missionaries.[40] It is understandable that those who adjusted to the mission – with resignation or enthusiasm – would fashion memories of their own responsibility for the mission's existence.⁴¹ It is likely that many of the ATF elders shared in a memory of Northern colonisation in which Aborigines were the willing hosts of colonising guests who brought much that was good. Now, worried by the evident indifference of the young to their traditions, they were pleased to find support from the ATF's white patrons, who approved a version of 'Aboriginal culture' – dancing the Law – as beautiful. The political and cultural agendas of white and black authority in Northern Australia had not merged to become identical, but they were sufficiently congruent to sustain programs such as the ATF and to give scope for the politics of the ATF to evolve as a celebratory performance of customary law. One can imagine the ATF activists' dismay in May 1973 when their Southern hosts in Canberra voiced suspicion of the ATF's patronage. The report of the seminar included a conciliatory 'statement by Aboriginal elders': 'We all agree we are Aboriginals. We, the tribal elders want to inform the Australian Government that all people who have been known in the past as mixed blood or part-Aboriginals are from here on fully recognised by us as Aboriginal people.'⁴²

Tasmania: sites in custody

The Hobart *Mercury*, reporting a statement supporting Tasmanian Aboriginal land rights on 17 November 1977, mentioned that the speaker (Heather Sculthorpe) was 'red haired and freckled'.⁴³ The paper implicitly invited the reader to compare Sculthorpe with Aborigines whose hair was dark (or perhaps grey), whose skin was darker than a double-shot café latte and whose quest for land rights was therefore credible. Sculthorpe was part of a population of Aboriginal descent that persisted on Bass Strait islands and other places, conscious of their difference but not acknowledged officially as Aboriginal. The view of the state government in the 1940s and 1950s was that the best future for these people was to be absorbed into the wider community, with migration to Launceston the most likely scenario for those on the islands. The government recognised, however, that the Bass Strait islands were sites of seasonal return (for commercial mutton bird hunting) and the basis of a sense of community among those of Aboriginal descent. In 1951 the government ceased to classify Cape Barren Island as 'reserve'. By then, some Cape Barren Islanders had taken leases which they fenced to run stock.[44] At least one report, in 1958, labelled them 'coloured'.[45] The government's neglect and the poverty of the mutton bird industry motivated emigration from Cape Barren Island. However, welfare agencies knew that while the migrants gained easier access to unemployment benefits in Launceston they also encountered racial discrimination; many sought refuge by returning to the island. The Cape Barren Islanders were regarded by such authorities as work-shy, stubborn in their squalor, too fond of alcohol; they were said to hate whites, unless they were 'rightly approached'.[46] In 1958, 120 residents remained on Cape Barren Island.[47] In 1960 one report had them down to fifty. 'Living in great adversity they refused to leave because they feared losing their land.'[48]

It was expensive to encourage the Bass Strait Islanders' emigration, and when the Commonwealth began to make grants to all states for 'Aboriginal programs', including housing, the Tasmanian government presented itself as eligible, joining the Conference of Commonwealth and State Ministers for Aboriginal Affairs in July 1968. However, it was not inevitable that Commonwealth grants would be directed towards persuading people to leave Cape Barren Island for Launceston or Hobart;

by the end of 1971, Commonwealth money was funding employment programs on Cape Barren Island. Abschol, a university student organisation, helped the Islanders to represent themselves effectively. In 1969 it reported that there were seventy people 'who were adamant they wanted to remain on the Island'.[49] In 1971 Abschol organised a conference of Islanders in Launceston. By 1973, with an increasing island population, the Islanders had formed a council.

The new 'race' question in the 1971 Census contributed to recognition of Tasmanians previously known to be only fractionally Aboriginal. Rosalind Langford and others in 1972 established the Aboriginal Information Service 'to assist people of Aboriginal descent with information and advice, and to unite them as one people'.[50] There were 671 people in Tasmania (not all of them on Cape Barren Island) who claimed this identity in the 1971 Census and 2942 in 1976.[51] In this 'ethno-genesis', grassroots action and targeted Commonwealth programs reinforced each other. In 1973, the Aboriginal Information Service became the home of the Commonwealth-funded Aboriginal Legal Service, and, in the same year, the new National Aboriginal Consultative Committee included an elected representative from Tasmania (Morgan Mansell). 'This acceptance by the more traditional Aboriginal groups on the mainland meant much to the Aboriginal Tasmanians,' writes Dennis Daniels, 'and further encouraged the expression of Aboriginality.'[52]

A 'people' must have 'heritage'. Australian archaeology has helped to ensure such recognised time-depth for 'Aboriginal Tasmanians'. University-based studies of ancient Tasmanian sites began in 1962 when, with the intention of curbing destructive data collection by amateurs, academics associated with the nascent AIAS began to survey sites, to exert influence over who could work on them and, in 1968, to lobby the state government to pass laws to protect them.[53] In the same year, Victorian Aboriginal activist Doug Nicholls advocated the preservation of rock carvings at Mersey Bluff. Nicholls' political associates found more carvings, 'but kept the locations secret for fear of vandalism'.[54] Bob Maza, of Victoria's Aborigines Advancement League, in July 1970 laid a wreath on the Mersey Bluff carvings. AIAS-funded fieldwork to study Tasmania's archaeological sites gave academic 'respectability to an interest in Aboriginal matters in this State'. Meanwhile, Aboriginal Tasmanians were beginning to attach a slightly different value and meaning to such 'heritage', as they 'discovered a reassuring cadence between the past and the present'.[55] They were the bearers, they insisted, of an ancient culture that was changing as it survived.

Accordingly, not long after academic archaeology had wrested control from blundering amateurs, Tasmanian Aborigines challenged archaeology in both the management and the interpretation of sites. Between 1973 and 1977, the Tasmanian Information Centre became the Tasmanian Aboriginal Centre (TAC). The state government granted the TAC's request for more respectful treatment of the remains of Truganini (1812–76), and her designation as 'the last Tasmanian' was increasingly challenged. The government authorised that Truganini's remains be removed from the Tasmanian Museum and Art Gallery and cremated, with ashes scattered in the D'Entrecasteaux Channel (her country), in May 1976. Further action over the management of heritage soon followed as part of the TAC's wider assertion that Aboriginal people had owned Tasmania and should be compensated for dispossession; they should now control all sacred sites, mutton bird islands and unalienated Crown land. Apart from the payment of compensation (which was not considered by the Australian parliament until the early 1990s), the demands by the TAC paralleled what was then considered due, by both sides of Australian politics, to Aborigines in the Northern Territory. However, the TAC was less credible, as the (freckled, red-haired) bearers of customary rights, than the 'real' Aborigines of remote Australia, and this contributed to prolonged opposition to their demand for land rights.

Meanwhile, the TAC pressed their claim to own sites of significance. At the Hobart conference of the Australian Archaeological Association in December 1982, the TAC's Rosalind Langford characterised archaeologists as 'invaders': 'you have tried to destroy our culture, you have built your fortunes upon the lands and bodies of our people and now, having said sorry, want a share in picking out the bones of what you regard as a dead past'.[56] She said that 19th century 'science' had been responsible for establishing that the Tasmanian Aborigines were a degenerating society that had become extinct (with the death of Truganini). Archaeology had been 'a science upon which the general community could rely to excuse gross atrocities committed against Aborigines'.[57] Refusing to thank archaeologists for supporting land claims, she criticised the probative process that burdened claimants. She contested that Aboriginal heritage was (quoting Mulvaney) 'the inheritance of all Australians', arguing that categories such as 'all Australians' and 'mankind' were, in effect, ways to maintain the white colonial control over the collection and analysis of data about the past: 'if we Aborigines cannot control our own heritage, what the hell can we control?'[58] 'We are the custodians. You can be either our guest or our enemies,' Langford concluded.[59] As 'hosts' Tasmanian Aborigines shared values with archaeology: preserving the environment and opposing the destruction of non-renewable resources.

However, 'we must be secure with control of our land and our culture'.[60] Langford did not say what steps the TAC wanted archaeologists to take to assure security, but 'we suspect that it will be a much larger step than you believe.'[61]

The TAC's agitation won it a role in the administration of the *National Parks and Wildlife Act* 1970 and the *Aboriginal Relics Act* 1975. However, in 1984, the two Aboriginal members of the 'Aboriginal Relics Advisory Council' resigned, obliging the government to find another way to show that Tasmanian Aborigines were allowed to influence the management of cultural heritage ('relics'). In 1992 the Parks and Wildlife Service began to refer applications for permits under the 'Relics' Act to the Tasmanian Aboriginal Land Council (TALC, founded in 1990), in the expectation that Aborigines would soon manage cultural heritage, within the framework of Tasmanian law. From their published discussions, it seemed that members of the Australian Archaeological Association supported this change: they expected to obtain permission from the Aboriginal owners of heritage sites before they began excavation, and they would not mind returning materials (their scientific data) to Aboriginal communities.[62] Australian archaeologists were thus in step with their disciplines' global response to Indigenous empowerment, particularly in the settler-colonial democracies.

It had been easy for archaeologists to obtain permission to dig: the government of Tasmania issued eighty-five such permits between 1975 and 1995.[63] From 1993 it became more difficult, due to TALC opposition, to get a permit for a new site and to renew permissions that had expired. It was becoming clear that Aborigines and archaeologists differed in their views about the proper disposal ('reburial') of the materials that archaeologists returned. From 1993 to 1995 the TALC clashed publicly with archaeologists at La Trobe University whose permits to excavate four sites – Bone Cave, Warreen, Pallawa Trounta and Warragarra – had expired in 1991 and 1992. By June 1994, it became clear to the La Trobe researchers that their permission might not be renewed, even after they had explained that their investigation (approved at its inception by the Tasmanian Aboriginal Centre) was not complete. Early in October 1994, they had received from the TALC the unwelcome news that by 1 November, they must send materials that they had gathered from these four sites to the TALC, at whose premises they could continue their study. The La Trobe researchers sought a meeting with the minister, but the minister deflected the researchers to the director of the Parks and Wildlife Service. Before the meeting could take place the TALC wrote to all researchers whose permits had expired; it demanded that another La Trobe researcher return material. The researchers then met with the Parks and Wildlife Service in January 1995; the TALC did not attend that meeting.

From the TALC's point of view, the researchers were ignoring a ministerial directive to hand back the material held in their laboratories. From the researchers' point of view, the TALC had not explained why it had advised the government not to permit continuing work on this material; the researchers also suspected that the TALC would not handle the returned material in such a way as to allow further study. They appealed to the Tasmanian government to establish a new system for the granting and renewal of permits. Each side was experiencing the other as unreasonable and as unwilling to meet and talk. Meanwhile, the Parks and Wildlife Service sought to mediate, knowing that both the minister and the wider discipline of archaeology were generally in favour of empowering Aboriginal people to manage cultural heritage. In June 1995 the prestigious journal *Science* described the dispute in terms that appeared, to the TALC, to sympathise with the La Trobe researchers' position. The TALC threatened legal action against La Trobe University (and urged the Parks and Wildlife Service to initiate it), while appealing to Koori organisations in Victoria not to work with the La Trobe researchers. In July 1995, action in the Federal Court by the Victorian Aboriginal Legal Service resulted in the La Trobe researchers losing custody of the materials gathered from five Tasmanian sites. The government of Tasmania then asserted legal control over the 'relics', taking them back to Tasmania.[64]

In 1996, the TALC again challenged Australian archaeologists, arguing that they had not yet conceded that 'we are the rightful owners and custodians of our heritage'; by presenting themselves as serving 'mankind', archaeologists were in effect assuming ownership of Tasmanian Aboriginal heritage and were using it to establish 'a reputation for your discipline and yourselves'.[65] Without explicitly setting aside Langford's host–guest suggestion, the TALC made a new suggestion: researchers (guests) and Aboriginal people (hosts) would be 'peers' as long as researchers conceded that Aboriginal understandings were 'knowledge'; as peers, Tasmanian Aborigines could cooperate with researchers in 'development of research questions and research methods'; 'our questions are ... relevant to your scientific enterprise'.[66]

Who speaks for the Ngarrindjeri nation?

Intervening in a debate about a proposed bridge and marina at Hindmarsh Island (Kumarangk) in 1994, the Ngarrindjeri people of South Australia argued that a bridge would spoil a place that was sacred to them. For apparently assimilated Aboriginal people to point to 'sacred sites' in long-settled Australia was controversial, and the response to their claim became even more polarised when it became clear that among the Ngarrindjeri there was disagreement about whether the site really was sacred. The state government supported the marina investors who wanted the bridge to be built, but the federal Minister for Aboriginal Affairs used the powers of the *Aboriginal and Torres Strait Islander Heritage Protection Act* 1984 to ban the bridge – two clashing levels of government, each citing opposed versions of Ngarrindjeri tradition. How was this possible?

Ngarrindjeri tradition had long proved to be a difficult object to represent to the wider world. It was plausible to say that it had disappeared after generations of colonisation. In 1859 a Christian mission had commenced on the banks of Lake Alexandrina, at Point McLeay, Ngarrindjeri country. Point McLeay continued under state administration from 1916 and was also known as Raukkan. The Ngarrindjeri residents had survived partly by paid work in the region's agricultural industries. When Ronald and Catherine Berndt visited the Lower Murray region in 1939, 1942 and 1943, they found that, with the passing of the old economy and with the attraction of many to the Christian faith, very little of classical Ngarrindjeri culture remained. The Berndts elicited traditional knowledge from Albert Karloan (1864–1943) and Pinkie Mack (1858–1954). Karloan was son of Taramindjeri, a native doctor of the Manangki clan.[67] He had been an eager pupil of elders who had died between the 1890s and the 1920s and he was known as the last man to undergo the entire initiatory sequence, in 1882. Mack was the daughter of George Mason, a government 'sub-protector', and she was raised in the Law of her mother. Diane Bell credits her as leading, with song, the Ngarrindjeri dances that graced the 1951 re-enactment of Charles

Sturt's arrival in her country.[68] The Berndts recalled Karloan and Mack as 'little islands of traditional knowledge hemmed in by an overwhelming alien culture that had become much less alien to them' who 'wanted to tell about the old life because they realised that a break with it had been made'.[69] Ngarrindjeri elders may have contributed to that break; it seemed to the Berndts that they had experienced 'a crisis of confidence in the ability, interest or worthiness of the younger generation's members to assume the heavy burden of responsibility that accompanies the receipt of [traditional] knowledge'.[70]

However, the evident vitality and content of Aboriginal 'tradition' are contingent on the approach taken by those who seek to describe it. European Australians' knowledge of what remains of the traditional past in the behaviours and world view of Aborigines is determined by 'the gulf that has always separated European and Aboriginal Australians'.[71] When the Berndts published their 1939–43 fieldwork in 1951, they were aware that the Ngarrindjeri may have chosen not to disclose everything. While some 'try to stress their relationship with the white group by sneering at any aspects of the old culture that may be mentioned in their presence', this stance was often 'a pretence, and does not long survive in sympathetic company'.[72] People knew the totems from which they were descended, the Berndts found in the 1940s, and they believed in the potency of sorcery.[73]

In 1993 the full results of the Berndts' many hours with Albert Karloan and Pinkie Mack were at last revealed in a new and much longer edition of their work *A World that Was*. By then, the Aboriginal 'thirst for knowledge of their unique heritage had never been greater'.[74] Whereas in 1951, some members of South Australia's Protection Board had criticised the Berndts for reviving interest in traditional culture among the supposedly assimilating Ngarrindjeri, by the 1990s Ngarrindjeri faced a more receptive and respectful world: official denigration had abated and public interest had grown.[75] Ngarrindjeri Sarah Milera immediately began reading *A World that Was* in order to teach the state government archaeologist, Neale Draper, as he began to document the Hindmarsh Island bridge site's Aboriginal heritage in late 1993.[76] However, the idea that the bridge site was of sacred significance to Ngarrindjeri women did not come from *A World that Was* but from a contemporary scholar of Ngarrindjeri history, Doreen Kartinyeri.

Born at Point McLeay in 1935, Kartinyeri had spent two years of her childhood at the Fullarton Girls' Home in Adelaide, before working as a domestic servant. As an adult living at Point McLeay and Point Pearce she had acquired knowledge and public respect as a genealogist of some of the large Aboriginal lineages of the southern regions of South Australia. At the University of South Australia, she had initiated a project called 'Finding my people'. Fay Gale, Professor of Geography at the University of Adelaide, had invited her to update anthropologist Norman Tindale's genealogies for the South Australian Museum, and for this she had obtained both Tindale's permission and AIATSIS funding. At the July 1994 NAIDOC Ball the premier awarded her 'South Australian Aboriginal of the Year'. In May 1995, the University of Adelaide recognised her achievements with an honorary doctorate.

Presented in the media as a spokesperson for the Ngarrindjeri opposing the bridge, Kartinyeri said that her Auntie Rosie had told her the myths of Kumarangk. In June 1994 she passed some of Auntie Rosie's Law to Cheryl Saunders and Deane Fergie, the lawyer and the anthropologist appointed to advise Minister Robert Tickner as he pondered whether to extend his interim ban on the bridge. She also committed to paper the more secret details of the Law of Kumarangk, on the understanding that only women could read this material.

The disagreement of some Ngarrindjeri with Kartinyeri's characterisation of the bridge site as sacred began quietly and obscurely: in November 1994, Dulcie Wilson (née Rigney) gave a talk to the Murray Bridge Rotary Club in which she said that she had never been told by Ngarrindjeri elders that the bridge site was secret and sacred to women. On 23 March 1995, a South Australian MLA read into the Assembly record a letter attributed to Nanna Laura Kartinyeri, the oldest woman of the Ngarrindjeri nation and daughter of Pinkie Mack; the letter declared support for those who were contesting the claim that the bridge site was secret and sacred. (Before Nanna Laura died a few months later she signed a statutory declaration that this unsigned letter misrepresented her.[77]) By 19 May 1995, Channel Ten was reporting 'dissident' Ngarrindjeri who had not ever heard that the site was sacred and who challenged the claim that it was.

The South Australian government, still committed to building the bridge, appointed Iris Stevens as Royal Commissioner to investigate the information on which Tickner had based his construction ban. Stevens concluded that the information about Ngarrindjeri Law supplied to Tickner had been fabricated. Public interest, by now, was intense and polarised. Most of the women who believed the site to be sacred (including Doreen Kartinyeri) refused to appear before Stevens, objecting that the state had no right to call into question the beliefs of Aboriginal people.

Subsequent legal processes in 1996 and 2000 presented opportunities to reconsider Stevens' finding. Because the Federal Court had declared Tickner's initial ban invalid on procedural grounds, the minister was obliged in January 1996 to commission a new review of the status of the bridge site. Justice Jane Mathews got submissions from both sides of the controversy; the authors of the alleged 'fabrication' agreed to allow two anthropologists seasoned by working in the Northern Territory land claims process, Diane Bell and Geoffrey Bagshaw, to present a version of the site's heritage that withheld its deepest secrets. Mathews came to two conclusions by September 1996: that both sides sincerely believed what they had been saying about the bridge site; and that while the proposed bridge site was a 'significant Aboriginal area', there was 'insufficient' reason to conclude that a bridge would 'desecrate this area according to these traditions'.[78] Meanwhile, as bridge construction commenced in 1999, the leading investors in the marina, Tom and Wendy Chapman, sued Tickner, Saunders and Fergie for the financial loss inflicted by the bridge's delay. In August 2001, Justice John von Doussa found that the Chapmans had not established that the secret/sacred Law had been a fabrication: the Stevens Royal Commission, he said, had insufficient basis for concluding that Kartinyeri and her associates had fabricated Ngarrindjeri law.[79]

The Hindmarsh Island bridge affair demonstrated how divided was the Australian public (including the media and anthropologists) about the cultural traditions of supposedly 'detribalised' Ngarrindjeri. The division was exacerbated by conflicting testimonies by Ngarrindjeri themselves. Which Ngarrindjeri represented their Law? According to Diane Bell's sympathetic exposition of the world of Doreen Kartinyeri and her associates, the credible Ngarrindjeri were those who 'pay attention to closeness of *ngatji* relationships, and *ngatji* affiliation is central to their identity as Ngarrindjeri'.[80] *Ngatji* she glossed as 'totem, friend, countryman, protector'.[81] The belief in totemic spirits, found in the 1940s by the Berndts, had evidently survived to the 1990s. However, other Ngarrindjeri – with whom Bell was not able to work – stated their disbelief. Dulcie Wilson wrote that such 'myths and legends … are simply stories, as the Loch Ness Monster is to the Scottish people and the leprechaun to the Irish'.[82] By Bell's criterion, Wilson's disbelief disqualified her as an authority on Ngarrindjeri Law.

However, Bell also recognised that 'At the core of the Ngarrindjeri world which I have come to know is the value placed on the maintenance of kinship ties and genealogies which bind Ngarrindjeri to land and to each other.'[83] That is, Ngarrindjeri who do not believe in *ngatji* might nonetheless value 'kinship ties and genealogies' and thus understand themselves to be living in the traditions of Ngarrindjeri. Dulcie Wilson presented herself as Ngarrindjeri in this genealogical sense: she and her dissenting associates 'can clearly demonstrate who our mothers, grandmothers and great grandmothers were and our links with the Ngarrindjeri people'.[84] Wilson portrayed Ngarrindjeri such as Doreen Kartinyeri as misrepresenting Ngarrindjeri culture, history and aspirations; she presented herself as a Ngarrindjeri Christian courageously standing up to the Aboriginal and non-Aboriginal 'proponents' of the secret and sacred law of Hindmarsh Island. Chris Kenny, the Channel Ten journalist who helped to bring public attention to objectors such as Wilson, reported that they saw themselves speaking for 'mainstream Ngarrindjeri'.[85] For Diane Bell, the more credible bearers of Ngarrindjeri Law were those who continued to believe in *ngatji*, such as Kartinyeri. Those hailed as 'dissidents', in her view, simply did not know and mistook their ignorance for the truth.

Dulcie Wilson presented herself not as ignorant but as properly sceptical of bogus tradition. Wilson was born on Raukkan in 1932; light-skinned, she grew up at a time when skin colour determined social position. 'We were never really accepted into the Aboriginal community because we were tainted by our European inheritance, nor were we accepted by the white community because we came from an Aboriginal Mission with the stigma of primitive man. We were people in limbo with nowhere to go.'[86] As an adult she learned from her uncle Bruce that she should not ask questions about her family's past; family trees, for people of mixed descent, could be contentious, and knowledge of the past had the potential to hurt and to 'disgrace ... the family name and honour'.[87] Dulcie's mother was a domestic servant of the mission school's head teacher, W.T. Lawrie; her father was a shearer, away for months at a time. When her mother died in 1944, Dulcie lived with her grandmother and her uncle Bruce. Dulcie left school in 1947 (when she was fifteen) to be a domestic servant in the household of the mission's dairy overseer. She married Lindsay Wilson (a Raukkan resident) in 1950, and they decided to leave Raukkan for Millicent, where the Salvation Army was active. Their move combined personal choice, labour market inducement and state government and Salvation Army encouragement to assimilate into the white community. Dulcie recalls assimilation as an opportunity that she grasped eagerly.

Assimilation did not mean that Dulcie and Lindsay turned their backs completely on Raukkan folk nor on their Aboriginal heritage. They gave their children holidays with her uncle Bruce and cousin Oky on Yalkuri Station (near Raukkan) and at the Coorong. Lindsay maintained a specific link with his Ngarrindjeri past. At the request of the Australian and South Australian museums, he applied himself to Aboriginal crafts in which he had been instructed by Ngarrindjeri elders in his boyhood. He made occasional use of the Ngarrindjeri language, and he served on a Heritage Committee whose concerns included maintaining an Aboriginal burial ground. Doctoral students in archaeology and anthropology interviewed Dulcie and Lindsay to gather data on Ngarrindjeri culture.

Having experienced assimilation as a benefit that did not cost her heritage, Wilson was uneasy about land rights policies, about special programs of Aboriginal support and about the sense of aggrieved racial separatism borne by some Aborigines – 'the notion that this is their land, that white Australians are intruders'.[88] When the state assists Aborigines on low income – to buy a home, for example – it is 'an act of gross discrimination against those Aboriginal people who are trying to rise above the generalised perception of Aboriginals by helping themselves'.[89] Why should those who have 'lazed about with the hand-out mentality' find it easier to get assistance, she wondered.[90] In her view, some Aboriginal people and their allies in governments and church organisations were upholding policies that were unfair to people such as herself, who had thrived by embracing assimilation. From her perspective, the presentation of Hindmarsh Island as a sacred women's site was a provocation to the Ngarrindjeri 'silent majority' to speak out.[91]

How could Ngarrindjeri history have produced the contrasting perspectives of Kartinyeri and Wilson? Bell argues that the cultural fissure so evident within the Ngarrindjeri nation in 1995 had resulted partly from elders' decision that some knowledge should not be entrusted to certain people. 'Elders must be wise in the ways of the land,' she wrote, 'and bestow their knowledge on members of their families who are worthy of such wealth.'[92] Such judgments were effective, she wrote, to the extent that Ngarrindjeri culture has remained 'oral'. 'It is easier to keep track of who knows what in an oral culture,' Bell contended, 'than in a culture that relies on written texts. If all important knowledge is transmitted orally, it is possible to know who has been told what.'[93] However, Bell also acknowledged that Ngarrindjeri literacy has been 'a boon for those who wish to know more of their forebears'.[94] Literate Ngarrindjeri such as Doreen Kartinyeri have supplemented their listening by reading the missionary Taplin and anthropologists such as Tindale and the Berndts.[95] Just as it has become possible to know Ngarrindjeri traditions from books, so it has become possible to question the veracity of statements sourced orally by asking: why aren't these sayings corroborated by written records? According to Bell, the Hindmarsh Island bridge controversy intensified Ngarrindjeri ambivalence about whether to transmit tradition in writing. Those 'who believe that no good can come of committing their knowledge to writing' contend with others who think that 'the time has come for their knowledge to reach a wider audience than is possible within an oral culture'.[96] Doreen Kartinyeri's autobiography dramatises this ambivalence. As a genealogist, she had used Tindale's field notes from the 1930s. However, state officials had added to Tindale's notes their comments on Aboriginal people under surveillance, and Kartinyeri recalls her horror at some of the officials' stories of sexual liaisons and fighting that appeared against the names of 'lovely people'. She also describes the rewards and hazards of taking Tindale's genealogies back to the people. The work was valued by an Aboriginal community whose relationships with kin had been severed by state actions and by the contingencies of the colonial economy; her work was now disclosing information about descent that was needed to reconnect kin. However, such disclosure can be perilous when it undermines strategies of forgetting or repressing: information about who had procreated with whom could be sensitive. Kartinyeri thus had to mediate two regimes of truth: one that presumed the benefit of disclosure for posterity, the other that discreetly elided, protecting family histories crafted to respect feelings now. 'Some people were saying that Tindale had no right to write their family's stuff down or to take their photos.'[97] 'Sometimes I got told off, I got cursed, told I shouldn't be doing this and it's not my fucking business and sometimes I got beer thrown in my face.'[98] She resolved to face such opposition, 'because if I didn't do it now, our grandchildren would not know anything'.[99] The controversy about Kumarangk intensified Kartinyeri's ambivalence about inscription, and in her autobiography she asked herself whether she endangered sacred Law by publicly claiming to know secrets and by writing them down.

As Elkin remarked in his 1938 synthesis of anthropological knowledge of Aborigines, secrecy has long been an Aboriginal strategy to protect the arcane knowledge that they believe to be the basis of power. Within that strategy there have been different tactics. One tactic is for those with knowledge to pretend that there is nothing to know. If this was Nanna Laura Kartinyeri's tactic, then it placed her ambiguously and enigmatically between those who said they knew sacred secrets but sought to police their circulation (Doreen Kartinyeri) and those who believed that there was nothing secret to know (Wilson). Nanna Laura's position – what she knew – remains one of the unanswered questions of the Hindmarsh Island bridge affair.[100] What we do know is that, through misadventure, what Doreen Kartinyeri knew and wrote down about Kumarangk got into the hands of white men. Eventually, she burned these pages: they had become too dangerous. Her autobiography, published in the year after her death, mingles indignation and self-laceration.

Healing the Stolen Generations

In the 1990s, public exposure of the damage that child removal had done became one of the self-defining campaigns of those once known as 'part-Aborigines'. Since the 1920s there had been occasional disquiet and sometimes intense controversy among some non-Indigenous Australians about the removal of Aboriginal children from their mothers (and sometimes fathers) to institutions and families where, it was officially assumed, they would have a greater chance of flourishing.[101] Australian governments continued to remove children, replacing natural parents with adult guardians of many shades of competence and morality – to the great detriment, as it is widely acknowledged now, of many thousands of people. In 1981, Peter Read's historical review of this practice in New South Wales – *The Stolen Generations* – gave this practice and its victims a name.[102]

Agitation against heavy-handed state intervention into Indigenous families led to the formation of Aboriginal Child Care Agencies (ACCAs) in the 1970s, presenting Aboriginal perspectives to state and territory child protection agencies. They formed a peak body, the Secretariat of National Aboriginal and Islander Child Care (SNAICC) in 1981, and in 1983 the Hawke government began to fund SNAICC as an aid to policy-making. The United States' *Indian Child Welfare Act* (1978) inspired SNAICC to formulate the Aboriginal Child Placement Principle (ACPP): 'children were to remain with their families, removals were to be a last resort and any children removed were to be placed with Aboriginal families.'[103] A child's rights, according to recent human rights standards, include their right to be socialised into the culture of their natural parents. SNAICC launched the annual National Aboriginal and Islander

Children's Day (NAICD) in 1988 to promote the importance of an Aboriginal child growing up with Aboriginal heritage. In 1990, SNAICC called publicly for a national inquiry into child removal: a public inquiry, rather than another research study, would allow those suffering to tell their stories. To hear such stories, activists known as Northern Territory Stolen Generations staged a conference in Darwin (3–6 October 1994). Invited to deliver the opening speech, Robert Tickner predicted that 'the tears will flow' were his government to initiate 'some form of further assessment, investigation' of the 'consequences' of child removal.[104] The Keating government announced on 14 May 1995 that the Human Rights and Equal Opportunity Commission (HREOC) would inquire into the Stolen Generations.

Both the removal and the supervision of the child were by now understood as 'traumatic' – that is, as leaving a wound in the mind and soul that generated ongoing mental illness and destructive behaviour. The Royal Commission into Aboriginal Deaths in Custody (1987–91) had reinforced the idea that Indigenous Australians were collectively traumatised. Although suspicion of police and prison officer foul play had motivated the Royal Commission, the commissioners' case studies had produced a more complex account: suicide and self-harm had contributed to the prison toll. Of the ninety-nine persons whose deaths were investigated, forty-three had been removed as children. This reframing of Aboriginal suffering as chronic mental illness was the result also of research by the Victorian Aboriginal Health Service, by the 1993 HREOC inquiry into the Human Rights of People with Mental Illness (Burdekin Report), and by a 1995 study of Aboriginal Australians by Pat Swan and Beverley Raphael, *Ways Forward*, commissioned by the Commonwealth government. A Commonwealth Aboriginal Mental Health

Action Plan, with $20 million to spend, commenced in October 1996. Tickner's advocacy of an inquiry succeeded partly because it joined a growing belief that the Stolen Generations must have the therapy of telling their own story.

Brian Butler, the chair of SNAICC, recalled in a 2004 interview that one obstacle faced by SNAICC in campaigning for an inquiry had been the growing public and governmental concentration on land rights: from the 1970s, campaigning for land rights had distracted activists from the issue of the forced removal of children.[105] The phrase 'Stolen Generations' named an Indigenous constituency that 'land rights' tended to exclude, for child removal had disrupted the transmission of knowledge now required in land claims. When the Darwin 'Going Home' conference in October 1994 heard the Stolen Generations' stories, they were not only of families torn asunder but also of land rights denied.

From the 1930s to the 1970s, people of Darwin who were of Aboriginal and non-Aboriginal descent had seemed the success stories of 'assimilation'. They had been distinguished legally from 'full-bloods' in 1953, gaining standard citizenship entitlements, and they had benefited from the 'Part-Coloured Housing Program' and other efforts to assimilate them. Their coexistence with whites contributed to Darwin's reputation as a successfully multi-racial town. Nonetheless, they had remained self-consciously 'Aboriginal', partly because their family lives had continued to be the concern of the Welfare Branch and through such institutions as the Retta Dixon Home. When the *Land Rights Act* came into force in 1977, it offered such people little: those whose estates had been alienated to townships could not claim land and those with ancestral connection to claimable land faced difficulties in demonstrating spiritual attachment to it because no-one had taught them the stories of that land. Through the 'Going Home' conference, these people presented themselves as people forgotten by 'land rights'. Some traced their ancestry back to the Larrakiah, the original owners of the land which Darwin occupied. Under the name Gwalwa Daraniki ('our land' in Larrakiah), they had begun publicly asserting their 'land rights' in 1971.[106] Such unsuccessful mobilisations had made the gulf between the winners and losers in land rights visible by the early 1990s. The *Native Title Act* 1993 reinforced that gulf because it also demanded that claimants present proof of continuing connection to country.

At the time of the 'Going Home' conference, the North Australia Aboriginal Legal Aid Service (NAALAS) was preparing an action in the High Court of Australia on behalf of several Aboriginal people, including Alec Kruger.[107] One of the five heads of damage claimed was lost or diminished entitlement to participate in land claims. Born a Mudburra (whose country is west of Katherine), but removed as a child to 'the Bungalow' in Alice Springs (Arrernte country), Kruger could not join the claim to his mother's ancestral land, because the Mudburra people felt he had been away too long to know his country. Accepting this decision because he had never learned Mudburra 'tribal songs, ceremonies and stories', Kruger was still hurt by the rejection.[108] When he attended a reunion of Bungalow residents, he realised that many who had been taken away from their families as children shared his feeling. 'Many spoke of a deep sense of personal rejection by the Aboriginal organisations and community, because of land claim problems. It was good for me and others to speak up about our anger at being humiliated by our own mob.'[109] As a stockman in the country of the Eastern Arrernte, he had learned from older stockmen some of the songs of that region. However, he was left out of the Loves Creek land claim as well, clashing with young Arrernte who thought that his Mudburra descent excluded him from an Arrernte claim. Land rights in the Northern Territory was, in his words, 'a humiliating and weakening process for the whole community almost everywhere it happens'.[110] When participants in Darwin's 'Going Home' event sought changes in the 'interpretation and implementation' of the ALRA, the land councils responded.[111] John Ah Kit, acting deputy chair of the Northern Land Council, acknowledged that the wishes of the Traditional Owners had sometimes been 'hurtful' to those raised in government or mission institutions not on their ancestral country.[112] Alison Hunt, a member of the Central Land Council, warned against seeking revision of the Act; she pleaded with the Act's critics to work with the council.[113] Galarrwuy Yunupingu, chair of the Northern Land Council, in a testy exchange with the Tiwi Land Council's Cyril Rioli, said that land councils could help those unable to claim land to re-establish their kin relationships with those who could; he reminded Rioli that the land councils were obliged to determine ownership by reference to the Act's definitions and to anthropological evidence.[114]

In 1994, it was useful to the Keating government's political agenda to address, conspicuously, those excluded from land rights. Responding to the Mabo judgment in 1992, the government had conceded that under the *Native Title Act* 1993 many Indigenous Australians would not be able to assert native title, just as they had not benefited from land rights laws in some jurisdictions. For those lacking demonstrable connection with the land that they might have claimed, Keating committed to negotiating a 'social justice package' – laws and programs that his government hoped would be recognised as compensatory by Indigenous Australians without title prospects. If the social justice package were to succeed politically, it had to be negotiated with such people and approved by them. The Stolen Generations, as a social movement, was well suited to present such interlocutors, for their defining narrative was that removal from kin had broken links to country. The 'Going Home' conference in Darwin in October 1994 was thus the result not only of SNAICC's agitation since the 1980s about broken families but also of the acknowledgment, highlighted in discussion of native title, that the recognition of custom was creating inequities among Aborigines. HREOC's inquiry recognised the distinct grievance of those deprived of 'tradition'.

However, it was not inevitable that a national inquiry into the Stolen Generations would take up these concerns about the inequities of 'land rights'. Among the four organisations prominent in promoting the inquiry – SNAICC, NAALAS, Link-Up and ALSWA (Aboriginal Legal Service of Western Australia) – priorities varied. Ronald Wilson and Mick Dodson, appointed to lead the inquiry, set up an Indigenous Advisory Council, and within this forum NAALAS became more distant and Link-Up more influential. Link-Up, founded in New South Wales in 1981 and formally incorporated in 1985, had established a casework approach to the Stolen Generations. Using government and church records and oral history, it tried to reconnect removed people with their families of origin. Link-Up was aware that one consequence of removal was that knowledge of country was not inherited. However, Link-Up's perspective on this problem was shaped more by experience in New South Wales, where Link-Up conducted twenty-two forums between November 1995 and March 1996 (including several in gaols). The New South Wales *Land Rights Act* 1983 did not demand of claimants that they pass a test of their continuing spiritual 'attachment'. To be of the Stolen Generations in New South Wales did not exclude a person from that state's land claim process to the extent that it had in the Northern Territory. In Link-Up's perspective, what was at stake for the Stolen Generations was less their land rights than their Indigenous selfhood. In Rebecca Devitt's words, 'For Link-Up, the finding of familial and cultural roots was essential to the recovery of the damaged subject.'[115]

The HREOC process was receptive to Link-Up's concern with damaged identity because this framing of the Stolen Generation's grievance, unlike the concerns generated by the Northern Territory's *Land Rights Act*, was not specific to a jurisdiction. The Stolen Generations people were differentiated, across jurisdictions, in their encounters with the land rights processes of each state or territory, but they had in common a story that their human right to culture, heritage and identity had been compromised.[116] As well as encouraging victims to tell their heartbreaking stories, Wilson and Dodson reinforced this psychological and cultural framing by calling expert witnesses – psychiatrists, psychologists and other health professionals – who represented the traumatic effects of removal. The experts' themes were the loss of the bond between parents and children; the loss of identity and Indigenous culture; racism and the denigration of Indigenous culture; and the intergenerational effects on parenting skills which compounded the original trauma of those removed and in turn contributed to the trauma of future generations, including emotional and sexual abuse. These experiences, the experts argued, 'have resulted in major depressive disorders, feelings of hopelessness and marginalisation, breakdowns in relationships, chronic grieving, anxiousness, suicidal ideation or symptoms of serious mental illness'.[117] Wilson reached out to mental health professionals during the inquiry. His address to the state Aboriginal Mental Health Conference in Perth on 21 November 1995 'outlined the existing evidence on the disproportionate incidence of mental illness in the Indigenous community'; he suggested that the inquiry process was healing not only the Stolen Generations but the nation.[118]

During the HREOC inquiry, NAALAS continued to represent its Northern Territory clients 'as survivors with rights to justice rather than victims in need of healing'.[119] Jacqui Katona, one of the editors of the 1994 'Going Home' conference report, addressed the National Press Club on 13 February 1996, demanding amendments to land rights legislation; she criticised the HREOC inquiry's trauma/healing model for exposing individuals to further psychological risk and for failing to 'assess the problems of the Stolen Generations group as a whole'.[120] In October 1996, NAALAS urged the recently installed Howard government to commit to reparations for survivors of removals and to changes in the land rights legislation.

Conclusion

The relationship of Indigenous Australians to other Australians has changed partly through expansion of the category 'Aboriginal' beyond Deakin's constitutional notion of 'Aboriginal native' as 'full-blood' to include those of mixed ancestry and those who had acculturated to the dominant way of life and who lived in towns and cities. The government's acceptance of self-identification from the 1971 Census acknowledged 'pan-Aboriginal' dynamics that some non-Aboriginal observers had noticed as early as the 1930s. In 1961, when the Select Committee on Voting Rights asked A.P. Elkin if Aborigines considered themselves a nation, he replied that the idea 'has built up during the last thirty years, particularly among the mixed-bloods. The latter are taking the full-bloods as a symbol of the idea of all being one aboriginal group ... I have been watching it since about 1936.'[121]

As the more inclusive sense of 'Aboriginal' proliferated in words and feelings and as it actualised in practices, the figure of the so-called 'part-Aboriginal' became problematic. What were they to be called? What did they want? What did they deserve? Was their Aboriginality 'informed' by knowledge of tradition? Was what they had lost recoverable? Now that Australian authorities were honouring the classical culture of some Aborigines in cultural programs and land tenure policies, how could others live as imperfect versions ('part') of what was now being idealised? What vibrant hybridity of survivals and innovations could 'part-Aboriginals' construct?

The educationalist Robert McKeich admitted at a 1974 conference that 'only part-Aborigines can really know their part-Aboriginal world', and he implied that they were not yet articulate about it.[122] Yet, as I have shown, by 1973 some of them were becoming forthright about what it meant for them to be recognised as 'Aboriginal'. In this chapter I have tried to show that it was *in dialogue* that so-called 'part-Aborigines' became articulate as 'Aboriginal people'. The dialogue was necessitated by unprecedented national forums such as the AAB, but it also took place in conferences with archaeologists, in court rooms and Royal Commissions, in the mass media. To be 'Aboriginal' has always been to occupy a position in a field of cultural identities constituted by colonial relationships. To change the meaning of 'Aboriginal', in the broadening way that I have described, required people to reposition themselves not only in a field of white/black, but also among 'blacks' themselves, *among all those of Indigenous descent*, for the inclusiveness of 'black' broke open old stereotypes and made new kinds of 'black' subjectivity both possible and contestable. Torres Strait Islanders, according to Eddie Mabo, had to reposition themselves in relation to Aborigines. Urban blacks had to come to terms with remote Aborigines who were not only enviable bearers of classical culture (their 'loss') but pitiable clients of government and mission patronage. Ngarrindjeri for whom assimilation had worked well had to reposition themselves, conspicuously, in relation to other Ngarrindjeri who were accentuating Ngarrindjeri tradition in what seemed (to them) aggressive and implausible terms. Those promoting the Stolen Generations as a constituency of grievance had to find national terms for suffering because the forum made available for storytelling was national: they found an idiom (suffering/healing) that was emerging elsewhere in public health policy. After the 1970s breakthroughs of pan-Aboriginality, the 1990s brought multiple 'Aboriginalities' into play.

11

The Indigenous middle class

Australia's experiments in self-determination have encouraged class formation in Indigenous Australia. In Chapter 8 I presented self-determination as a combination of five strands, all of which were continuous, in some respects, with what had been achieved under programs of assimilation: the removal of 'caste' distinctions from the enumeration of the Aboriginal and Torres Strait Islander populations, so that respondents could no longer be graded by others in their degree of Indigeneity; the grant of limited powers of self-management to recognised Aboriginal or Torres Strait Islander communities; the endowment of assets (land and capital funds) to Indigenous collectives; the encouragement of Indigenous collectives to incorporate as publicly funded service organisations; and the formation of representative bodies to articulate Indigenous wishes – regional and national – to state agencies and corporations.

One of the lasting results of these initiatives is thousands of organisations making up the 'Indigenous sector', the joint product of Indigenous political mobilisation and state funding and legislation. The Indigenous sector enables Indigenous Australians to be responsible for decisions and for carrying them out; non-Indigenous Australians serve as employees or consultants. That many Australians wanted Indigenous Australians to take responsibility for themselves was demonstrated by market research, when the Council for Aboriginal Reconciliation sought to discover what the public thought 'reconciliation' was. Donovan Research found that about one third had no idea what 'reconciliation' meant. To fill that void Donovan prompted each respondent with some possible meanings of 'reconciliation'. Ninety-five per cent of respondents supported the proposition that 'reconciliation' should include 'Aboriginals becoming more responsible for their own lives'.[1]

The skills and outlooks required for being 'responsible' – whether as individuals or as organisations – included literacy, numeracy and familiarity with formal organisations. These were among the talents of citizenship that assimilation programs were supposed to impart to Indigenous people. However, the distribution of such training had proved uneven, for two reasons. First, the colonial occupation of Australia had taken almost two centuries, and in the regions occupied most recently the culturally transformative processes have been less demanding; people from these regions were less acculturated to mainstream Australia, more immersed in the old Law. Second, Australian governments had been discriminating in their programs of acculturation. They had acted on the racial distinction between 'full-blood' and mixed descent, selecting children of mixed descent for more intensive training. In Northern Australia, this governmental discrimination by 'caste' had sometimes been matched by missionaries and pastoralists who delegated some of their authority over 'full-bloods' to Aborigines who were 'half-castes'. In the longer-settled Southern regions, although nearly all the 'full-blood' Aborigines had died out by the 1950s, distinctions of caste and colour had remained significant. Colour consciousness – among whites and blacks – had regulated access to the education system and this meant that the internal stratification of the Indigenous population along 'caste' and 'colour' lines was reproduced, over two or three generations, as an internal stratification based on unequal possession of the cultural capital necessary to function in wider Australian society.

Because some had acculturated more than others to mainstream Australian skills, norms and patterns of behaviour, Indigenous Australians have been differentiated in their experience of the formal equality that resulted from assimilation. When governments began to solicit 'self-determination' in the early 1970s, some people were better equipped than others to step into the roles that 'self-determination' created. Some could readily be leaders, entrepreneurs and functionaries in the Indigenous sector; others could not, and these less-skilled or motivated people became the clients and constituencies of those who could. This transition has tended to favour the employment of Indigenous women in administrative work, contrasting with the declining demand for Indigenous men in manual occupations.[2]

The differentiating dynamics of this assimilation–self-determination sequence have been experienced through an ideology of pan-Aboriginality that muffles such distinctions. Becoming powerful in the final third of the 20th century, as a critical response to distinctions imposed by governments and public opinion, this ideology emphasised the commonalities of 'Black' Australians. Black 'ethno-genesis' challenged governments and the public to no longer use 'caste' and colour distinctions to reckon degrees of Aboriginal authenticity. To notice class differences within Indigenous Australia, as I will in this chapter, is to apply distinctions that question 'Black' commonality. Class analysis has been criticised by Louise Taylor for alienating '"professional" Aboriginal people from our remote or rural (read real, authentic) brothers and sisters', just as past government policies alienated 'half-castes' from 'full-bloods'.[3] Class analysis, Taylor continues, fails to see how much Aboriginal elites share with Aboriginal non-elites; it undermines the credibility of Aboriginal elites that 'authoritatively speak on ... subjects which are of major significance in rural and remote communities'.[4] This critique of a class analysis of Indigenous Australia mobilises a historical narrative – strongly supported in revisionist historical scholarship – of shared suffering and common resistance as a colonised people.

However, by the 1990s, some Indigenous intellectuals were insisting that 'class' differences were real. Their class analysis encouraged a positively self-conscious Indigenous middle class whose careers would possibly include serving as the functionaries of 'self-determination'. Ngarrindjeri academic Maria Lane wrote in 1997 of several conditions required for self-determination. Three of them were

> that rural communities could either bring about the
> education of their own young people where they are, or
> attract, voluntarily, large numbers of skilled and educated
> indigenous people from the cities ... [that] the bulk of
> the educated indigenous work force, based in the cities,
> feel that their contributions might at last be valued by the
> communities and that ... educated people are allowed to
> participate fully in the decision-making of community,
> regional and other deliberative bodies in an atmosphere of
> mutual respect rather than hierarchy;[5]

Lane worked at the University of South Australia, supporting Indigenous Australians to get tertiary qualifications.[6] She was worried that Aboriginal organisations were slow to see the value of Indigenous graduates or qualified tradespeople, and she welcomed ATSIC's policy of recruiting qualified Indigenous Australians.[7] To explain the disconnection of the more educated from the less educated, Lane sketched a social history of South Australian Aborigines, contrasting two trajectories: the 'opportunity-oriented' migrants from settlements and missions to cities and large towns who sought education, who intermarried with non-Indigenous people and who enabled their own participation in Australia's 'open' or 'civil' society; and the 'welfare-embedded' Aborigines who had kept to their home region, limited their aspirations for education, employment and income and, by their marriage choices and other behaviours, reproduced an inward-looking social milieu.[8]

> There are now (at least) two distinct Indigenous socio-economic, or class, populations: a potentially Open Society, work- and opportunity-oriented population; and a Welfare-Embedded, work-averse, security-oriented population. This differentiation is a result of a process which has taken the best part of sixty years, three generations, and has been more or less confined to the closely settled areas of southern and eastern Australia.[9]

Another Indigenous academic, Larissa Behrendt, led a 2011–12 review of Indigenous participation in higher education. She envisaged 'a class of Aboriginal and Torres Strait Islander professionals who can respond to the needs of their own communities'; her panel saw such people as 'vital to meeting Closing the Gap targets'; they would emerge from 'success in higher education'.[10] Marcia Langton, in the published version of her 2012 Boyer Lectures, cited statistical evidence of an Indigenous middle class in order to criticise the stereotype of Indigenous Australians as 'the poor, undereducated, unemployed and disempowered'; she regretted the persistent influence of this typification on 'policymakers, educators and police'.[11] The Indigenous academic Anthony Dillon has similarly complained that

> Aboriginal people are portrayed as the victims of history (colonisation), racism, and government policies. Inequalities in health and well-being are cited as evidence for victimhood. But these factors alone cannot explain the high degree of dysfunction, disadvantage, and discontent of so many Aboriginal people.[12]

He drew attention to 'the Aboriginal people who are doing exceedingly well'.[13]

Many of the Indigenous middle class are white-collar employees of public sector agencies.[14] Kerryn Pholi, a former 'mid-level Aboriginal bureaucrat', objected to policies discriminating in favour of individuals on the basis that they are 'Aboriginal'.

> When we define people by one variable, in this case 'Aboriginal', they become a homogeneous collection of indistinguishable, interchangeable units, whose fate is somehow linked. As an Aboriginal person I belong to a statistically disadvantaged Aboriginal population; therefore, I am 'disadvantaged'.[15]

Refusing the help to which her Aboriginal status entitled her, Pholi was criticised for being unable – because of her pale skin and professional success – to share in and acknowledge the experience of Aboriginal oppression. This possible disconnection was studied by Elizabeth Ganter, a former (non-Indigenous) public servant in the Northern Territory, where a high proportion of her former colleagues were of Aboriginal or Torres Strait Islander descent. Asking seventy-six such people to reflect on the ways that they were 'representative of' and 'different from' the Aboriginal people of the Northern Territory, she found that many saw themselves as 'role models' (their term) whose practice included 'corrective governing' (Ganter's term) of any Aboriginal people whose comportment fell short of what governments and other citizens expected of them.[16] The interviewees saw themselves as both part of and not part of the Northern Territory Aboriginal population: they 'wanted to tackle the Northern Territory's deep historical problems because they had been affected by them and emerged relatively unscathed'.[17] As role models, Ganter's interviewees strove to be not only close to the people for whom they were models – 'not too flash' – but also professionally effective.[18] Their very existence challenged stereotypes of Aboriginal people as 'mere policy subjects or the passive recipients of welfare'.[19]

'Class' is increasingly salient in Indigenous accounts of themselves, for several reasons. First, since the 1960s, Indigenous intellectuals have been learning from commentaries on the contemporary situation of African Americans, and such writings have recently included a class-based critique of the stereotyping of all African Americans as poor and helpless. Noel Pearson has drawn on this strand of contemporary Black American social commentary to show what he considers to be the unfortunate complicity between 'Black' victim senses of entitlement and 'white' liberal shame for historic racism.[20] Dillon also draws on Black American writings about the psychological appeal and political rewards of victimhood.[21]

Second, the formation of a professional middle class is a consequence of the recent successful promotion of formal education to Indigenous Australians. Such government effort is likely to continue, and families that embrace higher education are likely to pass on their ambition for education and higher income to their children. From 2006 to 2011, the proportion of the Indigenous working-age population with a post-school qualification increased from 39 per cent to 44 per cent. Most of the growth in the proportion of Indigenous Australians with post-school qualifications between 2006 and 2011 was due to an increase in those with certificate-level qualifications.[22] Crawford and Biddle hail this as 'a remarkable investment in education by a population that, until relatively recently, was excluded from formal education, and even now reports a high level of discrimination and locational disadvantage in the education system.'[23] This investment is paying off, according to Biddle's analysis of 2011 Census data.[24] 'Indigenous males who had completed a degree had an income that was on average 2.91 times as high as those who had not completed Year 12 and had no qualifications. The ratio for Indigenous females was 2.68.'[25] An Indigenous person was more likely to engage in post-school education if he or she grew up in a home with a relatively high income and under the care of a mother with a post-school qualification.[26]

While some Indigenous families may be passing on to their children a disposition to take up post-school education, there are factors – not necessarily within any family's control – that continue to inhibit this Indigenous push into post-secondary education and higher incomes. They must complete secondary education: a smaller proportion of Indigenous than non-Indigenous students does so. And academic strengths of Indigenous students, at secondary level, are less likely to be in English, mathematics and science.[27] Having completed school, Indigenous youth are less likely than non-Indigenous youth to live near a university or training institution.[28] Young Indigenous adults are more likely to have caring duties – for children and for aged and disabled relatives – than are non-Indigenous youth.[29] Those studying at the level of bachelor degree or above were less likely than non-Indigenous Australians to study management and commerce, engineering, natural and physical sciences, and information technology; they were more likely to have studied education, or society and culture.[30] This pattern of study is related to a stronger female commitment to higher education. In 2011, 'among Indigenous Australians with higher levels of education (including both bachelor degree and above, and diploma or advanced diploma) there were about twice as many women as men'.[31] Such women were comparatively well rewarded: 'Indigenous females with a degree … had a slightly higher average income than non-Indigenous females with a degree.'[32]

The third reason why an Indigenous middle-class identity may be consolidating is that their role in self-determination – spending 'tax-payers' money' – requires them to articulate an ethical program. Writing on 'good governance' with anthropologist Diane Smith, Mick Dodson has evoked an ethical culture of Indigenous professional–managerial class service that would result in profitable Indigenous enterprises and 'political and business stability'.[33] The institutional requisite of an effective Indigenous managerial class in Indigenous incorporated bodies is 'a clear separation between the powers and responsibilities of leaders and boards, and the daily management of community businesses and services'.[34] Dodson and Smith list core ingredients and principles of good governance, including respect for the 'rules of the game', such as those found in publications of the Australian Stock Exchange; commitment to procedures of appeal and dispute resolution; and the ability to explain financial management systems to governing boards.[35] Scaling up Indigenous collective action beyond the local is another skill that Dodson and Smith hope to see emerge.[36] These are the capacities and virtues that governments and corporations promote, addressing the aspirations of an Indigenous constituency. In New South Wales Koori politics, according to Heidi Norman, the implementation of the *Land Rights Act* since the 1980s has encouraged the convergence of norms of good governance held by government and by Indigenous political elites. This evolution in political culture has been controversial among Kooris, she reports, as some see in the professionalisation of Indigenous governance the domestication of leaders, alienating them from the 'grassroots'.[37]

Class formation within Indigenous Australia has excited the creative imagination to perform drama – both serious and satirical – that expresses the reflexivity of the Indigenous middle class. The television drama *Redfern Now* (ABC TV) dramatised emergent differences of socio-economic fortune, aspiration and political sensibility. Some episodes focused on representative figures conflicted between duty to public office and the appeal of community loyalties, or who were fashioning a new sense of self from the diverse regimes of value and honour to which they were subject as community members and leaders. ABC TV's *Black Comedy* parodied some orthodox senses of victimhood and identity (anxieties about becoming 'white').

Anxiety about the emergence of the Indigenous middle class may persist at a personal level. Indigenous sociologist Bronwyn Carlson has told of the personal cost of competing within 'the world of identified Aboriginal employment': when recruitment to certain jobs defines 'Indigeneity' as a desired or necessary attribute applicants may find it an ordeal to authenticate their Aboriginality.[38] Those recognised as 'Aboriginal' may be troubled by that label's demands. A theme of Stan Grant's autobiography *The Tears of Strangers* (2002) is the question: has success made me less 'Aboriginal'? After growing up in a poor Wiradjuri family in a milieu in which Aborigines were sometimes bitterly divided among themselves about how to be 'respectable' and whether even to try, Grant attended university and then found success as a journalist – at first in radio, then in television and subsequently as an author. His tale implied a choice to be respectable, to negotiate white Australia on white Australia's terms and to distance himself from a certain way of being Aboriginal – resentful, defiantly unrespectable – that he referred to as 'Abo'. Grant wrote of being troubled by the thought that 'If Aborigines are poor, I'm not an Aborigine; if Aborigines are coal black, I'm not an Aborigine; if Aborigines are the victims of injustice and bigotry, I'm not an Aborigine.'[39] Presented as a role model, 'my example ... was in the futility of community life and the salvation of selfish individualism. I could have been a poster boy for assimilation.'[40] He has since become more content in his 'middle-class' identity.[41]

As these Indigenous intellectuals have differentiated themselves from what they see as a stereotype – the poor, dark-skinned victim – they have raised the question of how to characterise Indigenous Australians who are not flourishing and whose 'disadvantage' has been made conspicuous by statistics on employment, income, education, health (physical and mental) and incarceration. Lane's social history represents these people as the products of choices made by themselves or their parents and grandparents. Their own limited aspirations have kept them down, she suggests, and the welfare-dependent have continued to refuse opportunities. Both Noel Pearson and Stan Grant have promoted Lane's voluntarist explanation of inequalities among Indigenous Australians.[42]

Historian and lawyer Pearson's influence in these discussions is an important part of recent history. A product of the Lutheran Mission at Hope Vale, followed by St Peter's Lutheran College in Indooroopilly and the University of Sydney, Pearson's path was all that an assimilationist might wish for, yet his first use of his great skills had been to join the Indigenous leaders in 1993 negotiating native title; he then criticised the resulting *Native Title Act* for the limits it placed on the Indigenous right to self-determination. In 1997, he began to develop a new theme, commenting on the Howard government's substitution of Indigenous 'self-empowerment' for Indigenous 'self-determination'. The government 'cannot deny our right to self-determination,' he wrote, 'but the concept of empowerment gives a refreshing emphasis to the fact that as bad as our situation is and as poverty-stricken and disadvantaged as the great majority of our people are, we have to engage in the solutions. We cannot just be passengers. We cannot just sit back.' Adding that 'self-determination is hard work', Pearson regretted that it was the government, not Aboriginal people, who had put forward 'self-empowerment' as a new theme for action. 'We should be the ones realising that we have to do it ourselves, and promoting this idea among our peoples.'[43]

Pearson's public reflections on the irresponsible condition (as he saw it) into which the Aborigines of Cape York had sunk drew on his University of Sydney history thesis about Hope Vale as a community morally reformed, in the period from the 1880s to 1950s, under Lutheran guidance. Pearson's self-published book *Our Right to Take Responsibility* (2000) depicted his people's degenerating capacity for collective action since the 1970s. 'Aboriginal society in Cape York Peninsula today is not a successful society,' he declared.[44] His people, particularly *his* people in Cape York, had been 'poisoned' since about 1970 by their access to cash welfare benefits and to welfare programs in kind. He insisted that 'we have … *a right to an economy*'.[45] His concept of 'economy' was moral, flowing from his judgment about what is good in human relationships. The 'real economy' is defined by institutionalising 'reciprocity'. Reciprocity, a traditional Aboriginal value, had been undermined by too-easy access to welfare benefits. People on welfare were not required to do anything in return; they were getting used to being passive and without power, and they had become righteous about their entitlement to receive without reciprocity. Administrators of Aborigines' welfare had too readily supported the recipients' rights, and they had assumed that the recipients lacked the capacity to act. Donors and receivers thus shared a self-perpetuating mentality. Pearson argued that this welfare-based economy – not just the longer-standing phenomena of racism and associated psychological trauma – had debilitated Cape York people. 'Children who have grown up in this passive welfare economy have little understanding of and have never experienced life in the real economy.'[46] For Pearson, Lane's 'bad choices' explanation of 'disadvantage' is the basis of an explicitly moral reform program that makes access to welfare payments a reward for prescribed behaviour modelled by respectable and successful Aboriginal people.[47]

Pearson has listed what he considers to be fundamental Aboriginal values: 'unity, cooperation, respecting rights, sharing power, taking responsibility, encouraging others, supporting each other'. He asserted that 'the promotion of these values throughout the community is the particular responsibility of leaders'.[48] 'We need a leadership that fosters the social support of individuals and which underlines the importance of individual engagement for success,' he wrote.[49] People will resist taking more responsibility, he anticipated, but good leaders can overcome this resistance (which he calls 'going against the instincts of many members of our community') without 'dictating' to people that they must change.[50] He remarked that 'there has to be a healthy tension between leadership (by community leaders and by family leaders) and individuals in working out what acts of reciprocity will be expected in return for these programs'.[51] For some recipients of welfare, the first step towards recovery will simply be to take responsibility for those aspects of their health that lie within their control, such as ceasing substance/alcohol abuse. Another step will be to engage in 'education and self-improvement'. Yet another is to be more considerate of the welfare of family members, especially the old and the young. Finally, people will be asked 'to contribute to the community at large'.[52] In Pearson's view, the state would not be able to oblige Indigenous Australians to improve in these ways because governments have forfeited moral authority. They were remote and lacked transparency; Aboriginal memory of unjust treatment at the hands of government was fresh. For reciprocity to become the welfare recipients' moral framework, 'it must be defined and imposed by the Aboriginal people of Cape York Peninsula and their leaders, possibly in partnership with government'.[53] Pearson persuaded the state to devolve to local Indigenous elites on Cape York the powers to discipline those who abused their entitlement to welfare. Government funding of the Cape York Welfare Trials in 2008 enabled respectable Indigenous people to use state resources and their own moral suasion to bring order to the disorderly lives of other Indigenous people.[54]

Pearson's project has at least two precedents. In his scornful lamentation of the culture of the New South Wales reserves ('the reserves are pest-holes'), Kevin Gilbert in 1973 urged Kooris to turn their communities into 'black Israels', run by committees with no tolerance for weaklings and committed to schooling their children off the reserves.[55]

> There must be discipline. Young men and not so young men who have never worked in their lives, who have bludged off women for years, must be given what will undoubtedly, at first, be a pretty big shock. The black community will have to decide on stern rules, tough rules that Aborigines do not like exercising against one another. Rules that say 'Work or get out'. 'Work or don't eat.' 'Work, or no grog.' The bludger's, the drunkard's, the house neglector's, the wife and child bashers' days must be numbered in any developing Aboriginal community ... Remember back, Kooris, when our society was 'specialized' to allow for survival? When every contribution, every grain of seed, every hunt counted? When bludgers could not be afforded? So it must be again.[56]

The more distant precedent of Pearson's call to an Indigenous stratum confident of its capacity and moral strength are to be found in the Aboriginal manifestos in the late 1920s and 1930s. As I showed in Chapter 5, Fred Maynard, a leader of the

Australian Aboriginal Progressive Association (AAPA), saw distinctions among Aborigines, but his were not the governments' distinctions of 'full-blood' from 'half-caste' or 'tribal' from 'detribalised' but distinctions of capability. Government should set aside reserves for 'the incapables of the Aboriginal community', and government should delegate to 'educated aboriginals' the supervision of such 'Homes, Hostels or Reserves'.[57] AAPA asked that the NSW Aborigines Protection Board be replaced by a 'board of management comprised of capable educated aboriginals under a chairman to be appointed by the Government'. In November 1927, Maynard envisaged that 'native communities' would be supervised not by white officials of state and church but by 'educated and capable aborigines'.[58] A deputation of NSW Aborigines, when presenting a long-range policy to Prime Minister Joseph Lyons on 31 January 1938, said:

> In regard to uncivilised and semi-civilised Aborigines, we suggest that patrol officers, nurses, and teachers, both men and women *of Aboriginal blood*, should be specially trained by the Commonwealth Government as Aboriginal Officers, to bring the wild people into contact with civilisation ... While opposing a policy of segregation, we urge that, during a period of transition, the present Aboriginal Reserves should be retained as a sanctuary for aged or incompetent Aborigines who may be unfitted to take their place in the white community, owing to the past policy of neglect.[59]

William Cooper and the Australian Aborigines' League (AAL) classified Aboriginal contemporaries under three headings: 'primitive aborigines' who needed reserves, rations and special courts based on customary law; 'semi-civilised and detribalised natives' who needed help to turn their land to agricultural use, 'the right to work for adequate remuneration or the provision of full rations and housing' and access to schools and to pensions; and 'civilised natives' (and he included all NSW Aborigines), who were entitled to what the 'semi-civilised' should have and, in addition, to vote and to receive the 'maternity bonus'. The 'civilized' – including Cooper himself – had a duty to defend the 'primitive' and to 'uplift them morally, socially, intellectually and spiritually'.[60]

These Aboriginal people, promoting their advanced selves as guardians of the advancement process, competed with a humanitarian discourse that applied a different conceptual scheme to the differences observed among Indigenous Australians: distinctions of 'caste' and 'blood', of 'tribal' and 'detribalised'. For Tom Wright, the 'half castes and others of mixed blood' were not Aborigines, but coloured workers who suffered racial discrimination. For Aborigines, Wright demanded absolutely inviolable reserves, with tribal ownership of mineral resources. Only secular organisations (and not missions) should be allowed to interact with these sovereign reserve-owners. Wright wanted the state to exclude not only missions from reserves but also people of 'mixed blood', so that they could not become 'focal points for disintegration'. Wright's feminist contemporaries distinguished between the 'half-caste' or detribalised mother who should be assimilated, and the 'full-blood', tribal mother who should be shielded from degrading contact by living on large isolated reserves. Female protectors would protect the tribal Aboriginal woman from the demands of men (white and black).

Such feminists and Wright shared three ideas: they attached significance to the distinction between those who were 'half-caste'/'detribalised' and those who were 'full-blood'/'tribal'; they advocated strict territorial segregation as a way to protect the 'full-blood'/'tribal'; and they recommended that the government entrust to enlightened whites the beneficial mediation of modernity to the people on reserves. I do not know whether the feminists of the 1930s were aware of the aspirations of self-styled 'civilised' and 'capable' Aborigines to lead the 'wild' ones towards modernity, and Wright explicitly criticised that idea.

The significance of this fissure within the reform discourse of the 1920s and 1930s has become apparent. By presenting people such as themselves as well suited to assisting less 'capable' and more 'primitive' Aborigines to take on the demands and benefits of modern civilised life, Aboriginal people such as Maynard, Patten, Ferguson, Gibbs and Cooper foreshadowed the class structure of the Indigenous engagement with 'self-determination' from the 1970s. They presented the 'capable' Aborigines as guardians of Indigenous development and themselves as exemplary of evolved capacity. The communist and feminist visions of the future, in the 1930s, did not foresee how potent pan-Aboriginal ideology would become and how this ideology would enable 'capable' Aboriginal people to present themselves as the authentic leaders and models, after assimilation worked its differentiating effects upon Indigenous Australians. In what the Australian government would call 'self-determination', this ideology of the essential unity of black experience and of the linearity of black development would qualify the 'capable' to speak for and lead for those not yet 'capable'.

The middle-class champions of Indigenous development now know that they face a formidable ideological obstacle: a continuing evocation of Indigeneity as essentially and justifiably unrespectable. Lane's analysis of Indigenous tertiary enrolments in the first decade of the 21st century persuaded her that 'the *Welfare-Oriented Population* may be shunning opportunity more than ever and turning to other, perhaps more pathological, pathways to maintain their lifestyles'.[61] A 'pathological' lifestyle maintained by 'shunning opportunity' could be lived and experienced as a positive and sustainable 'Aboriginal' identity. This is evident in the words of one admired Indigenous writer, Ruby Langford Ginibi. Conscious of her people's high rates of incarceration and dwelling on the example of her sometimes imprisoned son Nobby, she presented her Aboriginality as defiance of imposed morality and law. Langford began by noting that 'we're the most incarcerated people in Her Majesty's jails in this country'. Asserting that Nobby's initial conviction had been 'wrongful', she continued:

> My son's not a bad, evil man. He's done some stupid things and been easily led and stuff like that, but we're all human, but nobody's been murdered or maimed, and his continual fight to just get justice, you know? And Aboriginal people don't have justice. How can we be the most bad, evil people in the whole of this now multicultural Australia when we're not quite two percent, as I said, of a total population which now stands at 18 million? You know? We don't have any justice because Aboriginal people always had to conform to the laws of the invading powers of our country, because we were never allowed to be ourselves. We had assimilation forced on us, had to give away language, identity and become like white people. And even today, governments do not classify urban Aboriginal people with a degree of Abo ... caste of, you know, caste in us, like half-caste, quarter-

caste, you can't say that today. You're either Aboriginal or white, but years ago it used to be you were half-caste, quarter-caste, full-blood, three-quarter-caste, one-eighth-octoroon, you know? This is how they defined us. But even today the governments of Australia define us, urban Kooris of mixed blood, as not real Aboriginals. Aboriginals here according to them are the traditional tribal ones out in the desert sitting on a rock with a spear in his hand. You see, this is how they've always defined us, but we define ourselves as the children of the Indigenous people, you know, the ancestors of the Indigenous people, and we're sick of other people telling us who we are.[62]

Langford combined several themes of contemporary Indigenous self-representation: that the unjust structure of Australian society stems from the unjust foundational act of colonisation; that this injustice has long been expressed in demands that Aboriginal people conform to colonial rules, a demand still enforced in the contemporary criminal justice system; that the categories imposed by colonial authority have harmed Aboriginal people by dividing them; that Aboriginal self-representation counters those divisions by asserting the common Aboriginality of 'urban' and 'tribal', 'half-caste' and 'full-blood'.

Certainly, Indigenous Australians are much incarcerated. In 2015 the Aboriginal and Torres Strait Islander imprisonment rate (prisoners per 100 000 Aboriginal and Torres Strait Islander population) was 2253, while the non-Indigenous imprisonment rate was only 146 prisoners per 100 000 non-Indigenous population. When age-standardised, the Indigenous rate was thirteen times greater than the age-standardised imprisonment rate for non-Indigenous persons (1951 per 100 000 compared to 153). Recent figures show Aboriginal and Torres Strait Islander prisoners as 27 per cent (9885 prisoners) of the total Australian prisoner population, about nine times larger than the Aboriginal and Torres Strait Islander proportion of the Australian population. Youth make up a large proportion of those imprisoned. Prisoners aged twenty-four years or under comprised 24 per cent (2368 prisoners) of all Aboriginal and Torres Strait Islander prisoners, compared to 14 per cent (3744 prisoners) of all non-Indigenous prisoners.[63]

There are broadly two rival explanations for the disproportionate incarceration of Indigenous Australians. One draws attention to class and regional differences, the other to the collective fate of Indigenous Australians as colonised people. The class/region explanation points out that a substantial proportion of the Indigenous population is well integrated into Australian society: they do not get arrested, tried, sentenced and imprisoned. Don Weatherburn shows that Indigenous people who do get arrested, tried, sentenced and imprisoned tend to churn through the law and order system, showing a high rate of recidivism; in this respect they are like other Australians with drug and alcohol problems, untreated mental illness, poor education, intergenerational unemployment and family problems. The significance of differences between jurisdictions has been highlighted by Roderic Broadhurst. He argues that some parts of Australia still have 'frontier' characteristics: a large quantity of land where Indigenous Australians continue features of Aboriginal culture, including language. Much of Western Australia, South Australia and the Northern Territory is 'frontier' in this sense but so are some regions within other states (for example western New South Wales). In such 'frontier' regions, low Aboriginal literacy, youth truancy and unemployment and a punitive settler–colonial political culture contribute to high incarceration.[64] The alternative explanation attaches less significance to class and regional differences, arguing that the criminality of Indigenous Australians continues their long-term collective political subjection, as a 'problem population' that continues to honour distinct ideas about right and wrong. Chris Cunneen and co-authors argue that 'the contemporary hyperincarceration of Indigenous peoples' is the latest form of the colonial heritage of institutionalising (missions, settlements, prisons) a dispossessed people who remain defiantly different in values and behaviour.[65]

The latter 'community of fate' view pays too little attention to significant regional and class differences. The class/region explanation recognises and seeks to explain not only the incarcerated but also the many Indigenous Australians who do *not* experience continuing adverse contact with the law. One of the striking features of Indigenous politics since the 1970s is the emergence of such 'respectable' Indigenous people's commentary on the pathologies of other Aboriginal and Torres Strait Islander families and communities, which is the topic of the next chapter.

12

Family, community and the crisis of self-determination

In previous chapters I have shown how 'detribalisation' has been an influential narrative for Australians making sense of Indigenous Australia. In 1988, Paul Hasluck recalled that assimilation was a constructive response to 'aboriginal society ... breaking down':

> tradition and tribal discipline were weakening and Aborigines themselves were being attracted more and more towards the ways of the white man and the benefits that come from conformity ... [They] had never known any other social organization than that of the Australian nation; and most of those who still lived in what is loosely termed 'tribal conditions' did not live wholly within an aboriginal tribal social organization.[1]

Hasluck's perception was right in one area: the weakening of 'tribal discipline'. As Aboriginal Australia came within reach of criminal law, it was less possible for adults with legitimate customary authority to apply the hardest sanctions of Aboriginal

Law: physical punishment and even death. By criminalising the Aboriginal social order's more severe punishments and by conspicuously subordinating senior tribespeople to new 'bosses' – pastoralists, missionaries, police and other government officials – the colonial encapsulation of Aboriginal society created conditions for individual preference to emerge, about where to live, how to sustain oneself, about sexuality and about the socialisation of the young. Against such wilfulness (not a new feature of Aboriginal society) men and women of authority now found themselves with fewer powers of restraint.[2]

However, the 'weakening' of senior figures in the kinship order does not mean that they lost all authority. Aboriginal Australians have been adapting, not losing, the social organisation through which they collectively regulated life's most important decisions. To comprehend social change as a reconfiguration of Aboriginal authority has been a task of anthropological research. Peter Sutton has synthesised research depicting Aboriginal kinship as it has become: the 'cognatic descent group' – a 'family of polity' 'formed by those who share recognised descent from a particular ancestor or set of blood-related ancestors, and who trace their links to such ancestors through either parent'.[3]

To constitute descent groups has been an ongoing political concern of Aboriginal people, and to constitute them pragmatically was a possibility built into their pre-colonial social system. The significance of such pragmatism has not faded, but grown, with colonial pressures on Aboriginal society. Though 'descent groups' have mattered most when land claims have been adjudicated, Aboriginal people lacking legal opportunity to assert title may retain a sense of regional belonging that is strong enough for their descent from country (from ancestors) still to matter. We should not underestimate the psychological importance of identities based on regional networks that consist of named and interacting family groups. Even in families that no longer live on their ancestral country, members share stories of having come from that country and of that country still being, in some sense, theirs by customary right.

The pressures creating new 'families of polity' – the 'post-classical' urban/rural cognatic descent groups, nowadays often referred to by their members as 'bloodlines' – have been summarised by Sutton:

> sudden loss of population, the arrival of children fathered by non-Aboriginal men, a decline of stability in marriage and of the very existence of marriage as an institution, a decline in the status and power of men, a rise in the role of personal choice in relationships, and a rise in the power and independence of women.[4]

The resulting 'family of polity' has the following characteristics. It is identified by a surname (which may be the name of an important male or female ancestor). It consists of a number of households; the links between households (which may be far apart) are sustained by visiting – especially for funerals, weddings and key sports events. Such activities are important to sustain an individual's recognised membership of his or her family. Membership is not voluntary as there must be 'bloodlines' to a parent or grandparent in the family, or there may be considered and acknowledged adoption. However, individuals are accountable for the effort they put into family membership; to exit the family (by transferring too much effort to non-Aboriginal friends or kin) is resented. Young people have more freedom to choose friends and sexual partners and spouses than in the 'classical' system. Individuals may belong to more than one 'bloodline', but they are expected to treat one as primary, and there may be competition between families for a person's primary allegiance and for the allegiance of offspring. Families may be associated with institutions that are formally voluntary but in whose affairs a family exercises great influence, so that it may require much political effort to distinguish the resources of the family from that of the organisation. The terms of kinship ('cousin', 'aunty'), while overlapping with Australian English, may have distinct Aboriginal English meanings.[5]

The 'politics' of constituting family and of interacting with other families is conducted not in parliaments but in domestic, local environments; it is a politics whose 'public' is a relatively small network of people known to one another, a politics in which there is no sharp and enduring distinction between leaders and led, elites and masses; it is a politics in which the state may play an unwitting part. A history of colonisation must try to understand the nature of this politics. Sutton's account of 'families of polity' corrects the supposition that 'detribalisation' amounted to the collapse of classical social structure into something inchoate.

This corrective is recent: recognition of families of polity as an evolved form of Aboriginal society has become necessary since the inception of native title, because native title processes ask: how has Aboriginal society in this place continued to work, through time, as a system for associating these people with this land/sea? However, a description that seeks to lay out the principles of orderly continuity is biased towards describing order; it understates and fails to explain disorder. This 'bias' does not render Sutton's synthesis untrue; rather, it means that contemporary Aboriginal society is a complex reality that looks different according to the angle from which we view it. The possibility of conflict within and between families is implicit in Sutton's description of families of polity, but a *focus* on tensions and violence among Indigenous Australians has come from other kinds of research.

Social scientists began with a study of domestic violence among Aboriginal and Torres Strait Islander people in Townsville in the 1970s.[6] Mortality data collected in the 1980s showed that 'injury and poisoning' was a major reason for Aboriginal men and women to be hospitalised and to die.[7] The political scientist Colin Tatz, who had emerged in the 1960s as a leading critic of state paternalism, admitted, in 1990, that after visiting fourteen places in New South Wales, eleven in Queensland, twelve in the Northern Territory, fifteen in Western Australia and nine each in South Australia and Victoria, over the period June 1989 to February 1990, he was losing faith in Aborigines' collective capacity.[8] There were no longer violent sanctions, within Aboriginal society, against 'rape, child-molestation and incest'.[9] What was going on?

Without dethroning the academic expert, 'self-determination' has given Indigenous people opportunities to describe problems and propose solutions. Indigenous agitation against heavy-handed state intervention into Indigenous families led to the formation of Aboriginal Child Care Agencies (ACCAs) in the 1970s and their peak body the Secretariat of National Aboriginal and Islander Child Care (SNAICC) in 1981. In 1989, delegates to SNAICC's annual general meeting complained of increasing violence and abuse of children in Indigenous families. SNAICC encouraged Maryanne Sam to publish *Through Black Eyes* (1991), a handbook for community activists. Brian Butler, SNAICC's chair, wrote in his foreword that 'violence in our families and Communities ... is no longer something to hide'.[10] In 1987, Queensland's Aboriginal Coordinating Council (made up of leaders of that state's former reserves and missions) met for five days to discuss child abuse and domestic violence; the discussion touched on alcohol and drug abuse, suicide, juvenile offences, adult imprisonment 'and other issues specific to social disintegration'.[11]

To become prominent in public reflections on disorder and on 'custom' Indigenous women had to reflect critically on 'custom'. When Torres Strait Islander nurse Ellie Gaffney complained in 1989 that very few women 'identified and accepted as Torres Strait Islanders are professionally qualified with experience', she observed that it 'is not for the want of trying, but more because of their cultural role initially than through lack of opportunity'.[12] With whom were such women to form alliances if they wished to speak on problems of their heritage? In 1989, anthropologist Diane Bell teamed with Topsy Napurrula Nelson to publish a paper about rape in Central Australian Aboriginal communities. Not only did they criticise Aboriginal leaders for not acknowledging and acting on the problem, the title of their paper asserted: 'Speaking about rape is everyone's business.'[13] Twelve Indigenous women disagreed: 'It is our business how we deal with rape and have done so for the last 202 years quite well.' While not commenting on the incidence of sexual violence against Aboriginal women, these women expressed solidarity with Aboriginal men against what they saw as a white feminist discourse – 'setting blacks against blacks'.[14]

That Aboriginal customary law was a contested resource in the campaign against family and community violence became evident to Audrey Bolger when she was commissioned by the Northern Territory police to talk to Aboriginal women. They distinguished violence 'sanctioned through formal social mechanisms' from contemporary male violence 'of a kind which would not have been countenanced in traditional society'.[15] One informant said: 'There are now three kinds of violence in Aboriginal society – alcoholic violence, traditional violence, and bullshit traditional violence.'[16] The substance of 'Aboriginal custom' was now in dispute among Aborigines themselves.

In October 1990, a 'Women's Issue' of the *Aboriginal Law Bulletin* editorialised that 'domestic violence has become the "norm" in some communities'.[17] Quoting women victims' criticisms of police responses, Judy Atkinson expressed dismay at the comment of 'a senior male Aboriginal public servant' that 'violence against women and sexual abuse of children was based on customary practice'.[18] Aboriginal practices of social control, although 'fractured and made inconsequential by the invading society', could revive, Atkinson wrote, if Queensland enabled local council by-laws to include 'issues of social disorder'. Such law reform would enable 'new law at a local level' that would, for example, ban pornographic videos.[19]

In 1992, the High Court's 'Mabo' judgment powerfully renewed the idea that Indigenous Australians' traditions of Law and government were in effect. Noting the High Court's recognition of 'the traditional laws and customs of indigenous Australians', SNAICC declared in 1995 that 'the principle of self-determination is indivisible ... Therefore we *must* see this principle extended to the issues of our child and family welfare.'[20] SNAICC wished to leave 'control of responses to abuse and neglect of Aboriginal children' to 'Aboriginal communities' resourced by governments: 'safe houses for women and children' and 'support and counselling services for abuse victims and their families, including Healing Centres which utilise the skills of Aboriginal healers'; Elders Councils should advise governments and community organisations.²¹ In contrast, the *Aborigines and Torres Strait Islander Women's Task Force on Violence Report* released in 1999 by the Queensland (Beattie) government, while noting that the Mabo judgment and other recent decisions demonstrated that 'courts are becoming more responsive to change', did not construe the High Court as presenting customary law as a source of discipline for disordered communities.²² The report was an initiative of fifty named Aboriginal and Torres Strait Islander women. The chair of the task force, Boni Robertson, had trained in social work at the University of Queensland in the 1980s before becoming director of the Gumurrii Centre at Griffith University. When the task force mentioned 'culture', recommendations referred not to Indigenous 'government' and 'law' but to 'identity' and 'healing': 'culture' as an attribute of effective personhood. Indeed the task force preferred the term 'lore' to 'Law'. The theme of the Queensland task force's recommendations was that governments had underserviced Indigenous communities – including in their policing; they lamented that previous calls for government to curb violence in Queensland communities had been 'dismissed as politically and culturally intrusive in the newly acquired autonomy of Indigenous communities'.²³ The task force authors were evidently not worried that a more responsible government would 'intrude', as they were convinced that the psychosocial bases of 'autonomy' were missing.

The 'Reconciliation decade' climaxed in the year 2000 without a clear resolution of the issues of whether and how law and public policy should combine with Aboriginal and Torres Strait Islanders' customs of social control. One journalist commented in 2002 that many who supported self-determination had found it difficult to acknowledge that psychosocial disorder undermined the exercise of the right self-determination. She noted that 'many conservatives' were using the mounting evidence of disorder 'to reprise a discredited political tune: that the solution lies in assimilation'.[24]

Indigenous critique began to point to self-censorship as an obstacle to the sharing of responsibilities between governments to Indigenous communities. The Aboriginal magistrate Sue Gordon made this point in 2002. Born on a cattle station near Meekatharra in 1943, Gordon had been removed from her mother at age four and educated at Sister Kate's Home in Perth. Upon finishing school in 1959, she had joined the Women's Royal Australian Army Corps (WRAAC), and then held a series of administrative positions, in the 1970s, in Aboriginal affairs, mostly in the Pilbara region. She became Western Australia's Commissioner for Aboriginal Planning in 1986 and then a magistrate of the WA Children's Court in 1988. When ATSIC commenced in 1990 with an interim unelected commission, she was one of five appointed part-time commissioners. In 2001, after the much-publicised death by suicide of a sexually abused Aboriginal teenager in Perth, the Western Australian government commissioned Gordon to inquire into 'Response by Government Agencies to Complaints of Family Violence and Child Abuse in Aboriginal Communities'. Gordon concluded from her scrutiny of government agencies that Aboriginal people were partly responsible for agencies' ignorance of problems. Having once solicited police investigation of alleged child abuse in her own family, Gordon had no illusions about the cultural and psychological barriers to such candour before police and social workers.[25] Her community visits presented some people with an opportunity to report things that, normally, they would not dare to speak of. She learned 'that people in positions of power in some communities ... hindered some of the programs ... that were designed to help women and children ... in some remote communities ... people were actively stopped from speaking to us'.²⁶

The 2003 SNAICC report on child abuse in the Northern Territory, *State of Denial*, criticised not only government agencies' limited response to notifications but also underreporting by affected families.²⁷ Aboriginal communities' shamed or fearful reluctance to speak was the topic of study by Indigenous researcher Kyllie Cripps; she called it a 'language of minimisation'.

> Phrases such as 'um [pause] well we were arguing', 'my husband was acting up', 'he was being cheeky', 'it was just a little fight' and 'we were drinking' are common phrases used in discussions about violence in Indigenous communities ... Terms common to professionals, such as family violence, domestic violence, sexual assault, or even rape, are very rarely utilised in [Indigenous] contexts as many people find these terms to be intimidating and are fearful of the consequences should they use them.²⁸

Frontier conquest, followed by 'protection', had ingrained in many Indigenous Australians fear, loathing and avoidance of police. It was rational, also, to be wary of the press. One Aboriginal school principal considered carefully what he could say to a television journalist about child sexual abuse in the community that his school served. He knew of staff at another school who had admitted that there was such a problem in their community; angry parents had forced them to leave. 'I shared their sense of wanting to be brutally honest about the despicable scourge of child sexual abuse' but not 'in front of a national television audience on a program more interested in airing the sensational'. He chose to deflect media interest in his school's achievements rather than to have to decide how frank to be about its problems.[29]

Indigenous institutions varied in their readiness to articulate problems in Aboriginal families and in community governance. ATSIC was ill-suited to becoming the platform of Indigenous intellectuals worried about violence in families. Although ATSIC was supposed to be the conduit of Indigenous advice to the national government on any issue that engaged its attention (including, in 1993, the Keating government's response to 'native title'), ATSIC's main responsibilities were housing and community development through local employment. ATSIC's knowledge and concerns did not extend to education, health and policing services that would be implicated in any state or territory governmental response to family violence. State and territory agencies had little contact with ATSIC, and the 'State Advisory Councils' on which ATSIC sat competed with many other lines of political pressure for a state or territory minister's attention. Health services had been among ATSIC's programs, until the National Aboriginal and Islander Health Organisation, the Australian Medical Association and the Royal Australian College of General Practitioners lobbied the Keating government to transfer funding of Aboriginal Medical Services to the Commonwealth Department of Health and Aging in 1995.[30]

In March 2003 the ATSIC board issued a 'Family Violence Policy Statement' affirming ATSIC's commitment to ending family violence and child abuse.[31] By then, the reputation of ATSIC's elected chair Geoff Clark was being undermined by press coverage of his alleged past, beginning with Andrew Rule's piece in the *Age*, 14 June 2001, conveying stories from four named women that Clark had raped them in the 1970s and 1980s. Although Clark characterised his accusers as politically motivated liars (a rebuttal endorsed by Aboriginal magistrate Pat O'Shane on ABC's *Lateline*) the dispute about his character damaged ATSIC's credibility on the topic of violence between men and women.[32] Clark declined to step down. The first elected chair of ATSIC (1999–2002 and for a second term 2002–2003), Clark steadfastly advocated the 'rights agenda' and the view that Indigenous Australians' culture was the foundation of sound law. His tainted advocacy made it easier for the public to suspect that the 'rights agenda' fudged the issue of Indigenous moral and political capacity.

By the end of 2003, the Indigenous assertion of a collective right of self-determination was in crisis. Self-determination rested on the evocation of an Indigenous 'self' whose vision and capacities commanded respect; the evidence before the public – sometimes presented with urgency by Indigenous Australians themselves – was of a people debilitated. The Howard government responded with three innovations in policy.

First, the government abolished ATSIC. In opposition, the Liberals had argued against ATSIC when legislated in 1989. In government (1996–2007), Howard faced a hostile Senate until 2004, and he learned to live with ATSIC. Indeed, he made it less accountable to the government: in 1999, the minister ceased to appoint the chair, enabling ATSIC's board fatefully to choose Geoff Clark. In 2003, arguing that ATSIC's elected leaders were in a conflict of interest whenever they were directors of organisations funded by ATSIC, the Howard government took $1 billion dollars from ATSIC and gave it to the new agency Aboriginal and Torres Strait Islander Services (ATSIS) to administer, pending a review of ATSIC. The reviewers were

Jackie Huggins (former DAA and ATSIC public servant, now an Indigenous academic and historian), John Hannaford (former NSW attorney-general) and Bob Collins (former Labor senator for the Northern Territory, 1987–98).

Submissions and hearings told them that people wanted ATSIC reformed: 'perceptions of failure permeated every meeting held with the review panel'.[33] 'Failure' themes included: that ATSIC, as an 'imposed western structure ... cannot achieve complete representation of all major cultural groups';[34] that ATSIC had not met expectations (a criticism perhaps reflecting the constituency's failure to appreciate how limited was ATSIC's role in the wider structures of government); that ATSIC was a 'top-down' body, too focused on 'Canberra', so that ensuring regional compliance with centrally determined programs had limited its attention to regions' opinions and needs. The reviewers recommended that ATSIC's elected board of commissioners be more accountable to the elected regional councils. 'ATSIC,' they warned, 'must go back to its people'.[35] In response, the government declared ATSIC a 'failed experiment'. To replace it, Minister for Indigenous Affairs Amanda Vanstone appointed an advisory National Indigenous Council (NIC), chaired by Sue Gordon. Vanstone wanted councillors who had 'jumped the hurdles, climbed the mountains' – role models, not representatives.[36]

The Howard government's second reform was to Northern Territory Aboriginal land tenure. The *Aboriginal Land Rights (NT) Act* 1976 (ALRA) recognised Traditional Owners and gave them legal form as land trusts. Land councils were obliged, by the ALRA, to consult Traditional Owners about land use matters, and they placed the rights of Traditional Owners above the rights of those Aboriginal and non-Aboriginal people who were merely resident on Aboriginal land. This pre-eminence of the

Traditional Owner was potentially in tension with the expectation that a local government area should serve and represent the entire resident community. As well, in 1999, a review of the ALRA (known as the Reeves Report, after its chair John Reeves QC) had argued that 'land rights' should not only safeguard Aborigines' customary property but also facilitate new wealth-creating uses of that property.[37] Critics of the ALRA, pointing to Traditional Owners' and other residents' persistent monetary poverty and poor health, asked: had the Act's focus on land as embodied 'spirit' smothered thoughts of land as 'asset'?

The Howard government amendments to ALRA sought to make it easier for Aboriginal land to generate income. Some amendments changed ALRA's approach to mining. The land councils and the Opposition parties were broadly approving of these amendments because they were the product of land councils' negotiations with the Northern Territory government and the Mining Council of Australia. However, the Howard government did not negotiate the amendments that defined new leasing arrangements on Aboriginal land and that further subjected land councils to the minister and to local majorities of Aboriginal residents. Before the amendments, section 19 of the ALRA had allowed Traditional Owners to lease portions of their land. The Howard government elaborated these leasing possibilities by allowing for a nested hierarchy of leases. That is, Traditional Owners could now agree to sign a ninety-nine-year 'head lease' with the Office of the Executive Director of Township Leasing – a body created by the Commonwealth government. That leasing body is able, in turn, to lease to particular persons or companies portions of that larger head lease. Three kinds of lessee were in mind: home-owners, private businesses and government agencies delivering services to residents. Though Traditional

Owners would not be obliged to sign head leases, during the parliamentary debate the Australian government said it would offer inducements: if Traditional Owners signed a head lease, the government would finance housing and other community assets.

Critics of the amendments objected that by signing a ninety-nine-year head lease the Traditional Owners would surrender to the state for four generations the customary powers recognised by the original ALRA. In particular, they would sign away their right to choose economic development suited to their cultural traditions, except by negotiating for certain restrictions to be written into the head lease itself. Critics also objected that by not negotiating certain amendments with the Traditional Owners or their representatives, the Howard government had broken with the spirit of the Act.

Aboriginal people respected and (in some cases) selected by the Howard government had helped to promote the ideas on which the amendments rested. In 2001 and 2004, Noel Pearson had praised the views of Hernando de Soto, who argues that private property is a much better basis for economic development than communal property.[38] In December 2004, Warren Mundine, chief executive officer of NSW Native Title Services, Deputy Mayor of Dubbo, a prominent member of the ALP and an appointed member of Howard's National Indigenous Council, urged Territory Aborigines 'to move away from communal land ownership and non-profit community-based businesses and take up home ownership, economic land development and profit-making businesses'.[39] Like many others in the ensuing debate, Mundine characterised existing Northern Territory Aboriginal tenure as 'communal' and called for tenure to be 'individual' and to be formalised (to give 'security').

According to legal scholar Leon Terrill, former counsel to

the Central Land Council, the problem that the government (endorsed by Mundine) sought to solve did not exist. Property arrangements that became effective on Aboriginal land in the thirty years prior to Howard's amendments were not 'communal'; they were, in each region, 'the negotiated outcome' of three interacting authorities: land trusts composed of recognised Traditional Owners, municipal bodies funded to service all residents, and the Australian and territory governments, with their control over funding – for housing, especially – and over land use planning.[40] The resulting tenure arrangements were 'modern-Aboriginal and part of something broader, relational and deeply engaged with governments'.[41] Mundine and others were not well informed, Terrill has argued, about the actual practice of property rights that had evolved in those parts of the Northern Territory where people reside in small townships (mostly former missions, settlements and pastoral homesteads) within larger tracts of Aboriginal land (former reserves and pastoral leases). In such places,

> the informal tenure arrangements ... provide individuals
> and organisations with relatively exclusive rights to
> particular land and buildings ... [T]he allocation of rights
> in communities is based on the exigencies of modern-day
> community life and the need for people living and working
> in communities (including governments and NGOs) to
> give order to the way in which land and infrastructure are
> utilised.[42]

The misleading description of Northern Territory Aborigines' property as 'communal' was politically influential partly because it came from Indigenous intellectuals such as Mundine.[43]

The NIC had advised that while Indigenous land title should remain 'communal' and 'inalienable', legislation should 'maximize the opportunity for individuals and families to acquire and exercise a personal interest in those lands, whether for purposes of home ownership or business development'. Traditional owners should not 'unreasonably' withhold granting leasehold to individuals, and only as a 'last resort' and with compensation on just terms should leases be created against Traditional Owners' wishes.[44] With such support – informed or not – from the government-appointed NIC, it was less costly in political terms for the Howard government to avoid negotiating these ALRA amendments with the Northern Territory land councils.

The new provisions for township leasing were intended to encourage private home ownership, small business formation and the payment of rent to Traditional Owners by private and public agencies that service such townships. As well, reformers probably hoped that, in the long term, economic development would enlarge the tax base (rates levied on residents) of the Northern Territory's rural shires, so that local governments would share the cost of programs currently funded by the Commonwealth and Territory governments. While it is too early to know these reforms' long-term effects on the quantity and quality of housing, on commercial development, on the incomes of Traditional Owners/rentiers and on the provision of infrastructure and services in the remote communities of the Northern Territory, the immediate effect was to transfer Aboriginal title not to entrepreneurial individuals but to a state agency that negotiates leases with other state agencies.

In 2013, when asked if the amendments had been effective, Mundine replied that it was a question of whether the land councils and Native Title Representative Bodies had lived up to the intentions of the architects of the reforms.⁴⁵ In projecting the ways that Northern Territory Aborigines could become more like other Australians in their approach to property and that Northern Territory shires could become more like (in fiscal terms) other municipal governments, Mundine has continued a tradition in which Aboriginal people (from the 'South') – acculturated to colonial expectations – have offered to be models for and tutors of remote Aboriginal people who are engaged with the challenges and opportunities of modern Australia. Seasoned by his involvement in the implementation of land rights in New South Wales, Mundine's advocacy of land as an asset may have been moulded by the accumulated distrust of government among New South Wales Aborigines. According to Heidi Norman, memories of government neglect and deceit have propelled Aboriginal people in New South Wales to use their land as economic leverage for wealth creation, to end historic dependency on welfare and to avoid vulnerability to governments.⁴⁶ However, in the short term, the reforms that Mundine has advocated in the Northern Territory have entrenched the power of the state over Aboriginal land and angered and bewildered many Traditional Owners.

The moral crisis of the remote community

At the turn of the 21st century the debate about 'self-determination' took a moral turn. Gary Johns, a former minister in the Keating government, summarised what he labelled 'inquiries into black morality' in five jurisdictions from 1999 to 2008.⁴⁷ In keeping with this atmosphere of dismay and censure, at least one MP (Senator Helen Coonan), debating the Northern Territory land tenure amendments, associated 'communal title' with 'the appalling levels of violence and abuse in many of these communities'. They were 'a stark reminder of the failed policies of the past ... The right of safety for women and children is a threshold issue.'[48] The 'safety' issue had featured in a *Lateline* (ABC TV) interview on 15 May 2006 with Northern Territory prosecutor Nanette Rogers, detailing cases of sexual abuse of young children. Responding partly to the furore that this interview aroused, the Northern Territory government on 8 August 2006 commissioned Patricia Anderson (a leader in Aboriginal health service delivery) and Rex Wild (a lawyer) to investigate the sexual abuse of children in Northern Territory Aboriginal communities.

Delivered on 30 April 2007, their *Little Children Are Sacred* report confirmed that the sexual abuse of children was widespread and underreported, and that many parents 'are failing to accept and exercise their responsibilities'.[49] However, the report said that Aboriginal communities were willing to tackle the problem with resources from governments. Aboriginal community leadership had been weakened, the report argued, by inappropriate, underfunded and short-term government programs. Calling on the Commonwealth and Northern Territory governments to coordinate their support and to 'commit to genuine consultation with Aboriginal people in designing initiatives', the report urged respect for local variation in corrective programs, while insisting that enforcing compulsory schooling should be common to all efforts. The report recommended principles of consultation: equal representation of all family groups, of men and women, of young and old. While urging respect for Aboriginal law, the report noted that many Aboriginal people did not yet understand Australian criminal law, including the concept 'sexual abuse'. 'It will require at least a generation for any real benefits to be achieved,' the report warned.[50]

Architects of 'self-determination' had anticipated that

different customs of sexuality could make difficulties for governments committed to cultural respect. In 1973, the Minister of Aboriginal Affairs Gordon Bryant had made a parliamentary statement, drafted by anthropologist William Stanner of the Council of Aboriginal Affairs, acknowledging the sensitivity of 'certain betrothal and marriage customs'. Polygyny should be recognised as part of the 'veritable systems of law' that Justice Blackburn had recognised in 1971, Bryant asserted, even if Aboriginal people were now 'voluntarily adapting their traditional practices to new circumstances' so that 'having several wives is no longer as fashionable as ... it used to be'. Australians will not have overcome 'proud and invincible ignorance', Bryant warned, if they were to interfere with this domain of Aboriginal law, 'unless for reasons of grave and compelling urgency. I do not think we have such reasons.'[51] Was the incidence of child sexual abuse, in 2007, presenting reasons?

Perhaps the Northern Territory government's pondering of this question explains why it took chief minister Clare Martin six weeks to release the Anderson/Wild report. Six days after it became public, and before the Martin government could announce its own response, the Commonwealth pushed the Northern Territory government aside. On 21 June 2007, in what became known as the 'Northern Territory Emergency Response' (NTER), the Howard government announced a package of measures in seventy-three Northern Territory communities that would apply for the next five years. Some focused on disorder in communities: alcohol restrictions on Aboriginal land; increasing the police presence in prescribed communities. Some were intended to change land and housing tenure in remote Aboriginal townships: the accelerated leasing of townships to government, funding town clean-ups through work-for-the-dole; rents for housing set at Northern Territory Housing levels. Some were designed to improve – morally and materially – the environments of children: restrictions on the expenditure choices made by adult recipients of 'welfare'; meals for school students (at parents' cost); obliging parents to send children to school, on pain of losing their income support; compulsory health screening for Aboriginal children (not implemented); banning X-rated pornography and auditing public computers for illegal material. Some measures were designed to improve public and government oversight: abolishing the requirement to get permission to enter certain areas of Aboriginal land; and appointing managers of government business in prescribed communities. The Commonwealth called for complementary actions by the Northern Territory government, including removing customary law as a mitigating factor in sentencing and bail. The intervention package required five pieces of legislation, introduced on 7 August and passed by both houses ten days later. While the Opposition complained of the speed of the legislation and of the absence of partnership with the Northern Territory government and the affected communities, it substantially supported the NTER and continued the policy, with modifications, after gaining office in November 2007.[52]

Since the Commonwealth had granted self-government in 1978, competition between political parties for the (sub)urban Territory vote had entrenched urban bias in the Northern Territory's public expenditure. Only the Commonwealth's fiscal authority could overcome this predominantly non-Aboriginal favouritism. The NTER increased Commonwealth grants to the Northern Territory; commitment to housing and police services directed that money to rural regions with a high ratio of Indigenous to non-Indigenous residents.[53]

In applying the NTER to a list of Territory communities the Howard government departed from the Council of Australian Governments (COAG) strategy of negotiating – community by community – Shared Responsibility Agreements (SRAs). In 2003, COAG had initiated SRAs in several communities across Australia. Ideally, a community's SRA would express its own priorities for self-improvement: in return for agreed actions, governments would guarantee support.[54] The Aboriginal and Torres Strait Islander Social Justice Commissioner (ATSISJC) Tom Calma had cautiously welcomed SRAs and suggested 'human rights' criteria by which each SRA could be judged. Governments had a responsibility, Calma warned, 'to find ways of negotiating [SRAs] with Indigenous communities that do not simply rely on existing community councils, regardless of whether they are inclusive, representative, well governed or the reverse'.[55] To be 'representative', the Indigenous party to the negotiation 'should ensure a gender balance and take into account the views of children and youth as relevant'.[56] In Calma's perspective, SRAs were experiments in Indigenous political development. When the Howard government unilaterally declared to which communities the NTER would apply, this experiment lapsed.

When the Minister for Aboriginal Affairs (Mal Brough) introduced the Northern Territory National Emergency Response Bill on 7 August 2007, he implied that in Aboriginal communities 'sexual abuse among Aboriginal children', the 'rivers of grog' and the 'free flow of pornography', were caused, at least in part, by the overcrowding of houses – a problem whose solutions included land tenure reform. 'We need to show people that it is possible to own and control your own house, which can only happen when you have a lease over the land that it is built on.'[57] He added: 'Banks will not lend money to start up small businesses because a committee decides what tenure arrangements will apply. People cannot even borrow to buy their own home because they cannot own or lease a block of land.'[58] Brough's Bill thus added to the recently legislated land tenure reforms, enabling the Australian government to acquire five-year leases over townships on land held under the ALRA, and in community living areas. Rent would be paid to Traditional Owners (whose underlying title remained) and the five-year leases would cease if the owners granted a ninety-nine-year township lease or if the community no longer required oversight.

The most contentious of these oversights was compulsory income management (CIM). To introduce it the Howard government had first to abolish Community Development Employment Projects (CDEPs), under which 'communities' had pooled unemployment benefit entitlements and received supplementary grants for local employment. Because transferring some people from CDEP jobs to welfare payments cleared the way for the government to manage their welfare income, the abolition of CDEP over the period 2007–12 has been credited to the NTER. However, sceptical appraisal of CDEP had been growing in the Commonwealth government since the 1980s. Against those who saw CDEP as a culturally appropriate, regionally adapted and community-empowering program, it was argued that some people had come to expect that participation in CDEP was for life, rather than a step towards more orthodox employment. Critics of CDEP also complained that it had become a cheap and second-rate way to provide government services that other agencies should have been providing. After the election of the Rudd government in November 2007, some CDEPs were reinstated, but in further changes in 2009 and 2012 the Commonwealth created thousands of public sector jobs as substitutes

Family, community and the crisis of self-determination • 425

for CDEP, and it foreshadowed that CDEP participants would be shifted to welfare payments if they could not find what some were calling 'real jobs'. The eclipse of CDEP was in this way determined by more than one strand of policy thinking.[59]

Debating the 'Intervention'

In winter 2008 the new Labor government led by Kevin Rudd appointed a panel to review the NTER. Peter Yu, Marcia Ella Duncan and Bill Gray visited thirty-one Aboriginal communities, spoke with representatives of fifty-six other communities, and read 200 submissions. They found considerable support for some features of the NTER: for the boost to policing, for measures to reduce alcohol-related violence, for extra money for housing and education. However, many complained that CIM was humiliating and racially targeted, and expressions of support for CIM were qualified by the criticism that it should not be applied indiscriminately to all Aborigines on welfare merely because they happened to live in one of the scheduled communities.[60] On 13 October 2008, Yu's board recommended a more targeted and reviewable approach to CIM (including allowing voluntary submission to it), supplemented by services for those CIM cases in which child protection and school attendance were problems.

If CIM were racial discrimination, could it be defended as a 'special measure', as allowed by the *Racial Discrimination Act* (RDA)?[61] That depended on whether the measures were publicly supported by the Aboriginal communities affected. The Rudd government continued with CIM, while canvassing the possibility of extending it on a non-racial basis. In consulting Aboriginal communities about the future of CIM, the approach by the Department of Families, Housing, Community Services and

Indigenous Affairs – particularly its selective disclosure of the submissions and testimonies received from Aboriginal people – attracted criticism from Aboriginal and professional organisations.[62] In *Will They Be Heard?* critics argued that the government was not 'consulting', but selecting evidence of community support.[63] Such critics did not deny that some Aboriginal people supported CIM.[64] Nor did the department deny that there was diversity of opinion; however, the department did not engage with critics of CIM other than to agree that non-Indigenous Australians should also be subjected to it.[65] The Rudd government sought to overcome the 'race discrimination' objection by amending the legislation underpinning the NTER in June 2010.

In July and August 2011 the Commonwealth convened meetings with Northern Territory communities to discuss a policy paper, 'Stronger Futures'. It then introduced the 'Stronger Futures' Bills on 23 November 2011. The Social Security Legislation Amendment Bill continued CIM. It enabled state and territory government agencies to refer a welfare recipient for management of their income and it authorised the minister to say in which regions recipients would be open to this management (and for the management to continue even if the recipient changed place of residence). The Bill created authority to oblige parents to enter into a school attendance plan (the School Enrolment and Attendance Measures, or SEAM); payment of part of their welfare income could be deferred until their child complied with the plan. The Stronger Futures in the Northern Territory (Consequential and Transitional Provisions) Bill repealed the *Northern Territory National Emergency Response Act* 2007. It continued, for another ten years, the restrictions on circulation of certain material (for example, pornographic DVDs) in certain areas. It restricted to certain heritage protection offences the consideration of customary law in bail and sentence decisions. The Stronger Futures in the Northern Territory Bill provided for ministerial oversight of local alcohol management plans and for an evaluation of such plans after three years by the Australian and Northern Territory governments; it enabled governments to regulate land tenure in community living areas and town camps, with the aim of increasing private home ownership and business development in such places. Finally, the Bill created a ten-year licensing regime for community stores, aimed at improving food security. The Bill also mandated an independent review of the operation of the Act after seven years (that is, in 2019).

The parliament immediately referred the Bills to the Senate Standing Committee on Community Affairs, which held hearings in the Northern Territory on 20–24 February 2012 and received 452 submissions (many of them form letters) from 560 individuals. Some critics objected to judges losing their discretion to consider customary law and cultural practice in bail and sentence hearings to do with violence and sexual abuse offences; judicial notice of traditional sanctions, critics suggested, reinforced Indigenous mechanisms of social control. Some critics argued that before changing land tenure laws governments should negotiate with the land councils. Alcohol management plans worried critics: the need for ministerial approval would slow their implementation; their penalties would be too harsh and would increase the Indigenous rate of imprisonment; government effort should focus more on treatment, rehabilitation and education; government restrictions on alcohol supply would be more effective. Store licensing aroused the comment that food security also required government action (for example, to diminish high freight costs) on the supply and quality of food. A consistent thread of concern across these points was that policy innovation seemed to be intensifying oversight and punishment of Aboriginal people. The Parliamentary Joint Committee on Human Rights expressed concern about whether the legislation complied with Australia's human rights obligations.[66]

The most criticised elements of 'Stronger Futures' were to do with the relationship between parental authority and state authority. How should parents be encouraged to take responsibility for their child's attendance at school? SEAM was being trialled in fourteen schools in the Northern Territory and Queensland in 2009, but the trial results were not yet well known, or their content was disputed, leading to the criticism that the measures were being continued without evidence of their effectiveness. Under SEAM, parents could lose part of their welfare income if the truancy of their child became entrenched. Denouncing this approach as too punitive, some critics demanded a more holistic approach – including improving the school and the health of pupils and more social worker contact for outstanding instances of truancy. Such critics wanted corrective action to work with the strengths of parents. A submission from seventy-one residents of Yuendumu complained that it was the governments' responsibility to restore a form of schooling that respected their culture: a bilingual program. When children learned 'mainly in English, their Warlpiri gets weak and they don't understand older people talking'. The Warlpiri had been willing to change, the submission continued, 'from living in humpies to houses, from men having two or three wives to one wife. We have no more forced promised marriages, and much less violence at sorry time. But we want to hold on to our language and important things in our culture.'[67]

Above all, critics deplored CIM as stigmatising, as failing to teach any skill, as inhibiting women who wished to leave violent partners. The Australian Indigenous Doctors' Association (AIDA) speculated that while the physical health and school performance of children might be improved by CIM, the mental health of communities, including children, would be damaged by a 'humiliating, discriminatory and racist' practice.[68] Some submissions said that a person's reference for CIM should at least be made more reviewable and that only a few competent agencies should be allowed to make such reference; others called for income management to be available only on a voluntary basis. The Aboriginal Medical Services Alliance Northern Territory (AMSANT) said that CIM 'punishes the majority who are effectively managing their money and fails to promote personal responsibility or improve money management skills for those that don't'.[69] However, AMSANT conceded that CIM could be trialled for selected parents – those abusing alcohol and/or not caring for their children – and then evaluated.[70] The Ngaanyatjara Pitjantjatjara and Yankunytjatjara Women's Council supported CIM's 'settling effect' in communities plagued by substance abuse and violence; it conceded that some individuals and communities could be 'stigmatised and hurt' by CIM, and it urged the government to better explain the objectives of CIM and why certain recipients were selected for it. Better case management was required to help such people.[71]

After the Senate Committee released its report on 14 March 2012, broadly endorsing the package (though with Green Senator Rachel Siewert's dissenting report), the Senate passed the Bills in June 2012.

Responsibility – a contested ideal

'Self-determination' was understood as enabling Indigenous Australians to take responsibility, but 'responsibility' has proved to be a politically charged idea, its meanings contestable. Market research for the Council for Aboriginal Reconciliation in 2000 showed the public to be sympathetic to Indigenous Australians' 'responsibility' in both the individual 'virtue' sense (each person/household succeeds or fails according to their self-disciplined efforts to make something of their lives) and the collective 'rights' sense (Aborigines and Torres Strait Islanders are entitled, as peoples, to self-determination through the state's recognition of their own culturally based institutions, including their land and sea estate). Both senses of 'responsibility' have resonated in public discussion.[72]

In June 2007, having become convinced of the irresponsibility of Aboriginal authority in many Northern Territory communities, the minister directing the NTER, Mal Brough, referred to his government's responsibility to protect children, even if that meant supervising Aboriginal adults' exercise of their responsibilities. 'While the government is ensuring welfare payments are spent on the priority needs of a person and his or her family, its objective is for the person to take responsibility for their own welfare and for the welfare of their family.'[73]

His words illustrate a tension within 'responsibility': it solicits the autonomy of Indigenous agency, while mandating the state to prescribe the shape of that autonomy.

Credible sources – both Indigenous and non-Indigenous – tell us that some Indigenous communities that were supposed to be practising self-determination were dangerous places to live – particularly for women and children. What was the responsibility of governments? Until the 1970s, government agencies who saw Indigenous family life as defective – by whatever criteria then current – could easily justify, to themselves and to much of the wider public, the physical removal of children. In the 1970s and 1980s, those asserting the cultural rights of the child had effectively questioned child removal; they persuaded governments that a removed child should be placed with an Indigenous family. By 1997, as a result of the Royal Commission into Aboriginal Deaths in Custody (1987–91) and the HREOC inquiry into the Stolen Generations (1995–97), the public had become convinced of the long-term mental health risks of removing a child to a setting that did not respect and foster his or her Aboriginal identity. To the extent that the Stolen Generations were heard in sympathy, the public and the Australian government found itself searching for alternative ways to deal with endangered children. Coalition and Labor governments since 2007 have sought to leave Northern Territory children where they are, but to reform the adults responsible. To attempt to shape the parent–child relationship has demanded that the Australian government (and on Cape York its delegate, the Family Responsibilities Commission) insert itself into the Indigenous social order.

The relationship of state responsibility to family responsibility is free of tension only when the norms and customs of state and family are congruent. The colonial relationship seeks to bring about such congruity by projecting models of responsible parenthood. Thoughtful debate about the methods and intensity of this colonial pressure cannot avoid raising profound and difficult questions about the allocation of authority, about measurement of 'well-being' – particularly the 'well-being' of women and children – and about the significance of 'culture' to mental health and to morality. Gordon Bryant, in 1973, invited

Australians to trust in the slow voluntary evolution of remote Aboriginal people's customs. However, trust between state and family is vulnerable when adult behaviour – particularly men's – is seen to fall below a certain standard. Trust is further damaged when the state, invoking emergency, acts unilaterally, as if Indigenous Australians were collectively irresponsible. The Senate Standing Committee on Community Affairs heard that in the preparation of 'Stronger Futures' there was a 'lack of consultation', suggesting that 'officers and consultants running the consultations need to be better prepared for the task, and that more time needed to be taken building relationships with people to support effective communication'.[74] The Australian government has recently initiated an intimate and in some respects adversarial relationship with remote Indigenous Australians, in response to real problems, advised by Indigenous people whom they have appointed or employed.

Alfred Deakin's avatars

The 'North' remains a problem for a settler-colonial nation-state that is still a 'Southern' continental projection. Immediately after Federation, Deakin and his colleagues could imagine a time when colonising laws reached into every part of the continent and when the nation included no distinct Aboriginal element. The first part of that vision has been realised: even the most remote region is under some degree of administration and law enforcement. However Indigenous Australia has not faded to insignificance but grown, presenting the moral, political and legal challenges of surviving colonised peoples.

What we mean by 'Indigenous Australia' has changed; we have learned to see Indigenous Australia more inclusively, accepting that light-skinned people who live like non-Indigenous Australians may nonetheless cherish, individually and collectively, their Aboriginal or Torres Strait Islander identity. At the same time, we have new ways to see the differences among Indigenous Australians. As well as becoming aware of the Torres Strait Islanders as a distinct Indigenous 'people', the terms of 'caste' distinction have been officially and authoritatively spurned; they remain in use among those Australians who doubt the authenticity of light-skinned Aboriginal people. Sociological distinctions among Indigenous Australians have become increasingly evident: between a flourishing 'middle class' and other Indigenous Australians who are measurably 'disadvantaged'.

One of the troubled beneficiaries of that more inclusive understanding was Indigenous journalist Stan Grant. In 2016 he sought to change the narrative of Indigenous Australia from disadvantage and failure to prosperity and success. Embodying success in 2016 less ambivalently than in 2002, Grant did not label or characterise those Indigenous Australians who are not prospering and not successful; but he was concerned for them, and he assumed that those not flourishing could and would, if only they would seize the opportunities that Australia offers, as he and his ancestors have done. Believing 'autobiography' to be 'essential to policy', Grant now offers his own history as the Indigenous paradigm of advancement.[75]

Jon Altman's response to Grant doubted that the minority of Indigenous Australians who now live on the Indigenous Estate, with their 'continuity of custom', would accept Grant's prescription to migrate from their homelands for formal education and employment. Altman argued that such people needed a different kind of schooling, in their regions, to prepare them for the Indigenous Estate's unusual economic potentials. Altman's point was that in those parts of Australia that the Bureau classifies as 'remote' and 'very remote' – approximating the regions to which I have referred as the 'North' – Indigenous Australians live differently and will continue to do so, because colonial history has dealt with them differently, affording continuing access to ancestral country on which there seem to be different opportunities to flourish: the arts, the application of knowledge to natural resource management, tourism as diplomacy. No matter how frequently and eloquently Grant narrates his family history of migration and his autobiography of astute choices and strenuous aspiration, the Grants cannot be paradigmatic for all Indigenous Australians, Altman argued.[76] A young Alice Springs woman of Warlpiri heritage, Jacinta Nampijinpa Price, responded to Grant by asking 'those who have made it' to 'reach out their hands in a practical way to help those who are trying to keep their languages and traditions intact and cope with the contemporary world'.[77] Like Altman, Price sees the prospects and problems of Aboriginal people of remote and very remote Australia as requiring their own difficult figuring.

Grant's response to Altman's invitation to consider remote Indigenous Australia as historically and culturally different was to deploy the 'Close the Gap' model of social justice. While conceding that the 'Indigenous life projects' of such neo-traditional residents of remote and very remote Australia 'may lead to more autonomy', Grant warned that such projects imply 'acceptance of a lower standard of living'. To 'close the gap' by 'selling labour ... will be the lot of most Aboriginal people, as it is for all Australians'.[78]

To think of 'social justice' as closing a measured socio-economic 'gap' has become possible because governments have revised Australia's statistics to enable us to compare all Indigenous Australians with the total Australian population. Comparison has exposed persistent deficits in Indigenous health, education, home ownership, income, employment and other dimensions of well-being. The premise of such comparisons is that when Australians aspire to a good life, they draw on a shared stock of values and feelings to which all individuals and households may commit. Insofar as 'Close the Gap' implies similarities of value and aspiration across all Australians, it has begged the question of whether the disadvantaged all want the same things as the advantaged. As a tool for reckoning our distance from social injustice, 'Gap' measurement attaches little if any importance to the possibility that some Australians (including some Indigenous Australians) have significantly different ideas about what is a good life. When Grant responded to Altman by referring to the Gap, he imagined Indigenous Australia as an ensemble of households and individuals with choices. He thus limited his cultural imagination to the Australia he knows from personal experience and family history; his often told autobiography makes him a compelling witness to a certain historic pathway, but his influence also limits our political imagination of other pathways.

It takes imaginative effort to see remote and very remote Indigenous Australians in terms that are grounded in *their* biographies and family experiences. Fortunately, Australia still funds ethnographic research. What readers of this research must consider is whether the differences revealed are viable or pathological and, to the extent that they are disturbing, whether corrective intervention by outside authorities is conceivable.

This question applies even to the efforts to close the mortality gap. Eirik Saethre, after working at Lajamanu, concluded that people there were intellectually open to western biomedical explanations and therapies, adding such ideas to their pre-colonial explanations and remedies. However, even people so eclectic are found by medical staff to be not compliant, to be unreliable and often hostile when treatment is offered. Saethre argues that when Lajamanu clients are 'difficult' it is not because they have no knowledge of, or belief in, western medicine; it is because they experience their illnesses (especially their chronic illnesses, such as diabetes) and the social interactions of the clinic as representative of their material poverty and of their subordination to non-Aboriginal institutions and laws. Affliction is meaningful to them not only as bodily or mental pathology, with causes and remedies, but also as their political condition. Thus, to credit a *ngangkari* (traditional healer) with one's recovery is not to reveal ignorance of biomedical explanation; it is rather to assert the value of Aboriginality.[79] Illness is not only a personal experience, but also 'a mode of social expression' and a 'political tactic'.[80] The afflicted and those whose vocation is to help them perform polarised identities made possible by a larger system of colonial authority.

Or consider the provision of more and better housing – surely a right and a benefit? At Yuendumu in the late 1990s, over 221 nights, Yasmine Musharbash recorded who slept in the house in which she slept and where and with whom they slept. She was exploring a theory about how the design of physical objects affects our 'dwelling' in the world (our basic, taken-for-granted thoughts and feelings about self and others). She wondered whether the physical structure commonly experienced by most Australians throughout their lives – a free-standing house with three or four bedrooms – gives rise to the same 'dwelling' when that structure is in Yuendumu, in Warlpiri people's use, as when it is your house or my house in a city or town. Musharbash concluded that Warlpiri 'dwell' differently; they 'camp' in houses – not through ignorance of 'proper' house use but in deeply grounded continuation of pre-colonial Warlpiri understandings of what a 'household' is, what a 'person' is, what 'intimacy' allows and what 'privacy' demands. Houses thus symbolise Warlpiri desires 'not to *be* like non-Indigenous Australians but to *have* what they have'.[81]

This strong desire for the material goods of the *munanga* (whitefella) world has been apparent also to Victoria Burbank, in her extended visits to Numbulwar. Like Musharbash, Burbank gained a strong sense of her hosts' self-conscious 'Aboriginal' identity and their commitment to its distinct purposes and values. She has evoked the ambivalence of their engagement with the *munanga* world. 'The Aboriginal cultural self' reproduced in Numbulwar today

> enables them to derive satisfaction and comfort from their family circumstances while it prevents them from engaging in the kinds of activities required for a satisfying and comfortable integration into the larger society. It is apparent the people of Numbulwar have never been provided with genuine opportunity or with an adequate preparation for such integration, but it is also apparent that such integration would require many, if not most, to abandon their selves in ways unacceptable to them.[82]

The least engaging feature of the wider Australian society, for Burbank's Numbulwar friends, is 'impersonality' – the idea, taken for granted by most Australians beyond childhood, that it is normal (if not beneficial) to allow certain parts of our lives to be structured by the routines and rules of institutions inhabited and run by strangers: the demands of school, the public transport schedule, the hours and social codes of our workplace, the trading times and exchanges of shopping, the rules applied by Centrelink, the newsreader's mode of address. Habituation to the impersonality of 'society' is so ingrained in most Australians that we easily concede its demands alongside the 'personal' demands of family, friends, lovers. But we cannot assume that this juxtaposition of the personal and the impersonal works effortlessly for those newly exposed to impersonality.

Schools – no matter how personable, skilled and caring the teachers – are frontiers of impersonality. David McKnight's many years with the Lardil and Kaiadilt peoples of Mornington Island showed him persistent resistance to schooling, giving rise to functional illiteracy. Of the situation in the late 1990s, he observed that

> in addition to being barely able to read and write they have trouble talking. Many people in their thirties and forties are unable to carry on a sustained conversation about complex matters, which the elders handled with ease in the 1960s. To a certain extent, this is a result of a loss of knowledge and an insecurity about what they may know, but it also reflects an inability to concentrate. Some adults are brain-damaged from alcohol, or from being bashed on the head, and they are punch-drunk from too many fights.[83]

The transition from a life supervised by strict and paternalistic missionaries or government officials (as recently as the early 1970s) to a life of collective self-determination has been both liberating and confronting for Aboriginal people of the 'North' because self-determination has made 'Southern' demands on them. Relief from paternalism supposed that people could rapidly develop from within themselves certain disciplined orientations to life that most Australians have been socialised to take for granted and to exercise with little effort. A psychiatrist working in the Kimberley in the 1980s, Ernest Hunter, argued in 1993 that these demands began in the 1960s when missionaries and pastoralists relinquished institutional authority and the state allowed access to alcohol; children raised in that new milieu of disrupted family life became a cohort given to self-mutilation and suicide.[84] Brian McCoy, an ordained Jesuit priest, has worked in Wirrimanu (formerly Balgo Mission), one of the communities studied by Hunter. McCoy portrays male youth as seeking *kanyirninpa* – 'to be held in the company of older men' – that is, to be mentored and nurtured in a fatherly way so as to qualify for manhood. Many forces have disrupted *kanyirninpa* – mission dormitories, the downgrading of adult male authority, high mortality and alcohol abuse among adult men – and so many young men find substitutes for *kanyirninpa* in petrol-sniffing gangs, in football tournaments, and in the social life of the prison. McCoy argues that the young men whom he got to know in 2001–04 cannot model themselves only on the masculine ideals projected in Australian schools and media. They look to their culture for sources of corrective ideals and emotional formation, including to mourning rituals, wherein grief enacts proper senses of being related to the deceased and to those who survive, and to the *maparn* (ritual healer), whose diagnosis and repair highlight the relationships vital to the young man's well-being.

McCoy's account is hopeful in that he sees some continuing strength in Western Desert traditions, but Balgo folk may not find all that they need in each other. The welcome achievement of recent ethnography has been to evoke the menace of emancipation. According to Diane Austin-Broos's recent work with the people of Hermannsburg, market society, a field of liberty, has intruded most forcefully (and righteously?) into their world as citizenship; welfare cash has included them in a world that routinely expresses value in monetary terms; and the authority of the state, since the 1970s, has eclipsed the mission's more familial authority under which Arrernte had lived for a century. The Arrernte meet the challenges of the impersonal as a people with a strong sense of belonging to country – that is, a conviction that social life re-enacts the sociality of ancestors that animate the country itself. This conjuncture of old and new senses of what is real is an enormous challenge to their imagination of themselves, writes Austin-Broos.[85]

Australians generally are unprepared to discover that, in the remote and very remote Aboriginal context, the meanings of 'freedom' and 'autonomy' have become so contestable. After doing two years of office work for an organisation servicing Ngaanyatjarra people, Tadhgh Purtill concluded that the autonomy of the Ngaanyatjarra from the demands of daily life, as experienced by other Australians, had locked them into an ever-narrowing world.

> What looks from the outside like freedom of choice – the freedom to ride around, to exit and enter the region, to live a largely unstructured existence, to do what one feels, to be unencumbered by the standards and expectations of mainstream society, to drift, to choose what to do with one's time rather than have to attend work or school – actually amounts, in the long term, to a lack of freedom.[86]

These people are equipped to live nowhere, he writes, but in the 'special zone' serviced by organisations whose interests are bound up in Ngaanyatjarra stasis and dependency. That this 'zone' is also their 'country' is their boon, and this is the rationale for wider Australia's unwillingness or inability to 'develop' the Ngaanyatjarra. Purtill challenges us to consider what 'autonomy' is, and it can be bewildering that what Purtill sees as confinement to 'country' results from the political success of the impeccably liberal critique of colonial paternalism in the name of human rights.

These ethnographies reveal a different world, subordinate to our best intentions as well as to our worst – a world that remains resistant to Australia's continental project of normalisation. It would be a mistake to overestimate the resistance. Indigenous Australians in very remote communities are struggling with one another about how to take on the forms of modernity that most Australians assume to be normal. In a discussion reported by Maggie Brady in 2005 about the terms of a liquor licence on a remote Northern Territory community, one person said:

> Grog is a big problem here. We are slaves to all you drunken mob … There's a lot of domestic violence and underage drinking. But we can't deny the drinkers' rights too. We gotta give them something too. Otherwise we should tell them to go to [nearest town]. We gotta balance their rights. Give them their rights too, all you sober people. So the community's got to support the drinking men … I'm starting to live with this grog problem. Balance it out, sober and drunken man. All these grog men say they agree as long as we give them something here so they stay and work. We can't frighten them by making them go to [nearest town].[87]

And in Numbulwar residents vary in their concessions to the impersonal, so that Burbank can distinguish 'the 9-5 crowd and the night life crowd':

> 9-5 have jobs, more education, live more by the western clock, more involved, e.g. jobs, with Western institutions. Night lifers sleep until late, stay up late, night probably long been a way of escaping white gaze. These are drinkers, ganja folk, more likely living off unemployment vs CDP [a form of welfare]. Younger people, perhaps, likely, more male than female. Christians would be 9-5.[88]

Readers of this book are almost certainly accomplished '9-5' people: we hardly have to think about the typical disciplines and emotions of being so adjusted to our version of modernity. But we Australians are not so 'modern' as to be free of our inherited colonial authority. In the first decades of the 21st century, as we look 'North' we are obliged to be more perceptive about the intrusion of our good order than Deakin was in 1904. In imagining in 2017 that disadvantaged Aboriginal people can and should make the effort to 'Close the Gap' by participating in the institutions that Australia offers – the school, the job, the local government – Stan Grant was the avatar of Alfred Deakin. Projecting a nation for a continent, Deakin imagined the law's territorial extension. Stan Grant represented many Australians in supposing that what remains to be extended is not the apparatus of law but the norms and daily practices of functional living.

Epilogue:
Within a single field of life

It would not have occurred to Alfred Deakin that Aborigines and Torres Strait Islanders – who did not participate in writing Australia's Constitution in the 1890s – would one day propose that the Constitution be amended to recognise them. With foresight, though, the men who wrote the Constitution provided Australians with a way to rewrite their vision of the nation.

Australians approach their Constitution in two ways – as a formal legal document that regulates the law-making powers of the Australian and state governments, and as a symbolic expression of the ideals that (should) bind Australians as a community. When Australians voted in 1967 to change the words of the Constitution, it was more real to them and better known to them in its symbolic dimension. Many people now recall the 1967 referendum as giving Aborigines the vote and the rights of citizenship; they recall the referendum as allowing Aborigines to be included in the Census. Such recollections of the 1967 referendum are false. However, these memories express a continuing desire that the nation's constitution be a statement of political values. When people voted 'Yes', this memory says, they were affirming equality and inclusion. Popular understandings then and collective memories since say that the original (1901) charter of the Australian people was flawed because it excluded Aborigines – by not 'counting' them and by not including them among the national government's responsibilities. In 1967, the people voted to make the nation's moral charter inclusive.

What did the 1967 referendum really do? The vote deleted section 127 – by then a dead letter. Once, it had forbidden states from using population data to cheat each other. If not regulated by section 127, states with a large estimated or enumerated non-voting Aboriginal or Islander population (such as Queensland and Western Australia) could have 'included' them in their population data when justifying claims to federal money or to seats in the House of Representatives; section 127 disallowed this way of using state population data. By the 1960s it was no longer necessary to forbid such 'reckoning' of numbers. Aborigines had been given the right to vote in Commonwealth elections in 1962 (so it was necessary to count them when deciding how many House of Representatives electorates should be in each state); and the processes for granting federal funds to the states had changed. By the mid-1960s, section 127 was a technical oddity, as removable as one's appendix.

Nonetheless, it felt good to get rid of section 127 because it was (and continues to be) widely misunderstood as forbidding counting Aborigines and Torres Strait Islanders in the Census. As I have shown, the Commonwealth had attempted to count them in every Census before 1967 (1901, 1911, 1921, 1933, 1947, 1954, 1961, 1966), but this has not stopped people believing that Aborigines could not be counted in the Census (and thus recognised as 'human') until the people voted 'Yes' in the 1967 referendum.

The other clause that the 1967 referendum changed was section 51. Part of that section had empowered the Commonwealth to pass racially discriminatory legislation – but not if the 'race' in question was the 'Aboriginal race'. The colonies, when writing the Constitution in the 1890s, had agreed that 'Aboriginal natives' would be the concern of the six states. The Commonwealth assumed responsibility for Northern Territory Aborigines in 1911, and from that time until 1967 many argued that, as a 'national' problem, all 'Aboriginal natives' should be among the national government's powers.

The campaign to write this power into the Constitution was in two respects ill-conceived. First, the Commonwealth already had powers to bring formal equality to 'Aboriginal natives' in every state: amendments to Commonwealth welfare laws in 1959, to the *Electoral Act* in 1962, and the 1966 'equal wages' decision empowered by the *Conciliation and Arbitration Act* 1904. The Commonwealth also already had the power to grant money to any state that agreed to spend it on Indigenous Australians in ways stipulated by the Commonwealth. Second, those campaigning for 'Yes' in 1967 assumed that the Commonwealth would exercise its new 'race' power to benefit the 'aboriginal native'. They ignored the advice of a constitutional lawyer, Prime Minister Sir Robert Menzies, who told the House of Representatives in 1965 that by withholding from the Commonwealth the authority to legislate about the 'aboriginal race', section 51(26) had been 'a protection against discrimination by the Commonwealth Parliament in respect of Aborigines'.[1] When Aboriginal and Torres Strait Islander people faced Commonwealth legislation that, in their view, discriminated against them, the High Court of Australia in 1998 confirmed Menzies' opinion: the 1967 referendum gave the Commonwealth power to legislate for or against the 'Aboriginal race'.

The 'Yes' voters of 1967 had voted as if the Constitution expressed their ideals about Australia as a fair-minded community. Rulings of the High Court show that the Constitution is less a charter of citizens or minority rights than – as the founding fathers intended – a rule book for dealings between the Australian governments. This painful lesson in constitutional law encouraged the idea that constitutional 'recognition' of Aborigines and Torres Strait Islanders must include writing into the Constitution some guarantee that legislation could never again discriminate against them.

In December 2010, the newly elected Gillard government, lacking a majority in the Senate and seeking to persuade Green senators to look kindly on Labor's legislative program, agreed to appoint an 'expert panel' on constitutional recognition. Reporting in January 2012, the panel (made up of Indigenous and non-Indigenous members) proposed five changes.[2]

First, get rid of any mention of Commonwealth power to deal with people as if they were members of a 'race', such as section 25 (allowing a state to exclude a 'race' from voting) and section 51(xxvi) (which allows the Commonwealth to pass laws about 'races', including Aborigines and Torres Strait Islanders).

Second, give the Commonwealth a new power – 'to make laws for the peace, order and good government of the Commonwealth with respect to Aboriginal and Torres Strait Islander peoples'. This would ensure the validity of Commonwealth laws such as the laws that protect Aboriginal and Torres Strait Islander heritage and that recognise 'native title' as a property right.

Third, the words describing this power would be part of a preamble – to be added to section 51 – that would recognise Aboriginal and Torres Strait Islander peoples as prior occupants of Australia with a continuing relationship to lands and waters and continuing culture; the preamble would also acknowledge these peoples' 'need' to 'secure [...] advancement'.

Fourth, insert words prohibiting racial discrimination by any government in Australia – unless the discrimination is intended to overcome disadvantage, or to reduce the adverse impact of racial discrimination in the past, or to protect culture, language or heritage.

Fifth, while acknowledging English as Australia's 'national language', the expert panel wanted Australians to recognise that there remain other Aboriginal and Torres Strait Islander languages.[3]

The fourth proposal was the most controversial. To put a 'right' (other than a right of a state) into the Australian Constitution confronted a widespread view that the national legislature, as the expression of popular sovereignty, should be the supreme body in defining the rights of Australians. If Indigenous Australians were given constitutional rights, the Australian parliament would become accountable to the High Court should anyone litigate legislation on Australia's Indigenous peoples. The major parties were prepared to discuss the wording of constitutional 'recognition' only on the condition that recognition made no difference to the authority of parliament. Many in the Indigenous community disagreed: the hard political effort of persuading Indigenous and non-Indigenous Australians to 'recognise' them would not be worth the trouble unless it resulted in constitutional recognition of their rights as a people.

From February 2012 the Australian government funded a publicity campaign by Reconciliation Australia to create a positive feeling towards constitutional recognition. Reconciliation Australia has always avoided saying what 'recognise' means: the word was iconic of some kind of fairness, but what would make the Constitution more fair? Reconciliation Australia considered its marketing successful if it attracted support for undefined constitutional change. The organisation's 2015–16 *Annual Review* celebrated consistently high levels of support, shown in 'eight consecutive large-scale polls by different organisations over four years'.[4] But 'Support for what?' became an increasingly pressing question, as a political stand-off became evident between 2012 and 2017. Those advocating the recognition of Indigenous sovereignty, through a treaty, were particularly scornful. The 'Recognise' campaign's deliberate vagueness and the opposition to the expert panel's fourth proposal confirmed their view that Indigenous Australians could not benefit from constitutional recognition.

However, some Indigenous intellectuals have continued to see possibilities in 'recognition'. Their challenge was to find a constitutional change that was substantive enough to meet Indigenous aspirations without compromising the legislature's supremacy as the expression of popular sovereignty and as the forum defining 'rights'. In 2015, Noel Pearson (a member of the expert panel) proposed a new question for a referendum: should the Constitution provide for an Indigenous representative body to be added as a new institution of Australian government? The proposed body would have the right only to comment on any matter before the Australian parliament, so it did not threaten the supremacy of the legislature; but it would institutionalise the Indigenous voice, a substantial 'recognition'. Pearson commissioned constitutional experts to draft designs.

With the 50th anniversary of the 1967 referendum looming, the Turnbull government and influential Indigenous intellectuals were united in their wish to progress an evidently stagnant debate on constitutional reform. The government had established a 'Referendum Council' in 2015, to advise the prime minister and the leader of the Opposition. To solicit ideas from

Indigenous Australians, the government funded an Indigenous assembly at Uluru in May 2017. Indigenous delegates deliberated for three days before issuing a two-part proposal to the Referendum Council: that the referendum question should be about creating an Indigenous deliberative and advisory body to whose concerns the national parliament would be obliged to respond; and that the government establish a Makarrata Commission to examine ways to proceed to a treaty between Australia and its Indigenous peoples. The Referendum Council has endorsed the Uluru statement, but at the time of writing no referendum had been announced.

The politics of 'recognition' necessarily highlights the symbolic dimension of the Constitution. Australians now dispute the significance of constitutional symbolism. Any idea for 'recognition' can be derided by pointing out that because it does not correct measured disadvantage it is 'merely symbolic'. Alternatively, 'recognition' can be promoted by arguing that the Constitution is necessarily a symbol of Australians' imagined community and that, currently, it imagines Australia as having no Aboriginal or Torres Strait Islander peoples: a Constitution that Australians 'unconsciously resolved not to discuss with them or treat with them about', to recall Stanner's words.[5] Constitutional recognition of Aboriginal and Torres Strait Islander peoples has become, for many Australians, a moral test of nationhood, welcomed and feared. Because the high 'Yes' vote in 1967 (91 per cent) is referred to by many as benchmarking Australians at their best, there is fear that a closer referendum result would reveal an equivocal nation, not a nation unified in goodwill. And how would Australians interpret a referendum on recognition that did not command a majority of voters in a majority of states?

References

Government publications

Commonwealth of Australia
Aboriginal Development Commission 1990 *Annual Report 1989–90* (to March 1990), Canberra: Australian Government Printing Service
Aboriginal and Torres Strait Islander Commission 1991 *Annual Report* (March–June 1990), Canberra: Australian Government Printing Service
—— 1992 *Annual Report* 1990–91
—— 1993 *Annual Report* 1991–92
—— 1994 *Annual Report* 1992–93
—— 1995 *Annual Report* 1993–94
—— 1996 *Annual Report* 1994–95
—— 1997 *Annual Report* 1995–96
—— 1998 *Annual Report* 1996–97
Aboriginal and Torres Strait Islander Social Justice Commissioner (ATSISJC) 2004 *Social Justice Report 2003*, Sydney: Human Rights and Equal Opportunity Commission
—— 2005 *Native Title Report 2005*, Sydney: Human Rights and Equal Opportunity Commission
—— 2006 *Social Justice Report 2005*, Sydney: Human Rights and Equal Opportunity Commission
—— 2011 *Social Justice Report 2011*, Sydney: Australian Human Rights and Equal Opportunity Commission
Anonymous 1929, *Finding of Board of Enquiry Concerning the Killing of Natives in Central Australia by Police Parties and Others and Concerning Other Matters* (unpublished report), National Library of Australia MS 744
Australia, Attorney-General 1998 *Native Title – Legislation with commentary / by the Australian Government Solicitor* (2nd edn), Fyshwick, ACT
Australia Council 1975 *Submission to the Senate Standing Committee on Education, Science and the Arts*, 'Vol. 2: Aboriginal Arts Board'
Australia Council and Australian Institute of Aboriginal Studies 1983 *Joint Submission to the Senate Standing Committee on Education by AIAS and the Aboriginal Arts Board*
Australia, Parliament, Select Committee 1961 *Commonwealth Parliamentary Papers*, 23rd Parliament, 3rd Session, 1961. Part 1 (No. H of R 1 [Group H]) *Report and Minutes of Proceedings* (including appendices), Part 2 *Minutes of Evidence* (No. H of R 2 [Group H])
Australia, Parliament, Senate Standing Committee on Community Affairs 2012 *Stronger Futures in the Northern Territory: Bill 2011 and two related bills*
Australia, Parliament, Senate Standing Committee on Legal and Constitutional Affairs 2006 *Unfinished Business: Indigenous stolen wages*

Australia, Review of the Aboriginal and Torres Strait Islander Commission 2003 *In the Hands of the Regions – A New ATSIC: Report of the Review of the Aboriginal and Torres Strait Islander Commission*, Canberra: The Review Panel

Australia, Royal Commission into Aboriginal Deaths in Custody 1991 *National Report: Overview and recommendations*, Canberra: Australian Government Publishing Service

Australia, Royal Commission into British Nuclear Tests in Australia 1985 *Report of the Royal Commission into British nuclear tests in Australia*, Canberra: Australian Government Publication Service

Australian Bureau of Statistics, *Prisoner Characteristics, Australia*, <http://www.abs.gov.au/ausstats/abs@.nsf/Lookup/by%20Subject/4517.0~2015~Main%20Features~Prisoner%20characteristics,%20Australia~28> (accessed 16 March 2016)

Australian Council for the Arts n.d. *First Annual Report, January–December 1973*, North Sydney: ACFTA

Australian Council for the Arts n.d. *Second Annual Report, 1974–75*, North Sydney: Australia Council

Commonwealth Bureau of Census and Statistics 1967 'Census of the Commonwealth of Australia 30 June 1966. The Aboriginal population: revised statement: States and Territories of Australia', typescript, AIATSIS Library

——— 1969 *Census of the Commonwealth of Australia, 30 June 1966. The Aboriginal population of Australia: Summary of characteristics* (Catalogue 2.23)

——— Yearbook no. 1 (1908); Yearbook no. 5 (1912); Yearbook no. 6 (1913); Yearbook no. 7 (1914); Yearbook no. 8 (1915); Yearbook no. 9 (1916); Yearbook no. 10 (1917); Yearbook no. 11 (1918); Yearbook no. 12 (1919); Yearbook no. 13 (1920); Yearbook no. 14 (1921); Yearbook no. 17 (1924); Yearbook no. 18 (1925); Yearbook no. 19 (1926); Yearbook no. 20 (1927); Yearbook no. 21 (1928); Yearbook no. 22 (1929); Yearbook no. 28 (1935)

Conference of Commonwealth and State Aboriginal Authorities 1937 'Aboriginal Welfare', initial conference of Commonwealth and State Aboriginal authorities, held at Canberra, 21–23 April 1937, Parliamentary Paper, Canberra: L.F. Johnston Commonwealth Government Printer

Department of Aboriginal Affairs 1976 *Joint Report and Financial Statements: Commonwealth capital funds for Aboriginal enterprises (1 July 1974 – 27 November 1974) and Aboriginal Loans Commission (28 November 1974 – 30 June 1975)*, Canberra: Australian Government Publishing Service

Department of Social Services 1967 *Twenty-sixth Report of the Director-General of Social Services for Year 1966–67* (Parliamentary Paper No. 92, 1967), Canberra: Commonwealth Government Printer

Department of Territories, Agenda, 1961 Native Welfare Conference, 'Progress in Health', A452, 1961/216 (digitised file, National Archives of Australia)

Human Rights and Equal Opportunity Commission (HREOC) 1997 *Bringing Them Home*, Report of the National Inquiry into the Separation of Aboriginal and Torres Strait Islander Children from Their Families, <https://www.humanrights.gov.au/publications/bringing-them-home-appendix-9-recommendations>

Indigenous Land Corporation 2014 *Annual Report 2013–2014*, Adelaide: Indigenous Land Corporation

Law Reform Commission 1986 *The Recognition of Aboriginal Customary Laws: Summary Report* (Report no. 31), Canberra: Australian Government Publication Service

McEwen, John 1939 *Commonwealth Government's Policy with Respect to Aboriginals*, pamphlet file, AIATSIS Library

McMahon, William 1972 *Australian Aborigines: Commonwealth policy and achievements*, Canberra: Commonwealth Government Printer

Report on the Administration of the Northern Territory for Year 1937–8 1939 Canberra: Commonwealth Government Printer (pp. 150 for 1937–38–39)

Spencer, W. Baldwin 1913 'Preliminary report on the Aboriginals of the Northern Territory', *Bulletin of the Northern Territory*, no. 7, Melbourne: Albert J. Mullett

Sweeney, G. 1956 'Census of Aboriginals – Northern Division of N.T. Graphs of population', 7 August, NAA (Darwin), F1 1956/293 PART 1 (folios 134–36)

New South Wales

NSW Parliament 1981 *Final Report from the Select Committee of the Legislative Assembly upon Aborigines*, D. West Government Printer, NSW, 1980 (Keane Report) in NSW Parliament, *Joint Volumes of Parliamentary Papers* 1980–81, vol. 4

Queensland

Archibald Meston 1896 *Report on the Aboriginals of Queensland*, Queensland, Votes and Proceedings of the Legislative Assembly, Session 1896, vol. 4, <aiatsis.gov.au/sites/default/files/docs/digitised_collections/remove/92163.pdf>

Queensland 1913 *Annual Report of the Chief Protector of Aboriginals for the Year 1912*, Brisbane: Government Printer

Queensland 1915 *Annual Report of the Chief Protector of Aboriginals for the Year 1914*, Brisbane: Government Printer

Queensland 1922 *Reports upon the Operations of Certain Sub-Departments of the Home Secretary's Department – Aboriginals Department – Information contained in report for the year ended 31st December 1922*

Robertson, Boni 1999 *The Aboriginal and Torres Strait Islander Women's Task Force on Violence Report* (Chair: Boni Robertson) (rev. ed.), Brisbane: Department of Aboriginal and Torres Strait Islander Policy and Development, <http://www.indigenouschamber.org.au/wp-content/uploads/2017/03/Aboriginal-Torres-Strait-Islanders-Womens-Task-Force-on-Violence-Report.pdf>

South Australia

Basedow, Herbert 1921 'Report upon the Third Medical Relief Expedition among the Aborigines of South Australia (typescript held by AIATSIS library)

Progress Report of the Royal Commission on the Aborigines Together with Minutes of Proceedings, Evidence and Appendices, Adelaide: Government Printer, Parliamentary Paper no. 26, South Australia Parliament, Parliamentary Papers 1913, vol. 2

Report of the Select Committee of the Legislative Council on the Aboriginal Lands Trust Bill 1966 (together with minutes of proceedings and evidence with appendices) (1967), South Australia Parliamentary Paper 98, 1966–7, second session of the 38th parliament. 28 September – 21 November 1966)

Western Australia

Annual Report of the Commissioner of Native Affairs for Year Ended 30 June 1938 1939 Perth: Government Printer

Bateman, F.E.A. 1948 *Survey of Native Affairs Western Australia*, WA Parliamentary Votes and Proceedings 1948, vol. 2, no. 19

Moseley Commission 1935 *Report of the Royal Commission Appointed to Investigate, Report, and Advise on Matters in Relation to the Conditions and Treatment of Aborigines*, W.A., Parliamentary Votes and Proceedings, vol. 1

——— 1935 *Transcript of Evidence* (Western Australia State Record Office Acc 2922/1-2, item 1 of 2)

Roth, Walter E. 1905 *Royal Commission on the Condition of the Natives: Report*, Perth: Government Printer

Non-government publications

Albrecht, Friedrich Wilhelm 1977 'Hermannsburg from 1926 to 1962' in E. Leske (ed.), *Hermannsburg: A vision and a mission*, Adelaide: Lutheran Publishing House, 42–89
Allen, Jim 1995 'A short history of the Tasmanian affair', *Australian Archaeology* 41, 43–48
Altman, Jon C. 1985 *Report of the Review of the Aboriginal Benefits Trust Account (and Related Financial Matters) in the Northern Territory Land Rights Legislation*, Canberra: Australian Government Publishing Service
────── 2009 'Indigenous communities, miners and the state in Australia' in Jon Altman and David Martin (eds), *Power, Culture and Economy: Indigenous Australians and mining*, Canberra: ANU ePress, 17–50
────── 2012 'Submission to Senate Community Affairs Standing Committee', 2 February 2012
────── 2014 'The political ecology and political economy of the Indigenous titling "revolution" in Australia', *Māori Law Review*, March, 1–17
────── 2017 'The Australian dream: correspondence', *Quarterly Essay* 65, Carlton: Schwartz Publishing, 123–27
Altman, Jon C., Frances Morphy and Tim Rowse (eds) 1999 *Land Rights at Risk: Evaluations of the Reeves Report*, Canberra: Centre for Aboriginal Economic Policy Research, Australian National University
Altman, Jon C. and John Nieuwenhuysen 1979 *The Economic Status of Australian Aborigines*, Melbourne: Cambridge University Press
Anderson, Chris 1983 'Aborigines and tin mining in North Queensland: a case study in the anthropology of contact history', *Mankind* 13(6), 473–98
Anderson, Pat and Rex Wild 2007 *Ampe Akelyernemane Meke Mekarle, 'Little Children Are Sacred': Report of the Northern Territory Board of Inquiry into the protection of children from sexual abuse*, Darwin
Anonymous 1985 *Victims or Victors? The Story of the Victorian Aborigines Advancement League*, South Yarra: Hyland House
Anonymous 1990 'Editorial', *Aboriginal Law Bulletin* 2(46), 3
Anthony, Thalia 2007a 'Criminal justice and transgression on northern Australian cattle stations' in Ingereth Macfarlane and Mark Hannah (eds), *Transgressions: Critical Australian Indigenous histories*, Canberra: ANU ePress, 35–61
────── 2007b 'Reconciliation and conciliation: the irreconcilable dilemmas of the 1965 "equal" wage case for Aboriginal station workers', *Labour History*, no. 93, November, 15–34
────── 2013 *Indigenous People, Crime and Punishment*, Abingdon: Routledge
Arrowsmith, H. M. n.d. *The Church Missionary Society and the Australian Aboriginal*, Sydney: Edgar Bragg & Sons
Atkinson, Judy 1990 'Violence against Aboriginal women: reconstitution of community law – the way forward', *Aboriginal Law Bulletin* 2(46), 6–9
Attwood, Bain 2003 *Rights for Aborigines*, Sydney: Allen & Unwin
────── 2005 *Telling the Truth about Aboriginal History*, Sydney: Allen & Unwin
Attwood, Bain and Andrew Markus (in collaboration with Dale Edwards and Kath Schilling) 1997 *The 1967 Referendum or When Aborigines Didn't Get the Vote*, Canberra: Australian Institute of Aboriginal and Torres Strait Islander Studies
Attwood, Bain and Andrew Markus (eds) 1999 *The Struggle for Aboriginal rights*, Sydney: Allen & Unwin
Attwood, Bain and Andrew Markus (eds) 2004 *Thinking Black: William Cooper and the Australian Aborigines' League*, Canberra: Aboriginal Studies Press
Attwood, Bain and Andrew Markus 2007 *The 1967 Referendum: Race, power and the Australian constitution*, Canberra: Aboriginal Studies Press

Australian Theatre Foundation Newsletter, May 1972 and May 1974

Austin, Tony 1993 *I Can Picture the Old Home So Clearly: The Commonwealth and half-caste youth in the Northern Territory 1911–1939*, Canberra: Aboriginal Studies Press

—— 1997 *Never Trust a Government Man: Northern Territory Aboriginal policy 1911–1939*, Darwin: NTU Press

Austin-Broos, Diane 2009 *Arrernte Present, Arrernte Past: Invasion, violence, and imagination in Indigenous Central Australia*, Chicago: University of Chicago Press

Australian Labor Party 1967 *Platform, Constitution and Rules as Approved by the 27th Commonwealth Conference, Adelaide 1967*, Canberra

Australian Labor Party 1969 *Platform, Constitution and Rules as Approved by the 28th Commonwealth Conference, Melbourne 1969*, Canberra

Baker, Gwen 2005 'Crossing boundaries: negotiated space and the construction of narratives of missionary incursion', *Journal of Northern Territory History* 16, 17–28

Bandler, Faith and Len Fox 1983 *The Time Was Ripe: The story of the Aboriginal-Australian Fellowship, 1956–69*, Chippendale: Alternative Publishing Cooperative Limited

Barwick, Diane 1998 *Rebellion at Coranderrk*, Aboriginal History Monograph 5 (edited by Laura E. Barwick and Richard E. Barwick), Canberra

Beazley, Kim E. 1964 'Dispossession and disease – or dignity?', *Provocative Pamphlet* no. 115, September–October

Beckett, Jeremy 1977 'The Torres Strait Islanders and the pearling industry: a case of internal colonialism', *Aboriginal History* 1(1), 77–104

—— 1987 *Torres Strait Islanders: Custom and colonialism*, Melbourne: Cambridge University Press

—— 2005 *A Study of Aborigines in the Pastoral West of New South Wales*, Oceania Monograph 55, University of Sydney

—— 2014 'The Murray Island land case' in J. Beckett, *Encounters with Indigeneity*, Canberra: Aboriginal Studies Press, 184–203

Behrendt, Larissa 2009 'Representative structures – lessons learned from the ATSIC era', *Journal of Indigenous Policy*, no. 10, 35–63

Behrendt, Larissa, Steven Larkin, Robert Griew and Patricia Kelly 2012 *Review of Higher Education Access and Outcomes for Aboriginal and Torres Strait Islander People, Final Report*, Canberra: Department of Industry, Innovation, Science, Research and Tertiary Education

Bell, Diane 1998 *Ngarrindjeri Wurruwarrin: A world that is, was and will be*, North Melbourne: Spinifex Press

Bell, Diane and Topsy Nappurrula 1989 'Rape is everybody's business', *Women's Studies International Forum*, 12(4), 403–16

Bell, James H. 1961 'Some demographic and cultural characteristics of the La Perouse Aborigines', *Mankind* 5(10), 425–38

Bennett, Mary M. 1933 'The Aboriginal Mother in Western Australia in 1933' (a paper read at the British Commonwealth League Conference, London, June 1933), Rischbieth papers, NLA MS 2004/12/215-34

Bent, Nagarta Jinny, Jukuna Mona Chuguna, Pat Lowe and Eirlys Richards 2004 *Two Sisters: Ngarata and Jukuna*, Fremantle: Fremantle Arts Centre Press

Berndt, Ronald M 1969 'Problems of change: progress and development toward full equality with other Australians' in R.M. Berndt (ed.), *Thinking about Aboriginal welfare*, Crawley: Department of Anthropology, University of Western Australia, 1–5

Berndt, Ronald M and Catherine H. Berndt 1951 *From Black to White in South Australia*, Melbourne: Cheshire

Berndt, Ronald M. and Catherine H Berndt 1987 *End of an Era*, Canberra: Aboriginal Studies Press

Berndt, Ronald M. and Catherine H. Berndt with John E. Stanton 1993 *A World that Was: The Yaraldi of the Murray River and the Lakes, South Australia*, Melbourne: Melbourne University Press at the Miegunyah Press

Berndt, Ronald M and E.S. Phillips 1978 'Looking toward the Aboriginal Arts' in *The Australian Aboriginal Heritage: An introduction through the arts*, Sydney: Australian Society for Education through the Arts/Ure Smith, 292–315

Biddle, Nicholas 2013a 'Income': CAEPR Indigenous Population Project, 2011 Census Papers, Paper 11

—— 2013b 'Indigenous and Non-Indigenous Marriage Partnerships', CAEPR Indigenous Population Project, 2011 Census Papers, Paper 15

Bishop, Catherine 1991 '"A woman missionary living among naked blacks": Annie Lock 1876–1943' (unpublished MA thesis, Australian National University)

Biskup, Peter 1973 *Not Slaves, Not Citizens: The Aboriginal problem in Western Australia 1898–1954*, St Lucia, Queensland: University of Queensland Press

Blake, Thom 1998 'Deported ... At the sweet will of the government: the removal of Aborigines to reserves in Queensland 1897–1939', *Aboriginal History* 22, 51–61

—— 2001 *A Dumping Ground*, St Lucia: University of Queensland

Bleakley, John W. 1929 'The Aboriginals and Half-Castes of Central and Northern Australia: A Report', Melbourne: Government Printer (*Commonwealth Parliamentary Papers* 1929)

—— 1961 *The Aborigines of Australia: Their history, their habits, their assimilation*, Brisbane : Jacaranda Press

Bolger, Audrey 1991 *Aboriginal Women and Violence*, Darwin: North Australia Research Unit

Bolton, Geoffrey C 1981 'Black and White after 1897' in C.T. Stannage (ed.), *A New History of Western Australia*, Nedlands: University of Western Australia Press, 124–78

—— 1989 'The spread of colonization' in J. Hardy and A. Frost (eds), *Studies from Terra Australis to Australia*, Canberra: Australian Academy of the Humanities, Occasional Paper 6, 183–93

Boughton, Bob 2001 'The Communist Party of Australia's involvement in the struggle for Aboriginal and Torres Strait Islander peoples' Rights, 1920–1970' in Ray Markey (ed.), *Labour and Community: Historical essays*, Wollongong: University of Wollongong Press, 263–94

Bonner, Neville 1967 'The referendum – now what', *OPAL* 4, 7

Bostock, Gerry 1985 'Black theatre' in Jack Davis and Bob Hodge (eds), *Aboriginal Writing Today*, Canberra: Australian Institute of Aboriginal Studies, 63–73

Bowman, Margaret (ed.) 2015 *Every Hill Got a Story*, Richmond, Vic.: Hardie Grant

Brady, Maggie (in press), *Teaching 'Civilised' Drinking? Clubs and pubs in Indigenous Australia*, Canberra: ANU Press

Brazil, P. and B. Mitchell (eds) 1981 *Opinions of Attorneys-General of the Commonwealth of Australia: With opinions of Solicitors-General and the Attorney-General's Department*, vol. 1: 1901–1914, Canberra: Australian Government Publishing Service

Brennan, Frank 1992 *Land Rights Queensland Style: The struggle for Aboriginal self-management*, St Lucia: University of Queensland Press

Brennan, Sean 2015 'The significance of the Akiba Torres Strait regional sea claim case' in Sean Brennan, Megan Davis, Brendan Edgeworth and Leon Terrill (eds), *Native Title from Mabo to Akiba: A vehicle for changer and empowerment?*, Annandale: Federation Press, 29–43

Brimblecome, J.K. et al. 2010 'After the intervention – research impact of income management on store sales in the Northern Territory', *Medical Journal of Australia* 192(10), 549–54

Briscoe, Gordon 2003 *Counting, Health and Identity*, Canberra: Aboriginal Studies Press

Briscoe, Gordon and Leonard Smith 2002 'The Aboriginal population in South Australia 1921–1944' in G. Briscoe and L. Smith (eds), *The Aboriginal population revisited: 70 000 years to the present*, Aboriginal History Monograph 10, Canberra: Aboriginal History Incorporated, 16–40

British Commonwealth League n.d. *A Report of Conference held June 30th and July 1st, 1927*, London

Broadhurst, Roderic 2002 'Crime and Indigenous people' in Adam Graycar and Peter Grabosky (eds), *The Cambridge Handbook of Australian Criminology*, Melbourne: Cambridge University Press, 256–80

Broom, Leonard 1970 'Educational status of Aborigines', *Australia and New Zealand Journal of Sociology* 6(2), 150–56

—— 1971 'Workforce and occupational statuses of Aborigines', *Australia and New Zealand Journal of Sociology* 7(1), 21–34

Broome, Richard 2005 *Aboriginal Victorians: A history since 1800*, Sydney: Allen & Unwin

—— 2015 *Fighting Hard: The Victorian Aborigines Advancement League*, Canberra: Aboriginal Studies Press

Burbank, Victoria K. 2011 *An Ethnography of Stress*, Basingstoke: Palgrave Macmillan

Butel, Elizabeth 1985 *Margaret Preston: The art of constant rearrangement*, Ringwood: Penguin

Carlson, Bronwyn 2016 *The Politics of Identity: Who counts as Aboriginal today?*, Canberra: Aboriginal Studies Press

Casey, Maryrose 2004 *Creating Frames: Contemporary Indigenous theatre*, St Lucia: University of Queensland Press

Chaney, Fred 2002 'Eddie Mabo memorial lecture Melbourne, 3 June 2002' <http://www.nntt.gov.au/Information%20Publications/Speeches%20Eddie%20Mabo%20memorial%20lecture%20Chaney%20June%202002.pdf> (accessed 22 August 2015)

Chase, Athol 1988 'Lazarus at Australia's gateway: the Christian mission enterprise in eastern Cape York Peninsula' in T. Swain and D.B. Rose (eds), *Aboriginal Australians and Christian Missions: Ethnographic and historical studies*, Bedford Park, SA: Australian Association for the Study of Religions, 121–39

Chauvel, Charles and Elsa 1959 *Walkabout*, London: W.H. Allen

Chesterman, John 2001 'Defending Australia's reputation: how Indigenous Australians won civil rights, part one', *Australian Historical Studies* 32, 20–39

—— 2005 *Civil Rights: How Indigenous Australians won formal equality*, St Lucia: University of Queensland Press

Choo, Christine 2001 *Mission Girls: Aboriginal women on Catholic missions in the Kimberley, Western Australia 1900–1950*, Nedlands: University of Western Australia Press

Clark, Jennifer 2008 *Aborigines and Activism: Race, Aborigines and the coming of the sixties to Australia*, Crawley: University of Western Australia

Clarke, Banjo (as told to Camilla Chance) 2003 *Wisdom Man*, Sydney: Penguin Books

Clarke, Bernard 2010 *Larrpan Ga Buduyurr: The spear and the cloud*, Tranmere, SA: Bernard Clarke

Cleland, John B. 1949 'The Australian Aboriginal: the significance of his past, the present, his future', Presidential Address to Section F (Anthropology), *Australian Association for the Advancement of Science Hobart Report*, 27th, Hobart, 1949; 66–78

Clendinnen, Inga 2005 *Dancing with Strangers: Europeans and Australians at first contact*, New York: Cambridge University Press

Clohesy, Lachlan 2011 'Fighting the enemy within: anti-communism and Aboriginal affairs', *History Australia* 8(2), 128–52

Cole, Keith 1980 *Dick Harris: Missionary to the Aborigines*, Bendigo: Keith Cole Publications

Conor, Liz 2008 '"Blackfella missus too much proud": techniques of appearing, femininity, and race in Australian modernity' in Alice Eve Weinbaum, Lynn M. Thomas, Priti Ramamurthy, Uta G. Poiger, Madeleine Yue Dong and Tani E. Barlow (eds), *The Modern Girl around the World: Consumption, modernity and globalization*, Durham and London: Duke University Press, 220–39

Cottle, Drew 2011 'The colour-line and the third period: a comparative analysis of American and Australian communism and the question of race, 1928–1934', *American Communist History* 10(2), 119–31

Cowlishaw, Gillian 1999 *Rednecks, Eggheads and Blackfellas*, Sydney: Allen & Unwin
Cox, Eva (ed.), 2011 'Evidence-free policy making? The case of income management', *Journal of Indigenous Policy* no. 12 (September), 1–98
Crawford, Heather and Nicholas Biddle 2015 'Education Part 3: Tertiary education', CAEPR Indigenous Population Project, 2011 Census Papers, Paper 17
Crawford, Ian M. 1978 'The Benedictine Mission at Kalumburu', *Studies in Western Australian History* 3, 43–47
Cribbin, John 1984 *The Killing Times: The Coniston Massacre 1928*, Sydney: Fontana/Collins
Cripps, Kyllie 2008 'Indigenous family violence: a statistical challenge', *Injury: International Journal of the Care of the Injured* 39S5, S25–S35
Cunneen, Chris, Eileen Baldry, David Brown, Mark Brown, Melanie Schwartz and Alex Steel 2013 *Penal Culture and Hyperincarceration: The revival of the prison*, Farnham: Ashgate
Curthoys, Ann 2002 *Freedom Ride: A freedom rider remembers*, Sydney: Allen & Unwin
Dalley, Cameo and Paul Memmott 2010 'Domains and the intercultural: understanding Aboriginal and missionary engagement at the Mornington Island Mission, Gulf of Carpentaria, Australia from 1914 to 1942', *International Journal of Historical Archaeology* 14(1), 112–35
Daniels, Dennis 1995 *The Assertion of Tasmanian Aboriginality: From the 1967 referendum to Mabo* (unpublished Master of Humanities thesis, University of Tasmania), <http://eprints.utas.edu.au/3585/>
Day, Bill 1994 *Bunji: A story of the Gwalwa Daraniki Movement*, Canberra: Aboriginal Studies Press
Deakin, Alfred 1968 *Federated Australia: Selections from letters to the 'Morning Post' 1900–1910* (edited and with an introduction by J.A. La Nauze), Melbourne: Melbourne University Press
De Costa, Ravi 2006 *A Higher Authority: Indigenous transnationalism and Australia*, Kensington: University of New South Wales Press
De Maria, William 1986 '"White welfare: black entitlement": the social security access controversy, 1939–59', *Aboriginal History* 10(1), 25–39
Devitt, Rebecca 2008 *'Sweat and Tears': Stolen generations activism and the National Inquiry into the Separation of Aboriginal and Torres Strait Islander Children from Their Families* (unpublished PhD thesis, Australian National University)
Dexter, Barrie 2015 *Pandora's Box: The Council for Aboriginal Affairs 1967–1976* (edited by Gary Foley and Edwina Howell), Southport: Keeaira Press
Dillon, Anthony 2013 'No more victims' in Rhonda Craven, Anthony Dillon and Nigel Parbury (eds), *In Black & White: Australians all at the cross roads*, Ballan: Connor Court, 75–90
Dixon, Rod 1990 'In the shadows of exclusion: Aborigines and the ideology of development in Western Australia' in Rod A. Dixon and Michael C. Dillon (eds), *Aborigines and Diamond Mining*, Nedlands: University of Western Australia, 155–68
Dodson, Mick 2003 'The end of the beginning: re(de)finding Aboriginality' in M. Grossman (ed.), *Blacklines: Contemporary critical writing by Indigenous Australians*, Melbourne: Melbourne University Press, 25–42
Dodson, Mick and Diane Smith 2003 'Governance for sustainable development: strategic issues and principles for Indigenous Australian communities', *CAEPR Discussion Paper* 250, Australian National University
Dodson, Patrick and Mark Liebler 2012 *Recognising Aboriginal and Torres Strait Islander Peoples in the Constitution: Report of the expert panel*, Canberra: Commonwealth of Australia
Donovan, Peter 1984 *At the Other End of Australia*, St Lucia: University of Queensland Press
Donovan Research 1992 'Aboriginal Reconciliation Study November/December 1991', Job No. 1121, West Perth
Doohan, Kim, Marcia Langton and Odette Mazel 2012 'From paternalism to partnership: the Good Neighbour Agreement and the Argyle Diamond Mine Indigenous Land Use Agreement in Western Australia' in Marcia Langton and Judy Longbottom (eds),

Community Futures, Legal Architecture: Foundations for Indigenous peoples in the global mining boom, London: Routledge, 231–50

Douglas, Heather and Mark Finnane 2012 *Indigenous Crime and Settler Law*, Basingstoke: Palgrave Macmillan

Downing, James H. 1971 'Consultation and self-determination in the social development of Aborigines' in R.M. Berndt (ed.), *A Question of Choice: An Australian Aboriginal dilemma*, Nedlands: University of Western Australian Press, 61–90

Durack, Mary 1969 *The Rock and the Sand*, London: Constable

——— 1971 'No longer just a dream', *Identity* 1(2), 17–18

Dussart, Francoise 2000 *The Politics of Ritual in an Aboriginal Settlement: Kinship, gender, and the currency of knowledge*, Washington: Smithsonian Institution Press

Edwards, William 1983 'Pitjantjatjara land rights' in M. Langton and N. Peterson (eds), *Aborigines, Land and Land Rights*, Canberra: Australian Institute of Aboriginal Studies, 294–304

——— 1999 *Moravian Aboriginal Missions in Australia 1850–1919*, Adelaide: Uniting Church Historical Society (SA)

——— 2012 *Mission in the Musgraves: Ernabella Mission 1937–73, a place of relationships*, Adelaide: Uniting Church Historical Society (SA)

Egan, Ted 1996 *A Justice All Their Own: The Caledon Bay and Woodah Island killings 1932–1933*, Melbourne: Melbourne University Press

Elkin, Adolphus Peter 1934a 'Anthropology and the future of the Australian Aborigines', *Oceania* 5(1), 1–18

Elkin, Adolphus Peter 1934b 'Missionary policy for primitive peoples', *Morpeth Review* 3(27), 1–15 (reprint)

——— 1938a *The Australian Aborigines: How to understand them*, Sydney: Angus & Robertson

——— 1938b 'Anthropological Research in Australia and the Western Pacific, 1927–1937', *Oceania* 8(3), 306–27

——— 1944 *Citizenship and the Aborigines: A national policy*, Sydney: Australasian Publishing

——— 1947 'Segregation would be the end of Aborigines', *Sun*, 22 January

——— 1951 'Aborigines and the Ministers' Welfare Council', *Australian Quarterly* 23(4), 9–20

——— 1954 *The Australian Aborigines: How to understand them* (3rd edn), Sydney: Angus & Robertson

——— 1964 *The Australian Aborigines: How to understand them* (4th edn), Sydney: Angus & Robertson

——— 1978 'Foreword' to Ella Simon, *Through My Eyes*, Adelaide: Rigby

Elliott, Brian 1979 'Introduction', *The Jindyworobaks*, St Lucia: University of Queensland Press, xvii–lxvi

Evans Raymond 1999 '"Steal away": the fundamentals of Aboriginal removal in Queensland', *Journal of Australian Studies* 23(61), 83–95, 226–28

Falkenberg, Johannes 1962 *Kin and Totem: Group relations of Australian Aborigines in the Port Keats district*, Oslo: Oslo University Press

Fink, Ruth A. 1960 *The Changing Status and Cultural Identity of Western Australian Aborigines: A field study of Aborigines in the Murchison District, Western Australia 1955–57* (unpublished PhD thesis, Columbia University)

Finnane, Mark 2011 'Settler justice and Aboriginal homicide in late colonial Australia', *Australian Historical Studies* 42(2), 244–59

Finnane, Mark and Andy Kaladelfos 2016 'Race and justice in an Australian court: prosecuting homicide in Western Australia, 1830–1954', *Australian Historical Studies* 47(3), 443–61

Fletcher, Jim J. 1989a *'Clean, Clad and Courteous': A history of Aboriginal education in New South Wales*, Carlton, NSW: self-published

Fletcher, Jim J. (ed.), 1989b *Documents in the History of Aboriginal Education in New South Wales*, Carlton, NSW: self-published

Foley, Gary 2001 'Black Power in Redfern 1968–1972', The Koori History Website, 5 October, <http://www.kooriweb.org/foley/essays/essay_1.html>

Fox, Charlie 2008 'The fourteen powers referendum of 1944 and the federalisation of Aboriginal affairs', *Aboriginal History* 32, 27–48

Frawley, Jack 2003 'People got a gun: the 1914 Melville Island Enquiry', *Journal of Northern Territory History* 14, 51–69

Furphy, Sam 2016 'Aboriginal Australians and the First World War Home Front' (unpublished manuscript)

Gaffney, Ellie 1989 *Somebody Now: The autobiography of Ellie Gaffney, a woman of the Torres Strait*, Canberra: Aboriginal Studies Press

Gale, Fay 1969 'A changing Aboriginal population' in F. Gale and G.H. Lawton (eds), *Settlement and Encounter: Geographical studies presented to Sir Grenfell Price*, Melbourne: Oxford University Press, 65–88

Gale, Fay and Alison Brookman (eds) 1975 *Race relations in Australia: The Aborigines*, Sydney: McGraw-Hill Book Company

Ganter, Elizabeth 2016 *Reluctant Representatives: Blackfella bureaucrats speak in Australia's north*, Research Monograph No. 37, Centre for Aboriginal Economic Policy Research, Australian National University

Ganter, Regina 1998 'Living an immoral life: "coloured" women and the paternalistic state', *Hecate* 24(1), 13–40

—— 1999 'Letters from Mapoon: colonising Aboriginal gender', *Australian Historical Studies* 113, 267–85

Gerritsen, Rolf 2010 'A post-colonial model for north Australian political economy: the case of the Northern Territory' in R. Gerritsen (ed.), *North Australian Political Economy: Issues and agendas*, Darwin: Charles Darwin University Press, 18–40

Gilbert, Kevin 1973a 'Of black patriots and a black intelligentsia', *Alchuringa* 1(4) January–March, 3–5

—— 1973b *Because a White Man'll Never Do It*, Sydney: Angus & Robertson

—— 1987 'Interview with Kevin Gilbert', *Ethnic Spotlight* no. 12, September, 17–22

Godden, Lee 2012 'Native Title and ecology: agreement-making in an era of market environmentalism' in Jessica K. Weir (ed.), *Country, Native Title and Ecology*, Canberra: ANU Press, 105–34

Goodall, Heather 1996 *Invasion to Embassy: Land in Aboriginal politics in New South Wales, 1770–1972*, Sydney: Allen & Unwin

Goot, Murray 2006 'The Aboriginal Franchise and its consequences', *Australian Journal of Politics and History* 52(4), 517–61

Goot, Murray and Tim Rowse (eds) 1994 *Make a Better Offer: The politics of Mabo*, Leichhardt: Pluto Press

Goot, Murray and Tim Rowse 2007 *Divided Nation? Indigenous affairs and the imagined public*, Melbourne: Melbourne University Press

Gordon, Christine 2002 *Punderlime: Brother John Pye, a Northern Territory legend*, Casuarina: Historical Society of the Northern Territory

Gordon, Deborah C 2004 *The Catholic Church and the Status of Aboriginal Women: Port Keats, 1935–1958* (unpublished PhD thesis, Charles Darwin University)

Gordon, Sue 2003 'The Gordon Inquiry, child protection and the role of the health worker', *Aboriginal and Islander Health Worker Journal* 27(5), 10–14

Grant, Stan 2002 *The Tears of Strangers – A memoir*, Sydney: HarperCollins

—— 2016 'The Australian dream: blood, history and becoming', *Quarterly Essay* no. 64, Carlton: Schwartz Publishing, 1–80

—— 2017 'The Australian dream: responses to correspondence', *Quarterly Essay* no. 65, Carlton: Schwartz Publishing, 131–37
Gray, Geoffrey 1991 'Aborigines, Elkin and the Guided Projectiles Project', *Aboriginal History* 15(1–2), 153–62
—— 1994 '"Piddington's indiscretion": Ralph Piddington, the Australian National Research Council and academic freedom', *Oceania* 64(3), 217–45
Grayden, William 1957 *Adam and Atoms*, Perth: Frank Daniels
Green, Neville 1995 *The Forrest River Massacres*, Fremantle: Fremantle Arts Centre Press
Green, Ribnga Kenneth 1980 'Aborigines and international politics' in Ronald M. Berndt and Catherine H. Berndt (eds), *Aborigines of the West: Their past and their present* (2nd edn), Nedlands: University of Western Australia Press, 388–92
Gruen, Fred 1966 'Aborigines in the Northern Territory cattle industry – an economist's view' in I.G. Sharp and C.M. Tatz (eds), *Aborigines in the Economy*, Brisbane: Jacaranda Press, 197–210
Gsell, Francis Xavier 1956 *The Bishop with 150 Wives: Fifty years as a missionary*, Sydney: Angus & Robertson
Haebich, Anna 1988 *For Their Own Good: Aborigines and government in the southwest of Western Australia 1900–1940*, Nedlands: University of Western Australia Press
—— 2000 *Broken Circles: Fragmenting Indigenous families 1800–2000*, Fremantle: Fremantle Arts Centre Press
—— 2004 'Bridging the gap: assimilation and Aboriginal women and their households', *Tasmanian Historical Studies*, 9, 4–20
Hall, Robert 1989 *The Black Diggers: Aborigines and Torres Strait Islanders in the Second World War*, Sydney: Allen & Unwin
Hannah, Mark 2005 *Constituting Marriage: Indigenous and inter-cultural marriage and power of protectors* (unpublished PhD thesis, the Australian National University)
Harman, Elizabeth J. 1982 'Ideology and mineral development in Western Australia' in E.J. Harman and B.W. Head (eds), *State, Capital and Resources*, Nedlands: University of Western Australia Press, 167–96
Harman, Kristyn 2013 'Protecting Tasmanian Aborigines: American and Queensland influences on the Cape Barren Island Reserve Act, 1912', *Journal of Imperial and Commonwealth History*, 41(5), 744–64
Harris, John 1990 *One Blood*, Sutherland: Albatross
—— 1998 *We Wish We'd Done More*, Adelaide: Openbook
Hartwig, Mervyn 1960 *The Coniston Killings* (unpublished BA thesis, University of Adelaide)
Harvey, Bruce 2004 'Rio Tinto's agreement making in Australia in a context of globalisation' in Marcia Langton, Maureen Tehan, Lisa Palmer and Katherine Shain (eds), *Honour Among Nations? Treaties and agreements with Indigenous people*, Melbourne: Melbourne University Press, 237–47
Haskins, Victoria 2005 *One Bright Spot*, Basingstoke: Palgrave Macmillan
—— 2009 'From the centre to the city: modernity, mobility and mixed-descent Aboriginal domestic workers from Central Australia', *Women's History Review* 18(1), 155–75
—— 2015 'The White Woman's Burden: encounters between white and Indigenous women in Australian domestic service,' *Journal of Australian Indigenous Issues* 18(1), 38–53
Hasluck, Paul M.C. 1953 *Native Welfare in Australia*, Perth: Paterson Brokensha
—— 1959 'Are our Aborigines neglected?' (unpublished paper, presented as PSA Service, the Lyceum, Sydney on 12 July 1959), Box 80, item 294, papers of A.P. Elkin, Fisher Library, University of Sydney
—— 1988 *Shades of Darkness*, Melbourne: Melbourne University Press
Hawke, Steve and Michael Gallagher 1989 *Noonkanbah: Whose land, whose law?*, Fremantle: Fremantle Arts Centre Press

Hegarty, Ruth 1999 *Is That You, Ruthie?*, St Lucia: University of Queensland Press
Henson, Barbara 1992 *A Straight-out Man: F.W. Albrecht and Central Australian Aborigines*, Melbourne: Melbourne University Press
Hey, Nicholas 1923 *A Visit to Mapoon*, Sydney: Presbyterian WMA Sydney
—— 1931 *A Brief History of the Presbyterian Church's Mission Enterprise among the Australian Aborigines*, Sydney: New Press
Hiatt, Lester R. 1984 'Traditional land tenure and contemporary land claims' in L.R. Hiatt (ed.), *Aboriginal Landowners: Contemporary issues in the determination of traditional Aboriginal land ownership*, Oceania Monograph 27, Sydney: University of Sydney, 11–23
Higman, Barry 2002 *Domestic Service in Australia*, Melbourne: Melbourne University Press
Hill, Barry 2002 *Broken Song: T.G.H. Strehlow and Aboriginal possession*, Milsons Point: Random House
Hill, Rosemary, Petina L. Pert, Jocelyn Davies, Catherine J Robinson, Fiona Walsh and Fay Falco-Mammone 2013 *Indigenous Land Management in Australia: Extent, scope, diversity, barriers and success factors*, Cairns: CSIRO Ecosystem Sciences
Hocking, Barbara 1981 'Is might right? An argument for the recognition of traditional Aboriginal title to land in the Australian courts' in E. Olbrei (ed.), *Black Australians: The prospects for change*, Townsville: James Cook University Students Union, 207–22
Hodson, Sally 1993a 'Nyungars and work: Aboriginal experiences in the rural economy of the Great Southern Region of Western Australia', *Aboriginal History* 17(1–2), 73–92
—— 1993b 'Making a rural labour force: the intervention of the state in the working lives of Nyungars in the Great Southern, 1936–1948', *Studies in Western Australian history* XIV, 26–41
Holland, Alison 2001 'The campaign for women protectors: gender, race and frontier between the wars', *Australian Feminist Studies*, 16(34), 27–42
—— 2005 'Saving the race: critics of absorption look for an alternative' in T. Rowse (ed.), *Contesting Assimilation*, Perth: API Network, 85–100
—— 2015 *Just Relations: The story of Mary Bennett's crusade for Aboriginal rights*, Crawley: University of Western Australia Press
Horner, Jack 1974 *Vote Ferguson for Aboriginal Freedom*, Sydney: Australian and New Zealand Book Company
Horton, Jessica 2015 '"Willing to fight to a man": The First World War and Aboriginal activism in the Western District of Victoria', *Aboriginal History* 39, 203–22
Huggins, Jackie and Jo Willmot, Isabel Tarrago, Kathy Willetts, Liz Bond, Lillian Holt, Eleanour Bourke, Maryann Bin-Sallik, Pat Fowell, Joann Schmider, Valerie Craigie, Linda McBride Levi 1991 'Letter to Editors', *Women's Studies International Forum* 14(5), 506–507
Hughes, Robyn 1995 *Australian Biography: Ruby Langford Ginibi* (full interview transcript), <http://www.australianbiography.gov.au/subjects/langford/intertext6.html> (accessed 1 August 2014)
Hunter, Ernest 1993 *Aboriginal Health and History*, Melbourne: Cambridge University Press
Ingamells, Rex 1938 *Conditional Culture*, Adelaide: F.W. Preece
International Labour Organization 2009 *Indigenous & Tribal Peoples' Rights in Practice: A guide to ILO Convention No. 169*, Geneva: International Labour Standards Department
Jack, R. Logan 1920 *Northmost Australia* (vol. 2), London: Simpkin, Marshall, Hamilton, Kent & Co.
Jacobs, Pat 1990 *Mister Neville*, Fremantle: Fremantle Arts Centre Press
Jebb, Mary Anne 1996 'High English for high people' (afterword) in Munro, Morndi, *Emerarra: A man of Merarra* (edited by M.A. Jebb), Broome: Magabala Books, 155–64
—— 2002 *Blood, Sweat and Welfare: A history of white bosses and Aboriginal pastoral workers*, Nedlands: University of Western Australia Press
Jenkin, Graham 1979 *Conquest of the Ngarrindjeri*, Adelaide: Rigby

Johns, Gary 2011 *Aboriginal Self-determination: The whiteman's dream*, Ballan, Vic: Connor Court
Jones, Edith [1933] 'The Australian Aborigine woman: is she a slave?' Rischbieth Papers NLA MS2004/12/Box 31/314
Jones, Frank Lancaster 1970 *The Structure and Growth of Australia's Full-blood Population*, Canberra: Australian National University Press
Jones, Frederic Wood 1934 *Australia's Vanishing Race*, Sydney: Angus & Robertson
Jones, Jennifer 2016 *Country Women and the Colour Bar*, Canberra: Aboriginal Studies Press
Jones, Philip 1990 'Ngapamanha: a case-study in population history' in P. Austin, R.M.W. Dixon, Tom Dutton and Isobel White (eds), *Language and History: Essays in honour of Luise A. Hercus*, Canberra: ANU Linguistics, 157–73
—— 2011 'The art of contact: encountering an aboriginal aesthetic from the eighteenth to the twentieth centuries' in Jaynie Anderson (ed.), *The Cambridge Companion to Australian Art*, Melbourne: Cambridge University Press, 22–37
Jordan, Kirrily 2012 'Closing the employment gap through work for the dole? Indigenous employment and the CDEP scheme', *Journal of Australian Political Economy* 69, 29–58
Kaberry, Phyllis 1935 'The Forrest River and Lyne River Tribes of North-west Australia', *Oceania* 5(4), 408–36
—— 1939 *Aboriginal Woman, Sacred and Profane*, London: Routledge
Kahn, M.W. 1980 'Wife beating and cultural context: prevalence in an Aboriginal and Islander community in northern Australia', *American Journal of Community Psychology* 8(6): 727–31
Kartinyeri, Doreen and Sue Anderson 2008 *Doreen Kartinyeri: My Ngarrindjeri calling*, Canberra: Aboriginal Studies Press
Katona, Jacqui and Chips Mackinolty (eds) 1995 *The Long Road Home* (report of the Going Home Conference, 3–6 October), Darwin: Karu Aboriginal Child Care Agency
Katz, Ilan and Margaret Raven 2013 'Evaluation of the Cape York Welfare Reform trial', *Indigenous Law Bulletin* 8(7), 19–22
Keen, Ian 1980 'The Alligator Rivers Aborigines – retrospect and prospect' in R. Jones (ed.), *Northern Australia: Options and implications*, Canberra: Research School of Pacific Studies, Australian National University, 171–86
—— 1989 'Aboriginal governance' in Jon C. Altman (ed.),) *Emerging Inequalities in Aboriginal Australia*, Oceania Monograph 38, Sydney: University of Sydney, 17–42
—— 2006 'Constraints on the development of enduring inequalities in late Holocene Australia', *Current Anthropology*, 47(1), 7–38
Kennedy, Rosanne and Tikka Jan Wilson 2003 'Constructing shared histories: Stolen Generations testimony, narrative therapy and address' in Jill Bennett and Rosanne Kennedy (eds), *World Memory: Personal trajectories in global time*, New York: Palgrave Macmillan, 119–39
Kenny, Chris 1996 *'It Would Be Nice if There Was Some Women's Business': The story behind the Hindmarsh Island affair*, Sydney: Duffy & Snellgrove
Keon-Cohen, Bryan 2013 *A Mabo Memoir: Islan kustom to native title*, East Malvern: Zemvic Press
Kerin, Rani 2009 'Dogging for a living: Aborigines and "undesirables" in South Australia' in B. Attwood and T. Griffiths (eds), *Frontier, Race, Nation: Henry Reynolds and Australian history*, North Melbourne: Australian Scholarly Publishing, 136–56
—— 2011 *Doctor Do-Good: Charles Duguid and Aboriginal advancement, 1930s–1970s*, North Melbourne: Australian Scholarly Publishing
Kidd, Rosalind 1997 *The Way We Civilise: Aboriginal affairs – the untold story*, St Lucia: University of Queensland Press
—— 2002 'Looking back: a historical overview of policy, legislation and administration relating to Indigenous child separation in Australia', Appendix A in A. Haebich and

D. Mellor (eds), *Many Voices: Reflections on experiences of Indigenous child separation*, Canberra: National Library of Australia, 247–64

Kolig, Erich 1987 *The Noonkanbah Story: Profile of an Aboriginal community in Western Australia*, Dunedin: University of Otago Press

Konishi, Shino 2016 'Bennelong and Gogy: strategic brokers in colonial New South Wales' in Tiffany Shellam, Maria Nugent, Shino Konishi and Allison Cadzow (eds), *Brokers and Boundaries: Colonial exploration in Indigenous territory*, Canberra: Australian National University Press 2016, 15–38

Kruger, Alec and Gerard Waterford 2007 *Alone on the Soaks: The life and times of Alec Kruger*, Alice Springs: IAD Press

Kyle-Little, Syd 1993 *Whispering Wind: Adventures in Arnhem Land*, Bowen Hills: Boolarong Publications

Lahn, Julie 2013 'Aboriginal professionals: work, class and culture', *CAEPR Working Paper* no. 89, Canberra: Australian National University

Lake, Marilyn 1998 'Feminism and the gendered politics of antiracism, Australia 1927–1957: From maternal protectionism to leftist assimilationism', *Australian Historical Studies*, 29, 91–108

Lane, Maria 1997 'Indigenous Australians and the legacy of European conquest: invasion and resurgence' in Elliott Johnston, Martin Hinton and Daryle Rigney (eds), *Indigenous Australians and the Law*, Sydney: Cavendish Publishing, 3–30

—— 1998 'The keys to the kingdom: effective student support mechanisms and mass Indigenous tertiary education success' in Roz Walker, Daphne Elliott, Kathryn Seymour and Gus Worby (eds), *Indigenous Education and the Social Capital: Influences on the performance of Indigenous tertiary students*, Perth: Black Swan Press, 19–30

Lane, Maria and Joe Lane n.d. 'HARD GRIND – The Making of an Urban Indigenous Population', <http://www.firstsources.info/twenty-first-century.html> (accessed 20 February 2017)

Langford, Rosalind F. 1983 'Our heritage – your playground', *Australian Archaeology* 16, 1–6

Langton, Marcia 1981 'Urbanizing Aborigines: the social scientists' great deception' *Social Alternatives* (special issue: Black Alternatives in Australia), 16–22

—— 1997 'Grandmothers' law, company business and succession in changing Aboriginal land tenure systems' in Galarrwuy Yunupingu (ed.), *Our Land Is Our Life: Land rights – past, present and future*, St Lucia: University of Queensland Press, 84–116

—— 2004 'The nations of Australia' in Pierre Boyer, Linda Cardinal and David Headon (eds), *From Subjects to Citizens: A hundred years of citizenship in Australia and Canada*, Ottawa: University of Ottawa Press, 191–209

—— 2013 *The Quiet Revolution: Indigenous people and the resources boom*, Sydney: ABC Books

—— 2014 'Koowarta: a warrior for justice: a brief history of Queensland's racially discriminatory legislation and the Aboriginal litigants who fought it', *Griffith Law Review* 23(1), 16–34

Langton, Marcia and Odette Mazel 2012 'The resource curse compared: Australian Aboriginal participation in the resource extraction industry and distribution of impacts' in Marcia Langton and Judy Longbottom (eds), *Community Futures, Legal Architecture: Foundations for Indigenous peoples in the global mining boom*, London: Routledge, 23–44

Langton, Marcia and Lisa Palmer 2003 'Modern agreement making and Indigenous people in Australia: issues and trends', *Australian Indigenous Law Reporter* 8(1), 1–31

Lapham, Angela 2016 'Stanley Middleton's response to assimilation policy in his fight for Aboriginal people's equality, 1948–62', *Aboriginal History* 40, 27–64

Lewis, Darrell 2012 *A Wild History: Life and death on the Victoria River frontier* Clayton, Vic.: Monash University Publishing

Link-Up (NSW) and Tikka Jan Wilson 1997 *In the Best Interest of the Child? Stolen Children: Aboriginal pain/white shame*, Aboriginal History Monograph 4, Canberra

Lippmann, Lorna 1973 *Words or Blows: Racial attitudes in Australia*, Ringwood: Penguin
Lockyer, Betty 2009 *The Last Truck Out*, Broome: Magabala Books
Lohe, M. 1977 'A mission is established at Hermannsburg' in E. Leske (ed.), *Hermannsburg – A vision and a mission*, Adelaide: Lutheran Publishing House, 6–41
Long, Jeremy P.M. 1966 'The numbers and distribution of Aborigines in Australia' in Ian G. Sharp and Colin M. Tatz (eds), *Aborigines in the economy*, Brisbane: Jacaranda 1966, 1–15
—— 1967 'The administration of the part-Aboriginals of the Northern Territory', *Oceania* 37(3), 186–201
—— 1970 'Change in an Aboriginal community in Central Australia' in A.R. Pilling and R.A. Waterman (eds), *Diprotodon to Detribalisation*, East Lansing: Michigan State University Press, 318–32
—— 1992 *The Go-betweens*, Darwin: North Australia Research Unit
Loos, Noel 1991 'From church to state: the Queensland government take-over of Anglican missions in North Queensland', *Aboriginal History* 15(1–2), 73–85
Loos, Noel and Koiki Mabo 1996 *Edward Koiki Mabo: His life and struggle for land rights*, St Lucia: University of Queensland Press
Love, James R.B. 1915 *The Aborigines: Their present condition as seen in Northern South Australia, the Northern Territory, North-West Australia and Western Queensland*, Melbourne: Arbuckle, Waddell and Fawckner
Loveday, Peter 1989 'Local governance in Aboriginal communities' in Jacquie S. Wolfe, *That Community Government Mob: Local government in small Northern Territory communities*, Darwin: Australian National University North Australia Research Unit, 13–35
Lydon, Jane 2012 *The Flash of Recognition: Photography and the emergence of Indigenous rights*, Sydney: NewSouth Books
Mabo, Eddie 1976 'Perspectives from Torres Strait' in Jim Griffin (ed.), *The Torres Strait Border Issue: Consolidation, conflict or compromise?*, Townsville: Townsville College of Advanced Education, 34–35
—— 1981 'Land rights in the Torres Strait' in Erik Olbrei (ed.), *Black Australians: the prospects for change*, Townsville: Students Union, James Cook University, 143–48
McAllister, Ian and Rhonda Moore, 1991 *Party Strategy and Change: Australian electoral speeches since 1946*, Melbourne: Longman Cheshire
McClure, Margaret 1998 *A Civilised Community: A history of social security in New Zealand 1898–1998*, Auckland: Auckland University Press
McCoy, Brian F 2008 *Holding Men: Kanyirninpa and the health of Aboriginal men*, Canberra: Aboriginal Studies Press
McCrae, Heather, Garth Nettheim, Thalia Anthony, Laura Beecroft, Sean Brennan, Megan Davis and Terri Janke 2009 *Indigenous Legal Issues: Commentary and materials* (4th edn), Sydney: Law Book Company
McGinness, Joe 1991 *Son of Alyandabu: My fight for Aboriginal rights*, St Lucia: University of Queensland Press
McGowan, Angela 1996 'A view from the castle: administering Aboriginal heritage legislation in a changing policy environment', *Tempus* 6, 301–309
McGrath, Ann 1987 *Born in the Cattle*, Sydney: Allen & Unwin
McGregor, Russell 1997 *Imagined Destinies: Aboriginal Australians and the doomed race theory, 1880–1939*, Melbourne: Melbourne University Press
—— 2009 'Another nation: Aboriginal activism in the late 1960s and early 1970s', *Australian Historical Studies* 40(3), 343–60
—— 2011 *Indifferent Inclusion: Aboriginal people and the Australian nation*, Canberra: Aboriginal Studies Press
McGuinness, Bruce 1972 'Black power in Australia' in F.S. Stevens (ed.), *Racism: The Australian experience, Vol. 2 Black versus White*, Sydney: Australia and New Zealand Book Company, 150–56

McIntyre, Greg 1981 'Aboriginal land rights – a definition at common law' in E. Olbrei (ed.), *Black Australians: The prospects for change*, Townsville: James Cook University Students Union, 222–33

McKeich, Robert 1977 'The construction of a part-Aboriginal world' in Ronald M. Berndt (ed.), *Aborigines and Change*, Canberra: Australian Institute of Aboriginal Studies, 252–65

McKenzie, Maisie 1976 *Mission to Arnhem Land*, Adelaide: Rigby

MacKnight, Campbell C. 1976 *The Voyage to Marege: Macassan trepangers in Northern Australia*, Melbourne: Melbourne University Press

McKnight, David 2002 *From Hunting to Drinking: The devastating effects of alcohol on an Australian Aboriginal community*, London and New York: Routledge

Maddock, Kenneth 1992 'Sanctity in Aboriginal landscape: problems of ascertainment and definition in Australia' in Henry Reynolds and Richard Nile (eds), *Indigenous Rights in the Pacific and North America: Race and nation in the late twentieth century*, London; Sir Robert Menzies Centre for Australian Studies, University of London, 111–22

Manning, Corinne 2005 '"If Aborigines are to be assimilated they must learn to live in houses": Victoria's transitional Aboriginal housing policy' in T. Rowse (ed.), *Contesting Assimilation*, Perth: API Network, 221–35

Mansell, Michael 1980 'Tasmania' in N. Peterson (ed.), *Aboriginal Land Rights: A handbook*, Canberra: Australian Institute of Aboriginal Studies 1980, 128–39

Marcus, Julie 2001 *The Indomitable Miss Pink: A life in anthropology*, Kensington: UNSW Press

Markus, Andrew 1990 *Governing Savages*, Sydney: Allen & Unwin

Martin, David 2009 'The governance of agreements between Aboriginal people and resource developers: principles for sustainability' in Jon Altman and David Martin (eds), *Power, Culture and Economy: Indigenous Australians and mining*, Canberra: ANU ePress, 99–126

Martinez, Julia 1997 'Problematising Aboriginal nationalism', *Aboriginal History* 21, 133–47

Mathews, Jane 1996 *Commonwealth Hindmarsh Island Report Pursuant to Section 10(4) of the Aboriginal and Torres Strait Islander Heritage Protection Act 1984*, Canberra: Australian Government Printer

Maushart, Susan 1993 *Sort of a Place Like Home: Remembering the Moore River native settlement*, Fremantle: Fremantle Arts Centre Press

May, Dawn 1994 *Aboriginal Labour and the Cattle Industry: Queensland from white settlement to the present*, Melbourne: Cambridge University Press

Maynard, John 2005 '"In the interests of our people": the influence of Garveyism on the rise of Australian Aboriginal political activism', *Aboriginal history* 29, 1–22

—— 2007 *Fight for Liberty and Freedom: The origins of Australian Aboriginal activism*, Canberra: Aboriginal Studies Press

—— 2015 '"Let us go … it's a 'Blackfellows' War": Aborigines and the Boer War', *Aboriginal History* 39, 143–62

Mazel, Odette 2006 'Returning *Parna Waru*: restitution of the Maralinga lands to traditional owners in South Australia' in Marcia Langton, Odette Mazel, Lisa Palmer, Kathryn Shain and Maureen Tehan (eds), *Settling with Indigenous People*, Annandale: Federation Press, 159–81

Mildren, Dean 2011 *Big Boss Fella: All same judge*, Annandale: Federation Press

Moorcroft, Heather 2015 'Paradigms, paradoxes and a propitious niche: conservation and Indigenous social justice policy in Australia', *Local Environment: The International Journal of Justice and Sustainability* 21(5), 1–26

Morton, Peter 1989 *Fire Across the Desert: Woomera and the Anglo-Australian Joint Project 1946–1980*, Canberra: Australian Government Publishing Service

Muecke, Stephen and Adam Shoemaker 2001 'Introduction: repatriating the story' in David Unaipon, *Legendary Tales of the Australian Aborigines* (edited by S. Muecke and A. Shoemaker), Melbourne: Melbourne University Press, xi–xliii

Muir, Hilda Jarman 2004 *Very Big Journey*, Canberra: Aboriginal Studies Press

Mullins, Steven 1999 'Internal colonialism, communalism, institutionalised racism, progressive reform, clash of administrative cultures, or all of the above: motivations for social control in Torres Strait, 1897–1911', *Electronic Journal of Australian and New Zealand History* 1999, unpaginated (hard copy in AIATSIS Library)

Mulvaney, John 1989 *Encounters in Place: Outsiders and Aboriginal Australians 1606–1985*, St Lucia: University of Queensland Press

——— 2004 *Paddy Cahill of Oenpelli*, Canberra: Aboriginal Studies Press

——— 2011 *Digging Up a Past*, Kensington: University of New South Wales Press

Munro, Morndi 1996 *Emerarra: A man of Merarra* (edited by M.A. Jebb), Broome: Magabala Books

Murphy, Craig 1994 *International Organization and Industrial Change: Global governance since 1850*, Cambridge: Polity

Murphy, John 2011 *A Decent Provision: Australian welfare policy, 1870–1949*, Farnham: Ashgate

——— 2013 'Conditional inclusion: Aborigines and welfare rights in Australia 1900–47', *Australian Historical Studies* 44(2), 206–26

Musharbash, Yasmine 2008 *Yuendumu Everyday: Contemporary life in remote Aboriginal Australia*, Canberra: Aboriginal Studies Press

Nannup, Alice 1992 *When the Pelican Laughed*, Fremantle: Fremantle Arts Centre Press

Neale, Timothy 2016 'Rereading the Wild Rivers Act controversy' in Eve Vincent and Timothy Neale (eds), *Unstable Relations: Indigenous people and environmentalism in contemporary Australia*, Crawley: UWA Publishing, 25–53

Neate, Graeme 2004 'Agreement making and the Native Title Act' in Marcia Langton, Maureen Tehan, Lisa Palmer and Katherine Shain (eds), *Honour Among Nations? Treaties and agreements with Indigenous people*, Melbourne: Melbourne University Press, 176–88

Neill, Rosemary 2002 *White Out: How politics is killing black Australia*, Sydney: Allen & Unwin

Neilson, Mahli 2008 *Hiatus or Catalyst? The impact of the Second World War on Aboriginal activism and assimilation, 1939–1953* (unpublished BA Honours thesis, Australian National University)

Ngaanyatjara Pitjantjatjara Yankunytjatara Women's Council (Aboriginal Corporation) 2012 Submission to Senate Community Affairs Standing Committee on the 'Stronger Futures in the Northern Territory Bill 2011
and two related bills'

Nicholson, Alastair (ed.), 2009 *Will They Be Heard? – A response to the NTER consultation (June– August 2009)*, Boulder, CO.: Indigenous Peoples Issues and Resources

Norman, Heidi 2015 *What Do We Want? A political history of Aboriginal land rights in New South Wales*, Canberra: Aboriginal Studies Press

Nugent, Maria 2012 'An economy of shells: a brief history of La Perouse Aboriginal women's shell-work and its markets, 1880–2010' in N. Fijn, Ian Keen, Chris Lloyd and Michael Pickering (eds), *Indigenous Participation in Australian Economies II: Historical engagements and current enterprises*, Canberra: ANU ePress, 211–27

O'Brien, Anne 2015 'Hunger and the humanitarian frontier', *Aboriginal History* 39, 109–34

Paisley, Fiona 1997 'No back streets in the bush: 1920s and 1930s pro-Aboriginal white women's activism and the Trans-Australia Railway', *Australian Feminist Studies*, 12 (25), 119–34

——— 1998 'Federalising the aborigines? Constitutional reform in the late 1920s', *Australian Historical Studies*, 29(111), 248–66

——— 2000 *Loving Protection? Australian feminism and Aboriginal women's rights*, Melbourne: Melbourne University Press

Palmer, Ian 1988 *Buying Back the Land*, Canberra: Aboriginal Studies Press

Palmer, Kingsley 1990 'Aborigines and Atomic Testing in South Australia', *Aboriginal History* 14(1–2), 197–207

Passi, Dave 1996 'Native title (Mabo) from a grass-roots perspective' in A. Pattel-Grey (ed.), *Martung Upah: Black and White Australians seeking partnership*, Blackburn, Vic.: HarperCollins, 86–91

Paterson, Alistair G. 2008 *Lost Legions: Culture contact in colonial Australia*, Lanham: AltaMira Press

Pearson, Noel 2000 *Our Right to Take Responsibility*, Cairns: Noel Pearson and Associates

—— 2009 *Up from the Mission: Selected writings*, Melbourne: Black Inc.

—— 2011 'Education and aspiration keys to membership of an open society', *Australian*, 23 April

Perez, Eugene 1977 *Kalumburu: The Benedictine Mission and the Aborigines 1908–1975: The history of Kalumburu Mission in north-western Australia*, Kalumburu Benedictine Mission

Peterson, Nicolas 1990 '"Studying man and man's nature": the history of the institutionalisation of Aboriginal anthropology', *Australian Aboriginal Studies* (2/1990), 3–19

Peterson, Nicolas and John Taylor 1998 'Demographic transition in a hunter–gatherer population: the Tiwi case, 1929–1996', *Australian Aboriginal Studies* (1/1998), 11–27

Pholi, Kerryn 2013 'Who are to speak? Silencing Aboriginal dissent' in Rhonda Craven, Anthony Dillon and Nigel Parbury (eds), *In Black & White: Australians all at the cross roads*, Ballan: Connor Court, 57–74

Piddington, Ralph 1933 'Psychological aspects of culture contact', *Oceania* 3(3), 312–24

Pohlner, Howard J 1986 *Gangurru*, Milton, Qld: Hope Vale Mission Board

Porteus, Stanley D 1969 *A psychologist of Sorts*, Palo Alto: Pacific Books

Powell, Robert (ed.) [1933] *The First Ten Years of Mt Margaret Mission WA*, Melbourne: Keswick Book Depot

Price, Jacinta Nampijinpa 2017 'Response to *The Australian dream*' in *Quarterly Essay* no. 65, Carlton: Schwartz Publishing, 103–105

Pryles, Lisa 2002 '"By the ABORIGINAL people": A history of the Northern Territory Council for Aboriginal Rights, 1961–1967' (unpublished Honours thesis, School of Historical Studies, Monash University)

Purtill, Tadhgh 2017 *The Dystopia in the Desert: The silent culture of Australia's remotest Aboriginal communities*, North Melbourne: Australian Scholarly Publishing

Pyne, Anthony 2012 'Ten proposals to reduce Indigenous over-representation in Northern Territory prisons', *Australian Indigenous Law Review* 16(2), 2–17

Radcliffe-Brown, Alfred 1977 *The Social Anthropology of Radcliffe-Brown* (edited by Adam Kuper), London: Routledge & Kegan Paul

Radford, Robin 1992 'Aspects of the social history of Hermannsburg' in J. Hardy, J.V.S. Megaw and M. Ruth Megaw (eds), *The Heritage of Namatjira: The watercolourists of Central Australia*, Port Melbourne: William Heinemann Australia, 63–96

Raftery, Judith 2006 *Not Part of the Public: Non-indigenous policies and practices and the health of indigenous South Australians 1836–1973*, Kent Town, SA: Wakefield Press

Raible, Reverend Otto 1938 'The Aborigines' in M.E. Dasey (ed.), *The Story of the Regional Missionary and Eucharistic Congress, Newcastle, NSW, Australia, 16–20th February 1938*, Newcastle (NSW): Specialty Publications and Sales Promotion Company, 272–76

Raynes, Cameron 2009 *The Last Protector: The illegal removal of Aboriginal children from their parents in South Australia*, Kent Town, SA: Wakefield Press

Read, Peter 1981 *The Stolen Generations: The removal of Aboriginal children in New South Wales 1833–1969*, Sydney: Government Printer

—— 1988 *A Hundred Years War: The Wiradjuri people and the state*, Canberra: Australian National University Press

—— 1990 'Cheeky, insolent and anti-white: the split in the Federal Council for the Advancement of Aboriginal and Torres Strait Islanders – Easter 1970', *Australian Journal of Politics and History* 36(1), 73–83

Reconciliation Australia 2012 *Australian Reconciliation Barometer 2012*, Sydney: Reconciliation Australia

Redmond, Anthony 2005 'Strange relatives: mutualities and dependencies between Aborigines and pastoralists in the northern Kimberley', *Oceania* 75(3), 234–46

——— 2012 'Tracking *wurnan*: transformations in the trade and exchange of resources in the northern Kimberley' in N. Fijn, I. Keen, C. Lloyd and M. Pickering (eds), *Indigenous Participation in Australian Economies II: Historical engagements and current enterprises*, Canberra, ANU Press, 57–72

Reeves, John 1998 *Building on Land Rights for the Next Generation: Report of the Review of the Aboriginal Land Rights (Northern Territory) Act 1976*, Canberra: Australian Government Publishing Service

Richards, Jonathan 2008 *The Secret War: A true history of Queensland's native police*, St Lucia: University of Queensland Press

Richards, Michaela 1985 'An Australian frontier … Aborigines and settlers at the Daly River 1912–1940' in J. Gleeson and M. Richards, *Mataranka and the Daly: Two studies in the history of settlement in the Northern Territory*, Darwin: NARU Monograph, 35–69

Riseman, Noah 2013 *Defending Whose Country? Indigenous soldiers in the Pacific war*, Lincoln: University of Nebraska Press

Roberts, Jan 1981 *Massacres to Mining: The colonisation of Aboriginal Australia*, Blackburn, Vic: Dove Communications

Robinson, Shirleene 2013 'Regulating the race: Aboriginal children in private European homes in colonial Australia', *Journal of Australian Studies* 37(3), 302–15

Roe, Michael 1986 'A model Aboriginal state', *Aboriginal History* 10(1), 40–44

Rose, Deborah Bird 1996 'Histories and rituals: land claims in the Territory' in Bain Attwood (ed.), *In the Age of Mabo: History, Aborigines and Australia*, Sydney: Allen & Unwin, 35–53

Ross, Tess and others 2012 Submission to Senate Community Affairs Standing Committee on behalf of 'Warlpiri people of Yuendumu' on the 'Stronger Futures in the Northern Territory Bill 2011 and two related bills'

Roughsey, Dick 1971 *Moon and Rainbow: The autobiography of an Aboriginal, Dick Roughsey*, Adelaide: Rigby International

Rowley, Charles D. 1970a *The Destruction of Aboriginal Society*, Canberra: Australian National University Press

——— 1970b *Outcasts in White Australia*, Canberra: Australian National University Press

——— 1978 *A Matter of Justice*, Canberra: Australian National University

——— 1979 'Aboriginal policy 1978', *Australian Labor Party National Committee of Inquiry – Discussion papers*, Bedford Park, SA: Australasian Political Studies Association, 102–27

——— 1980 'Aboriginal Land Fund Commission' in N. Peterson (ed.), *Aboriginal Land Rights: A handbook*, Canberra: Australian Institute of Aboriginal Studies, 254–66

Rowse, Tim 1987 '"Were you ever savages?" Aboriginal insiders and pastoralists' patronage' *Oceania* 58(2), 81–99

——— 1988 'Paternalism's changing reputation', *Mankind* 18(2), 57–73

——— 1998 *White Flour, White Power: From rations to citizenship in Central Australia*, Melbourne: Cambridge University Press

——— 2000a 'Housing and colonial patronage, Alice Springs, 1920–65' in P. Read (ed.), *Settlement: A history of Australian Indigenous housing*, Canberra: Aboriginal Studies Press, 85–98

——— 2000b 'Hindmarsh revisited' *Oceania* 70(3), 252–62

——— 2000c *Obliged to Be Difficult: Nugget Coombs' legacy in Indigenous affairs*, Melbourne: Cambridge University Press

——— 2002 *Indigenous Futures: Choice and development for Aboriginal and Islander Australia*, Kensington: University of New South Wales Press

——— 2006 'The public occasions of Indigenous selves: three Ngarrindjeri autobiographies', *Aboriginal History* 30, 187–207

―――― 2010 'Knowing and not knowing: the Ngarrindjeri dilemma', *Life Writing* 7(3), 245–58
―――― 2011 'Global indigenism: a genealogy of a non-racial category' in A. Holland and B. Brookes (eds), *Rethinking the Racial Moment: Essays on the Colonial Encounter*, Newcastle upon Tyne: Cambridge Scholars Publishing, 229–53
Rowse, Tim and Leonard Smith 2010 'The limits of "elimination" in the politics of population', *Australian Historical Studies* 41(1), 90–106
Rowse, Tim and Elizabeth Watt 2017 '"The North" – colonial hegemony and Indigenous stratification' in Jenny Gregory, Lenore Layman and Stuart Macintyre (eds), *A Historian for All Seasons: Essays for Geoffrey Bolton*, Clayton: Monash University Publishing, 204–35
Ryan, Lyndall 1996 *The Aboriginal Tasmanians* (2nd edn), Sydney: Allen & Unwin
Saethre, Eirik 2013 *Illness Is a Weapon: Indigenous identity and enduring afflictions*, Nashville: Vanderbilt University Press
Sam, Maryanne 1991 *Through Black Eyes: A handbook of family violence in Aboriginal and Torres Strait Islander Communities*, Fitzroy, Vic.: SNAICC
Sanders, William 1982 'From self-determination to self-management' in P. Loveday (ed.), *Service Delivery to Remote Communities*, Darwin: Australian National University North Australia Research Unit, 4–10
―――― 1985 'The politics of unemployment benefits for Aborigines: some consequences of economic marginalisation' in Deborah Wade-Marshall and Peter Loveday (eds), *Employment and Unemployment: A collection of papers*, Darwin: North Australia Research Centre Monograph, 137–62
Sarra, Chris 2014 *Good Morning, Mr Sarra*, St Lucia: University of Queensland Press
Scarlett, Phillipa 2015 'Aboriginal service in the First World War: identity, recognition and the problem of mateship', *Aboriginal History* 39, 163–82
Schapper, Henry P. 1969 'Present needs of Aborigines' in D.E. Hutchison, *Aboriginal Progress: A new era?*, Nedlands: University of Western Australia Press, 143–75
―――― 1970 *Aboriginal Advancement to Integration: Conditions and plans for Western Australia*, Canberra: Australian National University Press
Schwartz, Michelle 2008 *A Question of Power: The Geoff Clark case*, Melbourne: Black Inc.
Seaman, Paul 1984a 'Discussion paper' (issued by the office of Paul Seaman), AIATSIS Library
―――― 1984b *The Aboriginal Land Inquiry* (report by Paul Seaman QC, September 1984), AIATSIS Library
Seccombe, Mike 2015 'Ayers and Disgraces', *Saturday Paper*, August 1–7, 10–11
Secretariat of National Aboriginal and Islander Child Care (SNAICC) 1995 *Our Children, Our Culture, in Our Hands*, Fitzroy, Vic.
―――― 1996 *Proposed Plan of Action for the Prevention of Child Abuse and Neglect in Aboriginal Communities*, Canberra: Department of Health and Family Services
Sharp, Ian and Colin M. Tatz (eds) 1966 *Aborigines in the Economy*, Brisbane: Jacaranda Press
Shnukal, Anna 2002 '"All cross blood": demography and Darnley Islanders 1870s–1928' in Gordon Briscoe and Len Smith (eds), *The Aboriginal Population Revisited: 70 000 years to the present*, Aboriginal History Monograph 10, Canberra: Aboriginal History Inc., 50–80
Short, Damien 2008 *Reconciliation and Colonial Power: Indigenous rights in Australia*, Aldershot: Ashgate
Skyring, Fiona 2012 'Low wages, low rents and pension cheques: the introduction of equal wages in the Kimberley, 1968–69' in Natasha Fijn, Ian Keen, Christopher Lloyd and Michael Pickering (eds), *Indigenous Participation in Australian Economies II: Historical and anthropological perspectives*, Canberra: ANU ePress, 153–70
Simons, Margaret 2003 *The Meeting of the Waters: The Hindmarsh Island affair*, Sydney: Hodder
Simpson, Colin 1951 *Adam in Ochre*, Sydney: Angus & Robertson
Smith, Leonard, Janet McCalman, Ian Anderson, S. Smith, Julie Evans, Gavan McCarthy and J. Beer 2008 'Fractional identities: the political arithmetic of Aboriginal Victorians', *Journal of Interdisciplinary History* 38(4), 533–55

Smith, Tony 2002 'Indigenous accumulation in the Territory in the early years of "self-determination" 1968–75', *Australian Economic History Review* 42(1), 1–33
—— 2006 'Welfare, enterprise, and Aboriginal Community: the case of the Western Australian Kimberley region 1968–96', *Australian Economic History Review* 46(3), 242–67
Spate, Oscar H.K. 1968 *Australia*, London: Ernest Benn Ltd
Spencer, W. Baldwin and F.J. Gillen 1899 *The Native Tribes of Central Australia*, London: Macmillan
—— 1904 *The Northern Tribes of Central Australia*, London: Macmillan
Stanner, William E.H. 1969 *After the Dreaming*, Sydney: Australian Broadcasting Commission
—— 2009 *The Dreaming and Other Essays*, Collingwood, Vic.: Black Inc.
Stevens, Christine 1994 *White Man's Dreaming: Killalpaninna Mission 1866–1915*, Melbourne: Oxford University Press
Stevens, Frank 1974 *Aborigines in the Northern Territory Cattle Industry*, Canberra Australian National University Press
Stirling, Edward C. 1914 'Aborigines' in D.J. Gordon and E.J. Ryan (eds), *Handbook of South Australia*, Adelaide: Government Printer, 281–98
Stokes, Geoffrey 1987 'Special interests or equality – the mining industries campaign against Aboriginal land rights in Australia', *Australia-Canadian Studies* 5(1), 61–78
—— 2002 'Australian democracy and Indigenous self-determination, 1901–2001' in Geoffrey Brennan and Frank Castles (eds), *Australia Reshaped: 200 years of institutional transformation*, Melbourne: Cambridge University Press, 181–209
Stone, Sharman (ed.) 1974 *Aborigines in White Australia*, Melbourne: Heinemann Educational Books
Strakosch, Elizabeth 2015 *Neo-liberal Indigenous Policy: Settler colonialism and the 'post-welfare' state*, Basingstoke: Palgrave Macmillan
Strehlow, Theodor G.H. 1936 'Notes on native evidence and its value', *Oceania* 6(3), 323–35
Sutton, Peter 1998 *Native Title and the Descent of Rights*, Perth: National Native Title Tribunal
—— 2009 'Australian anthropologists and political action 1925–1960', *Oceania* 79(2), 202–18
Taffe, Sue 2005 *Black and White Together*, St Lucia: University of Queensland Press
Taft, Ronald 1970 'Attitudes of Western Australians towards Aborigines' in R. Taft, J.L.M. Dawson and P. Beasley, *Attitudes and Social Conditions*, Canberra: Australian National University Press, 1–72
Tasmanian Aboriginal Land Council 1996 'Will you take the next step?', *Tempus* 6, 293–99
Tatz, Colin M. 1990 'Aboriginal violence: a return to pessimism', *Australian Journal of Social Issues* 25(4), 245–60
—— 2012 'Genocide in Australia: by accident or design?' *Indigenous Rights and History: Occasional Papers*, Clayton, Vic.: Monash University
Taylor, John 2012 'Measuring Indigenous outcomes from mining agreements in Australia' in Marcia Langton and Judy Longbottom (eds), *Community Futures, Legal Architecture: Foundations for Indigenous peoples in the global mining boom*, London: Routledge, 59–75
Taylor, Louise 2003 '"Who's your mob?" – the politics of Aboriginal identity and the implications for a treaty' in *Treaty – let's get it right!* (no editor), Canberra: Aboriginal Studies Press, 88–99
Terrill, Leon 2015 *Beyond Communal and Individual Ownership: Indigenous land reform in Australia*, Abingdon: Routledge
Thomson, Donald 1931 'In camp with the stone-age men', *Queenslander*, 22 January
—— 1947 *The Aborigines and the Rocket Range*, Melbourne: Rocket Range Protest Committee, AIATSIS Library
—— 1983 *Donald Thomson in Arnhem Land* (edited by Nicolas Peterson), South Yarra: Currey O'Neil

Thomson, Neil 1991 'A review of Aboriginal health status' in Janice Reid and Peggy Trompf (eds), *The Health of Aboriginal Australia*, Marrickville: Harcourt, Brace, Jovanovich, 37–79

Tindale, Norman B. 1940–41 'Survey of the half-caste problem in South Australia', *Proceedings of the Royal Geographical Society of Australasia (South Australian branch)*, XII, 66–161

Tomasetti, W.E. 1967 *Our People of Australia League*, pamphlet held by National Library of Australia, dated 8 May 1967, unpaginated

Tonkinson, Robert 1993 'Introduction' to R.M. Berndt and C.H. Berndt with John E. Stanton, *A word that Was: The Yaraldi of the Murray River and the Lakes, South Australia*, Melbourne: Melbourne University Press at the Miegunyah Press, xvii–xxi

Torres, Dom Fulgentius 1987 *The Torres Diaries 1901–1914: Diaries of Dom Fulgentius (Anthony) Torres y Mayans, O.S.B. Abbot Nullius of New Norcia, Bishop Titular of Dorylaeum, Administrator Apostolic of the Kimberley Vicariate in North Western Australia* (edited by Rosemary Pratt, John Millington), Perth: Artlook Books

Trebeck, Kathy 2009 'Corporate responsibility and social sustainability: is there any connection?' in Jon Altman and David Martin (eds), *Power, Culture and Economy: Indigenous Australians and mining*, Canberra: ANU ePress, 127–47

Unaipon, David 2001 *Legendary Tales of the Australian Aborigines* (edited by Stephen Muecke and Adam Shoemaker), Melbourne: Melbourne University Press

Urry, James and Michael Walsh 1991 'The lost "Macassar language" of Northern Australia', *Aboriginal History* 5, 91–108

Van den Berg, Rosemary 1994 *No Options, No Choice: The Moore River experience*, Broome: Magabala Books

Walden, Inara 1995 '"That was slavery days": Aboriginal domestic servants in New South Wales in the twentieth century', *Labor History* no. 69, November, 196–209

Walker, Kath 1966a 'Discussion of Mr Long's Paper' in I.G. Sharp and C.M. Tatz (eds), *Aborigines in the Economy*, Brisbane: Jacaranda Press, 13

—— 1966b 'Discussion of papers by Bishop O'Loughlin and Rev. Albrecht' in I.G. Sharp and C.M. Tatz (eds), *Aborigines in the Economy*, Brisbane: Jacaranda Press, 184–87

—— 1966c *The Dawn Is at Hand*, Brisbane: Jacaranda Press

—— 1970a 'Aboriginals: the smell of frustration', *Politics* 5(1), 89–93

—— 1970b *My People*, Brisbane: The Jacaranda Press

Walter, Father Georg [1928] 1982 *Australia: Land mission people*, Pallottine Society Limburg, 1928 (all references to the 1982 edition, translated by Inge Danaher, published by Lahn-Verlag, Limburn)

Weatherburn, Don 2014 *Arresting Incarceration: Pathways out of Indigenous imprisonment*, Canberra: Aboriginal Studies Press

Webb, Thomas T. 1934 *The Aborigines of East Arnhem Land, North Australia*, Melbourne: Methodist Laymen's Missionary Movement

—— 1938 *Spears to Spades*, Sydney: Department of Overseas Missions

—— n.d. *Aboriginals and Adventure in Arnhem Land* (typescript, AIATSIS Library)

Wells, Ann E. 1963 *Milingimbi*, Sydney: Angus & Robertson

Wells, Edgar 1972 'The missions and race prejudice' in Frank S. Stevens (ed.), *Racism: The Australian experience* (vol. 2), Sydney: Australia and New Zealand Book Company, 243–249

—— 1982 *Reward and Punishment in Arnhem Land 1962–1963*, Canberra: Australian Institute of Aboriginal Studies

Wentworth, William C. 1969 'The role of the Commonwealth' in D.E. Hutchison (ed.), *Aboriginal Progress: A new era?*, Nedlands: University of Western Australia Press, 176–89

West, Ida 1984 *Pride against Prejudice: Reminiscences of a Tasmanian Aborigine*, Canberra: Australian Institute of Aboriginal Studies

Western, John 1969 'The Australian Aborigine: what white Australians know and think about him', *Race*, 10(4), 411–34

—— 1973 'The attitudes of white Australians to Australian Aborigines – some survey results' in Donald Tugby (ed.), *Aboriginal Identity in Contemporary Australian Society*, Brisbane: Jacaranda Press, 53–74

Williams, Magdalene 1999 *Ngay Janijirr Ngank: This is my word*, Broome: Magabala Books

Wilson, Bill and J. O'Brien 2003 '"To infuse an [sic] universal terror": a reappraisal of the Coniston killings', *Aboriginal History* 27, 59–78

Wilson, Dulcie 1998 *The Cost of Crossing Bridges*, Mitcham, Vic.: Small Poppies Publishing

Wilson, John 1961 'Authority and leadership in a "new-style" Australian Aboriginal community: Pindan, Western Australia' (unpublished MA thesis, University of Western Australia)

—— 1980 'The Pilbara Aboriginal social movement: an outline of its background and significance' in R.M. Berndt and C.H. Berndt (eds), *Aborigines of the West: Their past and present*, Nedlands: University of Western Australia Press, 151–68

Wise, Tigger 1985 *The Self-made Anthropologist: A life of A.P. Elkin*, Sydney: George Allen & Unwin

Worms, Ernest A 1970 'Observations on the mission field of the Pallottine Fathers in north-west Australia' in A.R. Pilling and R.A. Waterman (eds), *Diprotodon to Detribalization: Studies of change among Australian Aborigines*, East Lansing: Michigan State University Press, 367–79

Wright, Tom 1939 *New Deal for Aborigines*, Sydney: Modern Publishers

—— 1944 *New Deal for Aborigines* (2nd edn), Sydney: Modern Publishers

Young, Diana 2010 'Dingo scalping and the frontier economy in the north-west of South Australia' in I. Keen (ed.), *Indigenous Participation in Australian Economies II: Historical and anthropological perspectives*, Canberra: ANU ePress, 91–108

Yunupingu, Galarrwuy 1997 'From the bark petition to Native Title' in G. Yunupingu (ed.), *Our Land is Our Life*, St Lucia: University of Queensland Press, 1–17

Notes

Introduction
1 Deakin 1968, 147
2 Barwick 1998, 299–300
3 Barwick 1998, 235
4 *Commonwealth Franchise Act* 1902, s. 4
5 Deakin 1968, 147
6 Deakin 1968, 147
7 Deakin 1968, 148
8 Deakin 1968, 149
9 Reconciliation Australia 2012, 53
10 Stanner 1969, 25
11 Bolton 1989
12 Bolton 1989, 193
13 Spate 1968, 153
14 CPD (HoR), 12 October 1910, p. 4426
15 CPD (HoR), 12 October 1910, p. 4427
16 Stokes 2002 has framed Australia's colonial history in continental terms similar to mine, though our accounts differ in many ways.
17 Keen 1989, Keen 2006
18 Keen 2006, 17
19 Bent et al. 2004, 93 (translation Eirlys Richards)
20 Clendinnen 2003, 150–51. And see Konishi 2016, 24.
21 Finnane 2011, 246–48
22 Finnane and Kaldelfos 2016, 453, 459. Western Australia may be the only Australian jurisdiction in which so much effort was put into criminalising Aboriginal violence *inter se* (see 452).
23 Kyle-Little 1993, 123
24 Kyle-Little 1993, 123
25 Kyle-Little 1993, 164
26 Law Reform Commission 1986, p 25
27 Biddle 2013b, 1
28 Anderson and Wild 2007, 74

1 Missions and the state in North Australia
1 Donovan 1984, 3
2 Meston 1896; Roth 1904; W.B. Spencer 1913
3 Torres y Mayans, 1987 (entry for 15 June 1908), 120
4 These details are drawn from Western Australia's *Annual Report of the Commissioner of Native Affairs for the Year Ended 30 June 1938*
5 *Annual Report of the Chief Protector of Aboriginals for the Year 1914*, Brisbane: Government Printer, 1915, 10–11
6 *SA Royal Commission*, 1913, p. viii. The Royal Commission did not report on the remote northern regions of the state. Herbert Basedow (Basedow 1921) presented a bleak account of Aboriginal health in the north-east around 1920.
7 Stirling 1914, 281
8 Anderson 1983
9 Chase (1988, 136) discerns a 'third complex, dating from the 1960s' – 'the direct bureaucratic control by the state government with the church formally powerless in the missions'
10 Quoted in Harris 1998, 209
11 Walter [1928] 1982, 157

12 Webb n.d., 276
13 May 1994, 136–37. And see Ganter 1999 on the ideologies guiding the formation of missions in Cape York.
14 A story collected by Jean Devanny and cited in May 1994, 139
15 Jack 1920, 679
16 Beckett 1987, 40
17 Beckett 1977, 86; Beckett 1987, 49–50
18 Edwards 1999, 23, and see Hey 1931, 11–12
19 Hey 1931, 10
20 Quoted in Chase 1988, 126
21 Choo 2001, 56
22 Durack 1969, 39–41
23 Williams 1999
24 Mulvaney 2004, 12
25 Spencer quoted by Frawley 2003, 57
26 Gsell 1956, 47–48
27 Gsell 1956, 41–42
28 I draw on Frawley 2003.
29 Keen 1980
30 Spencer 1913, 19, 26
31 For more on the historical demography of this region see Keen 1980.
32 MacKnight 1976; Urry and Walsh 1981
33 Lewis 2012, 85–122
34 How to characterise the agency of Aborigines in this time of dependency and opportunity is the theme of Richards 1985, 35–69. Stanner evoked the region's disorder in his 'Durmugam, a Nangiomeri' in Stanner 2009, 19–57.
35 Lohe 1977, 6–41, 17
36 Stevens 1994, 140
37 Jones 1990
38 Kerin 2009; Young 2010, 91–108
39 Schenk diary excerpt, in Powell ed. [1933], 37
40 Edwards 2012; Kerin 2011, 50–51
41 Ganter 1999 emphasises missionaries' concerns about Cape York Aborigines' sexuality.
42 Raible 1938, 275
43 Gsell 1956, 69
44 Gsell 1956, 69
45 Walter 1982, 24
46 Perez 1977, 27
47 Perez 1977, 31
48 Perez 1977, 33
49 Stevens 1994, 231–32, 241
50 Cole 1980, 12
51 Arrowsmith n.d., 41
52 Perez 1977, 51
53 Webb n.d., 244
54 O'Brien 2015
55 Albrecht 1977, 46
56 Gordon 2004, 197–98
57 Falkenberg 1962, 18; Gordon 2004, 194
58 McKenzie 1976, 81
59 Arrowsmith n.d., 41
60 Williams 1999, 85
61 Webb 1934, 31
62 Webb 1934, 37
63 Webb 1938, 59
64 Webb n.d., 155
65 Webb n.d., 156
66 Hey 1923, 12, 19
67 Hey 1923, 27
68 Hey 1923, 29
69 Hey 1923, 29
70 Pohlner 1986, 104–105
71 Chase 1988, 131
72 Beckett 1987, 39
73 Beckett 1987, 43
74 Beckett 1987, 47
75 Beckett 1987, 48
76 Raible 1938, 274
77 Webb n.d., 163
78 May 1994, 138, 143
79 Walter 1982, 200
80 Durack 1969, 210–11
81 Walter 1982, 203
82 Durack 1969, 212
83 Walter 1982, 174
84 Beckett 1977, 83
85 Beckett 1987, 53
86 Beckett 1987, 53
87 Wise 1985, 130
88 Cole 1980, 61
89 Kaberry 1939, 88
90 Kaberry 1939, 272
91 Kaberry 1939, 108
92 Webb 1938, 66
93 Webb 1938, 27

94 Webb n.d., 68
95 Webb 1938, 32
96 Love 1915, 49
97 Love 1915, 49
98 Beckett 1987, 43–44, 119
99 Pohlner 1986, 72–73
100 Pohlner 1986, 72–73
101 Hey 1923, 22–23
102 Dalley and Memmott 2010, 120–22
103 Harris 1998, 330
104 Gsell 1956, 75
105 Gordon 2004, 148
106 Gordon 2002, 20
107 Falkenberg 1962, 178–79
108 Choo 2001, 103
109 Choo 2001, 86
110 Lohe 1977, 30
111 Radford 1992, 80–81
112 Neville's comments in Smith [1933], 15
113 Crawford 1978, 45
114 Choo 2001, 221
115 Williams 1999, 77
116 Raible 1938, 278
117 Lockyer 2009, 53
118 Dussart 2000
119 Gordon 2004, 189

2 Knowing and ruling Northern Aborigines

1 Thomson 1931, 4
2 Elkin 1938a, 149
3 Elkin 1934a, 16
4 Elkin 1944, 22–23
5 Peterson 1990, 5
6 The words of a 1921 resolution from the Australian Association for the Advancement of Science, quoted in Peterson 1990, 7
7 Elkin 1938b
8 Elkin 1938a, 150
9 Elkin 1938a, 149–50
10 Elkin 1938a, 151
11 Elkin 1938a, 152
12 Elkin 1934b, 3
13 Quoted by Choo 2001, 197
14 Webb n.d., 67
15 Webb n.d., 90
16 Webb 1934, 35
17 Smith [1933], 45
18 Cole 1980, 16
19 Kaberry 1935, 420
20 Kaberry 1935, 434
21 Kaberry 1935, 411
22 Kaberry 1935, 422–23
23 Kaberry 1935, 417
24 Cole 1980, 22
25 *The World*, 14 January 1932, quoted in Gray 1994, 222
26 Piddington 1933, 320
27 Piddington 1933, 319
28 Piddington 1933, 319–20
29 Piddington 1933, 324
30 Green 1995, 117
31 Green 1995, 120
32 Green 1995, 123
33 Green 1995, 226
34 Henson 1992, 29
35 Hartwig 1960, 10
36 Albrecht quoted in Henson 1992, 26
37 Wilson and O'Brien 2003, 71
38 Hartwig 1960, 35–36
39 Hartwig 1960, 34
40 Hartwig 1960, 38
41 Hartwig 1960, 40–41
42 The findings are reprinted in Cribbin 1984, 155
43 Hartwig 1960, 47–50; Markus 1990, 68
44 Hartwig 1960, 50
45 Anonymous 1929, *Finding*, 38
46 Anonymous 1929, *Finding*, 22
47 Anonymous 1929, *Finding*, 22
48 Anonymous 1929, *Finding*, 23
49 Anonymous 1929, *Finding*, 27
50 Anonymous 1929, *Finding*, 36–37
51 Anonymous 1929, *Finding*, 21
52 Anonymous 1929, *Finding*, 38
53 Anonymous 1929, *Finding*, 38
54 Anonymous 1929, *Finding*, 31, 33, 34
55 Anonymous 1929, *Finding*, 26
56 Anonymous 1929, *Finding*, 27
57 Anonymous 1929, *Finding*, 36
58 The letter is among Elkin's papers, reproduced in Bishop 1991, 233.
59 Bishop 1991, 233
60 Hartwig 1960, 79
61 *Finding* 1929, 28
62 The CMS Committee resolution is quoted in Harris 1998, 235.

63 I follow the account, based on CMS archives, in Harris 1998, 237.
64 Quoted in Harris 1998, 250
65 Quoted in Egan 1996, 151
66 See Mildren 2011, 111–12
67 Webb n.d., 248
68 Webb n.d., 274
69 Strehlow 1936 is a published version of his advice.
70 Markus 1990, 137–38
71 Enquiry recommendations quoted by Hill 2002, 235
72 Strehlow, letter to Secretary, Department of Interior, 17 October 1936 F1/38/636, Australian Archives, NT Branch

3 Governments, churches, parents, spouses and children, 1897–1940

1 Rowley 1970b, 219
2 Rowley 1978, 113
3 *Yearbook Australia* no. 17 (1924), 957
4 Harman 2013, 760
5 The *Aboriginals Protection and Restriction of the Sale of Opium Acts Amendment Act* 1934 (Qld); the *Aboriginals Ordinance* 1936 (NT) criminalised miscegenation.
6 *Aborigines Act Amendment Act* 1936 (WA); *Aborigines Act Amendment Act* 1939 (SA)
7 Stirling 1914, 289, emphasis added
8 Goodall 1996, 119
9 Read 1988, 48
10 Fletcher 1989a, 83
11 'The Aboriginal school syllabus, 1916' in Jim Fletcher, ed., 1989b, 119–21
12 Fletcher gives examples of Aboriginal parents' protests between 1902 and 1946 against the exclusion of their children (1989a, 76, 112–13, 115, 119, 121–22, 127, 132, 142–43, 150, 168, 221, 227).
13 New South Wales Parliamentary Debates (NSWPD), 27 January 1915, p. 1951
14 NSWPD, 27 January 1915, p. 1951
15 NSWPD, 27 January 1915, p. 1953
16 NSWPD, 27 January 1915, p. 1953
17 NSWPD, 27 January 1915, p. 1957
18 NSWPD, 27 January 1915, p. 1957
19 NSWPD, 27 January 1915, p. 1958
20 NSWPD, 27 January 1915, p. 1958
21 NSWPD, 27 January 1915, p. 1958
22 NSWPD, 27 January 1915, p.1965. A member of the APB itself, Mr Scobie (Murray), objected that the board had enough power: a better funded board could support Aborigines without severing children from parents.
23 NSWPD, 27 January 1915, pp. 1965–67
24 Raynes 2009, 5–14
25 Haebich 2000, 179–81
26 Broome 2005, 134–36
27 Broome 2005, 192
28 Haebich 2000, 167–68
29 Blake 1998, 52
30 Evans 1999, 86–87
31 Dalley and Memmott (2010, 118) recommend that we distinguish removal from separation.
32 Haebich 2000, 174–75
33 Blake 2001, 57–67
34 Hegarty 1999, 26
35 Hegarty 1999, 31–32
36 Hegarty 1999, 75
37 Haebich 2000, 227
38 Roth 1904, 8–9, 16–18, 23–24, 25
39 Roth 1904, 25
40 Haebich 2000, 237–38
41 Haebich 2000, 243
42 Haebich 2000, 233, 235, 237, 239
43 Haebich 2000, 249
44 Van den Berg 1994, 106
45 Van den Berg 1994, 109
46 Van den Berg 1994, 155
47 For the 'total institution' argument see Haebich 1988, 199–21. Nannup 1992 and Maushart 1993 tell stories about residents' survival tactics and room for manoeuvre.
48 Spencer 1913, 27
49 Markus 1990, 22–37; HREOC 1997, Chapter 9; Austin 1993
50 South Australian Royal Commission, Minutes of Evidence (SARCMoE) 1913, paragraph 599
51 SARCMoE 1913, paragraph 605

52 SARCMoE 1913, paragraph 679
53 SARCMoE 1913, paragraph 695
54 SARCMoE 1913, paragraphs 715–17
55 SARCMoE 1913, 36
56 SARCMoE 1913, 37
57 Haebich 2000, 317
58 QPD, 26 September 1899, p. 118 The home secretary denied that the amendment was directed at 'Asiatic aliens who are really among the very best employers that can be found of the main land aboriginals ... there are scoundrels belonging to every race' (p. 117). For a contrary view, see Ganter 1998.
59 QPD, 3 September 1901, p. 613
60 Roth 1904, 41
61 Western Australia Parliamentary Debates (WAPD) (new series), 13 December 1905, p. 427
62 WAPD (new series), 13 December 1905, p. 432
63 South Australia Parliamentary Debates (SAPD), 13 December 1910, p. 727
64 SAPD, 13 October 1910, p. 728
65 SAPD, 13 October 1910, p. 728
66 SAPD, 13 October 1910, p. 728
67 SAPD, 9 November 1910, p. 956
68 SAPD 13 October 1910, p. 728
69 Hannah 2005
70 Spencer 1913, 17
71 Spencer 1913, 17
72 Spencer 1913, 17
73 Spencer 1913, 21
74 Spencer 1913, 21, and see Austin 1997, 40
75 Bleakley 1929, 28
76 Bleakley 1929, 28
77 Bleakley 1929, 28
78 *Annual Report of the Northern Territory Administration for 1937–38*, 24
79 Haebich 1988, 117
80 Haebich 1988, 117
81 Biskup 1973, 135–39
82 Jacobs 1990, 82–83
83 WAPD (new series), 11 December 1929, p. 2101
84 WAPD (new series), 11 December 1929, p. 2102
85 WAPD (new series), 11 December 1929, pp. 2103–2104
86 WAPD (new series), 11 December 1929, p. 2107
87 Hodson 1993a
88 Hodson 1993a, 75
89 WAPD (new series), 10 December 1929, p. 2059
90 WAPD (new series), 12 December 1929, p. 2168
91 WAPD (new series), 3 December 1929, p. 1904
92 A point made about Roth's report by Bolton 1981, 131
93 Moseley Transcript, 650
94 Moseley Transcript, 13
95 Moseley Transcript, 32
96 Moseley Transcript, 65–66
97 Moseley Transcript, 68, 637
98 Moseley Transcript, 39–40
99 Moseley Transcript, 65
100 Moseley Transcript, 603
101 Moseley Transcript, 638
102 As Neville attested, Moseley Transcript, 57–58
103 In Chief Secretary William Kitson's words: WAPD (new series), 22 September 1936, p. 712
104 WAPD (new series), 3 December 1936, p. 2374
105 WAPD (new series), 3 December 1936, p. 2377
106 WAPD (new series), 3 December 1936, p. 2393
107 WAPD (new series), 3 December 1936, p. 2394
108 WAPD (new series), 10 December 1936, p. 2618
109 WAPD (new series), 10 December 1936, p. 2619
110 Rowley 1970b, 61

4   Did 'protection' protect?

1 Elkin 1934a, 15
2 Brazil and Mitchell eds 1981, 24
3 *Yearbook Australia* no. 1 (1908), 145
4 See Broome 2005, 198
5 *Yearbook Australia* no. 1, 1908, 144
6 *Yearbook Australia* no. 1, 1908, 144
7 *Yearbook Australia* no. 5, 1912, 120

8   See *Yearbooks* no. 6 (1913, 108), no. 7 (1914, 93–94), no. 8 (1915, 93–94), no. 9 (1916, 99–100), no. 10 (1917, 107–108), no. 11 (1918, 109–10), no. 12 (1919, 103–104), and no. 13 (1920, 89).
9   *Minutes of Evidence of Aborigines Royal Commission* (SA 1913), 8
10 *Minutes of Evidence of Aborigines Royal Commission* (SA 1913), 10
11 *Progress Report of Aborigines Royal Commission* (SA 1913), v
12 *Progress Report of Aborigines Royal Commission* (SA 1913), viii
13 Mullins unpaginated
14 Tatz 2012, 29
15 Queensland 1913, 14
16 Queensland 1913, 18
17 Queensland 1913, 30–38
18 *Minutes of Evidence of Aborigines Royal Commission* (SA 1913), 86
19 *Minutes of Evidence of Aborigines Royal Commission* (SA 1913), 88
20 *Minutes of Evidence of Aborigines Royal Commission* (SA 1913), 98
21 *Minutes of Evidence of Aborigines Royal Commission* (SA 1913), 85
22 Queensland 1922, 7
23 Douglas and Finnane 2012, 67–68
24 Richards 2008, 138–39
25 *Yearbook Australia* no. 14, (1921, 1128)
26 *Yearbook Australia* no. 18 (1925, 919)
27 On the revision of South Australia's remote estimates after 1921 see Briscoe and Smith 2002, 29.
28 *Yearbook Australia* no. 18 (1925, 919)
29 *Yearbook Australia* no. 19 (1926, 880); *Yearbook Australia* no. 20 (1927, 882); *Yearbook Australia* no. 21, (1928, 911); *Yearbook Australia* no. 22, (1929, 915)
30 Briscoe and Smith 2002, 29
31 *Yearbook Australia* no. 28 (1935, 548)
32 McGregor 1997, 124
33 McGregor 1997, 124–34
34 McGregor 1997, 116
35 Choo 2001, 203–205, 222–23
36 Shnukal 2002, 77
37 Peterson and Taylor 1998
38 Queensland 1922, 7
39 Passages that hint at the connection between 'protection' strategies and improved health can be found in Briscoe 2003, 121–22, 129–30, 147, 149–50, 255–56, 279, 291, 294, 307.
40 Briscoe 2003, 294
41 Blake 2001, 103
42 Blake 2001, 92
43 Blake 2001, 88–89
44 Blake 2001, 90
45 Blake 2001, 93, 102
46 Blake 2001, 99, 104
47 Blake 2001, 114
48 Blake 2001, 116
49 Smith et al. 2008, 550
50 Smith et al. 2008, 551
51 Jenkin 1979, 88
52 Jenkin 1979, 124
53 Gale 1969, 82
54 Crawford 1978, 45–46
55 Cleland 1949, 70, 75
56 Berndt and Berndt 1987, 199
57 Simpson 1951, 187. Simpson also challenged the assumption that 'half-castes' were not 'Aboriginal'.
58 Sweeney to Chief Welfare Officer, 7 August 1956, F1 56/293(1). According to Long (1992, 127–28) Sweeney believed that missions should give every opportunity for Aborigines on reserves to remain decentralised.
59 Sweeney to Chief Welfare Officer, 7 August 1956, F1 56/293(1)
60 Sweeney 1956
61 Long 1970, 320
62 Agenda item 1(c), *Proposed Native Welfare Conference – Commonwealth and State Authorities – 1959, 1960 and 1961*, NAA A452 1961/216, p. 247
63 Elkin 1964, 367
64 Rowley 1970a, 246
65 *Census of the Commonwealth of Australia, 30 June 1966*, p. 3
66 *Yearbook Australia* no. 17 (1924, 960)
67 *Yearbook Australia* no. 17 (1924, 960)
68 *Yearbook Australia* no. 28 (1935, 548)

69	McGregor 1997, 122	17	Wilson 1980, 155
70	McGregor 1997, 129	18	Wilson 1961, 27
71	McGregor 1997, 200	19	Wilson 1961, 37
72	McGregor 1997, 180	20	Wright to McLeod, 10 May 1946, Wright Papers, Noel Butlin Archives (ANU), Box 8
73	The demographer Frank Jones (1970, 2, 6) cautiously estimated in 1968 that the nadir of the 'full-blood' population had occurred in the 1950s.	21	McLeod to Wright, 17 June 1946, Wright Papers, Noel Butlin Archives (ANU), Box 8
74	Long 1966, 3	22	Wright to Wardlaw, 20 September 1951, Wright Papers, Noel Butlin Archives (ANU), Box 8
75	McGregor 1997, 203–205		
76	Bleakley 1961, 143		
77	Worms 1970, 374	23	Paisley 2000, 46–47
		24	British Commonwealth League (n.d.), 5

5 Global awareness and the recession of race

1	Worsnop, quoted by Jones 2011, 31	25	Paisley 2000, 28
2	Jones 2011, 31. And see Spencer and Gillen 1899, 1904.	26	Bennett 1933
		27	Lake 1998, 100
3	Butel 1985, 50	28	McGregor 1997, 241–49; Marcus 2001, 213
4	Unaipon 2001, 4		
5	Muecke and Shoemaker 2001, xxxviii	29	Holland 2001, 33. See also Paisley 1997.
6	As noted by Butel 1985, 51–52. Jones (2011, 32–33) says that Norman Tindale, in 1932, was the first to say that Aboriginal testimony was essential if outsiders were to understand the admired forms and motifs.	30	Jones 1933
		31	Paisley 1998, 253
		32	Holland 2015, 118–23. 'Polygamy' should be read, here, as referring to the specific practice of 'polygyny' – the customary entitlement of a man to more than one wife at a time.
7	Hill 2002, 394	33	British Commonwealth League (n.d.), 30
8	Elliott 1979, xxxvi–xxxvii		
9	Ingamells 1938	34	Paisley 2000, 54
10	Ingamells 1938	35	Paisley 2000, 89
11	Cottle 2011, 130–31; see also Boughton 2001	36	Jones 1934, 34, 17
		37	Paisley 2000, 67
12	*Workers Weekly*, Friday, 24 September 1931, p. 2 (italics added), <www.reasoninrevolt.net.au/objects/pdf/a000219.pdf> (accessed 24 January 2017)	38	Paisley 2000, 68
		39	British Commonwealth League (n.d.), 29
		40	Paisley 2000, 6, 137
		41	Maynard 2005, 14
13	Wright 1944, 30	42	Maynard 2007, 99–100
14	Wright 1944, 5. Donald Thomson agreed. See D. Thomson to T. Wright, 20 August 1944, Wright Papers, Noel Butlin Archives (ANU), Box 8	43	*Sydney Morning Herald*, 15 November 1927, reprinted in Attwood and Markus eds 1999, 70–71
		44	Maynard 2007, 125–30
		45	Attwood and Markus eds 2004, 65
15	Wright 1944, 31	46	Attwood and Markus eds 2004, 59, 49–50, 65
16	Wright to Curlewis, 13 May 1948, Wright Papers, Noel Butlin Archives (ANU), Box 8.	47	Attwood and Markus eds 2004, 51
		48	Attwood and Markus eds 2004, 75

49 Attwood and Markus eds 2004, 80
50 Attwood and Markus eds 2004, 38, 39, 43–44
51 Attwood and Markus eds 2004, 68–69
52 Attwood and Markus eds 2004, 74
53 Attwood and Markus eds 2004, 43–44
54 Attwood and Markus eds 2004, 38, and see 51, 92
55 Attwood and Markus eds 2004, 41, 44, 60, 47
56 Attwood and Markus eds 2004, 66
57 Attwood and Markus eds 2004, 65,103
58 Attwood and Markus eds 2004, 49
59 Attwood and Markus eds 2004, 51–52
60 Attwood and Markus eds 2004, 68, 78, 80, 95, 96, 105
61 Attwood and Markus eds 2004, 47
62 Attwood and Markus eds 2004, 94
63 Department of Interior 1937, 3 (emphasis added)
64 Conference of Commonwealth and State Authorities, 1937, 3
65 McEwen 1939, 1
66 Hasluck 1953, 16
67 Hasluck 1953, 17

6 World Wars and the Cold War

1 According to Furphy (n.d.), the outstanding 'nations' were the Ngarrindjeri in south-eastern South Australia, the Gunditjmara in western Victoria, the Cape Barren Island community in Tasmania, and the Barambah (later Cherbourg) Mission in Queensland.
2 Maynard 2015; Scarlett 2015, 165; Furphy n.d.
3 Horton 2015, 206
4 Horton 2015, 204
5 Quoted by Horton 2015, 214
6 *West Australian*, 25 September 1925, Document 60 in Attwood and Markus eds 1999, 118
7 *Age*, 16 March 1933, Document 72 in Attwood and Markus eds 1999, 143
8 Cooper to Lyons, 31 March 1938, Document 63 in Attwood and Markus eds 2004, 92
9 'Petition of "half-caste" women', January 1935, Document 66 in Attwood and Markus eds 1999, 132
10 Quoted in Scarlett 2015, 174
11 Hasluck 1988, 71
12 As A.P. Elkin understood the clause. See excerpt from Elkin 1944, reprinted in Attwood and Markus eds 2007, 97.
13 Fox 2008, 35
14 Quoted in Hall 1989, 149
15 Hall 1989, 189
16 Hall 1989, 144
17 Hall 1989, 36–37
18 Hall 1989, 163
19 Hall 1989, 186
20 Hall 1989, 169
21 Hall 1989, 170
22 Hall 1989, 138
23 Hall 1989, 180, 183, 186
24 Hall 1989, 174
25 Hall 1989, 176
26 Hall 1989, 150, 154; Rowse 2000a, 90
27 Rowse 1998, 95–96
28 Cole 1980, 32
29 Harris 1998, 273–76
30 Kruger and Waterford 2007, 121
31 Kruger and Waterford 2007, 124
32 Roughsey 1971, 118
33 Roughsey 1971, 121
34 A. Cameron to J.S. Collings, 26 January 1944, NAA A452 55/506, 'Employment of Aborigines in cattle industry – NT'
35 Berndt and Berndt 1987, 175
36 Bell 1961, 426
37 Broome 2015, 22
38 Broome 2015, 13; Broome 2005, 290
39 Hodson 1993b, 33–36
40 Hall 1989, 13–14
41 Pearl Gibbs, radio broadcast, 8 June 1941, Document 44 in Attwood and Markus eds 1999, 97
42 Hall 1989, 34
43 NAA: MP508/1, 82/712/670, letter, William Ferguson to Prime

44 Minister Robert Menzies, 8 July 1940, cited in Neilson 2008
44 NAA: MP508/1, 275/750/1310, letter, Ruth H. Swann, Secretary of the Association for the Protection of Native Races, to F.M. Forde, 20 April 1942, cited in Neilson 2008
45 National Film and Sound Archive (NFSA), AVC010218, Australia's World War II Newsreels, narration by Charles Lawrence, 00:20:00:00–00:20:53:00, cited in Neilson 2008
46 *Herald* (Melbourne), 25 November 1944
47 NAA: SP112/1, 265/1/34, memo, Commonwealth Department of Information, from Secretary to Deputy Director, 25 December 1940, cited in Neilson 2008
48 NAA: MP742/1, 164/1/283, letter, Michael Sawtell, Chairman of Committee for Aboriginal Citizenship, to Prime Minister Robert Menzies, 21 October 1939, cited in Neilson 2008
49 Hall 1989, 79
50 Clarke 2003, 109
51 Clarke 2003, 113
52 McGinness 1991, 24
53 Muir 2004, 78
54 Muir 2004, 75
55 Muir 2004, 82
56 Muir 2004, 79
57 Muir 2004, 80
58 Muir 2004, 80
59 Muir 2004, 85
60 Muir 2004, 84
61 Long 1967, 194
62 A.R. Driver to Secretary Interior, 6 July 1949, NAA F1 43/24
63 Bateman 1948, 18
64 Morton 1989, 59
65 Tindale 1940–41, 68
66 Palmer 1990, 197
67 Morton 1989, 69–70
68 Broome 2015, 30
69 Blackburn's speech is in CPD, 6 March 1947, 435–38
70 Thomson 1947 (reprinted 1957), unpaginated
71 Morton 1989, 73
72 Duguid, quoted in Kerin 2011, 49
73 Kerin 2011, 51–55
74 Quoted in Kerin 2011, 58
75 Elkin to Dedman, 4 March 1947, Australian Archives, Papers of Sir Frederick Shedden (MP1217), Box 1656, File 'Long Range Weapons Project Protection of Aborigines'
76 McGregor 2012, 32
77 Elkin 1944, 37–38
78 A.P. Elkin, 'Segregation would be the end of Aborigines', *Sun* (Sydney), 22 January 1947, p. 4
79 The words of the Guided Projectiles Committee, as quoted by John Dedman, CPD, 1 May 1947, pp. 1831–32
80 Gray 1991, 156
81 Thomson 1983, 110–11
82 Riseman 2013, 42
83 Thomson's report to the Army is reproduced in Thomson 1983, 132.
84 Thomson 1983, 117–18
85 Riseman 2013, 45–46
86 Riseman 2013, 49
87 Thomson 1983, 130
88 Thomson 1983, 137
89 Thomson 1983, 134
90 Thomson 1983, 135
91 Riseman 2013, 65
92 *Report of the Royal Commission into British Nuclear Tests in Australia*, 158
93 *Report of the Royal Commission into British Nuclear Tests in Australia*, 170, 173–74
94 *Report of the Royal Commission into British Nuclear Tests in Australia*, 323
95 For the film's reception, see Lydon 2012, 198–207.
96 Grayden 1957, 33–43. For sceptical responses to the Grayden Report, see Grayden 1957, 53–56, 68–79, 82, 113–34, 144–53.
97 Morgan Gallop Poll, subscriber report numbers 410 (February–March 1947) and 1233 (February–March 1957), and no. 1229–1240, February–March 1957

7 Towards racial equality

1. The Howard government's *Hindmarsh Island Bridge Act* 1997 removed an area in South Australia from the protection of the *Aboriginal and Torres Strait Islander Heritage Protection Act* 1984. To the dismay of those who had presumed the positive character of the 'Aboriginal race' power, the High Court of Australia ruled in *Kartinyeri v Commonwealth* 1998 that the power could be wielded for or against the interests of the 'Aboriginal race'.
2. Roberton in CPD, 3 September 1959, 930
3. A resolution of the fourth conference of the Aborigines Progress Association in 1940, in Horner 1974, 91
4. Murphy 2013, 212
5. Quoted in Murphy 2013, 212
6. Murphy 2011, 169
7. De Maria 1986, 29
8. De Maria 1986, 30
9. Investigation has shown that governments mismanaged these trusts: see Senate Standing Committee on Legal and Constitutional Affairs 2006.
10. Quoted in Murphy 2013, 216
11. De Maria 1986, 31
12. Murphy 2011, 204
13. Murphy 2013, 219–20
14. McClure 1998, 121
15. Murphy 2013, 219–20
16. Quoted in Murphy 2011, 210
17. De Maria 1986, 37
18. Elkin 1951, 16
19. Whitlam, CPD HoR, 20 August 1959, 46–63
20. Chesterman 2001, 27–29
21. Roberton, CPD HoR, 3 September 1959, 928
22. Roberton, CPD HoR, 3 September 1959, 931
23. Bryant, CPD HoR, 24 September 1959, 1412
24. Raftery 2006, 196–97
25. Director-General of Social Services 1967, 5. Promoters of this change continued to criticise the government for allowing an elastic interpretation of 'primitive and nomadic' to continue to exclude many people and for not paying cash directly to those who were included (Chesterman 2001, 31). Will Sanders has traced the steps by which 'nomadic' ceased to be an operative exclusion by 1975 (Sanders 1985).
26. Australia. Parliament, 1961. This parliamentary paper falls into two 'parts'. Part 1 (No. H of R 1 [Group H]) *Report and Minutes of Proceedings* (including appendices) and Part 2, *Minutes of Evidence* (No. H or R 2 [Group H]). I will refer to these two items respectively as *Report* and *Minutes*. The committee chair was George Pearce; other members were C.E. Barnes, K.E. Beazley, P.G. Browne, P. Howson, A.S. Luchetti and J. N. Nelson. Here I am drawing on *Report*, 5.
27. *Report*, 2
28. Cited in Goot 2006, 525
29. Fink 1960, statutory declaration reproduced at 47
30. Fink 1960, 183–84
31. *Minutes*, 261
32. *Minutes*, 209
33. *Minutes*, 212
34. *Minutes*, 20
35. *Minutes*, 189
36. *Minutes*, 75
37. *Minutes*, 77
38. *Minutes*, 78
39. *Minutes*, 138
40. *Minutes*, 88–89
41. *Minutes*, 91–92
42. *Minutes*, 287–88
43. *Minutes*, 352
44. *Minutes* (Peter Bush) 371–72; (Silas Roberts) 373; (Gertie Huddleston) 373; (Gula) 377; (Nabilya) 378
45. *Minutes*, 384–86
46. *Minutes*, 388–90
47. Charcoal Dulung, Wallaby Jangbagari, Humbert Tommy,

Nguringari, Kelly Wimud, Peter Du'Ulmaki, Frank Dangaro, Kinijo'or, Cloud Kanalagari, *Minutes*, 405–406
48 Abe Jangala, Annie Ngagita, Sandy Jurra, Morris Jibarula [sic], Peter Blacksmith, Florrie Blacksmith, Freddie Jigali and Molly Namjimba, *Minutes*, 406–409
49 *Minutes*, 413
50 Johnny Lynch, Benjamin Ebatarinja, *Minutes*, 431, 436
51 *Minutes*, 436
52 Chauvel 1959, 189
53 May 1994, 168
54 Paterson 2008, 220
55 Anthony 2007a, 47
56 See Cowlishaw 1999; Jebb 2002; May 1994; McGrath 1987; Redmond 2005; Rowse 1987; Rowse 1988
57 Porteus 1969, 116
58 Redmond 2005, 236
59 Redmond 2012, 69
60 Bowman ed. 2015, 77
61 Bowman ed. 2015, 77
62 Bowman ed. 2015, 85
63 Bowman ed. 2015, 68
64 Bowman ed. 2015, 63
65 Bowman ed. 2015, 64
66 Munro 1996, 59–60
67 Jebb 1996, 157
68 Porteus 1969, 110
69 Stevens 1974; Rowse 1998, 120–23
70 Stevens 1974, 76
71 Jebb 2002, 244. Anthony 2007a states the case for seeing pastoral colonialism as a distinct 'feudal' order.
72 May 1994, 105–106
73 May 1994, 115
74 May 1994, 119
75 Stevens 1974, 197
76 See Stevens 1974, 189–205 for summaries of the different submissions, Gruen 1966 for an economists' view, and Rowse 1998, 119–46 for the Central Australian context of the case. Anthony 2007b offers a critical reading of the proceedings of the commission.
77 Altman and Nieuwenhuysen 1979, 64–68; Rowse 1998, 175–78
78 Hasluck 1959
79 Robinson 2013
80 Higman 2002, 107–108
81 On the Cootamundra Home for Girls see Mulvaney 1989, 199–205
82 Walden 1995
83 Haskins 2015, 49, and see Conor 2008, 228: 'white employers and the state construed Aboriginal young women [in the 1920s] as both an anomaly to the modern Australian scene and its necessary recruit to meet the aims of assimilation'.
84 Haskins 2009, 158, 170
85 Haskins 2009, 164; Haskins 2005
86 Higman 2002, 62–63
87 Manning 2005
88 Haebich 2004
89 Jones 2016
90 Elkin 1978, unpaginated
91 Student Action for Aborigines (SAFA), based at the University of Sydney, angered many whites by demanding the end of racial segregation in several NSW towns in 1965, but got sympathetic press coverage: see Curthoys 2002.
92 Tomasetti 1967, unpaginated
93 The name OPAL was the acronym of 'One People of Australia' or 'Our People of Australia'.
94 Tomasetti 1967, unpaginated
95 Tomasetti 1967, unpaginated
96 For a detailed exposition of studies by Lippmann 1973, Taft 1970, Western 1969, 1973 see Goot and Rowse 2007, 27–60.

8 From the referendum to 'self-determination'

1 Stanner 2009, 201
2 Broom 1970, 150
3 Broom 1970, 153
4 Broom 1970, 155
5 Broom 1971, 22–23
6 Maynard 2007, 53–54
7 McGregor 2012, 109
8 Hasluck 1959
9 Bandler and Fox 1983, 116

10. Cited in Lapham 2016, 36. And see Biskup 1973, 250.
11. Transcript of Aboriginal Welfare Council meeting, 1965, Papers of Barrie Dexter, File 2, AIATSIS Library
12. Rowse 2000c, 22
13. Statement by Mr Len King reprinted in Stone ed. 1974, 232
14. Stone ed. 1974, 233
15. Wentworth 1969, 183
16. Wentworth 1969, 188
17. Quoted by Sanders 1982, 5
18. Walker 1970a, 91
19. Schapper 1970, 93
20. Walker 1970a, 92
21. Rowse 2000, 107; McAllister and Moore 1991, 109
22. Dexter 2015, 303
23. Thus Schapper 1970, 92: 'Political self-determination is one of the necessary requirements for Aboriginal integration.'
24. Replaced by *Equal Opportunity Act* 1984 (SA) and *Racial Vilification Act* 1996 (SA). Each Australian jurisdiction followed South Australia by outlawing racial (and other forms of) discrimination: the Commonwealth in 1975 (*Racial Discrimination Act*), New South Wales in 1977 (*Anti-Discrimination Act*), Western Australia 1984 (*Equal Opportunity Act*), Victoria in 1984 (*Equal Opportunity Act*), Australian Capital Territory in 1991 (*Discrimination Act*), Queensland in 1991 (*Anti-Discrimination Act*), Northern Territory in 1996 (*Anti-Discrimination Act*), Tasmania in 1998 (*Anti-Discrimination Act*).
25. Gale and Bookman eds 1975, 86–88
26. One of the first Aboriginal framings of Aborigines as a Fourth World people was by Ribnga Green (Green 1979). For a brief account of these excursions and arguments see Ravi de Costa 2006, 129–46.
27. Rowse 2011
28. Attwood and Markus eds 1999, 176–77
29. This disclaimer is expressed in ILO 2009, 26
30. www.un.org/esa/socdev/unpfii/documents/DRIPS_en.pdf (accessed 5 January 2017)
31. CPD Senate, 19 November 1979, 2427
32. Kath Walker 1966a, 13
33. Rowse and Smith 2010, 96–99
34. Commonwealth Bureau of Census and Statistics Press Release 1967, 1
35. Dodson 2003, 32, 39–40
36. Downing 1971
37. *Aboriginal Affairs Act Amendment Act* 1966–67 (SA), s. 41. For the Commonwealth's councillor training programs, see Loveday 1989.
38. Dexter 2015, 305
39. Department of Aboriginal Affairs, 1976, 11–13. The fund was administered under the *Aboriginal Enterprises (Assistance) Act* 1968.
40. Loans and grants for home ownership commenced in 1974 (*Aboriginal Loans Commission Act* 1974), aimed at Aboriginal people who were making their way as employed persons in cities and towns.
41. May 1994, 172–73; Skyring 2012
42. For this account of state and Commonwealth policy in the Northern Territory and Kimberley from 1968, see Smith 2002 and Smith 2006. And see Rowse and Watt 2017.
43. Pryles 2002, Chapter 1
44. McGuinness 1972, 153; Rowse 2000c, 74
45. That Cold War anti-communism contributed to Aborigines' ethnic honour is a theme of Clohesy 2011.
46. Foley 2001, 5–10
47. Rowley 1970b, 425
48. Short 2008, 152
49. Bonner 1967, 7
50. Walker 1966b, 186
51. Walker 1966b, 186

52 Walker 1970b, 80. Reprinted by permission of John Wiley & Sons, Inc.
53 Gilbert 1987, 18
54 Gilbert 1973a
55 Gilbert 1973b, 178
56 Gilbert 1973b, 97
57 Gilbert 1973b, 111
58 Gilbert 1973b, 132
59 Perkins told me in 1991 that he had been successful on five occasions in taking legal action against his critics.
60 Gilbert 1973b, 150
61 Gilbert 1973b, 153
62 Gilbert 1973b, 147

9 The Indigenous Estate in Land and Sea

1 Hill et al. 2013, 1. And see map at 20. Altman (2014, 5) gives a slightly different breakdown: land claimed or automatically scheduled under land rights law (an estimated 969 000 sq km); 92 determinations of exclusive possession under native title law totalling 752 000 sq km; and 142 determinations of non-exclusive possession under native title law totalling 825 000 sq km.
2 However, the ILC's purchasing ability has been weakened by its need to service debt incurred when it purchased the Ayers Rock Resort: see Seccombe 2015.
3 Alison Holland (2005) shows that, without using the phrase 'land rights', many critics of government policy in the 1930s argued that government should recognise Aboriginal rights to reserve lands. Bain Attwood (2003, 215–16) argues that 'land rights' became current as a phrase in public protest against excision (for mining leases) from remote reserves.
4 *Yarmirr v Northern Territory* (1998) 156 ALR 370 (*Yarmirr*)
5 Frank Walker, NSWPD, 24 March 1983, p. 5091
6 However, the extinguishing of native title must be financially compensated by the government, if the extinguishing act occurred after 31 October 1975 when the *Racial Discrimination Act* became law: see Australia, Attorney General 1998, 3–5.
7 Kidd 1997, 192–207, 214–26; Roberts 1981, 96–105
8 Loos 1991
9 Anonymous 1985, 69–85; Broome 2015, 99–107
10 See Wells 1982, 103–108 for newspaper coverage of the petitions from Yirrkala.
11 This is evident in writings by Methodist Pastor Edgar Wells: see Wells 1972, 243–49 and Wells 1982, 81–85. Harris 1990, 815–20 also discusses the debate among Christians on land rights and 'development'.
12 Harris 1990, 815
13 Bandler and Fox 1983, 98
14 Attwood 2003, 215–16
15 Taffe 2005, 209
16 Anne Wells 1963, 136–38 depicts the moment when her husband, Edgar, first realised that he was being instructed in Yolngu law.
17 McMahon 1972, 9
18 Australian Labor Party 1967, 26
19 Australian Labor Party 1969, 27
20 Smith 2002, Smith 2006
21 Stokes 1987
22 Edwards 1983
23 Mazel 2006
24 On the stance of the Western Australian government see Dixon 1990; Harman 1982; Hawke and Gallagher 1989. For Queensland's see Brennan 1992, Chapters 1 and 2. On Holding's political difficulties 1983–86, see Goot and Rowse 2007, Chapter 2.
25 Quoted in Brennan 1992, 58
26 Robert Katter, QPD, vol. 298, 3 April 1985, pp. 4896–97
27 Brennan 1992, 68
28 Brennan 1992, 73
29 See Langton 2014 for the circumstances and effects of Goss's laws.

30 Norman 2015, 71
31 Mansell 1980, 132
32 Tasmania, PD, 24 October 1995, p. 4596
33 Tasmania, PD, 18 March 1999, <http://www.parliament.tas.gov.au/ParliamentSearch/isysquery/3079b7d0-e6eb-4fca-b19d-df29ba0b6cf6/2/doc/H18MAR2.htm>
34 Rowley 1980, 259
35 Queensland cabinet decision of 1972, quoted in Palmer 1988, 67
36 The agreement was the 1965 *International Convention on the Elimination of All Forms of Racial Discrimination.*
37 Aboriginal Development Commission 1990, 43. Thus, I infer 89 purchases by the ADC.
38 I estimate from figures given by ATSIC in the following *Annual Reports*: March–June 1990, three properties; 1990–91, 12 properties; 1991–92, 11 properties; 1992–93, 74 'acquired or in process of being acquired'; 1993–94, 45 properties; 1994–95, 21 properties; 1995–6, 26 properties; 1996–97, 19 properties.
39 Indigenous Land Corporation, *Annual Report*, 2013–14, 32
40 Rowley 1980, 257–58
41 Office of the Registrar, 'Aboriginal Land Rights Act 1983 (NSW)', Land rights in New South Wales overview, <www.oralra.nsw.gov.au/landrights.html>
42 Norman 2015, 114–18
43 Radcliffe-Brown 1977, 132
44 Hiatt 1984, Maddock 1992, Sutton 2003, 26–32
45 Langton 1997
46 Rose 1996 evokes the energies, for claimants, of the land claim process.
47 Hocking 1981, 207
48 McIntyre 1981, 223
49 Beckett 2014, 187
50 Mabo 1976, Mabo 1981
51 Keon-Cohen 2013, 219, 33
52 Passi 1996
53 'The Cabinet's guiding principles on native title', reprinted in Goot and Rowse eds 1994, 220–25. Such legislation would need to have authorised state and territory parliaments do likewise, as these legislatures were responsible for many of the titles of doubtful validity.
54 Pearson quoted in *Australian Financial Review*, 4 June 1993
55 'The Cabinet's guiding principles on native title' in Goot and Rowse eds 1994, 223
56 John Hewson, 'Leader of the Opposition's address to the nation' in Goot and Rowse eds 1994, 241
57 HREOC 1998, 85; Neate 2004
58 Chaney 2002, n.p.
59 Langton and Palmer 2003, 25
60 This is the personal assessment of Bruce Harvey 2004, 247, while CRA's chief advisor on Rio Tinto's Aboriginal and Community Relations. See also Trebeck 2009, 137–39.
61 Doohan, Langton and Mazel 2012
62 Trebeck 2009, 135. For analysis of the difficulties of implementing this agreement see Martin 2009, 103–108.
63 Yunupingu 1997, 12
64 Altman 2009, 32, table 2.1
65 Altman 2009, 33, table 2.2
66 Taylor 2012, 67
67 Langton and Mazel 2012
68 Meston 1896, 14
69 Roth 1905, 28
70 Altman 1985, 18
71 Select Committee of the Legislative Council [South Australia], 1966, 28 September 1966, p. 14. For more instances of this phrase in South Australia's parliamentary proceedings, see Rowse 2012, Chapter 4.
72 NSW Parliament 1981, x
73 Rowley 1979, 110
74 Rowley 1979, 110
75 McCrae et al. 2009, 348

76 Notes taken by the author on discussion of a paper by Glen Kelly at the National Native Title Conference, Port Douglas, 18 June 2015.
77 Murphy 1994 has argued that the aspiration and right to socio-economic development has been the globally hegemonic ideology since World War II.
78 Brennan 2015
79 Norman 2015, 135–36
80 Kolig 1987, 157
81 Seaman 1984b, 35
82 Seaman 1984b, 40
83 Seaman 1984b, 36
84 Seaman 1984b, 36
85 Seaman 1984a, 43
86 CPD (Senate) (Crowley) 21 September 1994, p. 1112
87 CPD (Senate) (Ellison) 9 November 1994, p. 2807
88 CPD (Senate) 9 November 1994, p. 2798
89 CPD (Senate) 9 November 1994, p. 2803
90 CPD (Senate) 9 November 1994, pp. 2797–98
91 *The Australian*, 16 May 2015
92 Godden 2012, 107
93 See Neale 2016.
94 For an overview of the intertwining of policies of conservation and Indigenous social justice policies see Moorcroft 2015.

10 Asserting 'Southern' Aboriginality

1 McGregor 2009, Martinez 1997, Attwood 2003, 312–21, 335–39
2 Martinez 1997; Marcia Langton 2004 has argued that regional land use agreements under land rights and native title law have given impetus to the re-emergence of Indigenous 'nations'.
3 Katona and Mackinolty eds 1995, 28
4 The *Aborigines Preservation and Protection Act* 1939 and the *Torres Strait Islanders Act* 1939
5 Loos and Mabo 1996, 100–101
6 De Costa 2006, 92–120; Clark 2008, 1–3, 164–68, 206–208, 228
7 West 1984, 22
8 West 1984, 85
9 Berndt 1969, 4, 1
10 Beazley 1964, 4–5
11 Hasluck 1988, 23
12 Langton 1981, 16
13 Philip Roberts, quoted in the Australian Security Intelligence Organisation report on the meeting, cited by Taffe 2005, 244
14 Read 1990, Clohesy 2011, Broome 2015, 145, Taffe 2005, 240–66
15 Quoted by McGregor 2009, 356
16 Nugent 2012
17 Bell 1961, 437
18 Australian Institute for Aboriginal Studies and the Aboriginal Arts Board 1983, 14
19 McGregor 2009, 357
20 Gilbert 1973, 7
21 Quoted in McGregor 2009, 357
22 Casey 2004, 5
23 Quoted in Casey 2004, 13
24 Bostock 1985, 64
25 Casey 2004, 56
26 Australia Council 1975, 4
27 Australia Council 1975, 5
28 Australia Council 1975, 81, 34
29 Australia Council 1975, 20
30 Australia Council 1975, 21
31 Australia Council 1975, 18
32 Australia Council 1975, 18
33 Australia Council 1975, 18
34 Durack 1971, 17
35 Australian Theatre Foundation *Newsletter* no. 1, May 1972, 12
36 Durack 1971, 18
37 Australian Theatre Foundation *Newsletter* May 1974
38 Australian Theatre Foundation *Newsletter* no. 1 May 1972, 10
39 Berndt and Phillips 1978, 308
40 Baker 2005
41 A recent (2010) biography of Gatjil Djerrkura (of Yirrkala, where Methodists arrived in 1934–35) presents the Yolngu as having been disturbed by the Methodists'

	immediate predecessors – aliens such as Japanese boat crews and Australian settlers: see Clarke 2010.
42	Australia Council 1975, 18
43	*Mercury*, 17 November 1977, 5
44	Ryan 1996, 248
45	Ryan 1996, 248
46	Ryan 1996, 249
47	Ryan 1996, 248
48	Daniels 1995, 9
49	Daniels 1995, 13
50	Daniels 1995, 19
51	Ryan 1996, 253
52	Daniels 1995, 20
53	Mulvaney 2011, 116–17
54	Daniels 1995, 12
55	Daniels 1995, 12, 22
56	Langford 1983, 2
57	Langford 1983, 6
58	Langford 1983, 4
59	Langford 1983, 6
60	Langford 1983, 6
61	Langford 1983, 6
62	McGowan 1996, 303–305
63	McGowan 1996, 306
64	This paragraph is based on my reading of documents and commentary assembled in Allen 1995.
65	Tasmanian Aboriginal Land Council 1996, 293–94
66	Tasmanian Aboriginal Land Council 1996, 296, 297, 298
67	Berndt and Berndt 1951, 203
68	Bell 1998, 145–55
69	Berndt, Berndt and Stanton 1993, 296, 299
70	Tonkinson 1993, xxi
71	Tonkinson 1993, xvii
72	Berndt and Berndt 1951, 229
73	Berndt and Berndt 1951, 230
74	Tonkinson 1993, xvii
75	Tonkinson 1993, xxiii
76	Kenny 1996, 57
77	Simons 2003, 293
78	Mathews 1996, 3
79	*Chapman and Ors v Luminis Pty Ltd*, Federal Court of Australia, no. SG 33 of 1997
80	Bell 1998, 207
81	Bell 1998, xiii
82	Wilson 1998, 145
83	Bell 1998, 599
84	Wilson 1998, 10
85	Kenny 1996, 234
86	Wilson 1998, 15–16
87	Wilson 1998, 19
88	Wilson 1998, 135
89	Wilson 1998, 64
90	Wilson 1998, 65
91	Wilson 1998, 150
92	Bell 1998, 47
93	Bell 1998, 402
94	Bell 1998, 135
95	Bell 1998, 423–24
96	Bell 1998, 371
97	Kartinyeri and Anderson 2008, 137
98	Kartinyeri and Anderson 2008, 137
99	Kartinyeri and Anderson 2008, 133
100	In this section I have drawn on Rowse 2000b, 2006, 2010.
101	Haebich 2000, 312–41
102	Read 1981
103	Kidd 2002, 261
104	Katona and Mackinolty 1995, 8
105	Devitt 2008, 42
106	Wells 2005, Day 1994
107	The major test cases: *Alec Kruger and Ors v The Commonwealth of Australia* (known as *Kruger*); *George Ernest Bray and Ors v The Commonwealth of Australia* 146 ALR 126 (known as *Bray*), both decided in 1997; and *Lorna Cubillo and Peter Gunner v The Commonwealth of Australia* [2000] FC (known as *Cubillo*).
108	Kruger and Waterford 2007, 328
109	Kruger and Waterford 2007, 332
110	Kruger and Waterford 2007, 111
111	Katona and Mackinolty 1995, 24
112	Katona and Mackinolty 1995, 17
113	Katona and Mackinolty 1995, 18–19
114	Katona and Mackinolty 1995, 24
115	Devitt 2008, 46. See Kennedy and Wilson 2003 for a sympathetic account of this therapy. Tikka Wilson was a major contributor to Link-Up's submission to the

HREOC inquiry: Link-Up and Wilson 1997.
116 The *Native Title Act* was in force from 1 January 1994. Of the few judicial determinations in the period of the HREOC inquiry (from 9 August 1995, with the final report delivered to the attorney-general on 5 April 1997), only in the Yorta Yorta case (*Members of the Yorta Yorta Aboriginal Community v Victoria* 1996) were native title claimants defeated by the argument that they no longer observed their traditional laws and customs; this judgment was immediately appealed, and the High Court of Australia did not rule on it until 1998.
117 Devitt 2008, 179–80
118 Devitt 2008, 187
119 Devitt 2008, 196
120 Cited in Devitt 2008, 196
121 Australia, Parliament 1961, *Minutes of Evidence*, 490
122 McKeich 1977, 252

11 The Indigenous middle class
1 Donovan Research 1992, table 17
2 Rowse 2002, 152–66
3 Taylor 2003, 92
4 Taylor 2003, 93
5 Lane 1997, 27
6 Lane 1998
7 Lane 1997, 29; Lane 1998, 27
8 Lane n.d., 'Hard grind – the making of an urban Indigenous population' <www.firstsources.info/twenty-first-century.html> (accessed 20 February 2017)
9 Lane n.d.
10 Behrendt et al. 2012, 3, 14
11 Langton 2013, 154
12 Dillon 2013, 78
13 Dillon 2013, 78
14 See Lahn 2013 for Census and ethnographic data on Aboriginal 'professionals'.
15 Pholi 2013, 63
16 Ganter 2016, 137–41
17 Ganter 2016, 142
18 Ganter 2016, 150
19 Ganter 2016, 146
20 Pearson 2009, 223–34
21 Dillon 2013, 79–83
22 Crawford and Biddle 2015, 4
23 Crawford and Biddle 2015, 4
24 Biddle 2013a, 10
25 Biddle 2013a, 14
26 Crawford and Biddle 2015, 20–21
27 Crawford and Biddle 2015, 9
28 Crawford and Biddle 2015, 8, 19, 25
29 Crawford and Biddle 2015, 22
30 Crawford and Biddle 2015, 10
31 Crawford and Biddle 2015, 5
32 Biddle 2013a, 14
33 Dodson and Smith 2003, 15, 20
34 Dodson and Smith 2013, 15
35 Dodson and Smith 2003, 14–17
36 Dodson and Smith 2003, 19
37 Norman 2015
38 Carlson 2016, 233, 269–70
39 Grant 2002, 53
40 Grant 2002, 54
41 Grant 2016
42 Grant 2016, 41–43 and Pearson 2011
43 *Courier Mail*, 6 February 1997
44 Pearson 2000, 15
45 Pearson 2000, 94 (emphasis in original)
46 Pearson 2000, 30
47 Pearson 2011
48 Pearson 2000, 59
49 Pearson 2000, 58
50 Pearson 2000, 58
51 Pearson 2000, 84
52 Pearson 2000, 86
53 Pearson 2000, 87
54 Katz and Raven 2013
55 Gilbert 1973, 194
56 Gilbert 1973, 196
57 Maynard to Lang, 28 May 1927, reprinted in Attwood and Markus eds 1999, 67
58 *Sydney Morning Herald*, 15 November 1927, reprinted in Attwood and Markus eds 1999, 70–71
59 Attwood and Markus eds 1999, 91 (original emphasis)
60 Attwood and Markus eds 2004, 51

61 Lane n.d. (original emphasis)
62 Hughes (Langford) n.d., 59–61. Langford's *Don't Take Your Love to Town* (1988) illustrates that often she *did* seize opportunities.
63 ABS 'Prisoner characteristics, Australia', <http://www.abs.gov.au/ausstats/abs@.nsf/Lookup/by%20Subject/4517.0~2015~Main%20Features~Prisoner%20characteristics,%20Australia~28> (accessed 16 March 2016)
64 See Pyne 2012.
65 Weatherburn 2014; Broadhurst 2002; Cunneen et al. 2013, 20

12 Family, community and the crisis of self-determination

1 Hasluck 1988, 23
2 For a vignette of what this has meant for kinship in a region of North Queensland, see McKnight 2004, 221–27.
3 Sutton 1998, 60
4 Sutton 1998, 67
5 Sutton 1998, 62–71
6 Kahn 1980
7 Thomson 1991, tables 2.9, 2.10, 2.17, 2.18
8 Tatz 1990, 250
9 Tatz 1990, 251
10 Sam 1991, v
11 Mentioned by Robertson 1999, xxxii
12 Gaffney 1989, 84
13 Bell and Napurrula 1989
14 Huggins et al. 1991
15 Bolger 1991, 49
16 Bolger 1991, 50
17 Anonymous editorial 1990, 3
18 Atkinson 1990, 6
19 Atkinson 1990, 7–8
20 SNAICC 1995, 8, emphasis in original
21 SNAICC 1996, 9. SNAICC was critical of one feature of 'custom': the persistence of 'payback', in some communities, as a means of addressing a wrong. This contributed to 'a culture and expectation of violence' (SNAICC 1996, 6).
22 Robertson 1999, 251
23 Robertson 1999, x
24 Neill 2002, 80
25 Gordon 2003, 11
26 Gordon 2003, 13
27 SNAICC 2003
28 Cripps 2008, S26
29 Sarra 2014, 231
30 Behrendt 2009
31 See HREOC 2004, 169–73 for ATSIC's recognition of family violence as a problem, in 2003.
32 Clark was also at this time (2003) awaiting trial on charges of riotous behaviour and assaulting police, after an incident in Warrnambool. Convicted in January 2004, he was suspended as chair of ATSIC by minister Amanda Vanstone. On appeal, one conviction was dismissed and the penalty for the other reduced. Clark also successfully appealed Vanstone's suspension, as unlawful and racially discriminatory, in the Federal Court in August 2004: see Schwartz 2008, 26–28.
33 Australia, Review of the Aboriginal and Torres Strait Islander Commission 2003, 29
34 Australia, Review of the Aboriginal and Torres Strait Islander Commission 2003, 29
35 Australia, Review of the Aboriginal and Torres Strait Islander Commission 2003, 32
36 'Vanstone in defence of "new order"', *Koori Mail*, 17 November 2004, 9. The National Indigenous Council (NIC) consisted of Sue Gordon (WA), chair; Wesley Aird (Qld); Archie Barton (SA); Mary Ann Bin Sallik (NT); Miriam Rose Baumann (NT); Joseph Elu (Torres Strait); Robert Lee (NT); Adam Goodes (Vic); Sally Goold (Qld); John Moriarty (NSW); Warren Mundine (NSW); John Proctor (WA); Michael White

(Qld); Tammy Williams (Qld). Only Mr White, chair of Central Queensland ATSIC Regional Council, had an association with ATSIC.
37 Reeves 1998. For critical responses to the Reeves Report, see Altman, Morphy and Rowse (eds) 1999.
38 Terrill 2015, 63, 69
39 Mark Metherell, 'Land system holds us back, says Mundine', *Sydney Morning Herald*, 7 December 2004, 6
40 Terrill 2015, 99
41 Terrill 2015, 111
42 Terrill 2015, 131–32
43 Fellow NIC members Wesley Aird and Joseph Elu endorsed Mundine's views: see Terrill 2015, 148 (n 39).
44 The NIC's 'Possible Indigenous Land Tenure Principles' are reproduced in HREOC 2005, 185.
45 'Warren Mundine's agenda for an Indigenous policy', *National Indigenous Times*, 4 September 2013, 19
46 Norman 2015, 120–21, 149–51, 164
47 Johns 2011
48 CPD (Senate), 20 June 2006, p. 64
49 Anderson and Wild 2007, 16
50 Anderson and Wild 2007, 15
51 CPD (HoR), 25 September 1973, pp. 1444–45: see Dexter 2015, 341–43.
52 *Northern Territory National Emergency Response Act* 2007; *Social Security and Other Legislation Amendment (Welfare Payment Reform) Act* 2007; *Families, Community Services and Indigenous Affairs and Other Legislation Amendment (Northern Territory National Emergency Response and Other Measures) Act* 2007; *Appropriation (Northern Territory National Emergency Response) Act (No. 1) (2007–2008)* 2007; *Appropriation (Northern Territory National Emergency Response) Act (No. 2) (2007–2008)* 2007.
53 Gerritsen 2010, 35–36
54 Strakosch 2015
55 ATSISJC 2005, 139
56 ATSISJC 2005, 143
57 CPD (HoR), 7 August 2007, p. 11
58 CPD (HoR), 7 August 2007, pp. 11–12
59 Jordan 2012
60 Income management has not necessarily been repugnant to Aboriginal people. In the 1980s, many clients of Tangentyere Council, the Alice Springs town camp administration, saw its income management service as a strategy for dealing with 'demand sharing'.
61 ATSISJC 2011, 183
62 Cox 2012, 21–32
63 Nicholson 2009
64 For example ACOSS, quoted in Cox 2011, 31
65 Department of Families, Housing, Community Services and Indigenous Affairs, *Report on the Northern Territory Emergency Response Redesign Consultations*, cited in Cox 2011, 34–35
66 <www.hrlc.org.au/news/parliamentary-joint-committee-finds-stronger-futures-legislation-threatens-human-rights> (accessed 12 March 2016)
67 Ross et al. 2012, 4
68 AIDA submission, in Cox 2011, 40–41
69 AMSANT submission, in Cox 2011, 42
70 AMSANT submission, in Cox 2011, 43. The only rigorous before/after study available at the time the Bills were debated was by Brimblecome et al. 2010; they concluded that CIM had had no effect on tobacco and cigarette sales, soft drink or fruit and vegetable sales.
71 Ngaanyatjara Pitjantjatjara Yankunytjatara Women's Council 2012
72 The polls are summarised by Goot and Rowse 2007, 156–59.

73 CPD (HoR), 7 August 2007, p. 3
74 Senate Standing Committee on Community Affairs 2012, 59
75 Grant 2017, 136
76 Altman 2017
77 Price 2017, 105
78 Grant 2017, 136
79 Saethre 2013, 95–97
80 Saethre 2013, 31
81 Musharbash 2008, 156–57
82 Burbank 2011, 158
83 McKnight 2002, 215
84 Hunter 1993, 182–99
85 Austin-Broos 2009
86 Purtill 2017, 230–31
87 Brady 2018 (forthcoming)
88 Field notes, in Burbank 2011, viii–ix

Epilogue: Within a single field of life

1 See Document 28 in Attwood and Markus eds 2007, 113, an excerpt from Menzies' speech in CPD, 11 November 1965, pp. 2638–39
2 Dodson and Liebler 2012. The members of the expert panel were: Patrick Dodson (co-chair), Mark Liebler (co-chair) Josephine Bourne, Graham Bradley, Timmy Djawa Burarrwanga, Henry Burmester, Fred Chaney, Megan Davis, Glenn Ferguson, Lauren Ganley, Sam Jeffries, Marcia Langton, Bill Lawson, Alison Page, Noel Pearson, Rob Oakeshott, Janelle Saffin, Rachel Siewert, Ken Wyatt, Jody Broun, Les Malezer and Mick Gooda.
3 Dodson and Liebler 2012, xviii
4 Reconciliation Australia, *Annual Review* 2015–2016, p. 17, <www.reconciliation.org.au/wp-content/uploads/2016/12/RA_Annual-review-2016_web_spread.pdf> (accessed 7 July 2017)
5 Stanner 1969, 25

Acknowledgments

The late Professor Geoffrey Bolton suggested I write this book. Probably I would not have attempted it without his expression of confidence (and this was not the first time). I did much of the writing while employed by Western Sydney University; WSU supported me also with research funds, from 2010 to 2015. I was lucky to have Dr Elizabeth Watt as an excellent research assistant. Peter Hutchings was my supportive Dean, and I enjoyed the camaraderie of my fellow historians at WSU. The History Department at the Australian National University hosted my research leave in 2014 and they have welcomed me again in my retirement. Over many years, I have learned much of what I know about the subject of this book by mixing with ANU colleagues, and I would like to thank in particular: Jon Altman, Maggie Brady, Ian Keen, Francesca Merlan, Nic Peterson and Will Sanders. I have been fortunate also in numbering among my recent graduate students Elizabeth Ganter and Charlie Ward. Other intellectual debts will be clear from my citations. The Library of the Australian Institute of Aboriginal and Torres Strait Islander Studies is the best place in the world to write a book such as this: I warmly thank the Library staff for their welcome and their support. Phillipa McGuinness picked up my manuscript when it was at risk of being orphaned by the decision of another publisher. The professional skill and good humour of Phillipa and her team – particularly Tricia Dearborn, Paul O'Beirne and Josephine Pajor-Markus – made the trip from manuscript to book seem effortless. Karina Pelling and Kay Dancey of CartoGIS, College of Asia and the Pacific, the Australian National University, were patient and precise in their map-making. Bain Attwood was kind enough to comment on a late draft. The home and family life that Jan Mackay and Anna Georgia Mackay continue to give me has sustained my many hours in the study.

Index

Aboriginal and Torres Strait Islander
  people
  And 'Asians' 2, 8, 23, 30–31, 35, 117,
    119, 121, 124, 126–127, 129, 147,
    226–227, 229, 254–255
  And 'assimilation' 264, 266–268,
    365–367
  Children 44–45, 98–116, 121, 125,
    131–132, 142, 155, 156, 175, 183,
    185, 195, 206, 210, 212, 219, 231,
    237–238, 240, 254–255, 259, 263,
    266, 274, 345, 351, 366, 370–377,
    381, 387–388, 392, 394, 404,
    406, 408, 410–411, 420, 422–423,
    428–431, 439
  Creative expression 269, 292, 339–351
  'Detribalisation' 24, 170, 173, 186,
    190–191, 193–195, 216, 324–328,
    337–338, 346, 350–351, 364, 395–397
  Distinctions among 136, 166, 174–176,
    193–197, 379, 381–382, 401
  Economic adaptation 49–50, 125–126,
    201–206, 242–257, 319, 320–321,
    328–331, 380–394
  Education/schooling 22, 53, 58–60,
    100–102, 107, 109–110, 113–115,
    125, 131, 142, 147, 151, 174–175,
    191, 206, 211–212, 216, 222, 247,
    259, 262–263, 266, 277, 284, 313,
    322, 336, 366, 387–388, 394, 396,
    411–412, 420, 422, 425, 426–429,
    433, 438, 440, 442
  Health 276, 277, 326, 337, 371–372,
    376–377, 379, 385, 391, 393, 412,
    415, 420–422, 428–429, 431–432,
    435,
  Individuals:
    Abbott, D 246

Adams, H 241
Ah Kit, J 374
Anderson, P 19, 420–421
Apuatimi, R 344
Atkinson, J 408
Barunga, A 156, 349–350
Behrendt, L 384–385
Bennelong 14
Bin Bin, D 180
Blair, H 344
Bodidji, U 43
Bon, L 239
Bonner, N 282–283, 285
Boorong 14
Breaden, B 248
Brindle, K 278
Briscoe, G 149–150
Carlson, B 390
Chuguna, JM 13–14
Clark, G 412–413
Clarke, B 209–210
Coe, P 340
Coffin, P 240
Colbung, K 344
Coolwell, G 239
Cooper, W 187, 190–192, 194, 196,
  199, 228, 254, 395–397
Corbett, T 109–110
Coyne, A 237
Cripps, K 411
Crocker, A 241
Dhakiyar 88–89
Dick, K 344
Dillon, A 385, 387
Dixon C 278, 344
Dodson, M 274, 375–376, 388–389
Doolah, J 239
Duncan, ME 425

Ferguson, W 208, 228, 397
Foley, G 278–279, 343
Foster, L 239–240
Gaffney, E 407
Gibbs, P 207, 397
Gilbert 284–286, 340–341, 394
Ginibi, Ruby Langford 398–399
Gooda, M 331
Gordon, S 410, 414, 492
Grant, S 390–391, 433–435, 442
Groves, B 264
Hammond, R 344
Harris, J 114
Hegarty, R 107
Hetherington, B 241
Huggins, J 407 (endnote 14), 414
Hunt, A 374
Johnson, E 241
Johnstone, F 237
Kartinyeri, D 362–365, 367–369
Katona, J 377
Koo'oila, E 344
Koowarta, J 305
Kropinyeri, M 115
Kruger, A 204, 373
Lane, M 383–384, 391–392,
Langford, R 354, 356–357, 359
Langton, M 310, 338, 385,
Law, V 239
Lennon, A 344
Leura, T Jabaljarri 344
Lockyer, B 62
Mabo, E 313–314, 335–336, 379
Major, S 241
Mansell, M 354
Marika, W 344
Mau 88
Maynard, Fred 188–190, 394–395, 397
McKenna, C 180
Miller, M 344
Muir H J 210–212
Muir, W 210–212
Mulinthin 62
Mundine, W 416–419, 492
Munkara, B 241
Munro, M 249
Narkaya 88
Natjelma 88
Nelson, T Napurrula 407
Nemarluk 38
Nicholls, D 221, 292, 355

Norman, H 329, 389, 419
O'Shane, P 413
Pareroultja, E 242
Passi, D 313–315
Pearson, N 315, 386, 391–394, 416, 448
Perkins, C 267, 278, 285
Pholi, K 385–386
Price, J Nampijinpa 434
Raiwalla 218
Rice, J 313
Rigney, P 114–115
Rioli, C 374
Roberts, S 237
Robertson, B 409
Robertson, E Jampijinpa 247–248
Roughsey, D 204–205, 344
Salee, C 313
Sarra, C 411
Shaw, G 246–247
Simon, E 258
Smith, S 278
Stanton, V 344
Taylor, L 382
Tipuamantumirri, B 241
Unaipon, D 113–114, 171–172
Walker, K (Oodgeroo Noonuccal) 266–268, 273, 283, 285, 341
WaveHill, J 248
West, I 336–337
Widders, T 344
Wilson, D 363, 365–367, 369
Wilson, J 114
Yu, P 425
Yunupingu, G 320–321, 374
Kinship/governance 10–12, 14–15, 17, 19, 73, 125, 137, 162, 166, 222, 318–319, 365, 388–389, 403–405, 412, 439
Languages 31, 59, 66, 70, 173, 177, 246, 266, 278, 334–335, 340, 366–367, 398, 400, 411, 428, 434, 447
Leadership 53, 189–190, 197, 276, 280–281, 284–286, 302, 306, 315–316, 321, 337, 349, 382, 389, 391, 393–395, 397, 405, 407, 413, 420
Literacy 263, 321, 368–369, 381, 400, 438
Population 3, 22, 134–168, 225–226, 256, 262–263, 272–274, 289, 321, 334–335, 354, 377, 387, 444
Poverty/disadvantage 229, 233, 262–

263 320–322, 381–382, 400–401,
434–435, 438, 442
Relationships with police and criminal
justice system 2–3, 15, 23, 24, 32,
37–38, 40, 41, 53, 59, 73–74, 76–90,
96, 98, 102–103, 105, 108–109, 110,
119–120, 129, 137, 141–143, 167,
174, 177, 179–181, 202, 204–206,
231–232, 234, 255, 260, 276, 279,
286, 299, 327, 351, 371, 385, 391,
398–401, 403, 407–408, 410–411,
421, 422
Secrecy 54, 63–64, 67, 349, 355,
363–369
Sexuality 10, 12, 21, 16–18, 41, 47,
54–60, 70–72, 147–148, 403, 421,
439
War/military service 198–210, 410
Whites' attitudes to 102–105, 116–119,
124–126, 130, 132, 200, 205–206,
223–224, 227, 260–261, 300, 330–
331, 364, 427–429, 430, 443–449
see also Anangu, Anmatjira, Arrernte,
Bardi, Bunuba, Dieri, Djaba Djaba,
Gagudju, Gurindji, Iwaidja, Kaiadilt,
Kuku-Yalanji, Kulin, Kunwinjku,
Lardil, Larrakiah, Ngaanyatjarra,
Ngaatatjara, Ngarrindjeri, Nyungar/
Noongar, Ngarinyin, Nyul Nyul,
Pintupi, Pitjantjatjara, Walmadjeri,
Warlpiri, Wiradjuri, Yamatji, Yolngu,
Yorta Yorta
Aboriginal Legal Service of Western
Australia (ALSWA) 375
Aboriginal Medical Services Alliance
Northern Territory (AMSANT) 429
Aboriginal Theatre Foundation (ATF)
346–351
Aborigines Friends Association 80, 90,
155, 184, 215
Aborigines Progress Association 277
Alice Springs 6, 24, 39, 80–81, 90, 96,
111, 160–161, 201, 203–204, 256, 344,
373, 434
Anangu 24, 40–41, 58, 297–298
Anmatjira 80
Arnhem Land 12, 16–18, 28–29, 34–37,
50, 56, 58, 67, 70, 86–89, 91, 96,
158–159, 218–219, 223, 269, 291–292,
294, 309, 321, 337, 348, 350
Appel, J 142–143
Archer River Station 305

Areyonga 160
Arrernte 91, 170, 172, 203, 373–374, 440
Australia, Commonwealth agencies and
instruments
Aboriginal and Torres Strait Islander
Commission (ATSIC) 280–282,
305–306, 330, 384, 410, 412–414
Aboriginal and Torres Strait Islander
Social Justice Commissioner 274,
331, 423
Aboriginal Development Commission
(ADC) 276, 305–306
Aboriginal Land Fund Commission
(ALFC) 305–306
Aboriginal and Torres Strait Islander
Commercial Development
Corporation 276
Australia Council (Aboriginal Arts
Board) 335, 344–346, 350–351, 378
Australian Institute of Aboriginal
Studies (AIAS) 335, 362
Australian Institute of Aboriginal
and Torres Strait Islander Studies
(AIATSIS) 335, 362
Australian National Research Council
(ANRC) 75
Department of Aboriginal Affairs (DAA)
280–281, 285, 335
Department of Families, Housing,
Community Services and Indigenous
Affairs 426–427
High Court of Australia 88, 288,
305, 313–315, 317, 326, 328, 373,
408–409, 445–447
House of Representatives Select
Committee on Voting Rights
235–241, 377–378
Human Rights and Equal Opportunity
Commission (HREOC) 371,
375–377, 431
Indigenous Land Corporation (ILC)
287, 305, 330
National Aboriginal Congress (NAC)
280
National Aboriginal Consultative
Committee (NACC) 280
Reconciliation Australia 447
Royal Commission into Aboriginal
Deaths in Custody 371, 431
Senate Standing Committee on
Community Affairs 432
Australia, historical geography (North and

South) 5–10, 19, 22, 24, 66, 68–69. 74, 123–130, 140, 169–170, 177, 182, 192, 199–200, 202, 204, 212, 220, 289, 290–291, 337, 339–340, 348–352, 364, 381–382, 416–419, 432–442
Australian Aboriginal Progressive Association (AAPA) 189–190, 192, 197, 264, 395
Australian Aborigines' League (AAL) 187, 190, 341, 395
Australian Indigenous Doctors' Association (AIDA) 429
Australian Labor Party 295
Australian Medical Association 412
Australian Mining Industry Council (AMIC) 316

Baillie, H 182, 187
Bandler, F 278
Bardi 33
Barambah 142, 150–151 *see also* Cherbourg
Basedow, H 7, 64, 65, 148
Bateman, FEA 213
Bates, Daisy 65, 214
Beazley, KE 337
Bell, J 339
Bennett, L 347–348
Bennett MM 182–187
Berndt, CH 157–158, 205, 251, 360–362, 364, 368
Berndt RM 157–158, 205, 238, 252, 337, 349–350, 360–362, 364, 368
Berrimah 157, 212
Birrundudu 157
Black, G 103–104
Blackburn, J 215
Blackburn, RA (Justice) 294, 296, 309, 348, 421
Bleakley, JW 81, 122, 142–143, 149, 167
Bloomfield, H 204
British Commonwealth League 182
Brisbane 141, 210–211, 259, 277, 279, 282
Broome 9, 20, 22, 30, 51, 59, 117, 179, 199, 331
Brough, M 423–424, 430
Brungle 100
Bryant, G 233–234, 280, 285, 346, 421, 431
Bunuba 299
Bungalow, The 24, 96, 111, 256, 373
Burdeu, A 254

Cahill, P 36
Cann, J 102, 104
Cape York 6, 20, 22, 27, 29, 31–33, 47–48, 58, 63, 67, 143, 291, 310, 317, 321, 323, 392–394, 431
Cairns 20, 30, 142, 344
Cameron A 205
Carrolup 96, 109, 206
Cawood, J 81, 86
Chaney, F 272, 318
Chauvel, C and E 242–243, 246
Cherbourg 22, 107, 239
Chifley, B 213, 230, 250
Chinnery, E 204, 229
Cleland J 90, 156–157
Collins, B 331, 414
Commonwealth Department of Health and Aging 412
Communist Party of Australia (CPA) and anti-communists 174–182, 213, 215, 222, 258–259, 278, 293, 397
Community Development Employment Projects (CDEP) 276
Compulsory Income Management (CIM) 424–426, 428–429
Cook, CE 111, 123
Cooke, CM 182, 187
Coolbaroo Club 277
Coombs, HC 268
Coonan, H 419–420
Cooper, J 34–35
Cootamundra Home for Girls 102, 256
Council for Aboriginal Affairs 268
Council for Aboriginal Reconciliation 381, 430
Council of Aboriginal Women of South Australia 277
Country Women's Association 257–258

Darkinjung Local Aboriginal Land Council 328
Darwin 16–18, 20, 24, 35–36, 54, 81, 85, 86, 88–89, 91, 96, 111, 123, 159, 201, 210–212, 252, 344, 348–349, 371–375
Davis, L 318–319
De Grey station 181
Deakin, A 1–4, 7, 9–10, 13–14, 136, 173, 377, 432, 442, 443
Delamere 37, 157
Derby 9, 22, 213, 237
Dexter, B 268

Dieri 38
Djaba Djaba 33
Douglas, J 32
Driver AR 213
Duguid, C 40, 215–218
Dunstan, D 297, 324–325, 327

Elkin, AP 54, 63–64, 66–67, 70, 74, 76, 90, 134, 162, 165, 208–209, 216–218, 220, 232, 258, 369, 377–378
Erub 147
Evans, EC 160, 348

Federal Council for Aboriginal Advancement (FCAA) 259, 271, 293
Federal Council for the Advancement of Aborigines and Torres Strait Islanders (FCAATSI) 259, 279, 285, 293, 334, 338–339
Finn, P 328
Foundation for Aboriginal Affairs 277–278, 285

Gagudju 36
Gale CF 124
Garvey M 188–189
Gillard, J (government) 446
Goss, W (government) 302
Gray, F 50, 87–88
Gray, W 425
Grayden, W 221–222
Gurindji 293

Haag, S 341
Haasts Bluff 160–161
Hannaford, J 414
Hart CMW 67, 148
Hasluck, PMC 196–197, 200, 222, 233, 253, 258, 264, 270, 323, 338, 348, 402
Hewson, J 316
Hocking, B 311–312
Howard, J (government) 280–281, 317, 377, 391, 413–418, 421, 423–424
Howard, RB 141–142
Howson, P 268

Indigenous Protected Area (IPA) 332–333
Ingamells, R 172–173
International Labour Organization 183, 271, 293
Isdell, J 108–109, 117

Iwaidja 35

Japan and Japanese 24, 30, 37–38, 48, 86–88, 121, 148, 179, 199, 208, 218, 223
Jones, E 182, 185–186
Jones, FW 186

Kaberry, P 54–55, 67, 72–73
Kahlin Compound 24, 96, 111, 210
Kaiadilt 438
Karunjie 245–246
Katter R 301–302
Keane, M 325–326
Keating, P (government) 287, 315–316, 330, 371, 374, 412, 419
Kernot, C 331
Kimberley 6, 12, 21–22, 29, 33, 55, 59, 61, 67, 79, 108, 148, 156, 159, 168, 186, 201, 244, 245, 251, 319, 321, 347–350, 439
Kinchela Aboriginal Boys' Home 102
Kingsley-Strack, J 256
Kuku-Yalanji 27
Kulin 1–2
Kunwinjku 34, 36
Kyle-Little, S 16–18

La Perouse 206, 339
Lajamanu (Hooker Creek) 159, 241, 435–436
Lang, J 227
Lardil 58, 291, 438
Larrakiah 373
League of Nations 65, 183–184, 196, 269
Legislation
  Australia
    Aboriginal and Torres Strait Islander Heritage Protection Act 1984 360
    Aboriginal Councils and Associations Act 1976 280
    Aboriginal Land Rights (Northern Territory) Act 1976 296, 307, 320, 323–324, 372-6, 414–419, 424
    Child Endowment Act 1941 231
    Commonwealth Electoral Act 1962 234, 445
    Conciliation and Arbitration Act 1904 445
    Corporations (Aboriginal and Torres Strait Islander) Act 2006 280
    Defence Act 1909 207
    Franchise Act 1902 231, 236

Invalid and Old Aged Pensions Act 1908 226
Nationality and Citizenship Act 1948 226
Native Title Act 1993 287, 315, 317–320, 373–374, 391
Northern Territory National Emergency Response Act 2007 426–427
Racial Discrimination Act 1975 305–306, 314–315, 425
Social Security Legislation Amendment Act 2012 426–429
Social Services Act 1947 226, 233–234, 238
Stronger Futures in the Northern Territory Act 2012 426–429
Stronger Futures in the Northern Territory (Consequential and Transitional Provisions) Act 2012 426–429
Great Britain (Imperial)
British Nationality and Status of Aliens Act 1914 183
Commonwealth of Australia Constitution Act 1901 1–2, 4, 136, 162, 166, 173, 200, 225–226, 228, 233, 260, 273–274, 293, 305–306, 316, 339, 377, 443, 445–449
New South Wales
Aboriginal Land Rights Act 1983 303, 307, 375, 389
Aborigines Protection Act 1909 95, 100, 102
Aborigines Protection Amending Act 1915 95
Neglected Children and Juvenile Offenders Act 1905 102
Public Instruction Act 1880 101
Northern Territory
Aboriginals Ordinance 1918 96
Welfare Ordinance 1953 235
Queensland
Aboriginal Land Act 1991 302, 307
Aboriginals Preservation and Protection Act 1939 96
Aboriginals Protection and Restriction of the Sale of Opium Act 1897 96, 116, 141, 323
Aborigines and Torres Strait Islanders (Land Holding) Act 1985 301
Elections Act 1915 235
Family Responsibilities Commission Act 2008 431
Industrial and Reformatory Schools Act 1865 32

Land Act (Aboriginal and Islander Land Grants) Amendment Act 1982 299
Queensland Coast Island Declaratory Act 1985 313–314
Torres Strait Islanders Act 1939 97
Torres Strait Islander Land Act 1991 302, 307
South Australia
Aborigines Act 1911 94, 105
Aborigines Act Amendment Act 1939 94
Aborigines (Training of Children) Act 1923 94, 116
Children's Act 1895 104
Licensing Acts Further Amendment Act (No. 2) 1915 94
Licensing Act 1917 94
Maralinga Tjarutja Land Rights Act 1984 298
Northern Territory Aborigines Act 1910 94
Pitjantjatjara Land Rights Act 1981 298
Prohibition of Discrimination Act 1966 270
Tasmania
Aboriginal Relics Act 1975 357
Cape Barren Island Reserve Act 1912 94, 304
Licensing Act 1932 94
National Parks and Wildlife Act 1970 357
Victoria
Aboriginal Land Act 1970 298
Aboriginal Land (Lake Condah and Framlingham Forest) Act 1987 299
Aboriginal Protection Act 1869 106
Aborigines Act 1890 94
Aborigines Act 1915 94
Aborigines Act 1928 94
Licensing Act 1915 94
Western Australia
Aboriginal Affairs Planning Authority Act 1972 300
Aboriginal Heritage Act 1972 299
Aborigines Act 1905 96, 108–109, 123–124, 127, 130
Aborigines Act Amendment Act 1936 96, 98, 130
Electoral Act 1907 235
Licensing Act 1911 96
Native (Citizenship Rights) Act 1944 235, 237
Limbunya 157
Link-Up 375–376
Long, JPM 161–162, 166
Lyons, J (government) 87, 191, 199, 395

Macaulay R 220
MacDougall, W 220–221
Makassan people 36
Manbulloo 157
Marrakai 158
McKay, I 256
McKenzie-Hatton, E 256
McIntyre, G 312–313
McLeod, D 180–181
McMahon, W 266, 295
Menzies R G 200, 228–230, 233, 445
Meston, A 21, 323
Middleton, S 265
Missionaries
   Albrecht, FW 40, 80, 203
   Chaseling, W 88
   Courbon, R 35
   Docherty, R 45–46, 58–59, 62
   Droste, W 61
   Duguid, C 40, 215–218
   Dyer, A 87–88
   Gribble, E 73, 77–78
   Harris, D 54, 73, 204
   Heinrich, H 82, 84–86
   Hey, N 32, 45, 47, 58
   Kramer, EE 80, 82–85
   Long, RCM 28
   Love JRB 56–57
   Our Lady of the Sacred Heart Sisters 58
   Raible, O 42, 49, 61
   Rowan, H 48
   Schenk, R and M 39–40, 60, 72, 128, 187
   St. John of God Sisters 51, 59
   Strehlow, C 60, 90
   Walker, FW 32
   Walter, G 28, 43, 45, 51–52
   Webb, TT and EM 28, 44–46, 49–50, 55–56, 58, 70, 71–72, 87, 89
   Wells, E and A 292
Missions
   general 348, 351–352, 366, 368, 374, 379, 381, 384, 396, 401, 403, 407, 417, 439
   Aurukun 25, 29, 67, 142, 201, 291, 302
   Balgo 26, 439
   Bathurst Island Mission 25, 34, 42, 57–58, 67, 148–149, 201, 241
   Beagle Bay 22, 25, 28, 33, 43, 45–46, 51, 54, 58–59, 61–62, 67, 124, 146, 202

Bloomfield River 25
Bomaderry 102
Colebrook Home 105
Croker Island Mission 26, 201
Daly River 25
Doomadgee 26, 29
Drysdale River/Pago/Kalumburu 21–22, 25, 43, 44, 59, 60, 61, 71, 201–202
Edward River 26, 201
Emerald River Mission/Angurugu 26, 50
Ernabella 24, 26, 40–41, 58, 95, 157, 215, 220
Finniss Springs 95
Forrest River 22, 54, 67, 72–73, 77
Goulburn Island Mission 26, 37, 96, 111, 201, 349
Hermannsburg (Finke River Mission) 25, 38–40, 44, 60, 65, 67, 80, 82, 84 157, 160, 246, 440
Hope Vale (Cape Bedford) 25, 47–48, 57, 67, 142, 202, 391–392
Jigalong 179
Killalpaninna 23, 38, 43, 95, 105
Lockhart River 26, 28, 48, 67
Lombadina 22, 25, 33, 201–202
Maloga 100
Mapoon 25, 29, 32, 47, 58, 67, 142, 201, 291
Mari Yamba 25
Milingimbi 26, 37, 44, 46, 56, 67, 70–71
Mitchell River/Kowanyama 25, 29, 67, 142, 201
Mornington Island Mission 26, 58–59, 201, 204, 269, 291, 302, 344, 438
Mount Margaret Mission 22, 26, 39–40, 60, 67, 72, 128, 187, 214
Nepabunna 26, 95
Oenpelli 26, 36, 43–44, 58, 72–73, 87, 170, 172, 203–204
Oodnadatta 95
Ooldea 26, 95, 157, 214, 221
Point McLeay (Raukkan) 23, 95, 105, 115, 154–155, 360, 362, 365–366
Point George IV/Kunmunya/Mowanjum 22, 25, 220, 349–350
Port Keats 26, 37–38, 44, 46, 58–59, 62, 67, 201
Quorn 95
Roper River 25, 44–45, 58, 87, 219, 241
Sunday Island 25, 33

Swan Reach 95
Warangesda 100
Warburton Mission 22, 26, 221–222
Weipa 25, 142, 201, 291
Yarrabah 25, 142
Yirrkala 26, 37, 45, 89, 201, 292–294, 296, 309, 350–352
Moola Bulla 22, 96, 251
Moore River 22, 96, 109–110
Mount Doreen 247–248
Mountford, CP 90
Moy FH 216
Moynihan, M (Justice) 314
Murray Island (Mer) 239, 313–314

National Aboriginal and Islander Health Organisation 412
National Farmers Federation 316
National Tribal Council 338
Native Welfare Council 277
New South Wales 3, 6, 8, 95, 182, 200, 257, 400, 406
  and laws, policies 95, 99–104, 113, 131, 174, 198, 227–278, 230–232, 290, 370, 375–376
  and land rights 198, 281, 288, 290, 296, 302–303, 306–307, 325, 337, 375–376, 389, 419
  population in 138, 144–145, 164, 288–289
  site of activism 188–192, 207, 257, 278–279, 281, 285, 288, 302–303, 344, 389, 394, 419
New Zealand 2, 103, 192, 226, 229, 231
Newcastle Waters 253
Ngaanyatjarra 429, 440–441
Ngaanyatjarra Pitjantjatjara and Yankunytjatjara Women's Council 429
Ngarinyin 12, 245
Ngarrindjeri 113, 115, 154–156, 171, 359–368, 379, 383
Ngaatatjara 312–313
Nockatunga 51
Noongar/Nyungar 125–126, 199, 327–328
Noonkanbah 299
North Australia Aboriginal Legal Aid Service (NAALAS) 373
North-West Reserve 23–24, 40, 297, 324–325

Northern Territory 8, 9, 16, 19, 20, 21, 23, 24, 148, 160, 174, 182, 191, 202, 205, 213, 216, 217–218, 221, 241, 243, 275, 290, 310, 348, 400, 406, 414, 445
  and laws, policies 24, 36, 39, 65, 79–86, 90–92, 93–94, 96, 111, 118, 121–123, 201–203, 209–210, 232, 235, 250, 252, 275, 292, 407, 419–428, 430–431
  and land rights 288, 292, 296–301, 307, 309–310, 319, 320, 323, 356, 364, 374, 414–419
  population in 123, 138, 143–144, 146, 158, 162–163
  site of activism 241, 277, 281, 292, 300, 339, 348–352, 371–377, 386, 411, 441
Northern Territory Council for Aboriginal Rights 277
Nullagine 178
Numbulwar 437–438
Nyul Nyul 33, 61
O'Dowd, B 170
O'Leary C 238
Olney, H (Justice) 326
One People for Australia League (OPAL) 258–260
Oodnadatta 6, 95, 140, 145, 214

Palm Island 22, 205, 239–240, 282, 332
Papua New Guinea 65, 76, 147, 274, 313
Papunya 160–161, 242
Penhall WR 216
Pilbara 109, 178–181, 213, 321, 410
Pine Creek 36, 111
Pink, OM 67, 184
Pintupi 7
Pitjantjatjara 118, 160, 216, 297–298
Porteus, S 67, 249
Prinsep 117, 123–124

Queensland 2–3, 6, 8, 9, 15, 20, 82, 172, 199, 200, 202, 257, 285, 291, 338, 406, 444
  and laws, policies 16, 21, 22–23, 29, 32–33, 47, 50, 52–53, 65, 81, 96–97, 106–107, 113, 116–122, 141–143, 226, 227–228, 232, 235, 238, 243, 251, 252, 258–260, 275, 323, 335, 428, 431

and land rights 288–290, 291–292,
299–302, 305, 309, 312–315, 320, 323
population in 138, 144, 146–147,
149–152, 163, 444
site of activism 199, 210, 238–240,
257, 258–260, 281, 282–284, 320,
323–333, 338, 344, 349, 407–409

Radcliffe-Brown, A 145, 308–309
Reconciliation Australia 3, 447
Rischbieth, B 182, 186
Roberton, H 233
Rockefeller Foundation 65, 75
Rogers, N 420
Roth, WE 2–3, 21, 33, 57, 64, 65, 96, 108,
112, 117
Rowley, CD 95, 132, 162, 279–280,
305–306, 326–327
Royal Australian College of General
Practitioners 412

Seaman, P 329–330
Secretariat of National Aboriginal and
Islander Child Care (SNAICC)
370–372, 375, 406, 408, 411
Sexton, JH 90
Siewert, R 429
Simpson, C 158
Smith, WR 172
South WG 139–140
South Australia 7, 8, 15, 20, 82, 90, 96,
139, 170, 189, 213, 400, 406
and laws, policies 23, 35, 36, 39, 40,
94–95, 98, 105, 113, 118–119, 121,
141, 214, 216, 220, 226, 228, 232,
234, 265, 270, 275
and land rights 23, 35, 270, 288,
296–299, 324–325
population in 105, 138–140, 144–145,
154–156, 157, 160, 163
site of activism 113–116, 344, 359–369,
384
Spencer, WB 21, 34, 36, 65, 111, 121, 170,
172, 323
Stanner, WEH 3, 38, 67, 165, 201, 262,
268, 421, 449
Stewart, F 229
Stirling, E C 23, 98–99
Sweeney, G 158–160

Tasmania 195, 200, 232
and laws, policies 94, 106, 336

and land rights 94, 290, 303–304
population in 138–139, 143, 215, 232,
304, 354
site of activism 336–337, 352–359
Tatz, CM 141, 406
Tindale, N 214, 362, 368–369
Torres, F 21
Torres Strait and Torres Strait Islanders 5,
8, 21, 22–23, 30–32, 48, 52–53, 57, 97,
142–143, 146–147, 149, 200–201, 208,
235, 238–239, 270, 273–274, 275, 276,
277, 302, 307, 312–315, 335–336, 340,
379, 406, 407, 433, 449
Trade Unions 181, 209, 241, 251–252,
254, 293–294, 336
Treaty 272, 448–449
Turnbull, M (government) 448

United Nations 212–213, 269–270, 271,
328
United States of America 103, 158,
188–189, 208, 210, 278–279, 285, 323,
336, 342, 370, 386–387

Vanstone, A 414
Victoria 97, 182, 195, 215, 305, 337, 406
and laws, policies 1–3, 94, 100, 106,
137, 152, 198, 257
and land rights 198–199, 290–292, 296,
298–299
population in 106, 138, 144–145,
152–154, 215
site of activism 209–210, 342, 344, 355,
359, 371
Victoria River Downs 37, 157, 241
Victorian Aborigines Advancement League
270, 277–278
Violet Valley 96

Walker, F 288
Walmadjeri 13–14
Warlpiri 79–80, 160, 247, 428, 434,
436–437
Waterloo 157
Wave Hill 157, 253, 293
Western Australia 184, 252, 349, 400, 406
and laws, policies 3, 8, 15–16, 20–22, 39,
65, 74–76, 77–79, 95–96, 108, 109,
113, 117–118, 123–125, 127, 132, 179,
200, 206, 209, 213, 216, 220, 221–222,
226, 228, 231–232, 235–236, 243,
250–251, 265, 275, 410–411

and land rights 288, 289, 291, 296–297, 299–300, 305, 319, 323, 327, 329–330
population in 139, 144, 146, 149–150, 160, 162–163, 166, 444
site of activism 189, 221–222, 266–267, 344, 375, 410–411
White, VJ 90
Wilcox M Justice 327
Wild, R 19, 420–421
Willeroo 157
Williams, M 33, 45, 61
Wiradjuri 99–100, 103, 284–285, 307 340, 390
Woolner 158
Woorabinda 22, 202

Wootten, H 279
Worms, EA 168
Worsnop, T 170
Wran, N (government) 288, 303
Wright, T 176–179, 181–182, 186–187, 194, 396–397
Wyndham 22, 77, 245

Yamatji 236–237
Yolngu 12, 16–18, 28, 36–37, 45–46, 49, 55–56, 72, 86–89, 91, 218–219, 292, 294–295, 337, 351
Yorta Yorta 190, 221, 326
Youth Club 277
Yuendumu 428, 436